MOREHEAD MEMORIES

*True Stories from
Eastern Kentucky*

A Gift to

_____

from

_____

_____, 20_____

Morehead ladies celebrate the 1956 Rowan County Centennial.
L to R: Terry Caudill, Beulah Williams, Lynn Sidney Evans,
Edith Crosley, Margaret Jayne

MOREHEAD MEMORIES

True Stories from Eastern Kentucky

Before Paving: 1922 Morehead, Ky. Main Street. This view looking west from in front of the old courthouse before Main Street was paved shows Battson Drug Store (R) at street level. Notice the "dip" in the road at that time.

After Paving: 1930's Morehead, Ky. Main Street.
This view looking west from in front of the old courthouse shows the Mills Theater (R) and the Greyhound Restaurant (L)

MOREHEAD MEMORIES

True Stories from Eastern Kentucky

by
Jack D. Ellis

Jack D Ellis
Aug. 23, 2004

The Jesse Stuart Foundation
Ashland, Kentucky
2001

Library of Congress Cataloging-in-Publication Data

Ellis, Jack D., 1927-
    Morehead memories : true stories from eastern Kentucky / by Jack D. Ellis.
        p. cm.
    Includes bibliographical references.
    ISBN 0-945084-92-7
        1. Morehead (Ky.)--History. 2. Rowan County (Ky.)--History. 3. Morehead (Ky.)--History--Anecdotes. 4. Rowan County (Ky.)--History--Anecdotes. 5. Morehead (Ky.)--Biography. 6. Rowan County (Ky.)--Biography. I. Title.

F459.M67 E45 2001
976.9'57--dc21

                                                            2001029228

Published by:
The Jesse Stuart Foundation
P.O. Box 669 Ashland, Kentucky 41105
2001

DEDICATED TO THE 5 JS
WHO ARE THE JOY OF MY LIFE

Janis

Jackie

John

Jeff

Jean

(and grandchildren)

Bird's eye view of Morehead, Ky. 1940's

ACKNOWLEDGMENTS

There are so many who helped in preparing this book that it is impossible to name them all. However, at the risk of missing some, I want to gratefully acknowledge many of those who have made special contributions. First, my deep appreciation goes to Mrs. Ruth (Crisp) Robinson, my former secretary at Morehead State University, who patiently typed and re-typed the manuscript and stored it onto a computer disk. Without her professional assistance there could never have been a book.

Secondly, I want to thank Dr. Thomas D. Clark, Kentucky's renowned historian for the thoughtful insight and critical analysis he presented in the Introduction to this book. His words have been a great source of encouragement to me. Also, during the 30 plus years I have been privileged to know him, he has been a great source of personal inspiration. Dr. Thomas D. Clark is my kind of historian. He has a keen understanding of the past, a firm foundation in the present, and eyes confidently toward the future.

A very special thanks goes to Dr. C. Nelson Grote, President Emeritus of Morehead State University. Throughout the writing of this book, he read much of the material as it appeared in *The Morehead News* and encouraged me to put it into book form. His encouragement is greatly appreciated.

As someone who has been a lifelong librarian, I can understand and appreciate the difficult mechanics of publishing a book. Therefore, I wish to express my appreciation to the staff of the Jesse Stuart Foundation; especially Dr. James M. Gifford and Brett Nance for their professional guidance throughout this process.

A special thanks to Morehead State University Library Director Larry Besant and the entire staff of the Camden-Carroll Library, including the Special Collections staff: Clara Keyes, Alma Fairchild and Teresa Johnson. Also, grateful recognition is given for the use of the Morehead State University Archives and the Roger and Marie Barbour photograph collection.

Additional Morehead State University personnel who were extremely helpful were: Timothy Holbrook, chief photographer, for his expertise in preparing the photographs; and Timmy Sloan, Information Technology Specialist in scanning the photographs onto a computer disk. Also, special recognition is given to retried MSU professors Carol Pierce, Gail Ousley, and Helen Northcutt for their editorial assistance.

Among others who were helpful in preparing this publication were members of the Rowan County Historical Society, as well as Rowan County Library staff members Frankie Calvert and Donna Johnson. Also special thanks goes to Sue Buchanan and her late husband Reuel for their research into Kentucky Methodism, and sharing that research with this writer.

Last, but not least in importance, I want to publicly thank Janis Ruth, my wife of over 50 years, for her valuable assistance and patience in putting up with me during my grouchy times of trying to write when the words wouldn't seem to flow.

Jack D. Ellis

TABLE OF CONTENTS

My Kentucky Hills

I'm like a fish that's out of water.
Like a bird without a nest,
When I am far away from you
These hills I love the best!

O'Kentucky hills, you've seen me happy,
Seen me laugh and seen me smile,
And when I have to leave you
I can only stay a little while.

You have also seen me crying
Tears of joy and tears of pain.
Your streams have caught my tears that flowed
And helped me live again.

You give me such security
From a world that doesn't care.
These hills are like a mother's arms,
An answer to my prayer.

No matter where I travel
And what beauty I may see,
It's back to my Kentucky hills
That I yearn to be.

So when I shall get to heaven
One wish I hope God fills,
That I may be surrounded by
My beautiful Kentucky hills.

Janis C. Ellis

PREFACE

Historic Rowan County lies nestled amid the foothills of the Appalachian Mountains. Morehead, the county seat of Rowan County, Kentucky, was first called "The City of the Hills" over 100 years ago by the local Commercial Club. Both city and county reverberate a rich and colorful history, but little has been recorded. This book chronicles the carving of a county and building of a city in the isolated hills of Eastern Kentucky. It documents many of the people, places, and institutions that were instrumental in making Morehead the home of a magnificent University, as well as the vibrant, modern, growing city it is in the year 2000.

Morehead Memories represents a three year labor of love. Much of this material was published in the "Morehead News" and has been extremely well received by the readers. They have encouraged the publication of this book since there has been little positive history written about this region. Eastern Kentuckians seem hungry for a history that will enhance their sense of self and pride of community. It is my sincere hope that this book will help meet that need and build a foundation for future generations.

Although this publication is based upon solid research, in order to make it more readable, there are no footnotes. However, there is a Bibliography of Sources and a record of over 100 people that were interviewed. Although some of the writing can be called anecdotal and autobiographical, both have almost always been documented by other sources. Readers from this region will recognize many of the people and places, and those outside this region should gain new insight into our Appalachian culture.

Jack D. Ellis

INTRODUCTION

By Dr. Thomas D. Clark
Kentucky History Laureate

Fewer words in the English language are more glibly uttered than the word "history." But every aspect of natural and human activity is in some respects of historical importance. Historical recordings rest upon so many foundations that consideration must be given to all of them to arrive at some appreciation of human progress and the dynamics of change. An important segment of American history rests squarely upon a local base.

There remains a constant value in Thomas Jefferson's theory that what happens at the local level of society is more important to the individual than what happens at the national and international level. Kentucky is divided into one hundred and twenty county units, and scores of towns, cities, and crossroad communities. Every one of these places has a history, but of even greater importance they have emotional and sentimental meaning to the people who live within their borders, as well as those who have moved away and carry with them the precious baggage of memories and lifetime attachments.

The history of a county in Kentucky is little short of being a microcosm of the state itself. It involves the politics of local government, the rise of institutions, the settlement, ownership, and transfer of the land itself. From that moment in 1780 when the three original counties in Kentucky were established, down to the present day, the county seat town with its courthouse has been the politcal, fiscal, and unifying institution which has held the county together in a cohesive whole. Nowhere in Kentucky has this fact been stronger than in Kentucky's 104th County of Rowan, located in the hills of Eastern Kentucky.

Dr. Jack Ellis has performed for Rowan County, Morehead, and the outlying communities an invaluable service. In the area of this kind of local history this type of reminiscent treatment is of greater importance than a more elaborate interpretive treatment. It is important to know something of the personalities who lived, performed public services, operated stores, shops of all kinds, and who served as supporters and officers of local institutions. In the history of Kentucky towns before World War II many merchants and their stores became as much social institutions as commercial ones. Both townsmen and countrymen alike accumulated memories of those tender youthful days of growing up when stores and streets were places which generated life-long memories.

Few American towns have escaped troubles and tragedies of varying natures. Both Rowan County and Morehead have memories of violent episodes, feuds, floods, fires, accidents, and other incidents which touched the lives of every person living within their boundaries. Dr. Ellis has written graphic accounts of these moments. Conversely there is the history of evolving institutions such as churches, schools, a university, medical services, hospital, local newspapers, and recreational and amusement centers. All those things go together to give substance to local history.

So much detailed information passes on unrecorded with the succession of generations, leaving serious voids in both the knowledge of the past and in a sense of changes which occur. There most assuredly will come a time when a historian will undertake the writing of a comprehensive history of Rowan County and its county seat and people. Dr. Ellis has broken the ground for him or her. He has done far more than this. He has recorded a multitude of facts, first-hand experiences, and the memories of other people which otherwise might well have slipped unnoted into oblivion.

Almost as a central theme of this collected chronological and analytical material is the fact of change. This book sets a dependable gauge by which future changes can be measured against the background facts of the past. No community can live only by the conditions of the present moment or by anticipation of the past without making costly repetitive mistakes. This book is rich in the presentation of the past in the context of decisions made, of failures and mistakes, and of the consequences of the collective experiences of the area.

In precise local Rowan County-Morehead historical terms, the deeply ingrained sense of place is evident in the facts of their emergence from a primitive economic, political, and social entity carved out of an Appalachian Highland ridge and valley. This collection of rich factual materials preserves in an indelible form the nature and depth of changes which have occurred, of personalities who gave spirit and substance to local history, of institutions which flourished and faded with the progression of modernization, and of local crises and calamities which shaped the turns of local history. This book gives Rowan County and its community a creditable place in the ever-growing list of books which bring the history of the Commonwealth itself into clearer focus.

Dr. Thomas D. Clark
Kentucky History Laureate For Life
May 11, 2000

Masterson's station in Fayette County was the first Methodist Church in Kentucky. The historical marker reads: in a cabin on this site Bishop Francis Asbury held the first Methodist Conference west of the Allegheny mountains on May 13, 1790.

CHAPTER ONE
Faith vs. Feuds: Church and Conflict

The Methodist Movement into Morehead was closely connected to the westward expansion of our nation, and the early pioneer settling of Kentucky. It was in 1783 that Daniel Boone moved his family to Limestone, (now Maysville) on the Ohio River. He opened a trading post there as families began to arrive by flatboats from up river. Those were long barge-like boats that were used only to go down river. When they landed they would usually use the wood to build cabins. They came from New York, Pennsylvania, Maryland, and Virginia. Many landed in Limestone, (now Maysville) and moved southward, settling in what is now the fertile farmland of Fleming, Fayette, and Mason Counties. In fact Dr. Thomas D. Clark, Kentucky History Laureate, told this writer "While no precise data is available, I believe more settlers came to Kentucky down the Ohio River through Limestone than came by way of the Wilderness Road blazed by Daniel Boone". When the pioneers began arriving in Kentucky the Circuit Riding Methodist Preachers came with them. In 1783 the first Methodist Church was established in Kentucky. Then in 1784 at a conference in Maryland the Methodist Episcopal Church of America was organized. It was only then that the Methodist Society, organized by John and Charles

Wesley in England, became the Methodist Episcopal Church of America. They elected Thomas Coke, and Francis Asbury as the first Bishops, and in 1786 (six years before Kentucky became a state) appointed Benjamin Ogden and Lee Roy Cole as missionaries to Kentucky County of Virginia.

Through the zealous evangelistic efforts of these early Circuit Riding Pioneer Preachers, churches began to appear in what is now Mason and Fayette Counties. The first Methodist Church built in Kentucky is thought to be a log church with a thatched moss roof built in Fayette County on land given by Richard Masterson (Lexington was first called Masterson Station). But the first Black Methodist Church organized in Kentucky, was called Lee's Chapel located in Lewisburg in Mason County. That church is still active today.

Collins' *History of Kentucky* credits Thomas Stevenson and his wife, from Maryland as the first converts to Methodism in Kentucky in 1786. They immediately organized a church and held services in their home. They lived in what is now Southern Mason County which would soon become Northern Fleming County. The Methodist Movement grew rapidly as more settlers moved into the area.

In 1790 Bishop Asbury made the first of his fifteen trips (on horseback) to Kentucky. Therefore, two years before Kentucky became a state, he presided over the first conference of the Methodist Church in Kentucky. It was held at Masterson Station in Fayette County. The minutes of this first conference read:

"And as the brethren in Kentucky appear to be in greatest need the conference voted that they be supported by L 24 (pounds) 3s (shillings), and 1 d. (penny) for the coming year."

Appointments of Preachers:

Limestone, (Maysville) Peter Massie

Danville, Thomas Williamson and J. Tatman

Lexington, Henry Birchett and David Hogg and

Walt River, Wilson Lee and Joseph Lillard.

This meant that these seven circuit riding preachers would have to provide for themselves, seven horses, four districts, and their churches for one year on about $25.00 per preacher per year.

It is important from time to time, that we be reminded that the privileges and benefits which we enjoy are ours, **not by achievement**, but by inheritance. This is especially true of our religious heritage. Therefore, it is our prayer, that this book will serve to remind us of the great sacrifices that were made by these early pillars of the church.

Let us never forget that we are drinking from spiritual wells they dug, eating spiritual food they planted, and reaping a spiritual harvest they have sown. God is active in each generation as they build for the next. May each of us continue to build upon a firm foundation, realizing that we are building for the ages.

Morehead Main Street 1884. Time of Rowan County War.

EARLY CIRCUIT RIDING PREACHERS MOVE TOWARD MOREHEAD

To understand how the Methodist Church was established in Morehead it is necessary to look at the history of Methodism in Fleming County. Fleming County was formed out of Mason County in 1798. Its boundaries extended to Triplett Creek, and included much of what is now Northern Rowan County. As the early settlers moved into what is now Rowan County, the Methodist preachers were there proclaiming the Gospel of Jesus Christ under extreme conditions. Those early circuit riders braved the elements, swam swollen streams, suffered summer heat, and waded winter snow. It was a life of hardships, cold, and loneliness for those early preachers. They often slept out in the open, but would usually be given shelter and food from parishioners along their route. But it was also dangerous. There were no hostile Indians, but there were robbers and murderers who would kill you for your horse. It is no wonder that the average life span of those great spiritual soldiers of the cross was only 38 years, and mere comfort was a great luxury to them.

Those circuit riding preachers usually served four or five churches called a "charge." They arrived at each church about once a month depending on the distance between churches. Each trip they would preach, serve communion, baptize, officiate at marriages and conduct the business of the church. Also, there was usually a lay pastor who served as shepherd of the flock in the interim. Those lay pastors served God by preaching, teaching, visiting the sick, and conducting funerals. They are the great unsung heroes of the church.

First Methodist Church built in Rowan County in 1840.

FIRST CHURCH FOUNDED IN ROWAN COUNTY

In the early 1800s, those circuit riding missionaries

fired by the great evangelistic revivals of that day began to conduct revivals in what is now northern Rowan County. The first
record of a Methodist Church in what is now Rowan County was
listed in *The Conference and Trial Journal of Fleming County Methodist
Churches 1810-1847*. It reported that a conference was held at Mt.
Pisgah April 11 and 12, 1840. It is unsure how long this church had
existed at that time. But the Mt. Pisgah (sometimes spelled (Pisga)
located about 10 miles north of Morehead on KY 32 was the first
Methodist Church in Rowan County. It was a log church about
30'x36'. It had hand hewn 16 inch logs and a dirt floor. The building remained at the same location until 1991 when an antique dealer
purchased the building and moved it to Olympia where it is used
as an antique shop.

METHODIST CHURCH ESTABLISHED
IN CRANSTON AREA

The first preacher is unknown but it is believed this church was
on a circuit with The Goddard Church, because it was established
in 1823, and was part of a circuit with other churches. Also, 10
years before Rowan County was formed, the 1846 Fleming County
Deed Book recorded six acres of land sold by Robert Triplett to the
Pine Grove Methodist Episcopal Church. This land was to be used
for a church and a cemetery. P.E. Kavanangh was listed as the
preacher in charge. Trustees for the Pine Grove Church were George
Hamm, Robert Hamm, Daniel Hamm, James Hartley, and Asabel
Swim. A school, cemetery and a church were constructed on the
site. The church was built of logs and covered with clapboard and
said to be about 24 x 24 feet with one door and twowindows. The
cemetery is perhaps one of the oldest in the county.

The site for this church and cemetery is now about one-half
mile north of the Cranston Road on the Rock Fork Road. It is close
to the present TGT pumping station and located on an early well-

traveled pioneer road. This early log church stood at its original site until 1920 when it was moved to the farm of George White.

METHODISM MOVES TO MOREHEAD

While the Methodist Episcopal Church began in Rowan County before 1840 at Mt. Pisgah (and possibly as early as 1835), Morehead is not mentioned in the church records until 1861, five years after Rowan County was formed. The Kentucky Methodist Conference met in Paris in 1861. So the year the Civil War began J.T. Smith was assigned to the Morehead Mission. He began holding preaching services in the Courthouse, and the response was excellent. God's spirit was in those early courthouse services, and many confessed Christ at the bar of justice in the courtroom.

CIVIL WAR SLOWS GROWTH OF METHODISM

But it was this same year that the bloodiest war in American History, split our nation asunder dividing communities and families. It also deeply divided our churches. Congregations were almost evenly divided between Union and Confederacy. Many Methodist churches in Kentucky split as a result of the war. The Goddard Church in Fleming County 15 miles north of Morehead was bitterly divided and considered a Union church. So during the Civil War many members (among them Joe Goddard, founder of the church) moved to Wallingford, and formed the Methodist Episcopal Church South.

From 1863-1865 the Kentucky Conference of the Methodist Episcopal Church did not meet because of the Civil War. Southern preachers had to go through northern lines and vice-versa; therefore, no appointments were made in Morehead until 1868 when L.C. Waters was then appointed to the Morehead Mission. That year Morehead recorded a membership of 90 and one local pastor.

MOREHEAD METHODIST CHURCH
WAS CHARGE HEADQUARTERS

From 1868-1873 the Morehead Mission became part of a circuit with two other churches. Those were Hogtown (Elliottville), and Epperhart (Epperhart was located on the head of Minor, and later became known as the Minor School). The 1869 records show Morehead with 132 members, and the other two churches had a total membership of 65. By 1875 W.D. Murphy, pastor of the Morehead circuit, reported three churches in addition to Morehead. These were Bangor (southern Rowan County), Epperhart, andHogtown, with a total of 660 members, 104 probationary members, and 380 enrolled in Sunday Schools. The three churches were valued at $1,000. H.C. Northcutt, Presiding Elder of the Maysville district reported there was still no church building in Morehead, and that services were held in the courthouse.

In 1876 the Bangor Methodist Church, a community in southern Rowan County near Morgan, Menifee and Bath counties, reported 300 members. It was a thriving community made up of farmers, loggers, and rafters. (It is close to what is now the high bridge across Licking River into Menifee County). A railroad was later built up Licking River to their community.

The record shows that Edgar P. Hill was appointed as pastor at Bangor (Rowan County). The church building was valued at $250. It was a long, narrow building constructed of logs covered with clapboard. It was about 40x20 feet with three windows on each side and one door. This building was adjacent to what later became the Mt. Hope School. It was owned by Labe McKinney and remained at its original site until the 1940s when it was torn down. There is now a small rural Church of God on this site.

Over the many years, at one time or another, the Morehead Methodist Church was assigned on a charge with: Owingsville,

Frenchburg, West Liberty, Hogtown, Epperhart School, Soldier, Olympia, Mt. Pisgah, Pine Grove, or Farmers.

REV. B.F. ONEY COMES TO MOREHEAD CHURCH

In 1883 the Kentucky Methodist Conference met in Winchester in early December. Rev. B.F. Oney was appointed to serve the Morehead Church, which was then considered to be a fine appointment. The Morehead Charge now included Morehead (which met in a school building), and four mission churches. Those churches were Mt. Pisgah (the first church building in (Rowan County), Pine Grove, Epperhart (met in school house), and Hogtown (later Elliottville).

Brother Oney was happy with his appointment, even though he wrote in his journal "I had no money at the time, not so much as to pay my fare on the train from Winchester to Morehead." But he did have a deep and abiding faith that God would provide a way. So he packed his meager belonging in his valise (suitcase) and bid goodbye to the other preachers.

A PRAYER IS ANSWERED QUICKLY

As darkness began to settle over Winchester, Brother Oney began wondering how he would reach Morehead as he walked down the street carrying his valise. As he walked by a church that was under construction he went into the shell of the building and spent some time in fervent prayer. He prayed that he might reach Morehead, and that God would use him in a special way at this appointment. He thought as he left the church, that this was probably the first prayer in this new church. (And little did he realize it might be the quickest ever answered).

After walking out of his personal, private, prayer time in the church under construction, he met Bud O'Rear, a great layman in the church, who invited him to have supper with him at the Turner

Hotel. He gladly accepted, having not eaten all day. After supper, Mr. O'Rear wished Brother Oney "Fruit for his labors" in his new appointment. Then he shook hands with him and slipped a dollar bill in his hand. Brother Oney wrote, "That dollar made it possible for me to reach the place of my regular appointment at Morehead," (God was indeed in the appointment process).

He caught train number 24 east out of Winchester that night, arriving in Morehead about 11 p.m. December 18, 1883. He followed a drummer (salesman) to the Raines Hotel on the north side of the old freight depot. He registered for lodging, and was sent out to a separate room apart from the main hotel with three or four other men already there. Brother Oney wrote in his journal, "That next day, one of the men complained to the owner, Dr. Raines, that he had no business putting just anyone who came down the road in the same room with them." Brother Oney thought the man was complaining about him. But since he wanted no trouble, he did not respond. He did not even say he was a preacher.

BROTHER ONEY MEETS WARREN M. ALDERSON

On December 19, 1883, a crisp cold morning, Brother Oney, carrying his valise made his way to Warren M. Alderson's General Store. Warren was chairman of the Board of Trustees and the two became close friends. He also invited Brother Oney to stay with him as long as he was in Morehead. He said he had a separate cabin where the preacher could live while in Morehead. Many wealthy laymen of that time keep a room reserved for their preachers.

RIDING A RENTED HORSE UP CHRISTY CREEK

Rev. Oney writes in his journal, "I rented a horse at the livery stable for 50 cents and started from Morehead to Epperhart Schoolhouse for my January appointment, a distance of 14 miles south of Morehead, however, before leaving it began to rain. From Rodburn to Hogtown you traveled along a beautiful crystal clear stream where you could see fish swimming at a considerable depth in the pearly waters. The hills on either side were high, rough, and steep, where every kind of tree native to the area grew abundantly. Once in a while you could see a cleared field where some crop had grown in the summer. There was an occasional house of humble appearance, usually built of logs. But the people were hospitable."

Early Circuit Riding Methodist Preachers in Eastern Kentucky suffered great personal hardships.

It would have been a pleasant journey had the weather cooperated. But as Brother Oney rode farther up Christy Creek the cold rain rapidly turned to sleet. It began to freeze in cakes on him and his horse, and, as darkness began to fall, he whistled to keep up his courage. He sang along the trail "A Charge of Keep Have I", and consoled himself by saying "I am suffering for the cause of Christ."

As it grew darker, colder, and began snowing heavily, he was able to gain shelter with a Mr. Williams, who lived along the road. He spent the night in a room with snow blowing in his face, but was grateful for shelter. His horse was almost frozen to death the next morning, so Brother Oney left before breakfast to continue on to Epperhart Schoolhouse where he was greeted by a congregation of 25 souls. They built a fire, but snow was blowing through the cracks in the wall while the meeting went on. Sometimes mere comfort is a great luxury, as all circuit riding preachers knew.

After preaching at Hogtown for about six months the church was suppose to pay him some of his expenses. So he passed an offering plate and got one copper penny with a hole in it. Brother Oney begin to chastise the people mildly, saying it costs me 50 cents to rent a horse each trip I make here. So the ladies of the church asked him to step outside and they did their own collecting. They collected $5.00 for his expenses for the first 6 months.

The summer of 1883 the Morehead Methodist Church with its mission churches at Mt. Pisgah, Pine Grove, Epperhart and Hogtown were growing. (Bangor had been placed in another charge.) Brother Oney, a man of great compassion, preached strong evangelistic sermons. Many found Christ, but as the upcoming events would soon reveal, Satan still had many disciples in Morehead and Rowan County.

ROWAN COUNTY FEUD DAMPENS THE FLAME OF FAITH

Election day in August 1883 was the day the infamous Rowan County War began. Brother Oney, had been back to his home for a visit, and returned to Morehead on election day. He had quietly cast his vote and gone to the home of James Clark, a local attorney and church member. He had no sooner arrived there, when they heard pistol shots and women screaming piteously. He ran over to one of the hotels where two men were taken after being shot. One man was mortally wounded and died that night, but the other man survived.

Brother Oney said he was well acquainted with all of the principals involved in the feud; and had been in their homes. He even knew the men who were accused of the shooting. But he said there were more than two men involved, so no one was ever convicted. It was the beginning of sorrow and darkness, in the darkest of the dark and bloody ground.

Though strife would seem to end for a time, the dark spirit of violence and murder still prevailed, and the fighting would be renewed. But peace would not return until nearly all hostile parties were killed. (That did not happen until June 22, 1887.) Brother B.F. Oney's appointment at Morehead ended in September 1884. He was not reappointed because of the danger that existed in Morehead. He received $60.51 for his nine months service in Morehead.

In 1888 R.W. Baird was brought to Morehead to serve God through the Methodist Church. He succeeded in working with the other pastors in the Christian and Episcopal Churches in building a union church. But it would be the assignment of Brother James E. Wright to Morehead in 1892 that would bring about the construction of the first Methodist Church building in Morehead.

LAND ACQUIRED AND FIRST BUILDING BUILT

On March 24, 1894 the land was acquired for the site of a Methodist Church in Morehead. The land is located at the present site of the church on Main Street and the deed was made to Warren M. Alderson, William Cooper, and James E. Clark, trustees of the M.E. Church South. The deed further stated that for the sum of $65.00 this land shall be kept as a place of divine worship for use of the members and ministers of the Methodist Episcopal Church South.

Trustee Warren M. Alderson (great-great grandfather of Jack D. Ellis), donated all the lumber and building material for the first church. Mr. Alderson was a wealthy Morehead merchant. James Clark was one of the areas best known attorneys, and William Cooper operated a planing mill in Morehead. Reverend James Wright provided the fervent spiritual leadership for this early church, and those businessmen provided sound business leadership for the first church building. The white wooden weatherboarded building was completed in 1896, and included not only the sanctuary but Sunday School rooms and a connecting parsonage. It had two towers on the front corners of the church, and opera seats. However no pictures can be found of this building.

NEW BRICK CHURCH CONSTRUCTED

That white frame church served its purpose well, but was torn down and replaced by the present brick structure in 1926. John Cecil (Jo Ann Needham's grandfather), local businessman, contractor, and hotel owner was the contractor for the construction of the church. There was a great deal of volunteer labor. For instance the steps were built by Matt Cassidy (Nell Collins' father). But don't blame him because they are so steep, because the building was already built and he couldn't run the steps out in the street.

But in any event, the Methodist Church in Morehead has endured and grown to amembership of 618. It has grown because its builder and maker is God. It will endure because the Methodist people of God have a vision that working with God in faith believing it will endure for the ages.

> *"Surely the Lord is in this Place"*
> *Build it well what'er you do;*
> *Build it straight and strong and true;*
> *Build it tall and build it broad*
> *Build it for the eye of God.*
>   *(Old English Nursery Rhyme)*

APPOINTMENTS TO THE MOREHEAD METHODIST CHURCH: 1861-1999

1861-1863	J.T. Smith - Leadership at the beginning of the Civil War
1863-1868	To be supplied (appointments unknown)
1868-1870	L.C. Waters - (90 members and one local pastor)
1870-1872	C. Foster
1872-1873	J.C. Morris
1873-1874	J.W. Simmons
1874-1875	Elkanah Johnson
1875-1876	T.W. McIntyre
1876-1880	J.E. Clark
1880-1882	W.B. Ragan
1882-1883	John Maley Wilson
1883-1884	C.F. Oney - Leadership at the Beginning of the Rowan County War
1884-1885	To be supplied (appointment unknown)
1885-1886	B.L.F. Hurt
1886-1887	R.A. Humphrey
1887-1888	W.B. Ragan
1888-1890	R.B. Baird
1890-1891	J.L. West
1891-1892	J.W. Hunter
1892-1896	James E. Wright - Leadership built first church
1896-1898	C.E. Boswell
1898-1900	L.C. Mann
1900-1902	S.M.R. Hurt
1902-1904	J.R. Ward
1904-1905	O.B. Crockett
1905-1906	George Froh
1906-1907	W.P. Fryman
1907-1911	C.M. Humphrey
1911-1912	R.B. Baird

1912-1914	George W. Hoffman
1914-1915	Green V. Todd
1915-1916	E.V. Caton
1916-1917	Ben T. Sewell
1917-1918	L.E. Williams
1918-1919	C.H. Caswell
1919-1920	J.L. West
1920-1922	R.C. Evans
1922-1923	E.G.B. Mann (died while serving Morehead)
1923-1925	W.S. Mitchell
1925-1928	C.R. Thomas - Leadership built present sanctuary
1928-1932	A.R. Perkins
1936-1939	H.L. Moore
1939-1941	L.Edward Mattingly
1941-1945	C.L. Cooper
1945-1946	E.A. Howell
1946-1950	David Sageser, organized Wesley Club (now Wesley Foundation), MSU
1950-1951	G.H. Bierly
1951-1953	Walter W. Garrett
1953-1957	Donald W. Durham, (directed building education building)
1957-1959	I.J. Scudder
1959-1960	Stanley Gwinn
1960-1966	Thomas W. Ditto
1966-1974	Larry R. Buskirk
1974-1976	Earl T. Curry
1976-1983	Harold W. Tatman
1983-1986	Glenn L. Courts
1986-1989	David C. Hilton
1989-1995	William E. Parker
1995-1999	Michael T. Powers
1999-	Larry Gardner

THE ROWAN COUNTY FEUD AND ITS EFFECT UPON THE MOREHEAD METHODIST CHURCH

Reported in the 1887 issue of *The Journal of the Kentucky Conference of the Methodist Episcopal Church.*

Darkest of the Dark and Bloody Ground
by
A Mountaineer

This chapter was written by a Methodist preacher assigned to Morehead at the 1883 Kentucky Annual Conference. According to the records, Rev. B.F. Oney was assigned to Morehead that year. He wanted to remain anonymous because of the violence connected to the feud.

MOREHEAD MISSION

By a combination of circumstances and events it came to pass that I went to Morehead to preach. It came to pass also that I had no money at that time; not so much as would pay my fare on the train to Morehead. But I packed my valise to start and went down to bid Brother Green and his wife and the other preachers good bye, who were stopping at Mr. "Bud" Orears. And as I took one brother by the hand, he laid a dollar in mine. That dollar made me able to reach the place where I was to begin work of the regular ministry, that night. I took supper that evening at the Turner Hotel with Mr. Asbury Orear. He found me at prayer in the new Methodist Church which was then just about half completed. Perhaps that was the first prayer ever offered in that church.

I reached Morehead that night (December 18, 1883) about 11 o'clock and followed a "drummer" into Raine Hotel. I was sent into a room apart from the main building, with three or four other men in it. One of them complained of the arrangement, and said that Dr.

Raine had no business to put them in a room with just anybody that happened to come along. He seemed to have reference it to me; but I was timid and made no reply. I did not make it known that I was a preacher. I paid my bill after breakfast next morning, and made my way to Alderson's store and there, to my great surprise, I met "Jim Lewis" Quicksall, a neighbor boy, who was my warm friend while I stayed on that charge. He was one of the salesmen in Alderson's store. Warren Alderson was the chairman of the Morehead Methodist Episcopal Church Board of Trustees.

The Morehead circuit was composed of five appointments; viz Morehead, Pine Grove, Mt. Pisgah, Epperhart's Schoolhouse, and Hogtown. You will get some idea of the physical features of Rowan County as well as the character of the people as the narrative continues.

I started from Morehead to Epperharts' Schoolhouse to my appointment in January, a distance of some 14 miles. I was directed to stop with one Brother W.overnight. A cold rain was falling, which turned to snow when I was about half-way. It settled down upon me and the horse I was riding in great cakes, and soon began to freeze. I "whistled to keep courage up." That is, I sung along the way to console myself; pondered the fact that I was in the Lord's work, and was suffering for His cause. I rode up to a shaggy rail fence and a rustic set of draw-bars--Hello! An old man made his appearance from the small log house a few yards away. "What will you have!" he said in a shattered voice. Is this where one preacher lives? "Yes sir." Could another little preacher get to stay all night with you?" "We'll do the best we can." Well that's a plenty. And so saying, I dismounted and commenced staying. But I did not like the shelter for my horse. It was a log stable with large cracks, and covered with nothing but corn-stalks which had been cut up with the fodder on them, piled up on the joists. It was not waterproof, and then the wet snow was already freezing on the horse. Brother W. explained that he was about to move up on the hill and go into the goods business. His wife complained at supper, and told me I was no account, because I only took a few sups of the coffee, which was made as black as tar, and just about as much to my taste as tar. I slept in a warm bed near the fire, and was only disturbed when the snow blew through the crevices and fell in my face. When morning came I found that the poor horse had eaten non of the soured corn that had been put in his trough, and there he stood humped up in one corner almost frozen to death. I found it was impossible to clean the snow and ice off of him without a currycomb, and that he would soon die in that condition. So I took the horse and left before breakfast to find comfort for my horse, that of myself being secondary importance. This I soon found at Brother Hayden Harris'. Sometimes mere comfort is a great luxury, as most itinerants know.

On Sunday morning I went to the little schoolhouse, where I was to preach. The floor was covered with snow. A few people came in, and, with their assistance, I got a large "back log" into the fire place, and soon started a blaze which steamed the snow off the wood, and made those comfortable who sat nearest to it, but is was still a few degrees past pleasant near the opposite wall. Then the floor was swept, and we commenced the service. I was interrupted in my sermon by a young man, who kept talking to another young man by his side. I reproved him twice very mildly, but not personally, but he gave no heed. I then pointed my finger right at him and said: Young man, I'll have you to behave! He stopped talking and looked right at me, but he looked awful mad. I finished my sermon, and then closed by saying: I have no desire to hurt anyone's feelings: but I have a message from the Lord for you. I came here to preach the gospel to you; but I can do you no good if you do not listen to me. And I don't intend that those who don't want to hear shall interrupt those who do.

After the service was dismissed, I went to the door and heard him cursing me, and threatening to whip me. I went on down past him and got on my horse and went out to Brother Harris' for dinner. The ruffian's uncle, Mr. Jededia Day, came in while we wereat dinner, and explained the matter privately to me. He told me that the young man I reproved was a desperate fellow, and was then dodging the Circuit Court--to escape justice. He thought it was not safe for me to go to Hogtown alone that night, and proposed to go with me. I said, well Brother, I will be glad to have you go along with me but I am not afraid. I am in the Lord's hands and he will take care of me. He went with me, and I preached that night, but I was not molested. And, strange to say, I had no more trouble from that source. But I had a great deal of trouble with dogs.

DOGS IN CHURCH

A large dog took possession of the aisle in the schoolhouse at Hogtown. He raised up and looked at me when I got up to preach very much like he intended to show me fight. I looked around and said if the owner of this dog is here, he will please take him out. But the owner was not found out in that way. So I put the chair under him, back downwards, and coasted him off toward the door. A boy in the congregation yelled out, "Don't you hurt my dog!" Then I left him to the care of the owner. I had found him.

ANOTHER INCIDENT AT HOGTOWN

I was on my last round of appointments. Brother Ward did not come to take the collection for me, as I had expected. At the close of the sermon I said, I have been coming up here to preach to you people once a month for three-quarters of a year, and you have not paid me enough to pay for the hire of my horse, and that is only fifty cents a trip. The Bible says "The workman is worthy of his hire," and now I am going to give you a chance to pay me something if you want to. I have not got money enough to take me to conference; but if you people don't pay it somebody else will. I appointed two young men to take the hat around, which they did hurriedly, and brought back one black copper cent with a hole in it. I thanked them kindly, thinking that might be all the money there was in the house. But the collection did not suit the young ladies. (I was a single man then, you see.) So they borrowed what money they could there, and then collected what they could in the village, and paid me about five dollars before I left that afternoon.

The way from Morehead to Hogtown is up a beautiful stream in which the silvery fish can be seen to a considerable depth, finning their way through the pearly waters. The hills on either side are high and rough and steep, with everything common to the forest growing upon them. Here and there may be seen a cleared field with a scanty growing crop, and a house of humble appearance usually built of hewn logs. But the people are kind and hospitable.

The country surrounding Morehead is of the same description--rougher, if possible, on the north side owing to the fact that one must travel over the hills instead of along the streams. Here, in this region, are the homes and hiding places of the feuding families of the Rowan County War. It began in August 1884, and resulted in much bloodshed over three years.

THE BATTLE BEGINS

You may suppose it was very discouraging to see my first year in the ministry close out with war on the very ground where I had labored hardest and preached most to establish the gospel of peace; and with no conversion, and only one addition to church, and that by letter.

The parties to the feudal war (I shall not name them, though I was personally acquainted with all except one) were in the midst of a political strife, each party trying to elect a man for sheriff. I returned on election day from a visit home. When I got off the train I saw the town full of people, and in great commotion. It seemed that the spirit of murder was reigning over the great mass of excited men thronging about the courthouse and the Cary Hotel. I went quietly to the polls and cast my ballot, and then sought the home of James Clarke, one of my stopping places. I was bout half away when I heard two pistol shots. The dominating spirit which had already wrought up the passions of men to the highest tension had now prevailed, and the work of murder had begun. Women were screaming piteously. Their awful expectations were beginning to be realized. Brother Clarke's little daughter came running to bring her father. I told her to go back and I would go and bring him myself. She turned again and reached her father before I did. Two men had been shot, one in the head, and one in the neck. We went into the hotel just in time to see one of them die. The other was breathing hoarsely, and bleeding at the neck, we thought he would soon die, but he recovered in a few days. The man who was accused of doing the shooting got on the train at Farmers as we passed. I knew him well—had been entertained at his house; and calling him by name, as he staggered to a seat in the car, I said: What is the matter with you? "Oh!" said he, "I've got the rheumatism so bad I can hardly stand up." He had taken a dose, I suppose, that morning. In the evening the two parties went away in separate groups, prepared to resist any attempt to arrest them. Several others were somewhat bruised in the fight. But this affair was only the beginning of sorrows.

Though the strife seemingly ended for the time, the spirit of murder still prevailed, and the battle was renewed time and again. During the fall and winter peace could not be enforced and was never restored until nearly all the hostile parties were killed.

Fortunately for me, my year closed about the last of September, and I was not compelled to witness the most horrible scenes of the war. I was paid sixty dollars and fifty-one cents for my first nine month's preaching.

FIRST CHRISTIAN CHURCH

"In the beginning... darkness was upon the deep". (Gen. 1:1-2)

Darkness was upon the land of Morehead from 1884-1887. The flame of faith was flickering faintly. Morehead was a town terrorized by a bloody feud between family factions and political parties. Innocent people were caught in the middle and were afraid to leave their homes at night. There were four saloons doing business openly in town, and not one of them legally authorized to sell whiskey. There were gunfights in the saloons, gun battles in the streets, and frequent assassinations. So because of booze, battles, and bullets, schools, courts, and churches were closed. Many citizens moved out of Morehead for safety. There was no law in Morehead, except the law of the gun. Church services were few and far between.

TEMPORARY PEACE COMES TO MOREHEAD

A fragile peace was negotiated between the feuding factions in April 1885. It lasted less than a month before being broken. Both sides hired gunfighters with questionable reputations. The fighting escalated, and many people were being killed or wounded. Therefore, at the request of many prominent Rowan County citizens, Governor Knott reluctantly ordered 100 fully armed troops to Morehead in July, 1885 to restore order. The men were from Company F of the 2nd Regiment under the command of Lt. R.D. Williams, Cpt. Cockerill, Cpt. Smith, Cpt. Veach and Major McKee. They were in Morehead for two months and bivouacked in the Courthouse yard. The men were given a unit citation for their exemplary behavior and restoring the peace while stationed in Morehead.

There would be peace in Morehead only as long as the troops remained. But as soon as they left, the fighting would escalate. For the next two years the citizens of Morehead were afraid for their lives. Many prominent people moved away. Those that remained were afraid to leave their homes after dark. Therefore church services were rare, and when services were held, they were held in the Courthouse.

The flame of faith flickered faintly from 1884-1887.

PERMANENT PEACE COMES TO MOREHEAD

In June, 1887, after the Governor refused to send troops to Morehead a third time, the good citizens of Morehead decided to act. They armed themselves, and on June 22, 1887, after a bloody gun battle that resulted in four people being killed, peace came to Morehead.

From August, 1884 through June 22, 1887, twenty people were killed and 16 wounded.

FAITH'S FLAME GLOWS MORE BRIGHTLY
In the Beginning, God Said: "Let There Be Light."

In the 1800's there was no problem with the "Church and State" issue, so church services were frequently held in Kentucky Courthouses. From 1884-1887, church services in Morehead, because of the terror that grasped the town, were infrequent and intermittent. Whenever church was held it was in the courthouse, since there were no church buildings in Morehead at that time.

It was during this time (1884-1887) that a young teenager by the name of Frank C. Button was studying at Midway College (then a college for girls) where he was given special permission to attend. His mother, a widow, was a teacher at Midway. After he completed his studies at Midway, he attended Lexington Theological Seminary. It was during this period of time Frank and his mother, Phoebe, would read the papers, and listen to the talk about the need for missionaries in Morehead. After much prayer, they decided to act.

In late September, 1887, Frank Button and his mother, Phoebe, with a deep faith that Jesus Christ was the great "Peacemaker", and that education and salvation was the answer to the Rowan County troubles they arrived in Morehead. Their vision was to open a school and found a church. The Kentucky Christian Board of Missions (Disciples of Christ) provided the support for this school. It was intended that young Frank C. Button (age 23) act as principal, and Phoebe serve as a teacher. Also, Frank was to serve as Pastor of the new Christian Church.

THE CHRISTIAN CHURCH AND NORMAL SCHOOL GROW TOGETHER

The Morehead Normal School was born October 3, 1887 with one student, in a small frame building near where the old Rowan County Jail is located. The parents of this "frail school" with such a humble beginning could never have dreamed of the giant institution it would become. However, what brought Frank C. Button to Morehead, was his missionary zeal to bring Christ to the community, peace to the people, and education for the future.

In 1888, a Presbyterian preacher by the name of Dr. Guerant, began to hold services in the Courthouse in Morehead. Since there was no church building in town, he succeeded in convincing the Christian (Disciples of Christ), Methodists, and Presbyterians to build a "Union" Church located on the present site of the Christian Church. Each church would hold services at their scheduled time. Since church services were being held intermittently, this arrangement worked well. The Kentucky Conferenceof the Methodist Church in 1890, mentions that the Methodists had a mission church in Morehead, and held a one-third interest in a church there, along with the Presbyterians and Disciples of Christ. Let it be said that Morehead was the cradle of ecumenism.

In 1892 the Presbyterians moved out of Morehead, and in 1896 the Methodists built their own building. The Christian Church then acquired sole ownership of the Union Church. They quickly repaired and renovated the building and the congregation grew rapidly.

Morehead Union Church built by Methodists, Presbyterians, and Disciples of Christ, 1880s.

From 1887 to 1900 was a period of rapid growth for the Christian Church and the Morehead Normal School. Students began arriving on foot, horseback, wagon and by train. With the financial support of William T. Withers of Lexington, and the Kentucky Christian Missionary Society, more land was acquired, buildings were constructed, and faculty was added.

In 1896 fifty acres of land in Morehead was deeded to the Kentucky Christian Women's Board of Missions by Colonel Warren M. Alderson (the writer's great-great grandfather). This land was "between the Bishop, Trumbo, and Dormitory land", and is located in the heart of today's Morehead State University.

As the Normal School grew the Christian Church grew. Those employed as teachers, and even the students had to maintain high moral character, Christian principles, and attend church regularly. Students were required to attend Chapel services each day. Most faculty members were faithful workers in the Church. The Christian Church (Disciples of Christ) grew to become the largest church in Morehead before 1900.

"Brother" Button as he was affectionately known throughout this community was the first "Shepherd of the Flock" at the First Christian Church in Morehead. He served as Pastor for a total of 21 years on three different occasions. His long and distinguished service as the first Principal of the Morehead Normal School, and first President of Morehead State College, has been well documented in many other sources and need not be recounted here.

THE VISION BECOMES REALITY

Brother Button's vision to establish a school at Morehead has succeeded beyond, I'm sure, his wildest dreams. Our great university is a magnificent monument to that vision. Also, he had another vision—that of establishing a church to provide for the spiritual welfare of the community. After one hundred years, as we look at these two institutions, we would say that today's university far overshadows the Christian Church. But when we remember the vision Brother Button and his mother had for Morehead was to bring:

(1) Christ to the community (there was no church then).

(2) Peace to the people (people were being killed).

(3) Education for the future (most schools were closed)

We can say all three of these goals were achieved.

Throughout the past one hundred years, hundreds of dedicated faculty members have worshipped in the Christian Church. Also, thousands of the prominent citizens of Morehead have worshipped there. The church now has a membership of 150. As they examine their heritage, may they continue the same vision Brother Button had for their community.

During the past one hundred years there have been twenty-five pastors that have served this church. (This writer has been privileged to know 13 of them, beginning with Gilbert Fern and extending to Rev. Bill Watson). May Brother Bill Watson and these people keep the flame of faith burning brightly.

Ministers

F.C. Button	1887-1892
Ralph Julian	1892-1895
R.C. Button	1895-1901
J.B. Dickson	1901-1093
H.B. Wade	1903-1904
D.G. Combs	1904-1906
W.F. Smith	1906-1909
F.C. Button	1909-1911
George Farley	1911-1914
Wesley Hatcher	1914-1915
N. Carpenter	1915-1920
W.S. Irwin	1920-1926
C.B. Cloyd	1926-1930
Robert Riddell	1930-1932
Gilbert H. Fern	1933-1937
Arthur Landolt	1938-1943
Charles Dietze	1943-1946
Elmore Ryle	1947-1951
Miller Dungan	1951-1955
Ray Allen	1956-1960
Charles Brooks	1961-1966
G.C. Banks	1966-1967
Alvin Busby	1967-1969
G.C. Banks	1969-1970
Roy Roberson	1970-1984
Tom Phelps	1984-1985
Harold Tackett	1985-1997
Bill Watson	1998-

Frank C. Button, Minister, Founder of Morehead Normal School, 1887.

MOREHEAD FIRST BAPTIST CHURCH

"And he was afraid, and said how dreadful is this place" (Gen. 28:27)

To really understand the genesis of the First Baptist Church of Morehead, you have to understand the conditions that existed in Morehead in 1885. Morehead was then a lawless town, and the only law was the law of the gun. It was at the height of the Rowan County War, a conflict between feuding families, and between feuding politicians, (1884-1887). It was under these conditions the Baptists would establish their church. During those dark years of Rowan County there was open warfare in the streets. Men were being killed from ambush, as well as in open shoot-outs. By April 1885 all the county officials had resigned except Sheriff Cook Humphrey and Taylor Young (County Attorney). Taylor Young was seriously wounded, and Deputy Sheriff Baumgarder was killed from ambush. Sheriff Humphrey survived an attempt on his life that burned his home to the ground, and he left Morehead and never came back. There was no law in Morehead except the law of the gun. Many of Morehead's prominent citizens moved out of Morehead to either Mt. Sterling or Maysville. Among them were Warren Alderson, James W. Johnson, Robert and James Nichels, James Thompson, William Trumbo, Z.T. Young, and their families. Many others followed over the next two years.

It was into this land of terror that these fearless founders of the Morehead Baptist Church were determined to hold up Christ as the "Peacemaker". They had the faith to believe that Christ was the answer to the violence that held the little town hostage. Headlines of *The Courier Journal* on April 4, 1885 reported: **"Riotous Rowan in deplorable state of affairs—A County without church or courts. There is an urgent need for missionaries in the county".** So it was in September of that same year that The Morehead Baptist Church would be founded.

Many people moved to Mt. Sterling for safety in April 1885, among them such prominent citizens as Z.T. Young, Jas. W. Johnson, Dr. H.L. Raine, Robert and James Nichels, James Thompson, William Trumbo, and Warren M. Alderson—whom *The Courier Journal* called "The richest man in Rowan County".

Troops on Guard at Rowan County Courthouse during the Feud, 1885.

While living in Mt. Sterling during the summer of 1885, many of those ex-Morehead residents attended the Baptist Church. While there, they succeeded in convincing the Baptists in Mt. Sterling there was a need for a church in Morehead, and that Morehead was a worthy missionary field for the Baptist church. Plans were made in the summer of 1885 for a revival in Morehead.

The Morehead Baptist Church had its genesis as the direct result of the revival held in Morehead beginning September 21, 1885. The services were conducted by James M. Wells, pastor of the Mt. Sterling Baptist Church. This was a very successful revival and many were led to Christ. Then on October 4, 1885, under the leadership of the Mt. Sterling church, about forty Morehead Baptists accepted the Articles of Faith and theChurch Covenant. Also, they joined together in the constitution of "The Baptist Church of Jesus Christ of Morehead". This brave band of Baptists, with many names representing some of Morehead's earliest families such as Rice, Logan, Layne, Coldiron,

Smith, Hamm, Johnson, Nichells, Oxley, Humphrey, Rose, Garten, Carter, Fultz, Hargis, and Havens, moved out on faith in establishing the Baptist Church of Jesus Christ in Morehead.

This group held their first business meeting on October 17, 1885, and selected Aurilla Layne as the Church Clerk, and called Rev. F.W. Carney, from Mt. Sterling, as the first Pastor. Brother Carney had led the music for their revival.

Services were held intermittently at first, usually on third Saturdays and Sundays in the Courthouse or in homes. Pastor Carney only remained until May 1886, leaving to accept a call to a church in Missouri. But it must be remembered that bullets were flying in the streets of Morehead and may citizens moved out, and those that remained were afraid to leave their homes after dark.

Much has been written about the founding of the Morehead Normal School in September 1887. That school was founded in an attempt to counteract the poor education in the area and hopefully end the violence. This was certainly true, but very little has been said about those who were here during those trying times of 1884-1887 among them that fearless flock of believers who founded a church in the midst of the reign of terror that existed in Morehead in 1885. Although there was no church building in which to meet, this faithful fellowship of believers continued to uphold the faith although there was little opportunity for the people to meet because of the fighting going on in the town. Most of the citizens who remained in Morehead were afraid to leave their homes after dark. But the flame of faith continued to faintly flicker, but never was extinguished even with the departure of their first Pastor in May 1885. The Morehead feud came to a violent end June 22, 1887, and peace finally came to Morehead again.

On April 19, 1891 Brother William Jayne became Mission Pastor, and that same year land was purchased in Morehead from a Mr. Oxley, one of Morehead's earliest families. Also, the first build-

First Baptist Church in Morehead, Established 1885.

ing committee was formed consisting of Rev. William Jayne, W.H. Avlick and Dr. L.P.V. Williams.

On November 1, 1891 the committee entered into a contract with J.Z. Haven to construct their first church building in Morehead. Financing the construction of the first church building in Morehead was difficult. There were no banks here at that time, and because of the recent feud in Morehead, surrounding banks were reluctant to loan the money for the building.

The local church membership contributed $307 to the building fund. Surrounding Baptist Churches gave cash and building materials. The Maysville church gave windows, the Brooksville Church gave furniture, and the Winchester Church gave the largest cash gift.

But they still would not be able to complete their church construction without more money. The committee turned to Colonel Warren M. Alderson for a loan. The Colonel loaned them funds needed to complete the building, and took a mortgage on the church property. (He was the father of Harvey G. Alderson, the first man to be ordained by the Church in 1895). (Harvey is this writer's great grandfather and Warren is my great-great grandfather).

On July 15, 1892 the little white church building was completed at a cost of $1,400.00 Two days later the building was dedicated with Rev. J.M. Prestridge of Winchester preaching the dedicatory sermon. He took his text from Genesis 28:17 which says:

"And he was afraid, and said, How dreadful is this place! This is none other than the house of God, and this is the gate of Heaven".

How marvelously appropriate was his text, and, as we try to understand the fear and dread that existed during those dark days we can even be more joyful to see this "House of God, and Gate to Heaven" arise in Morehead.

During the same month the church was dedicated, a Sunday School was established with Dr. Luke William serving as the first Sunday School Superintendent.

In 1893 it was taken into the Bracken Association Baptists, and became known as the Morehead Baptist Church. They also licensed Brother H.G. Alderson to preach the Gospel. Financial support for Brother Alderson included "a few $5.00; a few $1.00; more $.50; and several $.25; and $.10." Brother Alderson became the first pastor of Slaty Point Baptist Church in Rowan County.

In looking back over the one hundred thirteen (113) years, the Baptists have been worshiping in Morehead, it is evident that God was in this place from the beginning. Their rich fertile history; the long line of thousands who have worshipped here; and the thousands of prominent Moreheadians whose lives have been influenced is an indication that Morehead is a much better place because this church is here.

The original forty who in faith founded this church in 1885, has increased to a membership of 680 in 1998. This is an indication that God is still working among his people, and may He continue to work until He returns.

During the past 113 years, this church has been serviced by 23 pastors. Also during that time 11 have been licensed to preach and 8 have been ordained into the ministry.

FIRST BAPTIST CHURCH
1885-1985

Called to Full-time Ministry

Licensed		*Ordained*	
1897	H.G. Alderson	1895	L.P.V. Williams
1898	Alonzo DeHart	1895	H.G. Alderson
1916	Robert Orville Black	1916	J.W. Black
1970	Ken Hines	1972	Gary Light
1975	James Earl Forrest	1977	Charles Stephens
1976	Charles Stephens	1980	David L. Adams
1977	Terry Murphy	1982	Roy Allen White
1978	Reuben DeBoard	1983	John Hillard Weaver
1979	Jeff Withers		
1981	Roy Allen White		
1984	Neal Alan Gordon		

FIRST BAPTIST CHURCH
1885-1985

1885	Rev. F.W. Carney
1892	Rev. William Jayne
1895	Rev. T.J. Riggs
1897	Rev. Luke P.V. Williams
1901	Rev. S.F. Caudill
1902	Rev. Luke P.V. Williams
1903	Rev. R.L. Baker
1904	Rev. A.T. Stout
1906	Rev. C.L. Craig
1906-1915	Records Missing
1915	Rev. H.M. Estes
1918	Rev. J.W. Black
1919	Rev. J.S. Thompson
1921	Rev. W.M. Smith
1923	Rev. W.C. Hale
1926	Rev. M.E. Staley
1930	Rev. B.H. Kazee
1952	Rev. J.C. Raikes
1963	Dr. Ralph Couey, Interim
1964	Rev. Kenneth Cole
1969	Dr. D.M. Aldridge, Interim
1970	Rev. Hugh Brooks
1974	Rev. R.D. Baker
1982	Dr. Alan Gragg, Interim
1982	Dr. R. Don Mantooth,

FIRST CHURCH OF GOD

"Go ye therefore and teach all nations, baptizing
them in the name of the Father, and of the Son,
and of the Holy ghost." (Matt. 28:10)

THE FORMATIVE YEARS

In 1893, J.N. (Jack) Howard of Nappanee, Indiana, inspired by
these words of Jesus, came to preach the gospel. He was thought
to be the first Church of God preacher to conduct revival services
in Morehead. He was a great orator and a nationally recognized
fiery evangelist, whose winsome messages attracted responsive listeners wherever he went. Morehead was no different as he began
holding revival services in the old courthouse. God was indeed in
these services, as many local citizens were won to Christ and soon
the courthouse would not hold the overflow crowds. (The flame
of faith was glowing brightly in the town.)

Brother Howard began looking for another place to hold services. The only other churches in town were the Union and the
Baptists. The Union Church was being renovated, so he asked the
leadership of the Baptist Church if they would allow the revival to
continue in their Church. But after some debate the leaders of the
Baptist Church refused to allow Mr. Howard to continue the revival in their Church. This was a deterrent to Brother Howard, but
he was determined to continue to preach in the courthouse.

COLONEL ALDERSON INTERVENES

It was at this time that prominent local businessman, Warren
M. Alderson, heard of the situation. Since he had heard of Brother
Howard's dilemma, he wanted to help. He sent word to the
preacher the next day to come by his store at 6 p.m. Warren also

asked the local Baptist Church leaders to come to his store at 6 p.m. So when they all arrived that evening, he closed his store and told those assembled he wanted to say something. He arose and said: "Friends, this man of God has been persecuted since he came to our community, and he needs a place to preach. Now I'm asking that you allow him to preach in your Church and if you don't let him preach in your Church, 'by gum' <u>I'll foreclose on your mortgage</u>. He preached in their church.

SOWING SEEDS BY PRAYER AND FAITH

But many of the people were unhappy and they noticed Brother Howard going up on the hill back of town at daylight each morning. They thought he was meeting a woman so two of them followed him up the hill one morning and found him under a giant oak tree praying fervently for the people of Morehead.

Brother Howard is credited with planting the seeds of the great Church of God Reformation Movement in Morehead. But he was followed by Brother W.A. Sutherland, Edward Ellis and many others who kept fanning the flame of faith that would eventually glow brightly into the Church of God.

ROWAN COUNTY WAS BOOMING

In 1898 Morehead was widely known as "The City of the Hills". It was a busy trading center, strategically located half way between Lexington and Ashland on the C&O Railroad. The chief industry was lumber and stone products. It was considered a beautiful mountain town with a population of 1,200, with great potential for growth. It had an active commercial club with dynamic leadership, and Morehead and Rowan County were booming.

Farmers, Kentucky was shipping more freight tonnage (lumber, stone) than any place on the C&O between Louisville and Ashland. Bronson, located three miles west of Morehead had a lumber yard

services in the courthouse. They were determined the flame of faith would continue to burn brightly. Miss Lena Cecil served as the first Pastor, and began to plan a church building. It was certainly highly unusual for a woman to serve as a pastor in those days. But she surely must have been called by God as their spiritual leader because it was under her leadership the Church began. Also she must have been a role model to the young teenager Cora Wilson to encourage her to become a leader in education.

FIRST BUILDING WAS 1900

After fervent prayer, planning, and hard work, plans for a new church building began to materialize. Judge Allie W. Young (father of Jane Young Holbrook) gave the land for a new church and his brother W.T. Young gave a generous cash donation to start the building. Miss Lena Cecil, Mrs. Dee Sims, and Mrs. Alice Mark headed a building fund drive and began receiving donations from many local citizens. As the building fund grew, and with the gift of land, a new church building was planned on Sun Street at North Hargis Avenue. Two years later a small boxed, unpainted building was completed, and in 1900 the congregation began meeting in their own building. It was the same year their first pastor Miss Lena Cecil moved to California and married a Mr. Carpenter. She remained active in the Church of God movement throughout her life time.

Brother Henry Dunnigan was the second pastor and he remained until 1903 and was followed by Samuel Ford, a pioneer Church of God preacher. Brother Ford moved and in 1905, the small congregation of about a dozen faithful followers called Reverend T.F. Lyons to become their Pastor. Brother Lyons would be used by God to make profound changes in the First Church of God in Morehead and throughout Kentucky.

On December 25, 1890, Turner Franklin Lyons married Sara Elizabeth Wells in Menifee County. This union would prove to have a profound effect upon the First Church of God in Morehead and the Church of God Movement throughout Kentucky. The Rev. I.T. Mark records in his early history of the Morehead Church of God that he believed Turner Lyons was led to Christ by one of these early evangelists.

First Church of God in Morehead. Established 1898.

REV. TURNER F. LYONS CALLED TO MOREHEAD

In 1900 at Morgan County, Kentucky, Turner Franklin Lyons was ordained as an Elder in the Church of God, and was authorized "To perform such duties as devolve upon a minister of the gospel." In 1905 he accepted a call from the Morehead Church and moved his family to Morehead where he purchased a small farm from the Mark family. The farm was located at Bronson about three miles west of Morehead, Bronson was a busy community located on the C&O Railroad. It had an extensive lumber mill with a payroll of $6,000 per month. Brother Lyons would later purchase the land behind the church and build his home on Lyons Avenue.

When Brother Lyons came to Morehead the church building was located at the corner of what is now Hargis Avenue and Sun Street. The building was a small boxed, unpainted building. It was lighted by kerosene, and heated with a wood stove. There were about 12 faithful members of the Church.

But God would use this beloved Pastor to build a great congregation at the Morehead First Church of God. He would also use

Brother Lyons as his instrument in building dozens of churches in Rowan County and Eastern Kentucky. He was a great evangelist and people responded to his messages of love and forgiveness. His home was a haven for the hungry and homeless. Many of the citizens of Morehead who did not want to be "bothered" by the hungry and homeless would send them to Brother Lyons' home. He never turned anyone away. He was poor in the eyes of the world but rich in God's eyes. His rich legacy continues today.

From the first revival in 1893, and the great tent meeting of 1898, when the first Church of God in Morehead was founded the church continues to grow. It was been blessed by God with great spiritual leaders and laity. The *Book of Acts* tells us that it was at Antioch that the people of God were first called Christians, it was in Morehead that the First Church of God member were first called Saints.

During their 100 years, the Morehead First Church of God has gone through several building programs:

100 YEARS OF BUILDING

1900   White weather boarded church on Sun Street and Hargis Avenue. (When this building was torn down 48 years later, the women's missionary Society sold souvenir nails to help pay for the new building.

1947   Built a parsonage beside the old white church.

1948   Brick church on the corner of Second Street and Hargis Avenue *(called Lyons Chapel). (Now owned by St. Claire Hospital)*

1948   Razed old building built in 1900

1960   Brick Cathedral on the corner of Sun Street and Hargis Avenue (now owned by St. Claire Hospital).

1981   Beautiful rounded Cathedral of Worship on Sunset Drive (behind WalMart).

1998   Began construction on the Rowan County Christian Academy on Sunset Drive.

Also located on Sunset Drive is the First Church of God's Rowan County Christian Academy which began major construction of a Christian School. This project has tremendous community support, and will prove to be an asset to the total community.

God has blessed this church in the past 100 years. In addition to great preachers, there have been scores of dedicated Sunday School teachers and dozens of great Christian laymen that have influenced each generation. It has grown from the small church with 12

First Church of God during Morehead Centennial, 1956.
R-1: ?, John J. Ellis, M.L. Tate, Pastor.
R-2: Jackie Ellis, Janis Ellis, Jack Ellis, Norma Tate, ?.

members in 1898 to a lovely cathedral with a seating capacity of 800 and average Sunday morning attendance of 350.

The people of the First Church of God realize they have been blessed by God with a rich heritage, and they are determined to keep the flame of faith burning brightly. With God's help they are determined to grow not only in bricks and mortar, but in grace, love, and faith in the Lord Jesus Christ.

100 YEARS OF PASTORS

Year	_Pastor_
1898	Miss Lena Cecil
1900	Henry Dunnigan
1903	Samuel Ford
1905	Turner F. Lyons
1923	R.C. Caudill
1925	Charles Richardson
1927	Turner F. Lyons *
1941	Raman Johnson
1944	James Wade
1946	B.W. Moore
1948	Marvin L. Tate
1960	John W. Conley *
1967	Dale R. Whalen
1969	Gerald Eggleston
1973	Richard Dillon
1976	Frank Fultz
1983	Mitchell Burch
1992	John W. Conley *
1992	Rodney Williams **
1995	Stephen Carney

* Served two separate appointments

** Interim appointment

Morehead's main business district on Railroad Street, 1890s.

Looking East on Morehead's Main Street at Hargis Avenue, 1930s.

CHAPTER TWO

Early Entrepreners:
Visions of the Future

As the end of each century approaches, there is a tendency of people and institutions to examine where they are, analyze how they got there, and project where they are going. This is true now as the leaders of business, industry, education, and other services face the fast approaching 21st century. So let us look back at early Morehead, 100 years ago. As the 19th century was coming to an end, what were their plans for facing an unknown 20th century.

Rowan County was formed in 1856. Morehead was then designated as the county seat. It is unclear who were the first settlers into Morehead. They probably came here following the Revolutionary War and received a land grant. One settler who preceded them was a Mr. Oxley. (This writer has seen a powder horn with J.R. Oxley 1817 carved on it.) The small stream up Wilson Avenue was called Oxley Branch by the early settlers in Morehead.

CIVIL WAR AND ROWAN COUNTY WAR

Within five years after the county was formed and Morehead named the county seat, this state and nation was torn apart by the bloodiest war in our history. Brother against brother and neighbor against neighbor prohibited much growth in Morehead.

On November 10, 1863, guerilla bands captured Morehead and terrorized the local citizens for several days. Then on March 21, 1864, the town was captured again and the courthouse burned to the ground.

Next the Tolliver-Martin feud, 1884-1887, slowed the economic growth of Morehead and Rowan County. Indeed a bill was introduced in the Kentucky Legislature to abolish Rowan County–but failed to pass due to mounted local opposition. Finally in June 1887, when peace was restored to Rowan County, business began to flourish again. The Morehead Normal School was then established in September 1887.

Following the end of the conflict and the establishment of the Morehead Normal School, the little town began to experience growing pains. Therefore as the 19th century drew to a close, the prominent citizens of Morehead, called "The City of the Hills", began planning for what they considered an exciting future in the 20th century.

In July, 1898, Schoolers Printery, a commercial printing company, of Morehead, Kentucky, publishers of "The Morehead Advance", included a "commercial club edition" extolling the virtues of Morehead, "The City of the Hills." "The Advance" was printed in pamphlet form on hand operated machines. The office was located on Railroad (First) Street across from the present freight station. Every member of the Commercial club passionately believed that Morehead and that Rowan County had potential for tremendous economic development and investment potential. They were determined to see the community prosper and grow.

A HEALTHY CITY

If you want health and wealth, come to Morehead, 'The City of the Hills' was the motto of the commercial club of Morehead 100 years ago." Their goal "was to show the outside world what was buried in these beautiful hills surrounding Morehead." They said, "All laws in the world cannot bring success to the town that lacks energy and push." These early citizens were totally dedicated to the commercial and industrial development of Morehead and Rowan County. This group believed that you could do no better than invest in Rowan County. Indeed the editor of "The Morehead Advance" said, "We have fought hard to see our city and county build up and will keep on hammering along this line as long as there is anything to hammer at."

INDUSTRY ARRIVES

Although the over exuberant claims of coal and iron being located in Rowan County were not true, the insistence that Rowan County contained some of the finest fire clay in the nation was prophetic. Because within 10 years, the Clearfield and Haldeman tile and brick companies located in Rowan County. These factories employed hundreds of men. It was also emphasized that this county had some of the finest hardwood timber every grown. This of course is still true 100 years later and continues to be one of the premier industries of our county. Although several sawmills and one planing mill were here, their goal was to establish a furniture factory close to the source of "the finest hardwood timber in the nation". This goal is still one of today's goals after 100 years.

RAILROAD PROPOSED

This group was visionary in that they proposed a railroad be constructed through southern Rowan County to Morgan County, for the purpose of opening to the world the rich coal, clay, and timber deposits of Rowan and Morgan counties. This indeed was a prophetic recommendation at that time, and did result in the construction of the Morehead and North Fork Railroad. This railroad extended from Morehead up Morgan Forkthrough the Clack Mountain Tunnel down North Fork of Licking through the Poppin Rock Tunnel and on to Wrigley in Morgan County.

This railroad resulted in the coming to pass of what was proposed by the Commercial Club. It did open up that region and brought great economic growth to our county during the first one-fourth of the 20th century.

Those early citizens, members of the Commercial Club, not only saw Morehead as having great potential as a place for people to work and invest in the future, but said,

"The 'City of the Hills', on account of its delightful location is one of the most healthy towns in the U.S. The malarial swamps that are in southern towns are not here. Also, the fatal fevers of the north are unknown here, and we are located midway between the frigid north and the torrid south. Therefore, our climate is moderate in summer and winter. The town also has a natural drainage that cannot be excelled."

MORALITY IMPORTANT

They were proud of this community, a safe and serene place to live and raise a family. They also emphasized the high moral and spiritual character of the citizenry. This is an obvious attempt to reverse the image of Bloody Rowan County and the Rowan County War. The carnage of that feud took the lives of 20, and wounded 16 people from 1884-1887.

The Commercial Club was anxious to change the image of Morehead and said "In morality, Morehead is not excelled by any town in the mountains. The town is inhabited by peaceful, industrious, sober, christian people who live upright and frugal lives". Also the publication pointed out the gracious hospitality extended by its citizens as it states, "Kentucky's greatest glory is its hospitality, and the people of Morehead and Rowan County indulge without restraint in that hospitality which has made Kentucky famous".

There were four churches in Morehead in 1898: Methodist, Baptist, Christian and Church of God. The Methodists and Baptists worshiped in their own building while the Christians and the Church of God worshiped in a Union Church. The Methodists, Christians and Baptists had well organized and flourishing Sunday School.

Those early visionaries of 100 years ago believed in the future of Morehead and Rowan County. They were pioneers in the area of economic development. They were devoted in their determination to see Morehead and Rowan County become a place where people could live, work, and be happy.

EDUCATION NOT IMPORTANT

In 1898 the citizens of Morehead did not seem to really consider education important in any future growth. Almost as an afterthought. They said that the "Educational facilities of Morehead is equaled by few an seldom surpassed by any town of the size". Also, we have a graded school with good teachers, and a school term of five months. Again, almost as an afterthought they said, "The Morehead Normal School is an excellent institution in a town of excellent people with a reputation state wide". Again it seems they were more interested in presenting the citizens of Rowan County as being an honest, peace loving, citizenry with high moral character, than as an educated citizenry.

ORGANIZATION IMPORTANT

In 1898, J.G. Whitt, a local attorney, was elected President of the Commercial Club of Morehead. This club must have been the forerunner of what we now know as the Chamber of Commerce. Its members included business and professional men who were excited about Morehead's potential and believed in its future as they moved toward 1900. They had a vision of what could happen when:

"the enterprising citizens of Morehead and Rowan County put their shoulders to the wheel, and if you hear anything drop you need not be alarmed. Because they mean to leave something to show their children, and their children's children what was done in the year of our Lord 1898."

SUMMARY OF BUSINESSES IN MOREHEAD 100 YEARS AGO

In 1898 Morehead, called "The City of the Hills" by the Commercial Club was located on the C&O Railroad half way between Ashland and Lexington. Its population was about 1,200 with 4,200 in Rowan County. It was a sixth class city governed by five trustees, a police judge and a marshall. "This beautiful city in the hills" commanded a large area of rich territory with enterprising merchants able to handle the business. The "Advance", Morehead's newspaper in 1898, was published and owned by J.M. Schooler. His economic survey of the city listed "eleven general stores, all doing a good business": J.M. Carey, Mark & Muse, H.M. Logan, W.A. Mocabee, A.W. Vinton, G.A. Nickell, O.S. Gilkerson, J.H. Fraley, B. Lipsitz, Mrs. Minnick and William Porter.

Colonel Warren A. Alderson, an early pioneer businessman in Morehead was then in his 80's, and had sold his business several years earlier. It was then known as Mark & Muse and was located on Main Street across from the Courthouse.

Evidently in 1898, the people in "The City of the Hills" were not sick very much, or wore a lot of hats because there were as many millinery stores as there were drug stores. Those included two first-class millinery stores, Bradley Brothers & Company and Mrs. Mary D. McBrayer; two drug stores, L. PickleSimer & Company and C.E. Bishops. Those were located on what is now First Street, across from the Depot.

LOTS OF LAWYERS - FEW DOCTORS IN TOWN

Nine lawyers were doing a brisk business in this beautiful "City of the Hills". This seems to me to be a good sign of the times, because at least the people were no longer settling their disputes with guns, but did, as we now do, litigate our disputes. These nine lawyers were: W. Clarke & Son, J.W. Riley, Will A. Young, C.E. Day, J.G. Whitt, J.R. Blair, T.W. Rose and C.S. Gilkerson.

Three country doctors practiced in Morehead 100 years ago. They were probably products of the University of Louisville College of Medicine. They made house calls on horseback, many times swimming streams and remaining all night in their patients homes. They dispensed their pills out of their "black" doctor bags and were greatly revered by their patients. These three physicians in Morehead were: Dr. J. Wilson, Dr. L.P.V. Williams and Dr. C.E. Saulsberry.

There must have been a lot of tourists, or traveling men in Morehead 100 years ago, because there were five hotels. Of course most of these were large homes with a hotel sign hung outside. Most were located on First Street (Railroad Street) on both sides of the C&O tracks. One hotel, The Gault House, was located on Main Street across from the Courthouse. This was the place following the famous gun battle of June 22, 1897, that ended the Rowan County War, where the dead were taken to be viewed by passengers that came into Morehead on the train that day. Those five hotels and their owners were: Cottage, Mrs. Raine; Gault, J.M. Carey; Bryan House, Mrs. J.R. Bryan; Hotel Hamilton, Mrs. Hamilton; Proctor House, C.S. Proctor; and Palace Hotel, Mrs. Watkins.

The ladies in Morehead did their own hair because there were no beauty shops in Morehead in those days. I'm sure none of them would have even entered either of the two barber shops in town 100 years ago. The two barber shops were owned by Jas. Lytle and Tom Bennet.

One of the main goals of the Commercial Club of Morehead in 1898 was to encourage greater investment and more capital to invest in the community. But only one bank was here at that time.

The Bank of Morehead, Sam Bradley, President, opened its doors for business January 3, 1898, and closed in 1928. Joel Head, Jr. was cashier and M. Paxton Davis was the assistant cashier.

Other businesses in Morehead, and the prominent citizens who owned them are ancestors of many Moreheadians today. Among those were Sam Allen, grandfather of John "Sonny" Allen; and Wilson Allen, grandfather of Robert and Hubert Allen. Allen's business is now operating in Morehead as Sloanes.

One grocery, J.R. Bryan; one livery stable, F.P. Blair; one blacksmith shop, Kennard & Smedley; one hoop factory, George Petty; one planing mill, William Cooper; one meat market, Wilson Allen; one confectionery, Sam Allen; one jeweler, Sherman Evans; and one shoemaker, Dock PickleSimer.

TAXES AND ROADS

Productive farm land was selling for 5 to 20 dollars per acre. Valuable timberland could be purchased for 4-6 dollars per acre. The county boasted a good system of public dirt roads maintained by the citizens living along said roads. Each citizen was required to work three days per year on said roads to keep them in good order. They also furnished their own equipment and tools. There was no taxation for roads in the county. The rate of taxation for county purposes was 50 cents per hundred. THE COUNTY HAD NO INDEBTEDNESS, EITHER BONDED OR OTHERWISE.

Clearfield and Haldeman, large population centers in the county in the early 20th century, had not yet been established. Also Farmers and Cogswell were major trading centers at that time because of their location on the Licking River.

Let it be said that these early citizens had a clear vision of what they wanted to see happen in this community in the 20th century. They worked hard, and they worked together. Many lived to see their dreams come to fruition without local-state-or federal grants. The railroads lines, clay mines, brick and tile factories, and stone quarries all came into being. But they were very short sighted to not see the potential economic impact of the Old Morehead Normal School upon the region, and the impact of education upon economic growth.

QUEEN CITY, KENTUCKY

So you thought Cincinnati was known as the Queen City? But almost 125 years ago when the county was barely 20 years old, plans were made by a "shady" real estate developer to build Queen City, Rowan County. You say you ever heard of it? Well, don't worry, not many people in Rowan County, and few people in Kentucky, ever heard about it either–but it once was printed on a map as one of the most promising cities in Kentucky. It was registered on an elegant plat in the Rowan County Court Clerk's Office in 1875. It was a very official looking document which said:

STATE OF KENTUCKY S.S.
County of Rowan
This is to certify that the plat of Queen City, as made out by the "Queen City Land and Building Association: is duly filed in this office, and that the title of the lands of said Company is good as shown by my official records. GIVEN UNDER MY HANDS AND SEAL,

James W. Johnson
Clerk and Recorder of
Rowan County, Kentucky
Morehead, November 8, 1875

While this appeared very legal and factual, it was the basis of one of the biggest, boldest, and most audacious land swindle in the state, and maybe, even the nation. It certainly rivaled many of the real estate "scams" in Florida that came 50 years later where innocent people bought worthless swamp land.

"SLICK SEWELL'S SHADY SCAM SWINDLES"

The Queen City Land and Building Association was the brain child of J.W. Sewell. Mr. Sewell was a native of Breathitt County, who moved to Covington, Kentucky. On his way to Covington, he came through Rowan County, and the seeds of the scheme were sown. After getting settled in Covington, he had no trouble getting financial backing and formed an Association with Mr. E. Wood of Cincinnati as president. He then returned to Rowan County and purchased 1800 acres of land four and one-half miles west of Morehead along the road to Olympia, in Bath County.

The Association then published an elegantly engraved plat of the city which included 368 blocks, each with 24 lots to the block. Each lot was 25 ft. by 100 ft. and sold for $4.50 to $6.00 per lot. The illustrated description of Queen City showed a symmetrically laid out city with 200 ft. wide boulevards and avenues. Streets were 80 ft. to 100 ft. wide, with such names as Grand Blvd., Lake Avenue, and Park Avenue. Many streets were named after past U.S. Presidents. A post office was actually established April 11, 1878, called Queen City, Kentucky. It was located three miles west of Morehead, and the postmaster was Mr. William Fowles. However the post office was discontinued May 15, 1882.

A PERFECTLY PLANNED CITY

This handsomely laid out city showed beautiful churches with lofty spires, large school buildings with modern equipment. A lovely park was located in the center of townwith two continuous fountains. Marble statues of Cupid and Aphradite all certainly captured the admiration of the reader. For the music lover there was a music bandstand and gazebo for outdoor concerts. For the water lover, there was a large lake called Silver Lake. The brochure showed a wide road around the lake side with people on horseback, in buggies, and strolling. There were several sailboats on the placid lake, with happy children in sailor suits sitting on their decks. The shrubbery, trees, and grass reflected the natural beauty of the surrounding countryside. Market Garden was the commercial district where business would flourish. The Lexington and Big Sandy Railroad showed two tracks adjoining this idyllic setting, where trains would bring the latest merchandise and tourists to Queen City.

Everything anyone would want in life was elegantly presented in their brochure. They did not even forget death because there on the edge of the city is beautiful Silver Lake Cemetery, arranged in circular format with three streets in an ever widening circle of grave sites. There was also a chapel for funeral services.

Everything anyone would want in life, and in death, was planned for the Queen City, Rowan County, Kentucky. With this strong sales pitch, "hundreds of lots were bought by people from all over the country–but in those days it was strictly a paper city."

SWINDLE DISCOVERED–BUYER BEWARE

James Appleby, a wealthy hotel owner in Montreal, got tired of the Canadian winters, and decided to move south. He traded his hotel for one block in Queen City plus several thousands acres in the surrounding country. After he received the deed from the Queen City Land and Building Association, he decided to go examine his purchase.

Arriving on the train at Mt. Sterling, he was informed that was as far east as the train ran. Mr. Appleby rented a horse and buggy, and began asking where Queen City was. No one, of course, knew about it, until he met someone who told him it was in Rowan County, 40 miles east. So Mr. Appleby came to Morehead and finally found "Queen City". There were no railroads, churches, houses, parks, or streets. He sued in Rowan Circuit Court to recover his hotel, but died before the case was settled.

Many others taken in by the swindle joined in the suit, but others fearing it was not worth the effort took their loss and went home. Some of the deeds were recorded in Rowan County, and each had a miniature copy of the brochure attached to the deed. Among those who were swindled by Mr. Sewell were: Hammond Smith (1883), William H. Main (1885), George H. Klugh (1886), Peter Vanderer (1876), Joseph Hersh (1888), Elizabeth Sharp (1877), Abraham Patterson (1876), and John P. Kelley (1886).

THE DECEPTION DEEPENS

This was not the end of the Queen City Land swindle, because although Mr.Sewell paid for the land, he had recorded it in the name of his sister, Abbie Grigsby. Therefore all the deeds for the land purchased and even recorded were worthless. In fact the Queen City Land and Building Association was worthless, and did not even own the land. Abbie Grigsby owned the land. There were many claims against the land. Suits and counter suits resulted. But on January 3, 1879, A.J. McKenzie, Sheriff of Rowan County, sold the land at auction at the courthouse steps. Warren M. Alderson purchased all the land in 10 different tracts. He bought a total of 2,387 acres, but no price was ever listed on a deed in those days. (I sure would like to know how much he paid for that land.)

"THE BAD GUY GETS HIS"

This was not the end of "Slick" Sewell's shady scam swindles. He disappeared for several years, but later re-appeared in Indiana and had the same type of scam going again. But this time one of the men he swindled hunted him down and put a forty-four bullet in his brain ending his life and works.

His death, and the purchase of the land by Warren M. Alderson, marked the end of Queen City, Rowan County. But if the dream had been legitimate who knows what Rowan County would look like today.

ELECTRICITY: LET THERE BE LIGHT

"Go not where the path may lead–go instead where there is no path..and leave a trail." (Ralph Waldo Emerson)

This writer has written much about the darkness that prevailed over Morehead in the early years. (Spiritual Darkness). But this is the account of the man who literally brought Morehead out of the darkness.

LOCAL LEGEND LOOMS LARGE OVER LOCAL LANDSCAPE

He was one of Morehead's early pioneers in business, industry, and utilities. Although he was not a large man, his early contributions in all of these areas looms large over the local landscape. He was responsible for bringing the mysterious magic of electricity to Morehead.

His name was E.E. Maggard, and everyone called him Ed, but really the E.E. could have meant "Early Entrepreneur". He was born in Elliott County, Kentucky in 1879 and moved to Morehead in 1903, because of the influence of Warren M. Alderson, who had extensive real estate holdings in Rowan and Elliott Counties. Colonel Alderson, a prominent pioneer businessman in Morehead, had just sold fifty acres to the Morehead Normal School for $250. He had also sold some of his other real estate holdings and due to poor health moved to Elliott County where he lived with a daughter. There he became friends with young Ed Maggard and encouraged him to move to Morehead where there was greater opportunity.

In 1903, Morehead had no paved streets, utilities, or city services. There were a few "coal oil" (kerosene) street lights that flickered faintly on Morehead's Main Street. The last local lamplighter in Morehead was Noah Kennard. As a young man, Noah was a deadly shot with a rifle or shotgun. He would put on local exhibitions of his skill with a rifle by hitting marbles as fast as you tossed them into the air. Noah later served as Morehead Mayor for many years. But he was proud that he was the last local lamplighter and that Ed Maggard put him out of a job.

E.E. Maggard was a man of vision. He had visited some of the surrounding cities and literally "had seen the light", by recognizing the importance of Thomas Edison's invention. He was determined to transform Morehead's dim coal oil illuminated streets into a new bright way. He also wanted to better illuminate Morehead's homes, schools and businesses. So after a few months in Morehead Ed formed the original Morehead Light company.

The Morehead Light Company was founded in 1903 by E.E. Maggard, J.M. Carey, C.A. Proctor, F.E. Webster, and W.F. Davidson. They began construction of lines and power plant immediately (without any government regulations). The first power plant was constructed about where the old dam is on Triplett Creek, as you go over to the city Park.

In a few months electricity was ready to be turned on in the village of Morehead. Most residents were excited, but many were afraid of this new invention of lights from a line. But nevertheless, electricity came to Morehead in 1903. There were of course no meters to measure the amount of electricity a customer used. The power was turned on for only five hours each evening (from 5 to 10 p.m.). Cost was determined by the number of light bulbs in the building. The charge was .50 per light bulb per month. (Notice there were no electrical outlets at this time). Later as electrical outlets were added there were additional charges based upon the number of outlets.

E.E. Maggard (R). Early Eastern Kentucky Entrepreneur.

The Morehead Light Company Power Plant burned down in 1906. But Morehead residents had "seen the light" and were determined not to live with coal oil light anymore. Therefore, the city of Morehead rebuilt the power plant and leased it to Ed Maggard, and he managed the operation until 1925.

During this time tragedy struck the Maggard family. It happened one evening during an electrical storm, when the power went off, as often happened. Of course if the power went out anytime except between 5-10 p.m. in the evening nobody noticed. But when it went out during the time that people were supposed to receive electricity many people would pound on Ed's door. (No phones yet).

One evening about dusk the power went out and Ed sent his only son (who worked for him) to restore the power. Tragically Ed's son accidentally came in contact with a bare high tension line and was electrocuted. Ed, had to be the one to turn the power off and get his son's badly burned body down from the pole. Of course he was profoundly affected because the thing he had created had destroyed his only son. (He had one daughter, Hildreth, who died in a local nursing home in 1998). Ed believed in the importance of his work and he continued to manage the Morehead Light Company until 1925 when it was sold to Barrett Waters and Associates from Augusta, Kentucky. It was later sold to the Kentucky Power Company who later became Kentucky Utilities Company.

A new power plant was built in 1925 about where the "Old Town Park" is now located. (There was a small dam across Triplett Creek there.) It supplied electricity to Morehead and part of Rowan County until the mighty Dix River Dam was completed in the 1930s. Then the Morehead Plant was used only as a supplementary emergency power source. It was torn down in the 1960s. Many Rural Rowan Countians remember Roosevelt and the Rural Electrification Act of the 1930s for their electricity. (My grandfather did not get electricity on his farm in Rowan County until 1945). But a "light" Morehead Memory should be of Ed Maggard who believed it was "better to light a candle (bulb) than to curse the darkness".) He was one who punched holes in the darkness of Morehead. He should be a MOREHEAD MEMORY when we turn on our lights tonight.

MOVIE MANUFACTURER IMPROVED ON THOMAS EDISON

The idea of moving pictures has long been a dream of mankind. But it wasn't until 1889 when Thomas Edison and George Eastman designed their celluloid strips that it became a reality. Even then, watching moving images was done on an individual basis, and involved great exertion. The viewer was required to turn a heavy crank on a primitive private appliance in order to watch short frames on small screens.

In 1891 Edison invented the movie camera, and then in 1898 he developed the Kinetoscope. These inventions formed the basis for filming and projecting moving images on a white surface. But Edison's silent projector left much to be desired, because the films were constantly fluttering and flickering which was irritating to the viewer. But in any event movie houses were born.

EARLY MOREHEAD MOVIE HOUSES

The *Rowan County News'* Centennial Edition reports that in 1904 the first movie house in Morehead was located on Trumbo Avenue, and was in a two story building called "The Nickelodeum." It was owned by Millard Stevens and for a nickel you could see a silent movie as it was projected on a sheet. These movies were either westerns or mystery films, with diabolical plots where the hero rescues the heroine at the last minute from in front of the approaching train.

Another Morehead movie house that did not last long was at the corner of what is now South Wilson Avenue and First Street where the Morehead Utility Plant Board offices are now located. It was owned by John Wall and closed in 1908.

MOREHEADIANS ENJOYED EARLY MOVIES

Elisha Edward Maggard, local businessman and highly respected inventor was convinced that this primitive invention of moving images had a future. So undaunted by two previous Morehead movie house failures he opened his own movie house in 1909, called the Nickelodeon. For a nickel you could see a movie and listen to Elizabeth Young as she accompanied the movie on the piano. The crescendo increased on the piano as the drama increased on the screen. (Also, when it rained on the tin roof of the building, she would start playing 'Showers of Blessings'.) Moreheadians flocked to see the movies and hear the music. They did this in spite of the fact that the city council enacted a law making it illegal for young boys to walk the streets of Morehead shouting the name of the movie playing that night. (This was Ed's method of advertising his movies.)

But Ed became dissatisfied with the quality of the image being projected (it constantly flickered), and, the dependability of the projector,(it constantly broke down). So Morehead's mechanical movie man believed he could improve upon Thomas Edison's movie projector. Undounted by the reputation of the great Mr. Edison he began blazing a new trail (a la Mr. Ralph Waldo Emerson) "Go not where the path may lead, but go instead where there is no path and leave a trail".

ED MAGGARD IMPROVES UPON EDISON'S INVENTION

Photo: Rowan County Historical Society.

Entrepreneur Ed decided one of the problems with the projector was it had too many moving parts. he theorized that if he could simplify the machine by reducing the number of moving parts he would have a more practical dependable machine. He was determined to improve upon the eminent Thomas Edison, who had invented the movie projector. So in reality he was determined "to build a better

Cosmograph Motion Picture Company owned by E.E. Maggard and Sam Bradley. 1910-1918.

mousetrap", and the world did beat a path to his door. In 1913 after receiving a patent for his invention, Mr. Maggard formed Morehead's largest enterprise to date. He then secured sufficient financial backing for a factory to produce movie projectors. It was called the Maggard-Bradley Company. Incorporators were E.E. Maggard, S.M. Bradley, B.S. Wilson, J.B. Peers, and A.M. Beatty. (Mr. Beatty of Denver, Colorado, was formerly with the Thomas A. Edison Company.) The company was incorporated at $250,000, a fortune for that time, and Mr. Beatty was appointed national sales manager.

COSMOGRAPH COMPANY COMMENCES

The Maggard-Bradley Cosmograph Company built Morehead's first factory on the corner of Railroad Street (now First Street) and Trumbo Avenue. It was constructed of native bluestone, and began production September 13, 1913. Fifty men were employed, with the production capacity of 50 to 100 machines per day.

COMPANY REACHES NATIONAL AND INTERNATIONAL MARKETS

The company opened offices at 95 Liberty Street, New York, NY. Also, offices were opened in Chicago, Illinois, and Denver, Colorado, and a national sales and publicity campaign began. The machine was advertised nationally as follows:

THE PERFECT PROJECTOR

"Uses standard film, can be attached to any ordinary lamp socket".

"This machine is the most simple in the world to operate as a simple part performs the work of three of the most important parts as employed by all other projectors, namely, the cam, shutter, and fly wheel. Also, the picture thrown by the machine is clearer and uncluttered".

A better mousetrap had been built; and national sales were brisk. Soon the 'Perfect Projector' was being sold internationally. No less than the Czar of Russia ordered several hundred to be used in Russia to help to educate the masses. (I don't know where the film was produced to do this). But the shipment was made, and a representative of the Czar was sent over with the money. In the meantime the Czar was overthrown, and his family was killed. (I just read in the paper that after 80 years, the Czar and his family had been given a proper burial).

The envoy never showed up with the money, therefore Morehead's largest enterprise to date -- THE MAGGARD-BRADLEY COSMOGRAPH COMPANY suffered a devastating financial loss. In 1919 the business was sold to the World Eye Company at Cleveland, Ohio, dismantled and moved to Ohio. So after six years of operation, Morehead's first manufacturing plant went out of business, but this was not the end of E.E. Maggard.

SELECTING A SITE FOR A NEW COLLEGE

In 1922 the Legislature in Frankfort was debating the most appropriate site for a new college recently authorized for Eastern Kentucky. The site selection committee was deeply divided between Morehead and Paintsville. Senator Allie W. Young was arguing valiantly that the most appropriate site should be Morehead. But the site selection committee seemed unimpressed, and it was at this point that Mr. Maggard entered with his movie magic.

MR. MAGGARD BEGINS HIS MOVIE

Ed Maggard produced a silent movie, documenting the many advantages of Morehead as the best site for a college. Many of Morehead's citizens actively participated in the movie. The plot went something like this:

On the scheduled day, dozens of Morehead citizens, dressed in their Sunday best (the men in suits and ties, the ladies in long dresses and hats) met at the Railroad Passenger Depot just as the noon train arrived. (This writer's father-in-law, Lindsay Caudill was a Railway Express agent on the train at that time). The local citizens then all boarded the train and it slowly <u>BACKED</u> out of the station for about a half a mile. Then as the train returned to the station, Ed filmed the train as it came chugging into Morehead. He then filmed all of these people as they got off the train, pro-

MSU Professor Steve Young demonstrates Cosmograph Motion Picture Projector manufactured in Morehead, 1912.

moting Morehead as a busy passenger terminal. In the meantime all the people who owned cars in Morehead (perhaps a dozen or more) had been scripted to drive along the dirt street now called First Street.

MOREHEAD CITIZENS PROVIDE THE ACTION

As all these people walked across Railroad Street, a policeman was on duty to stop the cars, and allow the people to cross the street. Of course, Mr. Maggard was filming all of this activity depicting Morehead as a busy, safe, yet modern community. The people then walked up the dirt street (Trumbo Avenue) to the corner of Main Street, and by that time the same dozen cars had circled the block. The sheriff was on that street corner stopping traffic (there were no traffic lights in Morehead then). As the people crossed the dirt street safely under the guidance of the sheriff, Ed's camera was grinding away.

Some of the people walked down the wooden sidewalks to the businesses in town, where they were filmed, and others went to their homes where they were filmed. Senator Allie Young was filmed going to his home where he picked up his newspaper and sat down on the porch to read. (His daughter, Jane Young Holbrook, told me that in this scene he was holding his paper upside down.) She said the family always had a good laugh over his big movie role when he was reading the paper upside down.

FILMING CONTINUES AT THE NORMAL SCHOOL

Many of the people were filmed as they walked over the grounds and through the buildings of the beautiful Morehead Normal School. This provided evidence that Morehead already was emphasizing the importance of education, and the Normal School could form a nucleus for a new college. Brother Frank Button, Morehead Normal School President was filmed in his office, and in chapel with the students. This showed educational and administrative leadership already in place in Morehead.

The newly produced film was sealed in a can and rushed off to Cincinnati to be developed. As soon as titled subheadings were spliced into the film, Senator Young scheduled a screening with the committee in Frankfort. It was then, Ed loaded one of his cosmograph film projectors, manufactured in Morehead (the committee must have been impressed by this), and, along with some of the city "fathers", boarded the train to the state capital.

FILM PREVIEWED IN FRANKFORT

The film was shown to the Site Selection Committee on Ed's "Manufactured in Morehead Perfect Projector". Senator Young provided appropriate narration to the silent film. Also it was evident that the film had a dramatic effect upon the committee, even though they had visited the Morehead site. It had a dramatic effect because of what is now known about the learning process; also, how a moving image and a sound tract can affect behavior, and change attitudes.

This writer, at one time served as a full-time Educational Consultant to CORONET Films. (A division of Esquire Inc.). We were the world's largest producer of educational films. This company was founded because the President (Mr. Abraham Blinder) had lived in Germany before WW II. He had viewed first hand Adolph Hitler's rise to power, and how the Nazis had used a moving image and a soundtrack to change behavior. This was primarily the way the "Hitler Youth" were trained, and they soon would turn against their own parents. So Mr. Blinder came to this country and founded CORONET Films, designed to help change the behavior of children through the use of educational films.

MR. MAGGARD "SELLS" MOREHEAD

When Mr. Maggard made this film designed to promote Morehead as a site for a college, he had no idea what an important tool he had discovered. He may not have been the first to recognize that a moving image, and a soundtrack could "sell" a product, (or then he may have been the first). Today, we are bombarded on every side with these moving images. We know that it can affect behavior. Looking at this incident through the telescope of time, it is apparent Elisha Edward Maggard was light years ahead of his time, when he produced this film to promote the image of Morehead.

Did the viewing of this film affect the vote of the Site Committee? The committee by a slim margin of one vote picked Morehead over Paintsville as the site for the new college. Now we have our fine institution, Morehead State University. We are all justly proud of Morehead State. But a mighty Morehead Memory (because of help from Ed Maggard) we can now say *Morehead State University* instead of *Paintsville State University*. (Perish the thought.)

TELEPHONES -MOREHEAD PHONE COMPANY - PHONE 1

Early entrepreneur Elisha Edward Maggard was a pioneer in many fields. He not only patented and manufactured a movie projector in Morehead, he also brought Morehead out of the darkness with his electric power plant. But he also brought thetelephone to Morehead. This invention was and is considered both a blessing and a cursing. But nevertheless, Mr. Maggard was credited with bringing Alexander Graham Bell's invention to Morehead (telephone). Mr. Bell's famous first phone message, "Mr. Watson come here", reverberated all the way into these Kentucky hills thanks to Ed Maggard.

CONNECTED BY "CENTRAL"

In 1919 Mr. Maggard established the Morehead Telephone Company and began stringing telephone lines on the electric poles he owned throughout the city (a master stroke of genius). The switchboard was located on the second floor of a building on Main Street. That's where the telephone operator, or "central" was located. She was called "central" if you didn't know her name. (But most everyone knew her name.) It was an exciting time in Morehead as the crude phones were hung upon the walls of Morehead homes. I say homes, because businesses had not yet seen a need for such a device. (They preferred personal contact). If you wanted to make a call, the procedure was, you picked up the receiver, attached to a cord from the phone on the wall. You held it to your ear, and cranked vigorously, and "central" would answer. Then you would yell into the phone on the wall "Esther get me Lindsay Caudill's house". Esther Ellington was one of the early switchboard operators. Some would just use a first name--nobody ever used telephone numbers. However, Ed Maggard's phone number was #1, and Calvert's Garage and Taxi Service was #2. (I'll bet they never forgot their phone number).

CONNECTED TO OTHER COMMUNITIES

Looking for ways to expand his communications empire, he purchased the Big Sandy, Farmers, and Salt Lick telephone companies. Then he consolidated the companies into a public service company. The Morehead Telephone Company was then able to provide much better service, not only to Morehead, but to these regions of Kentucky.

In 1925 Mr. Maggard sold the Morehead Phone Company to a Mr. Brown, who sold it to a Mr. White, who then sold it to a Mr. Sparks. Mr. Sparks later sold out to the Kentucky Telephone Company, which became the General Telephone Company.

Another famous first for Morehead's Ed Maggard was the gramaphone. He was credited with being the first to demonstrate this device in Morehead. (The gramaphone was the invention of Thomas Edison which reproduced music or sound on a wax disk). It was at the July 4th 1920 celebration on the Courthouse lawn Ed demonstrated the gramaphone music from a wax disk. He cranked up the old music box and presented a concert. The "canned concert" was a great success as Moreheadians marveled at music from a box, even though a live band also performed.

MOREHEAD'S "MR. COOL"

Another famous first for Mr. Maggard was helping to cool Morehead. No, air conditioning had not yet been invented, but the process of freezing water into ice had, and Ed brought it to Morehead. In 1920, Mr. Maggard established the Morehead Ice and Bottling Company. (Phone 71). I'm not sure what they were bottling but the business was located on the East end of Railroad Street. The ice was frozen from pure healthy water (as stated in their advertisements). It was frozen in 100 lbs. blocks, then it was stored in an ice house with thick walls heavily insulated with sawdust. Before the ice was sold it was chipped with a sharp ice pick into 50 and 25 lb. blocks then it was ready for sale. (There was a real art to chipping the ice without losing small chunks).

Home Ice Delivery Comes to Morehead

Mr. Maggard's partner and early ice company manager was C.B. Daugherty, who would later become successful as a stockholder in the Citizens Bank. (C.B. Daugherty Branch Bank in Trademore Shopping Center). Later a young J. Wallace Fannin was employed as the delivery man. Delivery was made to the homes in Morehead on a regular basis. Each customer was given a card with a large 25 printed on one side, and 50 on the reverse side. If you wanted ice you stuck the card in your window with the 25 or 50 showing how many pounds you wanted.

Delivery was made from a wagon pulled by a team of mules. The wagon was filled with sawdust, and the ice placed in the sawdust and covered with a heavy wet tarpaulin for insulation. Wallace Fannin would then drive the ice route delivering ice to homes and businesses. He carried the ice from the wagon to the delivery point with large ice tongs. The ice was carried all the way to the wooden ice boxes of customers.

Wallace Fannin Kind to Kids

Years later (in the mid-1930's) J. Wallace Fannin was still delivering ice in the mule drawn wagon. But this writer's family did not ever have a wooden ice box--we could not afford ice. We kept our milk and butter in a water tight bucket hanging submerged in the well in our yard. But on hot summer days, as Wallace made his rounds in the ice wagon all the neighborhood children would surround the wagon, some riding on the rear "tongue" of the wagon "mooching" small chips of ice. Wallace would always run us off-- but only after we had grabbed a large chunk of ice to cool us off on a hot day. Years later, I realized that Wallace deliberately left some large chunks, and gave us time to get them before he would run us off. Eating ice from the back of the old ice wagonremains a Morehead Memory, as well as the early phone service when we were on a first name basis with central (operator).

UTILITIES – WATER, GAS AND SEWER

In baseball there is usually a utility man. This is a man who can perform well at several different positions. Mr. Maggard was such a man. He was the Utility Man for many Morehead utilities. He performed well at every position.

WATER AND GAS COME TO MOREHEAD

In the 1922 general election, the city of Morehead voted to put water in Morehead. In 1924, twenty five thousand dollars in bonds were sold to install water lines in Morehead homes. A dam was erected on Tripplet Creek and Morehead built its first water treatment plant. Norman Wells had the contract to lay the first water lines to the homes and businesses. In the early 1930s natural gas was brought to Morehead by the L.C.Young Company. The first gas fields to supply the city were located on Long Hungry, about six miles west of Morehead. During these early days there was weak water pressure and low gas pressure. Moreheadians shivered in the winter time and had trouble getting water pressure. Then Mayor Noah Kennard (Morehead's last Lamplighter) called upon the man who had ended his lamplighting job by bringing electricity to Morehead many years ago, to help. He appointed an elderly Ed Maggard as water and gas commissioner with the assignment to remedy the situation. Ed located another large gas field toward Lewis County and piped the needed gas to Morehead. This move helped meet the demand for more gas until the giant Tennessee Gas Transmission lines came to Morehead in the 1940s.

MR. MAGGARD, THE DANIEL BOONE OF INDUSTRY

Water pressure was improved under Maggard's supervision by installing new pumps, building a new water tower and locating leaks. Whenever, and wherever there was a problem with any of Morehead's utility services, Mr. Maggard was the "trouble-shooter" they called. He could usually locate and solve the problem.

Mr. Maggard might be called the Daniel Boone of his day. Daniel would discover new territory, settle it, and move on. This seemed to be Ed's major formula. He would move into a new business territory, establish it, and move on to new territory.

In his later years, Mr. Maggard was involved in many business ventures. He was one of the men who established the Citizens Bank. He was one of the owners of the Consolidated Hardware Company (phone 92) located on Main Street. Also, he went into the construction business and built many fine home homes and businesses in Morehead.

The last building he built was on Main Street was where the McBrayer Furniture Store was located. When Mr. Maggard decided to build, his intention was to join his building with the Peoples Bank building next door and completely cover his lot. C.P. Caudill, president of the Peoples Bank offered him $1,000 if he would leave a five foot easement between the buildings. Mr. Maggard agreed, and since the total cost to construct his building was eleven hundred dollars the building only cost him $100.00. I'm sure the rent he collected from Mr. McBrayer paid for the building several thousand times.

Mr. Elisha Edward Maggard was a major force in bringing Morehead from a small town without utility services, to a thriving community with all utilities and services. He <u>was</u> recognized by many of his contemporaries as a "mechanical and electrical genius", and as a "real asset to Morehead". Although the Bible tells us that "A Prophet is not without honor, except in his own land," Ed <u>was</u> honored and respected in his own land.

DYING IN MOREHEAD BETTER
THAN LIVING IN ARIZONA

Ed had a deep love for Morehead, and devoted his life to enhance its growth. As he grew older his health began to fail, and his doctor told him that if he wanted to live he would have to move to Arizona. After several agonizing days of decision, Ed packed up and boarded the train for Arizona. One cold snowy day less than a month later this writer saw him in the Post Office. I was surprised to see him and said: "Ed, I though the doctor told you to move to Arizona if you wanted to live?" He said: "I'd rather die in Morehead than live in Arizona". Yes, Mr. Maggard loved Morehead, and in less than three months he was dead. (March 1, 1948). But he should remain a Morehead Memory because of his Famous Firsts:

> Established first viable movie house in Morehead.
> Established telephone service in Morehead.
> Established first factory in Morehead (Cosmograph).
> Established first ice plant in Morehead.
> Demonstrated first Victrola in Morehead.
> Helped to establish viable gas and water service here.
> Also, successful builder and businessman.
> Helped establish Citizens Bank.

Although he did not own the first car in Morehead (Sam Bradley was given that honor), he went to Lexington with him to buy the car, (a chain drive Ford). Ed drove the car back for Sam since he had not yet learned to drive. When they came to the LickingRiver at Farmers, they had to wait over night for the water to recede so they could ford Licking River. As they traveled through Farmers and Morehead the next day they attracted a large crowd.

Ed Maggard did not own the first Model T Ford car in Morehead, but he was probably the first man in Rowan County to wreck his car. It was on a trip out in the country, and he was driving his Model T too fast, and hit a large rock in the road, lost control, and turned the car completely over one revolution and landed right-side-up. A farmer that witnessed the accident came running over to see if Ed was hurt. He was not injured, in fact he was sitting behind the wheel and still had his hat on and his cigar was still in him mouth.

MONEY MANAGERS

"Why didn't you deposit the money in the bank, so that I could at least get some interest?" (Luke 19:23)

BEFORE BANKS

It is claimed that the first bank in this area was the Kentucky Bank, chartered in Mason County in 1793. In 1835, it became the Bank of Maysville. It is still in business in Maysville today. However, banks have only been solid sound financial institutions for less than one hundred years. Bank robbers, unscrupulous bankers, and unsure economic conditions caused many people to be suspicious of banks. Indeed, there was a bank panic in Kentucky in 1819 as a result of an economic depression and many failed. Also several of the banks in our state were called "Forty Thieves," when they foreclosed on borrowers creating a panic. Banks even printed their own currency. In 1822, the Bank of the Commonwealth in Lexington and Louisville, printed their own dollars which were worth fifty cents. However, by that year they had loaned 2 million Commonwealth Dollars, but only held three thousand dollars of hard currency. Many borrowers and creditors went bankrupt, and it was over fifty years before Kentuckians would have confidence in banks again.

MOREHEAD BB (BEFORE BANKS)

Morehead's wealthy early pioneer settler, Warren M. Alderson

(1819-1903) never trusted banks. Therefore since there were no banks in Rowan County, Colonel Alderson with his personal wealth, became a banker to Rowan Countians. Although he was robbed several times, he still refused to deposit his money in a bank. He was Morehead's leading dealer in dry goods, groceries, and general merchandise in the late 1800s.

BANKER WITHOUT CHARTER

From 1873, Warren M. Alderson was the private personal bank for Rowan County businesses, churches, and citizens. He loaned money to build the first Baptist church in Morehead in 1885. But he insisted upon a mortgage. He would accept mortgages on land, buildings, cattle, horses, or furniture. He kept his money and account books in his saddle bags. While out collecting on his mortgages, he stopped to spend the night at John Ellis's house. He left his saddle bags on the front fence all night. When he went out to get them the next morning they counted $5,000 (nothing was missing). Mr. Alderson wrote his own mortgages and recorded them in the courthouse. In looking through the old mortgage books in Rowan County, this writer found on record in 1898 that Colonel Alderson had released a $400 mortgage he held on T.C. Tippett's furniture. It was released when Mr. Tippett died so as "not to burden his widow with the bill".

When Mr. Alderson loaned money, he required adequate security for the loan. In 1887 John W. Rice wanted to get in the sawmill business, and Colonel Alderson loaned Mr. Rice $796.98 for sawmill equipment. Evidently Mr. Alderson did not have much faith in the future of the sawmill business, because he required much more than just the sawmill equipment for security. Mortgage Book Number 1 in the Rowan County Courthouse lists the following as security for the loan:

1 Sawmill and all fixtures, 2 bay horses, one with one white foot, and the other with a bald face. One bay horse-pigeon toed (10-11 years old). One large black mare mule, one sorrel horse (7 years old), one four-horse wagon, and one two-horse wagon. (The date of this mortgage was August 1, 1887. Just a few days before the start of the Rowan County War). Payment was to be made at the rate of $50.00 every six months plus interest.

FORECLOSED ON HIS OWN RELATIVES

Certainly Colonel Warren Alderson required sufficient collateral before loaning money. (The same secret of success for today's banks.) Warren Alderson was never reluctant to go to court to foreclose on anyone who defaulted on his loans. He was fearless in that respect. Before moving from Logan County, West Virginia to Morehead in 1873, Colonel Alderson loaned money to 10 nephews in West Virginia. He held a mortgage against each piece of property. All 10 nephews defaulted on their loan. During the period from 1876-1879, after moving to Morehead, Colonel Alderson returned to Logan, West Virginia and sued each in Court, and won every case, and foreclosed on his nephews. By the way every one of them was named Hatfield. Warren Alderson' wife was the aunt of Anderson (Devil Anse) Hatfield; and "Devil" Anse Hatfield, the patriarch of the Hatfield (McCoy) Feud, was one that lost his land due to Colonel Alderson's fore closure.

Also in February 1897, court records show Colonel Alderson sold "50 acres of land in or near the city of Morehead" to the Kentucky Women's Christian Missionary Convention (a corporation under the laws of Kentucky). The land was for expansion of the Morehead Normal School and the price was $450, payable by $50 down and $100 a year for four years. Although he had no charter, it can safely be said that Colonel Warren M. Alderson was the first banker in Rowan County.

FIRST BANK: MOREHEAD STATE BANK

On January 3, 1898 the Morehead State Bank became the first banking institution established in Morehead. It was located across Main Street from where the Citizens Bank is now located. The officers were considered outstanding community leaders. They were: Samuel Bradley, President; Joel Head, Jr., Cashier; Paxton Davis, Teller; and Hiram Bradley, Board Member. Calling it "the pride of the hills" was a way of putting a positive spin on the opening of the new bank. In an obvious attempt to overcome the negative image of banks, the Morehead State Bank called itself "one of the most substantial banking institutions in the State, and if people wish to place their money where it will be protected, they could do no better than deposit it in the Morehead State Bank".

Using the same logic used by Morehead businesses for the next 100 years, they emphasized that "now our citizens don't have to travel to other cities to do their banking, or run around for 2 or 3 hours to cash a check". They should also "deposit their mite in the local bank and show their support for their community". President Bradley said, "When the bank has been here a year, its customers will wonder how they ever did business without it". Each staff members was portrayed as honest, hard working industrious, and a great asset to Morehead.

EARLY BANK MERGERS AND LOSSES

In 1902 the Lenora Deposit Bank opened its doors in competition with the Morehead Bank. Local physician, and Baptist Preacher L.P.V. Williams was president. The Lenora Deposit Bank did not survive very long. In 1905 it merged with the Lenora National Bank, and immediately merged with Sam Bradley's Morehead State Bank.

Following that merger, the Morehead State Bank moved into a new two-story brick building on Railroad Street across from the old Passenger Depot. (That was the heart of the business district then.)

Sam Bradley and Paxton Davis continued to help manage Moreheadians money through their bank until 1928. However, in the early 1900's they financed some un-wiseinvestments by accepting mortgages on land in the territory of Arizona (it was not yet a state), in the city of Phoenix. This investment turned sour when the owners defaulted on the land leaving the Morehead State Bank as the owners of a good portion of Phoenix. This cut drastically into the bank's reserves and it began to struggle to stay afloat. In 1927 with capital stocks of $15,000, and a surplus of $18,000, and deposits totaling only $213,000, the bank stockholders began to get nervous. By 1928 the Morehead State Bank was out of business, purchased by a new bank opening up in Morehead called The Citizens Bank.

PEOPLES BANK ORGANIZES

On August 15, 1906, a plan for another bank in Morehead was conceived at the Abel Caudill Family Reunion at Waggoner in Rowan County. Abel was born February 4, 1843 in Letcher County, Kentucky. His father (Samuel) and grandfather (Matthew) were born in Wise County, Virginia. They migrated to Letcher County, Kentucky in the early 1800s. Abel served in the Confederate Army during the Civil War. When the war ended he moved to Rowan County and married Mary Ann Hall on November 15, 1866. They became the parents of 15 children. Many of these children distinguished themselves in the business and financial world.

On September 25, 1906, following that famous family reunion, an organizational meeting was held at the Peoples Hotel on Railroad Street (First Street). There were 17 people at that meeting including Abel and all of his sons. Two hundred shares of stock were

Morehead State Bank. 1898-1928.

sold at 100 dollars per share, for a total of the $20,000 capital investment needed to obtain a bank charter. Since the organizational meeting was held in the Peoples Hotel, and the bank was located in an office in the Peoples Hotel, it was decided to name the new business "The Peoples Bank of Morehead".

The first bank officers elected were: F.P. Webster, President; Abel Caudill, Vice President; and D.B. (Dan) Caudill, Cashier. Other original stockholders were: S.M. Bradley, Hiram Bradley, H.H. Caudill, D.G. Bales, J.N. Caudill, C.L. Clayton, S.M. Caudill, Robert E. Caudill, John T. Caudill, Ben T. Head, C.P. Caudill, H.H. Lewis, G.W. Caudill, and W.C. Caudill. The Peoples Bank (could have been called the Caudill Bank) officially opened its doors for bank business in the Peoples Hotel on Railroad Street on January 1, 1907. (In today's banking world January 1 is a holiday.)

CAUDILLS - PIONEER BANKERS

As the bank began to grow, Abel Caudill succeeded F.P. Webster as the bank president, and served several terms until his death in 1925. Following his death he was succeeded by his son, D.B. Caudill. In 1926, however D.B. withdrew from the MoreheadPeoples Bank and established the Peoples Bank of Sandy Hook, Kentucky. His Brother, Dave, succeeded D.B. as president of the Morehead Peoples Bank. Dave was succeeded by his brother, C.P. Caudill, as president of the Peoples Bank of Morehead in 1937. Following the death of C.P. Caudill, his son, Roger became president and C.E.O. and served until his death. Following his death, Roger Caudill's sons James and Donald, served as president and C.E.O. of the bank. Therefore, there were four generations of Caudills that served as president and C.E.O. of the family owned Peoples Bank before it was sold.

Abel Caudill worked hard all of his life to raise a family of 15 children. But he combined that hard work with a vision and optimism for the future of Morehead and Rowan County. He imparted that vision to his children, and together they set out to build a banking business that would parallel the growth of the bank, with the growth of the community. C.P. Caudill once said: "their eyes were upon the future of Morehead to an even greater Morehead of tomorrow."

The loan officers of the Peoples Bank were not necessarily known as your friendly bankers, where just anyone could walk in and get a loan. However, the bank combined sound business practices with excellent service to their customers. That helped both customers and the bank to prosper. The Peoples Bank remained on first Street until 1937 when it moved to a new building on Main Street. In 1956 the bank built a new and modern bank across the street and is still at that location today. However the bank is no longer owned by the Caudill family. It's name has changed several times since it was sold. It has been Peoples First, Trans Financial, Star, and First Star Bank. (Mr. Perry Allen is the Bank Manager of the Downtown Branch.)

BANK AND CITY GREW TOGETHER

The Peoples Bank of Morehead grew as the community grew. By 1910 the $20,000 resources needed to open the bank had grown to $72,468. By 1920 their resources had grown to $116,060 and after 30 years their resources reached $810,771. In those early days, the bank officers divided their profits at the end of the year by sitting around a table and counting out the cash to each owner. During that era Morehead's economy had grown from a crossroads community to regional commercial center. Its education had grown from a struggling Normal School to a rising regional College. Its city services had grown from mud streets to paved streets, from wooden sidewalks to cement walk ways, and from kerosene to electricity. Also, instead of well water, there was city water, and instead of outhouses, there was indoor plumbing. All of this growth was amazing when the population of Rowan County had grown only from 8,277 in 1900 to 12,734 by 1940, (about 50 percent) in 40 years. Although he did not live to see it come to fruition, Abel Caudill had built a bank that grew as Morehead grew.

SURVIVED CRASH OF 1929

The Peoples Bank of Morehead prided itself on being a sound solid financial institution, with integrity that promoted confidence by its depositors. That confidence proved true during this nation's financial collapse in 1929. Many banks closed during that time, many went out of business, but the Morehead Peoples Bank did not close its doors. It remained open, and not a single depositor lost a penny during those depression days. That remains a Morehead Memory of the days when Morehead's money managers provided financial assistance to economic growth, and remained afloat during those dark depression days.

Peoples Bank officers and employees, 1940. F-R: Hobert Lacy, Dave Caudill, Mary Caudill, Roy Caudill, Roger Caudill, Dudley Caudill, C.P. Caudill.

CITIZENS BANK

On September 21, 1928, Articles of Incorporation for a new Morehead bank were signed and submitted for approval to the Kentucky Banking Commission. It was approved on September 22, 1928 and the Citizens Bank of Morehead was born. The articles of incorporation listed the capital stocks at $15,000. The Incorporators listed were H. Van Antwerp, E.E. Maggard, C.E. Dillon, Squire Hogge, and Frank Havens. Three hundred shares of stock were sold at $50 per share to forty-four Rowan County citizens. The initial bank officers were: Dr. T.A.E. Evans, President; E.E. Maggard, Vice President; and J.W. Hogge, Cashier. The Board of Directors were H. Van Antwerp, C.B. McCullough, M.F. Moore, Tom Harmon, Squire Hogge, and Frank Havens.

The reason there were so many original stock holders (44) was that the Citizens Bank took over the assets and liabilities of the failed Morehead State Bank. Many of the 44 stockholders in the failed bank were permitted to exchange their stock in that bank for stock in the Citizens Bank. Among those original 44 stock holders were: Allie Young, Dr. H.L. Nickel, William Parker, Silas Black, Martha Ellington, Callie Calvert, Beulah Williams, W.G. Blair, and H.M. Turner.

The Citizens Bank opened its doors for business September 28, 1928 on Railroad Street (First Street). Their slogan was "Grow With Us." Their goal was to serve the financial needs of all the citizens of Rowan County as well as businesses. The first employees were Tom Hogge, cashier; Pruda Garey, teller; and Elizabeth Davis, bookkeeper.

DIFFICULT DEPRESSION YEARS

Just one year after the Citizens Bank began business in Morehead, the nation experienced the worst banking crisis and economic depression in history. Also, the Citizens Bank had the liabilities of the old Morehead State Bank. That in itself caused an early crisis in the Bank. Mr. C.B. Daugherty (who was President of the bank at that time) and Mark Logan, took the mortgages held by the Citizens Bank on Arizona land to Phoenix, and sold them to Phoenix banks. That helped relieve some of the critical need for capital, but the economy was depressed and the bank was barely able to continue. Mr. Daugherty had to appear before the Kentucky Banking Commission to get special approval to continue the business. Indeed, there were many times Mr. Daughtery would sell Citizens Bank notes to Cincinnati Banks, in order to meet their own obligations.

Mr. C.B. Daugherty decided they needed new leadership in the bank. He brought the former State Assistant Banking Commissioner, Glenn W. Lane, to Morehead as the new cashier. Mr. Lane began immediately to turn the bank around, and get it on a sound financial basis. Gradually the bank began to grow and to make a profit. By 1933 when President Franklin D. Roosevelt started the Federal Deposit Insurance Corporation (F.D.I.C.), the bank began to move forward. The FDIC insured depositor accounts up to $5,000. (Now accounts are insured up to $100,000)

CITIZENS BANK ROBBED

On Oct. 12, 1939 Morehead experienced its one and only bank robbery. The bank was then on Railroad Street (First Street) and thieves used a crow bar to break in the rear door. They drilled through the safe, blew the door off, and escaped with $6,600 dollars in paper, and $1,400 in silver. It was similar to robberies at the Salt Lick, West Liberty and Sandy Hook banks a few months earlier. G-men were called in but the money was never recovered. However, it was insured and the bank suffered no loss as a result of the robbery.

ALPHA IN THE BEGINNING

"Alpha" is the Greek word for "beginning." "Alpha" Hutchinson was not present at the beginning of the Citizens Bank, but he did arrive almost at its beginning. Alpha Hutchinson, the present Chairman of the Board of the Citizens Bank, is a real life Horatio Alger. He began his career as one of Morehead's Money Managers on October 7, 1940. An article from the October 17 issue of *The Morehead Independent* printed the following news: "Alpha Hutchinson has left his employment at Curt's Transfer, and will be employed at the Citizens Bank as a clerk-bookkeeper. Mr. Hutchinson's many friends who are glad to learn of his new job wish for him every success".

Alpha Hutchinson was born April 13, 1919 at Elk Fork, Morgan County, Kentucky. He is the son of David Roscoe Sr., and Marinda (Conley) Hutchinson. Mr. & Mrs. Hutchinson were the parents of six children. These were: Curt, Dora, Alpha, Dorothy, Clifford, and David Roscoe, Jr. In 1923, Mr. Hutchinson moved to Morehead with his family and entered the mercantile business.

Alpha attended the Morehead Public Schools, and graduated from Morehead High School in 1938. He was an outstanding football player and was elected most popular boy in his class. Alpha served as President of the Dramatic Club where he was cast as "Paul Webster" in the senior play "Keep Off the Grass." He was also elected by his peers as the best all-around student. Alpha's leadership abilities emerged early in his life.

ALPHA MARRIES MILDRED

After enrolling at M.S.T.C., the dapper Mr. Hutchinson soon met and married Mildred Randall, who was one of Morehead's most popular young ladies. (Today, they are the parents of one daughter, Susan Neff, and grandparents of Heather and Ryan Neff, and Jennifer Markwell.) Soon after marriage, Alpha dropped out of college and began working for Curt's Transfer and the Railway Express Agency. Work was going well and the future looked bright when quite un-

Alpha Hutchinson,
Citizens Bank employee 60 years.
President and CEO 1999.

expectedly, Mr. Glenn Lane, cashier of the Citizens Bank, offered him a job as clerk-bookkeeper.

Alpha and Mildred discussed the offer together. The question was whether it would be better to keep his present job at $50 per week? They decided that there was a better future by accepting the bank job, even though it meant taking a 20 percent cut in salary. After a few weeks the janitor quit and Alpha agreed to take that duty for another $5 per week. Alpha's banking career and Horatio Alger story had begun. He began his banking career at the bottom, and worked his way to the top.

When Mr. Hutchinson began his banking career at the Citizens Bank in 1940, he was the fourth employee. That year the bank moved to the Cecil Building on Main Street across the street from its present location. In 1956 the bank moved to its present location. In 1940, the total bank assets were $154,029.98, but soon began to grow rapidly. With Mr. Glenn Lane as his mentor, Alpha learned the banking business from the ground up. He was gradually promoted through the ranks, and held every position in the bank. When Mr. Lane retired in 1970, Alpha Hutchinson was elected President and C.E.O. Gradually over the years he and his family acquired controlling interest in the bank. (Now the only other stockholder in the bank is Mr. J.T. Daugherty with 15%). Today, Mr Hutchinson is proud that the Citizens Bank is a five star rated bank. (Highest rate given.) Also, he is proud to say the Citizens Bank is one of the few private family owned banks in Kentucky. His son-in-law, Robert Neff, is now President and C.E.O. Also grand children Heather, Ryan, and Jennifer (Markwell), are learning the banking business under Mr. Hutchinson's tutelage.

BANK GROWTH AND TECHNOLOGY

In almost 60 years in the banking business in Morehead, Alpha has seenphenomenal growth in Rowan County and the Citizens Bank. The bank's resources grew from $154,029.98 in 1939 to $45,716,167.00 in 1999. All that growth while the Rowan County population increased only 100 percent (10,893 to 20,353). The number of employees grew from four to 29 today. Mr. Hutchinson is quick to recognize the many excellent bank employees who have contributed to the bank's success.

During Alpha's years at the bank, many changes have occurred in the banking business, e.g.: ownership changes, technological changes, adding new services, (ATM machines, drive-in banking, and direct deposit); also dropping old services, such as no longer returning your canceled checks. However, checks are still returned by the Citizens Bank and the phone is answered by a person (Vicky Blakeman), not a machine. Also, branch banking has brought better service to the people, and the Citizens Bank was the first in Morehead to open a Branch Bank in the Trademore Center. It was named for C.B. Daugherty, early chairman of the Board of Directors.

The private family owned Citizens Bank Board of Directors today include Alpha and Mildred Hutchinson and Neff and Markwell Families. Also, Dr. Adron Doran, former President of MSU; and Lawrence E. Forgy Jr., past un-successful candidate for Governor, are board members. Today, the bank has a core capital of $4,875,541, plus $380,850. It is a solid substantial bank with a 5 star rating (highest rating given by FDIC).

Citizens Bank officers and employees, 1956. L-R: Glenn Lane, Ruby Wood, Ruth Litton, Jean Wells, Beulah Green, Jo Thomas, Nettie Jamison, Alpha Hutchinson.

ALPHA ACTIVE IN COMMUNITY AND POLITICS

Mr. Hutchinson, a life long Republican, says he supports the man and not necessarily the party. Always active in political affairs, he has served on major state, local, and national political campaigns and committees. Alpha has also been active in local clubs and community activities, and has received numerous civic awards. He is a 50 year member of the Morehead Masonic Lodge and the Kentucky Bankers Association. (He's almost eligible for 60 years.) He was selected by the Morehead Lions Club as their "Man of the Year," and has received dozens of personal, professional, and political awards. Alpha is a faithful member of the Morehead Methodist Church. He is faithful in attendance, service, and support. He also supports about every worthwhile community drive for funds.

The venerable Mr. Hutchinson, looking much younger than his age, came to work everyday for almost 60 years. His wife, Mildred, remains as always, the motivating, yet stabilizing force in the Hutchinson family as well as in the Bank. Therefore, loosely quoting the article in the old MOREHEAD INDEPENDENT published October 17, 1940: "Alpha Hutchinson is currently employed at the Citizens Bank. Mr. Hutchinson has many friends who are glad to learn of his position and wish for him every success in the future." That is true today as it was almost 60 years ago–HIS FRIENDS WISH HIM EVERY SUCCESS IN THE FUTURE.

D.B. CAUDILL ESTABLISHED PEOPLES BANK

In 1926, one group of Morehead's Money Managers purchased the Martin Bank of Sandy Hook, and on December 6 of that year established the Peoples Bank. The initial stockholders were: John Thompson, Drew Evans, H.W. Wheeler, G.W. Fannin, H.C. McClain, G.W. Pritchard, Dave Caudill, and Daniel B. Caudill.

The founding officers were: D.B. Caudill, President, D.C. Caudill, Vice President, H.W. Wheeler, Vice President, W.E. Mobley,

Cashier, and Mary Vansant, Asst. Cashier. The bank opened with an initial investment of $15,000 of capital stock, and was located in the old Bank Building at Sandy Hook. The bank achieved success from the beginning and grew rapidly. In 1955, the old building was replaced with a modern banking facility. Mr. D.B. Caudill emphasized the impor-

Peoples Bank of Sandy Hook Presidents:
L-R: Boone Caudill, D.B. Caudill, Jane Caudill.

tance of good character, respect, and reputation for a successful bank. The motto of the bank from the very beginning and remains appropriate today, was: "Confidence is the Greatest Word in Banking." Mr. Caudill said, "Without confidence, you cannot get depositors, and without depositors, you might as well close your doors."

CAUDILL REFUSED STOCK IN ANOTHER BANK

Daniel Boone (D.B.) Caudill seemed to have banking in his blood. He seemed to attract banks through his personal reputation. In fact he was voted shares in the old Morehead Lenora Bank without his knowledge. But he returned the stock saying he did not want to be connected with that bank. Mr. Caudill attended the Morehead Normal School, and studied banking and law at Valapariso Normal School in Indiana. He was admitted to t he Kentucky Bar Association in 1906. In 1908, he married local beauty, Miss Etta Procter, in a ceremony conducted by the Reverend F.C. Button, President of the Morehead Normal School. Their children included Kentucky philanthropist, Lucille (Caudill) Little, retired dentist Dr. Milton Caudill, Patty (Caudill) Eubank, the late Boone Caudill, as well as the late beloved Dr. Claire Louise Caudill. (She remained chairman of the Board of Directors until her death.) Also her sister-in-law the late Jane Caudill, was an officer in the bank for over 60 years, and President at her death.

MODERN BANK OPENS IN MOREHEAD

By 1956 the bank had grown to a capital of $30,000 with a surplus of $40,000, and resources of over $100,000. In 1998 a new modern Peoples Bank opened on Morehead's Flemingsburg Road. Officers in the new bank were: Dr. C. Louise Caudill, Jane E. Caudill, B. Procter Caudill (grandson of Dan Caudill), Roberta H. Caudill, and Boone P.Caudill III. Also, there are 31 additional employees and officers in the bank. In 1988 the total assets of the bank reached $48,828,112.00. A far cry from the $15,000 initial investment in 1926.

Money is the engine that oils the economy. Without financial capital, the economy grinds to a halt. Morehead has been fortunate throughout most of its history to have money managers with a vision of what the future holds, and as a result, Morehead continues to reach toward the future.

FIRST FEDERAL SAVINGS & LOAN

For over 50 years Morehead's money managers (bankers) were men of the Citizens and Peoples Banks. Long-term loans for homes and businesses were difficult to obtain. Large down payments, irregardless of credit rating, made it difficult to obtain local loans. Therefore, many people had to finance their homes and businesses through lending agencies in Ashland, Lexington, and Cincinnati.

On a warm spring day in 1962, a group of local business buddies were having their usual coffee in the Eagles Nest Restaurant on Main Street. While enjoying their coffee, the conversation turned to the need for a new bank in Morehead. That group included businessman Roy Cornette, whose vision it was to see another bank in Morehead. He soon convinced his business partner in the Monarch Company, and Morehead Postmaster, Claude Clayton, of the need for a bank. Later, Claude Clayton saw J.E. Duncan at a Little League game and said, "Gene, we're having a meeting tomorrow at the Eagles Nest to discuss a new bank in Morehead. If you are interested, we'd like you to be there." Gene said, "I'll be there." Others who were at the meeting were: Clyde Bruce, Thomas R. Burns and L.G. Bishop. But all those interviewed agreed Roy Cornette was the motivating force behind the bank plans. Planning sessions were later held at Roy's house. After more planning, they asked Attorney Thomas R. Burns, for legal assistance. After several weeks of discussion, the group decided to apply for a Federal Savings and Loan bank rather than a full service bank. They believed that was needed more, and had a better chance for approval.

APPLICATION SUBMITTED

Mr. Burns did the preliminary investigation and obtained the necessary papers. The group visited the regional Savings and Loan Bank in Cincinnati, where they were encouraged to continue. Attorney Burns began collecting the mountains of socioeconomic data required for a bank charter. He said, "It took almost a year to collect, assemble, organize, and present the data required by the Federal Savings & Loan Board in Washington, D.C. But finally, in February 1963, the completed application andsupporting data were forwarded to Washington, D.C. for approval. Before approval could be granted, a public hearing was held in Washington to hear witnesses for and against approving the bank.

Attending that hearing were Morehead Bankers Alpha Hutchinson and J. Roger Caudill, along with their attorneys. They argued vehemently and eloquently that Morehead had no need for another bank. Attorney Thomas R. Burns presented very persuasive arguments as to why another bank was needed in Morehead. He was supported by the seven original board of directors. After a brief delay, a decision was reached in favor of "a new bank in Morehead."

ROY CORNETTE FIRST PRESIDENT

*Roy E. Cornette,
Morehead Savings and Loan
First President, 1953.*

On Tuesday, July 8, 1963, at 4 p.m., an organizational meeting of stockholders was held in the old Citizens Bank building on Main Street in Morehead, Kentucky. The First Federal Savings and Loan Bank of Morehead was then a reality when those magnificent seven, risking reputation and capital, were elected Board of Directors. Those men were: Roy Cornette, L.G. Bishop, J.E. Duncan, Claude Clayton, Glennis Fraley, Clyde Bruce, and Attorney Thomas R. Burns. The officers were Roy Cornette, President (he remained president until his death in April 1981, when he was replaced by Thomas R. Burns); L.G. Bishop, Vice President; and J.E. Duncan, Secretary-Treasurer. J.A. Shackleford was the executive manager, and Virginia Hibberd, his assistant.

The new mutually owned Morehead bank opened its doors on July 21, 1963. The bank opened with 275 stockholders (the federal government required 250 minimum), with an investment of $300,000 in capitol stock. The bank paid 4 percent interest on passbook savings, and made home and commercial loans, and all accounts were insured by the F.D.I.C. for $10,000 (now $100,000). Under the watchful eye of President Tom Burns, the bank maintains sound business practices and it is on a sound financial basis.

EXPANDS INTO NEW BUILDING

The bank's assets have grown from $621,000 after two years to over $36,000,000 today. It is considered one of the most financially sound banks in the area. In 1963, it opened with two employees, and now has seven. The First Federal soon out grew its quarters, and purchased the Cecil property at the corner of Main and Hargis. Now there is a new modern building on that site, with a large parking lot for future expansion across the street. Like the classic children's book, *"The Little Engine That Could,"* the train was pulled across the mountain by the little engine that could. "The Little Bank That Could," has pulled the train of Morehead's economy across the mountain of resistance, and all have benefitted.

In the classical American movie *"It's a Wonderful Life,"* Jimmy Stewart gives up his dreams of becoming an architect and remains in his hometown as president of the family-owned Bailey Savings and Loan Bank. At the end of the movie, he believes himself a failure, until all the local townspeople rally around him in his time of need. They helped him because, they said, he had helped them in their time of need. Perhaps the First Federal Savings and Loan Bank is now helping many Moreheadians in their time of need to purchase their own home or business. If so, then it has been of great value to this area. That was the object of the bank, and objective accomplished.

MOREHEAD NATIONAL BANK

In the spring of 1981 a group of Morehead physicians, citizens and Ashland attorneys and architects began the long process needed to establish another bank in Morehead. The Ashland architect was David Osborne, and the attorneys were William H. Jones, Gregory L. Monge, and Howard Van Antwerp. The early Morehead organizers were former Morehead Mayor Crayton Jackson, MSU Professor Alex D. Conyers, and local physicians Warren

Proudfoot, and Charles Franks. Mr. George Archbald was the chief organizer and was elected interim president of the new bank.

In the late fall of 1981 the original organizers offered 150,000 shares of common stock with a par value of $5 for a sales price of $10 per share. The minimum investment was $1,000 and all stocks had to be sold before the bank could be chartered. Also, the comptroller of currency had to examine, and approve the stock sale. Within a few months the stock was all sold, and the sale approved, and the application submitted.

FOURTH BANK ORGANIZED

The opening of a fourth bank in Morehead was a long and complicated process. It began with the application to the Kentucky Banking Commission for approval of another bank in Morehead to be called The Morehead State Bank (That was the name of a bank in Morehead in 1907). All three of Morehead's local banks (Citizens, Peoples and First Federal Savings) opposed the charter approval, saying there was no need for another bank in Morehead. The state charter was denied. Not to be deterred, the determined group began looking toward Washington, D.C. and in December 1982, applied for approval of the Morehead National Bank. After some delay, the new bank was approved in 1984.

HISTORIC HOME PURCHASED

In November, 1984, the new bank officers purchased the Lane Funeral Home property at the corner of Main Street and Carey Avenue. It was Morehead's oldest brick building in Morehead at the time it was torn down to make way for the new bank. The stately old brick residence was originally built in 1904 as a private residence for prominent Morehead attorney, Bill Young (brother of Allie Young). In 1903, Mr. Young signed a contract with a Louisville building contractor to build the home. While it was under construction, Mr. Young and his wife were on a grand tour of Europe. The contractor made a mistake laying out the foundation, and had to reduce by a few inches the size of each room from the original specification. When Mr. and Mrs. Young returned from Europe, the house was completed. But when Mr. Young discovered the rooms were smaller than specified, he refused to pay for the house. He sued the contractor, and won in court and did not have to pay one penny for his new home. The home remained a private residence until 1956 when it was purchased by the Lane Funeral Home.

NATIONAL BANK OPENED IN 1984

On November 19, 1984, the Morehead National Bank, with faith in the future, opened for business in a small trailer at the rear of their property. The bank conducted business as the old brick home was being torn down. It would be the site of a new modern bank building with over 4,000 square feet. The bank was designed by the Ashland architectural firm of Kensco Associates. The construction cost was $600,000 plus $50,000 for furniture, and the cost of the land was $197,500. The Morehead National Bank opened with the motto "More than a new bank--a new attitude." But they had no idea of the approaching turmoil in America's financial institutions. Interest rates went as high as 18 percent, people were defaulting on loans, and banks were caught in the middle. The newly organized Morehead National Bank was almost doomed to failure from the beginning. It soon was sold.

A WHITTAKER BANK

In March 1988, the Whittaker Bank Group took over the Morehead National Bank, and brought Mr. Terry Ensor as the new President and C.E.O. The knowledgeable, friendly, and outgoing Mr. Ensor gradually began to turn the bank around. Today, the modern, service oriented Morehead National Bank, located at the corner of Main and Carey Avenue, exemplifies the goal of the original founders which is a Morehead Memory: "More than a new bank—a new attitude."

MOREHEAD BANKS
1898-1999

Name of Bank	Year Established
1. Bank of Morehead	1898
2. Lenora Deposit Bank	1903
3. Lenora National Bank	1904
4. Morehead State Bank	1905
5. Peoples Bank of Morehead	1907
6. Citizens Bank	1928
7. First Federal Savings and Loan	1963
8. Morehead National Bank	1984
9. Peoples First Bank	1986
10. Trans Financial Bank	1994
11. Star Bank	1998
12. Peoples Bank	1998
13. First Star Bank	1999

CHAPTER THREE

Building Businesses:
Sales and Service

ALLEN'S MEAT MARKET

Allen is a name closely connected to Rowan County for over 140 years. Indeed, there is substantial evidence that they did not move to Rowan County, but Rowan County moved to them. The early Allens emigrated from Virginia, and were living in the Morgan County section that in 1856 became a part of Rowan County. In other words the Allen family did not move to Rowan County, but Rowan County moved to them. William S. Allen (Grandfather of Hubert and Bobby Allen) owned a farm in the Farmers section of Rowan County prior to the Civil War. But when the war began he enlisted in the Union Army in 1862, and proudly served until 1865, when the war ended.

WILLIAM ALLEN RETURNS FROM THE CIVIL WAR

Following the Civil War, William Allen returned to his farm in Rowan County and soon became successful in his chosen work. He then married Martha Cassity and they began raising their family. Three sons were born to William and Martha Allen. They were: George Wilson (b. 1868), Samuel (b. 1874), and John A. Allen (b. 1876). Two years after John was born William Allen died, leaving

Martha the responsibility of the farm and rearing the three boys. But the work, and responsibilities were too much for her and sadly she died when John was nine, and Samuel was eleven. Both William and Martha Allen are buried in the Siloam Cemetery in Rowan County.

ALLEN BOYS SENT TO ORPHANS HOME

Following their mother's death, John and Sam were sent to the Masonic Children's Home in Louisville. It was a "hard knock life" for these two young boys living in an orphans home so far away from family. Even though they saw each other during the day, they had little chance to be together. Sam and John slept on cots in a large one room dormitory. They were not permitted to have their cots together and one boy was at one end of the room and the other at the opposite end. At night after the lamps were turned out, Sam would crawl underneath all of the other bunks and quietly whisper encouragement to John, his younger brother. They decided to run away, so one night they packed all their earthly belongings in a pillow case, climbed over the fence and slipped out into the darkness of the city.

THE RUNAWAYS RETURN

They slowly made their way back toward Morehead, walking most of the way, but occasionally hitching a ride in a wagon going east. After reaching Lexington, they hopped a slow moving freight train toward Morehead. It was as if an invisible magnetic force was drawing them slowly toward Morehead. As many of the old timers have said, "Once you've taken a drink from Triplett Creek, you will always come back." They came back, and never left.

John A. and Sam showed up cold, hungry, and tired on the porch of their older brother G.W. who, by that time had moved into Morehead. He took them into his home, cared for them, and sent them to the local pubic school. John and Sam Allen grew up in Morehead doing odd jobs for local shopkeepers and farmers.

SAM ALLEN MARRIES AND OPENS STORE

Samuel Allen soon met Nora Ellis, a young lady from Logan, West Virginia, sent to the Morehead Normal School to keep her from marrying a local boy. Her family wanted her to get an education, but shortly after arriving in Morehead, she met and married Sam Allen instead. Shortly after marrying Nora Ellis, Sam opened the first Allen's Grocery Store in Morehead in 1897. It was a small grocery store on Railroad Street across from the freight depot. (At that time that was the heart of the Morehead business district.) Sam and Nora had three children, John Edward, Sr.; Samuel Elwood; and Thelma. (John Edward was the father of John Sonny Allen). Samuel Allen successfully operated his grocery store on Railroad Street for over fifty years. This writer can remember as a small child spending the night with his cousin John "Sonny" Allen. When they got up the next morning for breakfast, there were two different kinds of dry cereal on the table, but not the kind "Sonny" wanted. So "Grandma" Allen walked down to the store before breakfast to get "Sonny" a box of Wheaties–"The breakfast of champions." (Perhaps that's why Sonny was an All-American athlete). But that remains a Morehead Memory for this writer, because it was the first time I had ever eaten "store bought" cereal. Any brand of cereal would have been fine with me, because I had never heard of "the breakfast of champions".

SAM ALLEN'S STORE BURNS DOWN

Sam Allen's store on Railroad Street burned in 1946 when the Proctor Hotelburned. But many Moreheadians' memories of that store remain clear. Some bought their first Coca-cola there, others purchased their first dry cereal, sliced bread, bologna, chewing tobacco, "jaw breakers," or "roll your own" cigarettes. Roll your own cigarettes consisted of a small cloth bag filled with loose tobacco and closed at the top with a tight draw string. Attached to the side of the bag was a package of tissue-thin paper about 3x5 inches. A bag of Bull Durham cost 5 cents and would roll about 25 or 30 cigarettes. If you were experienced you could roll your own cigarette with one hand and use one hand and your teeth to tighten the draw string.

SHERIFF GEORGE ALLEN

George Wilson Allen (John and Sam's older brother) was elected sheriff of Rowan County on the republican ticket in 1906. He named younger brother John A. to serve as his deputy. This was the same year that Eva Sexton and her sister came to Morehead from Boyd County to attend the Morehead Normal School. During that year their father (A.J. Sexton) and mother came to visit them. They did not think the girls were eating right while in school so he moved to Morehead and bought a farm in town so the girls could live at home.

John A. Allen, deputy sheriff of Rowan county met Eva Sexton a student at the Normal School, and they were married in 1907. A.J. Sexton then sold the farm consisting of 17 acres of what is now Allen Addition to John Allen, and returned to Boyd County. (He would later move back to Rowan). Then John and Eva moved into their first home located on what is now Knapp Avenue, just off West Second Street. (At the present site of Eddie & Jane (Allen) Holbrook's home.) John and Eva settled down in their new home. But a tragedy would soon change their lives.

Sheriff G.W. Allen was walking down the main street of Morehead (then Railroad Street) when a runaway team of horses suddenly scared by a loud train whistle, ran wildly up the street. George rushed out and grabbed the reins, holding on tightly as he was being dragged along the street. When he finally stopped the runaway wagon, he had a severely broken leg. His leg was set by a local doctor. Medicine was primitive then, with no x-rays or antibiotics, and the leg became infected. Soon gangrene developed, and he was taken to the St. Joseph Hospital in Lexington, where he died seven days later.

SHERIFF ALLEN DIES—BROTHER APPOINTED

With the death of the elected Sheriff G.W. Allen, his deputy J.A. Allen was appointed sheriff in 1908. Being sheriff in Rowan County in 1908 was a difficult, thankless, and dangerous job. There were no state police, or other law enforcement agencies to help keep order in the county. (Morehead had one constable). Bootleggers,moonshiners, land disputes, gun fights, serving warrants, and collecting taxes kept the sheriff busy day and night. It was a dangerous job with poor pay and leaving Sheriff Allen little time with his family.

J.A. ALLEN RESIGNS—OPENS MEAT MARKET

It was September 12, 1908, after the county taxes had been collected, that John Allen came home from work and told his wife Eva, "I can't make a living on a sheriff's salary, so I'm going into business for myself." After talking with his brother Sam, who had been in the grocery business for 10 years, Sam advised him on what he needed to do. John and Sam agreed that he would specialize more in meats and produce and not locate too close to Sam's store. The next day John went to Cincinnati and purchased $168.52 worth of butcher shop equipment. Then on a crisp clear day in late September 1908, John Allen opened his grocery store and butcher shop in the first floor of a two story building on Fairbanks Avenue (South Wilson).

BUILT ICE HOUSE FOR MEAT

When John Allen announced his plans to open a butcher shop, many predicted it would fail because every one butchered their own meat. Also, there was the problem of preserving the meat. Since there was no method of cooling, John built a sturdy well-insulated ice-house behind his store. The walls were one foot thick filled with sawdust, and four feet of sawdust on the floor. In the sub-zero winter weather John would take his ice saw and horse drawn wagon to frozen Triplett Creek, and saw heavy blocks of ice. He would stock the ice in the ice-house, and cover it with four feet of sawdust, and the ice would last through most of the following summer. He also sold ice during the summer months. (The winters were so much colder then, because Triplett Creek seldom freezes anymore).

Contrary to popular predictions the butcher shop was very successful and became known far and wide for their quality meats. As the family grew, the older children were all expected to work in the store, along with their mother. This allowed John time to travel throughout the county and purchase stock for butchering. He much preferred doing this than actually working in the store. So Eva and the children managed the store, while John did the buying and butchering. He also slaughtered cattle and hogs for other people. One man would bring his own beef on the hoof every year for John to slaughter. He then left it hanging in a building for two or three months until the mold covered the outside. (A process he believed help give the beef a better flavor.) He would then come in pick up his beef, cut off the mold and take it home. John's stock were kept on the farm in what is now Allen Addition. As the beef, pork, and chicken supply ran low at the store, John would just butcher a fresh supply and bring it in for sale. (No frozen foods, only all fresh meat then.)

BUTCHERING MEAT HARD WORK

"Hootie" Allen recalled as a young boy his job was to help in the butchering process on the farm. He would draw the water from the well (which is still located just a few yards from where he now lives.) He would then fill the large iron kettles and boil the water needed for cleaning, cutting, and scraping. Also, his job was boiling the fat for rendering lard which they also sold in the store.

"Hootie" remembered "Ma" Catlett, Breckinridge science teacher, bringing her anatomy class to the farm. They were to observe the butchering process as a laboratory to locate certain muscles, ligaments, and bones of the animals. But the process was not very pretty, and many of the class members chose not to participate.

ALLEN'S MEAT MARKET MOVES TO MAIN STREET

By 1926 Morehead's business center was moving to Main Street, and Mr. Allen decided to move also to Main Street. That year he build a new modern meat market on Morehead's Main Street. It was a two story building with office space on the second floor. It was no sooner finished than Mrs. Allen said "John, I'm tired of living in the country, and I want to move into town and live over the store." (She considered the corner of Second Street and Allen Drive "the country", so she moved into town.) Needless to say the upper level of the store had to be remodeled into family living quarters. But there he reared his family with everyone helping in the business.

FATHER DIES—SONS OPERATE BUSINESS

John A. Allen was active in Rowan republican politics, and was party chairman for many years. In 1943 while helping count votes, he suffered a heart attack and died. His son, "Hootie" was in the Army Air Corps at their meterological school at the University of

Chicago. (Bobby Allen called his older brother "Hootie" as a child and the name stuck.) He came home on emergency leave and the family decided that Clarence, would purchase and operate the store. Clarence decided that doing your own slaughtering was too much work and in 1948 ended that aspect of the business. He then begin purchasing meat from commercial meat processing plants. It was more convenient by then with frozen foods, and refrigeration. But the choice cuts of fresh meat in Morehead were about to pass from the scene, replaced by frozen meat.

POLICE CHIEF SHOOTS HOG AND DOG

This writer recalled the last experience his family had with butchering their own meat. It was 1942 when meat was scarce because of rationing, and my dad kept a hog in the back yard to be fattened and slaughtered. In latter November at hog killing time (cold weather for butchering) my Dad said its time to butcher our hog. Dad would not allow me to shoot the hog for fear of an accident, so he asked Ed Hall, Morehead's Police Chief, to come and shoot the hog. Ed came down and loaded his 30/30 rifle and carefully took aim while resting his gun on the fence. He killed the hog on the first shot and the butchering was completed just before dark. Shortly thereafter a next door neighbor came over and announced his dog had been killed. Chief Hall come back to investigate the crime and concluded he had shot and killed the hog and the bullet ricocheted off the hogs head killing the neighbor's dog. That was the last time this writer's Dad butchered his own meat and even with meat rationing, he began buying meat at Allen's Meat Market.

HUBERT AND BOBBY PURCHASE STORE

When "Hootie" Allen returned from WW II in 1946, he returned to college and completed his degree at the University of Kentucky. By that time Clarence became restless and unhappy in the store and in 1949 sold the business to Hubert, and moved to California. Hubert ran the store until 1953 when younger brother Bobby returned from the military service he sold him a one-half interest in the store. They began to purchase new products, modernize and upgrade their equipment and services. They opened charge accounts, and offered free delivery service to your home or business. Therefore, in 1953 there were two Allen Brothers in grocery business in Morehead again, almost fifty years after Sam and John Allen began their first grocery stores.

As the business grew it also became more competitive. The postwar boom in production was flooding the market with new products. Also, TV was just reaching Morehead, and advertising began to influence consumers' selection of these new products. So Bobby and Hootie began to look for local land on which to expand. They soon located land just one block west on Main Street and made plans to build a new store.

Allens Meat Market established 1908. (Photo 1947)

MOREHEADS MEAT MARKET MOVES AGAIN

After thirty years in their first Main Street location, Allens new modern IGA Foodliner opened for business in 1957 (on the site of Slones Market). It was a gala opening celebration with a formal ribbon cutting by Mayor Bill Layne, a band playing, and the awarding of prizes. There was a great deal of publicity and people came from many other counties. The first prize awarded by a drawing was a new 1957 Chevrolet. Also, all the grocery carts were numbered, and periodically throughout the day, a numberwas drawn to correspond to a cart, and whoever had that cart number won a free grocery shopping spree. Many people thought that everyone who attended would win free groceries so the crowds were large. There were also many special sales, eg. One cent sales on ice cream, buy one gallon for 89 cents, and get one more gallon for one cent.

Bobby and "Hootie" pioneered the concept, that for a business to be successful the owner must be on the premises. Therefore, no matter what time you were in Allens IGA, either one or both brothers, were there working and greeting customers. Price, products, publicity and personal relationships provided the formula for the growth of their business. Their business was always well organized, spotlessly clean, and well maintained, and a real asset to Morehead. They next opened a second store in Morehead on East Main Street. Shortly thereafter they opened another Allens IGA in Olive Hill on East U.S. 60.

ALLEN STORE NOT IN TRADEMORE CENTER

When the new Trademore Shopping Center opened in Morehead, the Allen Brothers submitted a bid to open a new store in that center. But they were denied the opportunity because the shopping center management wanted a store to compete with Allens. Therefore the Allen brothers began acquiring property around their West Main Street business and opened their own shopping center called The Morehead Plaza. It now houses 16 business establishments anchored by Slone's Market and Battson Drug Store. It is typically well organized and maintained and remains a real asset to Morehead's downtown area.

ALLENS—PLACE FOR SHOPPING AND TALKING

A Morehead Memory of Allens was that it provided a place for meeting your friends. Also, you would usually spend more time talking than shopping. You could quickly find what you were looking for, whether it was Premier Coffee, bluing, Argo Starch, lye soap, lard, Spry or Swan Soap. You ordered your hamburger, steak or pork from an open tray in the meat cooler. It was then weighed, priced and wrapped for you to take home. You usually brought your steak home, beat it with a heavy metal beater and fried it in a skillet of lard. There was no broiling or grilling, only fried. (Cholesterol had not yet been discovered).

Allens was the first store in Morehead that sold commercially prepared dog food. This writer did a "double take," and sure enough there it was, Purina Dog Chow. Of course every one knew that Purina made chicken feed, but dog food? Everyone knew dog food was left over people food. Why would anyone ever want to buy dog food? But today, pet food is a billion dollar industry in this country. This was another indiction Allens kept aware of consumer trends.

Allens was where many Moreheadians bought their first frozen meats and vegetables. It was also where they bought their first coffee beans directly from a 100 lb. "Coffee sack." Each home had their own hand cranked coffee grinder, and you ground your own coffee from the beans. (Many gourmet stores today sell the beans for grinding your own coffee.)

Many Morehead Memories are centered around Allen Stores. Two brothers, (Sam and John) began the Allen dynasty in 1897, and two brothers (Hootie and Bobby) sold their stores in 1989. But they retained ownership of the Morehead Plaza and plan to continue their ninety two year tradition of making Morehead memories.

BISHOP DRUG STORE

BIG LITTLE BOOKS AND PEGGY BENTONS

A modest headstone set in the Bishop Family Plot in Morehead's Lee Cemetery tells all who pass by about the earliest Bishop family member in Morehead. It says simply Stephen Bishop born Cranbrook, England 1830, died Morehead, Kentucky 1926. But he and his wife, Emma (1852-1920) had a major influence upon the growth of the little town of Morehead.

STEPHEN STARTS OVER—THREE TIMES

Stephen Bishop sailed for the United States aboard a Windjammer in 1849, but only two days out of port the ship ran into a terrible storm. This ship was blown off course, and wrecked upon a rocky island. Miraculously, no one was lost, but when they were rescued from the rocks by a passing ship they had to return to England. This was the first time he had to start all over again, but it was not the last. This time he started over again with his sister, and they arrived safely in the U.S. After becoming a naturalized citizen, Stephen migrated across Pennsylvania, and down the Ohio River, and settled in Galliopolis, Ohio. Mr. Bishop was a master cabinet maker, and he opened a factory specializing in extension tables. Soon he became quite successful as he sold his furniture which was shipped down river to Cincinnati. But as is so often the case, fate or providence entered in, and his factory was destroyed by fire. From there he moved to Cattlettsburg, Kentucky and founded furniture factory number 2. But here a major Ohio River flood washed much of his furniture back down river toward Cincinnati. After the flood in Cattlettsburg, he moved to Rowan County in the middle of a feud. Stephen Bishop said it took a shipwreck, fire, flood and feud to get him to Morehead. (Talk about hardships of life - Stephen Bishop had them.) But he never gave up! Each time his business was destroyed, he would say to his wife, "Mrs. B., we'll just have to start overagain." He seemed to be always starting over. He was like many of Rowan County early pioneers, they had strength of character, and a spirit of determination never to give up.

BISHOPS ARRIVE IN ROWAN COUNTY

Stephen Bishop along with his wife and family packed up and moved to Rowan County. They settled at Hogtown (Elliottville) before moving on to Morehead. There Stephen began to build furniture. He had a limited market, and had limited success. After the railroad came through Morehead he moved his family to the county seat. There he opened a furniture factory on the corner of Fairbanks Avenue and Railroad Street (now First Street). He specialized in making caskets. His wife, Emma, would sew the material and prepare the inside while Stephen finished the outside.

Stephen Bishop also served as a funeral director. He purchased a horse drawn hearse and in those days the bodies were always "laid out in their homes". Therefore, a funeral home was not necessary. But he received lots of business as a result of the carnage in the Rowan County War.

C.E. BISHOP OPENS FIRST DRUG STORE 1896

Charles E. Bishop, along with his sister Hattie, were born in Galliopolis, Ohio. But they moved to Morehead at an early age. In 1896, Charles opened a drug store in a building in the heart of Morehead's business section. It was at the corner of Fairbanks Avenue and Railroad Street (First Street). (At that time you were trained as a druggist under a physician and served a residency.) (Mr. Bishop's pharmacy license was dated June 23, 1898.) But he remained there only a few months before moving to the first floor of a two story building on the corner of Carey Avenue and Railroad Street. When they opened the new drugstore it was first called the City Drug Store. Morehead was a primitive place with no paved streets or city services. The only connection with the outside world was by train or telegraph.

BISHOP DRUG STORE ADVERTISES IN MOREHEAD PAPER

Early drugstore publicity advertised in the 1898 *Morehead Advance* proudly proclaimed, prescribed prescriptions "would be filled exactly as written without substituting other medicines in place of those prescribed." Also, the drug store was "stocked with many rare chemicals, and new remedies usually found only in large city drug stores".

This early drug store also carried a full line of cigars, chewing tobacco, perfumes, and face powders. Also, it was well established in the brush business, carrying tooth, hairand clothes brushes. The name was soon changed to Bishop Drug Store, and it would be called that the remainder of its existence.

C.E. BISHOP DIES— YOUNG ROBERT MANAGES BUSINESS

Mr. C. E. Bishop died in 1929 at the age of fifty-six, and his son Robert continued to operate the business. The friendly, congenial Robert Bishop sadly recalled the early days after his father's death when he began to manage the drug store. It was 1930 the height of the depression and business was very slow. He recalled they purchased chemicals in bulk from such drug companies as Merck, Eli Lilly, and Upjohn (companies still in business). These orders were shipped by train, and the prescriptions were compounded by the pharmacists.

EARLY PRESCRIPTIONS LABOR INTENSIVE

He described a common prescription formula in the early days as a "paper box." The medicine was in powder form. It might call for 24 "charts." The druggist would cut out 24 small square pieces of white tissue paper and place the paper on a glass sheet. He would then pour out the granular medicine into the paper, fold the paper very neatly and insert the ends of the paper tightly so the powder would not spill. (There was a real art to this.) Then, the process was repeated 24 times and the papers were packed in a box for the customer. (This was called a "paper box.") The patient would then open the paper and take the medicine as prescribed. (Usually in a glass of water, or milk.) After capsules became available, the pharmacist would compound the prescription, often using a mortar and pestle. Then he would fill the capsule. The capsule then would be weighed and packed in a bottle for the customer, who would now swallow the capsule instead of pouring out the powder in water.

"DEAR KISS" PRODUCTS SOLD— BUSINESS MOVES TO MAIN STREET

Robert recalled an early brand name of cosmetics they sold was called "Dear Kiss." There were Dear Kiss powders, perfumes, and beauty aids. This was about the time the store was moved to its first Main Street location about 1938. Then on June 26, 1948, it moved to the last location on the corner of Main Street and Fairbanks Avenue (now South Wilson.)

ROBERTA BISHOP GRADUATES FROM PHARMACY SCHOOL AT PURDUE

During WW II when it was difficult to find pharmacists, Roberta Bishop (Razor)returned to Morehead. She was a graduate of Morehead State College when she decided to attend Purdue University, where she received her degree in pharmacy. Her goal now

Bishops Drug Store. In business 1896-1987. (Photo 1935)

was to help Robert with the Drug Store. Together, they hoped that the Bishop Drug Store could reach a grand total of 100 years in Morehead (1896-1996). Realizing that neither wanted to work until 1996, they brought their nephew Charles Bishop into the business.

Nephew Charles Bishop lived in Pittsburgh, Pennsylvania, where he graduated from Pharmacy College at the University of Pittsburgh. He them moved to Morehead and Robert and Roberta began looking forward to retirement. Sadly, it was not to be, because young Charles developed a kidney disease that eventually took his life.

ROBERT AND ROBERTA CONTINUE STORE AFTER NEPHEW'S DEATH

Brother and sister continued operation of the drug store for several years after their nephew's death. But they began to "grow weary with well doing," and wanted to explore other options. (Robert had been in the business 56 years and Roberta 37 years.) They decided to liquidate the business and retire. The drug store could have been sold, and there could have been a drug store by the name of Bishops, operated by someone else, but they elected <u>not</u> to do this.

Because both Robert and Roberta valued the name "Bishop" so much, they could not allow some one to use their name in a business over which they had no control. Therefore, they liquidated the name of Bishop's Drug Store that lasted in Morehead only ninety years, instead of their goal of 100 years. However, if you consider Stephen Bishop's furniture factory and funeral home, there was a Bishop in business in Morehead for well over 100 years.

DRUG STORE MEMORIES IN SMALL TOWN AMERICA

The corner drug store is an icon of America's small town culture. It was popularized by the paintings of Norman Rockwell on the *Saturday Evening Post* covers. While the corner drugstore is a part of our national memory, Bishop's Drug Store remains our Morehead memory.

Robert Bishop always made you feel welcome when you entered the drugstore. It was a place you could get a fountain Coke for a nickel. Bishops charged 5 cents for a coke and never increased the price of a 6 oz. Coke in the more than fifty years they sold this product. When Robert was asked how he could afford to sell cokes for 5 cents, he said 1 oz. of Coke and 5 oz. water is a small price to pay for customers' good will. A nickel Coke was un-heard of in 1986, and the store gained wide-spread publicity for that "special."

MEDICINE—BIG LITTLE BOOKS—SOFT DRINKS— PEGGY BENTONS

Bishop's was a place you took your girl for a Coke after a movie, or where you met your friends on Saturday afternoon before going to a movie. It was a place where you bought medicine, candy, ice cream, magazines, cokes, coffee, comic books and Big Little

Books. These were small books, printed on pulp paper and were 4 inches tall, 3 inches wide, and 2 1/2 inches thick. They were usually western adventures with a colorful binding. At the fountain you could also get a "Peggy Benton." This delightful delicacy consisted of sliced bananas in the bottom of a glass with layers of ice cream, chocolate syrup and whipping cream topped with nuts and cherries. (Those were the days, my friend, there were no calories then.)

Eccentric Professor Gets Angry At Closing

Dr. Wilhelm Exelbirt, the late beloved professor of history at Morehead State University was a regular customer of the drug store for many years. He came in two or three days a week and sat on the same stool. If someone was already sitting there, they would be asked to move. Dr. Exelbirt would always order a cup of coffee with half of it cream, stir it vigorously, sip it slowly, then buy a pack of chewing gum on the way out. After the drug store closed, Mr. Bishop saw Dr. Exelbirt out on the street and said, "Dr. Exelbirt, how are you, I never see you any more." Dr. Exelbirt replied very gruffly in his thick German accent, "You should not have closed the store! Every time I walk by there I get mad!" There were many Moreheadians who echoed that sentiment.

Memories of Moreheadians

Not only do Moreheadians cherish their memories of Bishop's Drug Store, but Robert and Roberta Bishop cherish their memories of many Moreheadians. They have a lifetime of memories of their valued customers and cherished friends. And, the many employees who worked there over the years. They emphasized that so many of their employees had gone on to become successful in education, medicine, politics, business, industry and life. They especially remembered Nellie Easton Ellis (no relation to this writer) who was a valued employee for 29 years. She was in charge of the cosmetics counter and the fountain and now owns a successful restaurant in Owingsville, Kentucky.

PAST AND FUTURE MESH

Robert especially mentioned his deep admiration <u>of</u> and respect <u>for</u> the early Morehead medical community in Morehead's pre-hospital era, for example: Drs. Garrad, Blair, Reynolds, Wilson, Evans, G.C. Nickel, Homer Nickel, and of course our belovedDr. Louise (Caudill) and Susie. He also expressed his wonder in a very positive way at the marvelous modern medical miracles and what the future holds for those involved in medicine.

BATTSON'S DRUG STORE

CHERRY COKES AND COMIC BOOKS

Battson's Drug Store remains a warm memory in the minds of many Moreheadians. But it would never have happened had Hartley Battson decided to ride his motorcycle back to his native Vancouver, British Columbia, instead of coming to Morehead.

FROM CANADA TO A KENTUCKY HOME

W. Hartley Battson was the grandson of a Missionary to New Zealand who emigrated from that British Colony back to Canada. Hartley's mother was born in 1868 aboard ship on that long dangerous voyage to Canada. The family settled in Vancouver, where Hartley was born in 1892. He grew up in that city, attended the public schools, and was a member of their World's Championship La Crosse Team. (Now we know where his sons Donald and Bill got their athletic ability). La Crosse was their equivalent of our basketball in terms of fan interest in Canada.

Mr. Battson attended Pharmacy College in his native city. It was an 18-month program in those days. After graduating in 1915, he came to the U.S. where he was employed as a chemist in a munitions factory in Steubenville, Ohio. After WW I (1918) he bought a motorcycle and planned to return to Vancouver. But, in the meantime, his father and mother had moved to Morehead and were teaching at the Morehead Normal School. So he decided to come by and visit them before returning home. While in Morehead he recalled pitching horseshoes with a group of men on unpaved Main Street. Mr. Battson's La Crosse experience lended itself well to the game of horseshoes and he soon became one of the best in Morehead. Hartley Battson was so impressed with Morehead and its people and its potential he decided to remain here and open a drugstore.

COMMUNITY INVOLVEMENT IMPORTANT

He never went back to Canada; in fact, his family said he never even had any desire to return and always regarded Morehead as his home. He was an elder in the First Christian Church, a member of the Masonic Lodge, Commercial Club of Morehead, and a member of the first organized fire department in Morehead in 1922. The Battsons' had two sons: Donald, a resident of Morehead, and William, now deceased.

CORNER DRUG STORE OPENS IN MOREHEAD

Battson's Drug Store opened its doors on the corner of Main Street and West College Blvd. in the new Cozy Building in August, 1920. It was called the Cozy Building because the movie theater of that name was housed in a part of the building. The building was built out of sawed stone the size of brick by Bert Willett. John Knapp and his son-in-law, Bert Willett, came to Morehead in the early 1900s. They operated the stone quarry at Bluestone, Kentucky, where the stone was sawed for the building. Mr. Knapp and Mr. Willett also owned property in Rosenberg, Texas. They sawed the stone at Bluestone for one other building (a drug store) in Rosenberg, Texas (suburb of Houston). The family owned this

Battson Drug Store. 1922-. (Photo 1922)

building until 1960. These are the only two buildings of this type of construction in the world, because brick was so much cheaper than sawed stone. Mrs. Maude Clay, a niece of Mr. Willett, still owns this beautiful historic building.

FIRST PRESCRIPTION FILLED

The first prescription filled in the new drug store was for Evelyn Royalty, a teacher at the Morehead Normal School, and the business was an immediate success. Soon it became apparent that Hartley had to have help. So after one month in business, a young lady from Farmers, Kentucky, by the name of Jewell Waltz enrolled in the Morehead Normal School and was hired by Hartley to help in the business. They became lifetime partners in marriage and in business.

JEWEL A REAL "JEWEL" IN HELPING HARTLEY

Jewel was just what her name implies, a "jewel," in the business and was friendly, efficient, and hard working. She recalled in the early days most prescriptions, and non-prescription products were compounded in the basement of the building. Such items were shaving lotion, face cream, corn cure, hair tonic, jewelry cleaner, croup medicine, whooping cough medicine, and many others. Mrs. Battson still had the recipe book used for these prescriptions when they sold the business in 1964. (Since then the business has changed hands many times, but Battson's Drug Store is still doing business in Morehead on West Main Street).

DRUG STORE "BASEMENT" HISTORY

The basement of the drug store was actually the basement of the old Gault House that was torn down before the new building was constructed. Mrs. Battson said she always enjoyed working in the basement where the giant oak beams joined to form the foundationof the old Gault House. This old hotel was the headquarters for one of the feuding factions in the Rowan County War in 1884-1887. The feuders frequently poked their guns out from between these beams of the old Gault House and took pot shots at their enemies. The Gault House also was where the bodies of the men that were killed June 22, 1887, the final day of the Rowan County War, were laid out for burial.

It was in this very same basement where men had waged war against people, that Hartley and Jewell Battson waged war against disease.

DRUG STORE EXPANSION BEGINS

Battson's Drug Store expanded many times in the many years they were in Morehead, offering many different products and services. There was Battson's Beauty Bar, offering a wide variety of cosmetics, creams, and lotions. They offered Richard Nudnutt, Yardley, and Evening in Paris products for the ladies.

EXPANSION BRINGS COKES, COMICS, AND KIDS

In the 1930's, soda fountain, lunch counter, magazine, and comic book sections were added. Among their specialities were delicious cherry Cokes, lemon Cokes and pineapple sundaes. The lunch counter proudly presented prepared on site: grilled ham salad, egg salad, pimento cheese and olive nut sandwiches. This writer can remember he had 15 cents for lunch and he bought a pimento cheese sandwich for 10 cents and a Coke for 5 cents. (Later on, however, these prices increased). But they were delicious! (This was certainly a mouth-watering Morehead Memory). After placing your order at the counter, you would sit down at one of the small white tables (usually with a flower and a vase on top) in one of the white triangular shaped chairs, waiting for your order to be filled. These tables just happened to be adjacent to the comics (funny books) section. There, while waiting for your order to be filled, you could enter into another world. The world of Superman, Batman, Archie, Tarzan, Zorro, Spider Man, Blondie, and Sheena of the Jungle. When your <u>name</u> (they knew you by name and not number) was called and your order was ready, you would pick it up at the lunch counter and return to your own private comic book world. There you would nibble on your sandwich, sip your Coke, and linger as long as possible in the fantasy of a make believe world.

RARE COMIC BOOKS DESTROYED

Many of the older editions of these comic books are extremely rare and valuable today. They are now collectors' items. Don Battson tells me that when these comic books were not sold, they burned them, and got credit from the company. He says he has burnedup a fortune in first editions of comic books.

The late Mr. and Mrs. Battson were always patient with young people without any money coming into the store and not buying anything. These youngsters would sit down on the floor and read the comic books. Should they notice a child sitting on the floor and just looking at the pictures they would tell them. "It's OK for you to examine the comic books, but don't just look at the pictures, <u>read them</u>."

NO SCHOOL LUNCHROOMS BRING KIDS TO BATTSON'S

In the days when there were no lunchrooms in the schools, and on those rare occasions when we did not bring our lunch or go home for lunch, but were given 15 cents, we headed for Battson's. (This writer's wife, Janis Ruth, tells me they had a charge account there that she sometimes abused.)

The delightful aroma of perfumes and powders by the comics and the smell of real butter as it sizzled on the grill remain a vivid memory. It seems all five senses were stimulated in the little drug store on the corner. Many times while sitting in school our thoughts were of getting out of there and heading for Battson's, especially on a cold winter day where it was a warm refuge. Also, those delicious grilled home-made pimento cheese sandwiches, cherry Cokes, and comic books remain a "Morehead Memory" at Battson's Drug Store.

EAGLES NEST

"And He saith unto them--come and dine" (John 21:12)

In 1920, two cousins, Virgil D. Flood, and James M. Clayton, migrated from this area to Ashland. In those days, Ashland was a growing community similar to Detroit, Michigan, and Dayton, Ohio. Virgil and James went to work immediately delivering milk for the Sanitary Milk Company, a new dairy just opening in the city. But both cousins had a dream of returning to Morehead and opening their own business.

TOWN AND COLLEGE GROWING

One of the customers on their milk route was a new restaurant called the Chimney Corner, that recently had opened on Ashland's

Central Avenue. Virgil and James watched the new restaurant grow rapidly into a thriving restaurant. They believed Morehead had the potential for such a business. After talking with the restaurant owner and getting some tips on opening a new restaurant, they left their jobs in Ashland to return to Morehead and open their own business.

The year they returned to Morehead was 1925. The new Midland Trail (U.S. 60) had just opened through the heart of downtown Morehead. The Morehead Normal School had just become a state college, and was be-

Austin Riddle, Eagles Nest Restaurant Manager, 30 years.

ginning to increase rapidly in enrollment, facilities, and faculty. There were no cafeteria or food services on the new campus. Also, a new hotel had just opened (Midland Trail). In addition, there was the Caskey and Peoples Hotel. Morehead was located half way between Ashland and Lexington, and was a major stop for salesmen traveling by train and automobile. Sometimes, they would rent cars and buggies to call upon clients in Elliott and Morgan counties. Therefore, Virgil D. Flood, known as "Mike," and James M. Clayton, known as "Chin," recognized the potential for a new restaurant and Morehead's business climate was excellent. But, when they moved their families back to Morehead, they had no idea the business would exceed their wildest expectations.

Virgil D. Flood and his wife, Nell (Shelton) Flood had four children: Gladys, Frances, Charles and Vivian. James Morgan Clayton and his wife, Lucille (Moore) Clayton, had three children: James, Lyda, and Laura. With their families growing up in Morehead, Mike and Chin were even more determined to become a success in business.

SITE FOR NEW BUSINESS SELECTED

In 1925, Mike and Chin rented a building from hotel owner, John Cecil, located on Morehead's Main Street (U.S. 60) between the Midland Trail Hotel and the Caskey Hotel. (Where Arby's is now located). They employed Noah Kennard, Morehead's last lamplighter, also a mayor, businessman, and excellent cabinetmaker. Mr. Kennard built the booths, fountain, counters and cabinets in the front and kitchen areas. He also built the famous blue mirror and clock that was

J.M. "Chin" Clayton, Co-owner of Eagles Nest 1925-1972.

behind the counter. (Now owned by George D. Alfrey, Jr.) It was later that the tables and chairs were added, and the oval shaped glass check out counter with display shelves. (Those display shelves later housed dolls representing MSU's Homecoming queens.)

NO-NAME RESTAURANT OPENED

The restaurant opened in the fall of 1925 with a gala celebration, attended by many local dignitaries. However, the restaurant had no name. So Mike and Chin, working with the students and faculty of the new Morehead State College, agreed upon a plan to name the restaurant. Since the college planned new athletic teams that had not yet been named, and the restaurant had not been named, why not name the two at the same time. Therefore, Mike and Chin sponsored a contest among the students to name the athletic team and restaurant.

NAME SELECTED

Among those names submitted were Lions, and Lion's Den, Hawks and Hawks Nest, Bears, and Bears Den, Bald Eagles and Eagles Nest. The group of student judges selected the winners (and the rest is history). The winning entry was submitted by freshman student, Peaches Ellis (this writer's aunt). She received a $25 savings bond for submitting the winning entry. Then, one of Morehead's most famous restaurants and local landmarks was born.

EAGLES NEST SERVED AS STUDENT CENTER

In the early days, with no food service on campus, the Eagles Nest catered to the college crowd. It served as a grill, cafeteria, and student center for many years. There was a piano in the restaurant, and students would gather in the evening and sing around the piano. Miss Olive Fannin, a student in college from 1928-1931, would often play dinner music in the evening. On Sundays, after church, many students would eat lunch at the Eagles Nest. Also, pep rallies were held there before football games. It was a popular social center for students and faculty before there was a cafeteria and student center on campus.

During the 1930s, as the college enrollment increased and new buildings and services were added on campus, student clientele at the Eagles Nest began to decrease. Also, the severe depression at that time meant most students had little money to spend at a restaurant. Most students were opening cans and eating cheese and crackers in their room (many still do that today), and there was a corresponding decline in the restaurant business in Morehead. The Eagles Nest was no exception, its business hit a low point.

The Eagles Nest was a family restaurant where you could take the children for a meal with good food, quiet atmosphere, and excellent service. When prohibition ended, Mike and Chin discussed selling beer and wine with their food. When Clyde Smith, a young college student came to work one evening and there were about 12 cases of beer in the kitchen, he asked Chin about it, and Chin said they were considering selling beer. Clyde Smith said, "You're making a mistake. You will hurt your business more than you will help it." Clyde came back to work the next day and the beer was gone and it was never mentioned again.

MOREHEAD'S MEETING PLACE

By the 1930's the Eagles Nest was the social, political and business center of Morehead. It was the place where local businessmen met for coffee each morning. They made deals, told tales, argued politics, and dreamed of a brighter future for Morehead and their children. That was all done over a cup of coffee, and the Eagles Nest coffee was reputed by well-traveled people to be among the best in the world. It was a work of art.

The world-famous Eagles Nest coffee began with a 100 pound bag of FleetwoodCoffee Beans purchased from salesman, William Kopp, of Ashland. (He said the Eagles Nest was one of his best customers.) The beans (enough to make six pots of coffee) were then hand ground into a six ounce Coca Cola glass. They made three pots at a time, and if they were not used in 30 minutes, the coffee was thrown out, and a new pot brewed. Their goal was to never have any coffee over 30 minutes old from the bean to the customer's cup. That insured that the taste and the aroma were delightful. Although the cost was 10 cents, which was high for that time, it was well worth it because it included unlimited refills. It served as the coffee house of its day.

The Eagles Nest Men's Coffee Club was made up of many Moreheadians. Among those were Bill Sample, Claude Clayton, Roy Cornette, C.B. Cornette, Glen Lane, Glennis Fraley, "Snooks" Crutcher, "Cap" Daugherty, Jack West, M.L. Tate, Oscar Patrick, Murvel Crosley, Boyd McCullough, and many, many more. Mr. Crosley would sip his coffee by the inch. The waitresses always said he would ask for more coffee when it was only one inch below the rim of the cup.

MOUTH WATERING MENU

In addition to the excellent coffee, the food was superb. When the restaurant first opened in 1925, their famous food menu included home-cured country ham, red eye gravy, roast beef au jus, oysters, chicken with little blue slick dumplings, country gravy, Kentucky Hot Brown, hot home-made yeast rolls, real cow butter, along with an assortment of vegetables, salads, and home-made pies. (Especially pecan pie.) Also, at each booth and table, there was a honey jar. The honey dippers were made from old iced tea spoons with the handle bent in a curved shape so it would not slide down into the honey.

The Eagles Nest was particularly known for their country ham. Mike and Chin purchased most of their country hams from Bath County resident, Gene Toy. They would always buy them in the late fall just after being slaughtered and cured. They then brought them to Morehead and let them cure for six months. Next, the hams were soaked in salt water for 24 hours before being fried in lard. (They also sold whole hams, always telling the customers to let them cure at least six months before cooking). Mike and Chin maintained close quality control over the food served at the Eagles Nest. That's why it became so widely known.

COMPLIMENTS TO THE CHEF

The Eagles Nest owners were quick to recognize that the cook was the essential ingredient of food service. It was then they hired Clearfield resident Martha (Stewart) Barndollar. After working for two years as a dishwasher, she replaced Mattie Jones as the cook, and remained for 37 years. When she began her cooking career, she cooked on a coalstove. In order for her to get to work, she walked 3 miles each way, 7 days a week. (Then she had to build a fire and get the old coal cooking range warmed up.) After cooking several years, she became more financially prosperous and only had to walk half that distance because she hired Ben McBrayer's Taxi one way each day.

Mrs. Barndollar's two daughters, Alice and Loretta, worked as waitresses in the Eagles Nest during their high school days. They said, "Mr. Clayton was very particular about cleanliness and service. He required all employees to wear hair nets and clean aprons." He always trained the waitresses "to be alert but not a flirt." Also, a pleasant smile was

Martha Barndollar,
Chief Cook at Eagles Nest 37 years.

a must. Mr. Clayton always said, "Be sure you're right then go ahead." And in those days the customer was always right. He believed excellent service made the good food taste better. Therefore, the Eagles Nest service was as famous as its food.

Mrs. Barndollar was famous throughout Eastern Kentucky for her cooking and baking. She was particularly known for her home-made pies. (This writer can still taste those pies just writing about them.)

On one occasion a TV crew from WSAZ in Huntington stopped to eat lunch at the Eagles Nest. They were so impressed with the food, they wanted to interview the cook on camera. But unlike the Martha Stewart on TV today, Morehead's Martha (Stewart) Barndollar was shy and refused. However, she did agree for them to take a picture of her holding one of her pies. It was later shown on WSAZ-TV in a program highlighting fine regional restaurants.

MANY MOREHEADIANS WORKED AT EAGLES NEST

To be able to get a job as a waitress in the Eagles Nest was the ambition of many Morehead maidens (and men). Among those people who worked there during the early Eagles Nest days were Bessie Binion, Bertha Pelphrey, Bessie Switzer, Lillie Jones, Mrs. LeMaster, Georgia Markwell, Essie White, Florcie Dulin, Monie and Sam Kidd, Vivian Flood, Barbara Hogge, Margaret Johnson and Dottie Highly. Other early employees included Clyde Smith, Surrena Hall, Judy Elam, Bonnie Johnson, Ruth and Irene Jackson, Betty Cassity, Betty Wallace, Jeri Runner, Goldia Smith, Charlene Alfrey, Mae Caudill and many, many more.

Martha (Stewart) Barndollar became a legend in her own time. After 37 years when the Eagles Nest closed, she opened her own restaurant on Carey Avenue (Old Johnson Boarding House). She was successful in that business for many years. She used to take food that was not sold to shut-ins and poor people. She never let good food go to waste and many who never went to her restaurant had a taste of her home cooking.

MIKE SELLS TO CHIN ON COIN TOSS

In 1933 at the height of the depression, the Eagles Nest was not making enough to support two families. Therefore, Mike and Chin decided one should sell to the other. They agreed on a price and flipped a coin to see who would buy the other's part. Mike lost and he sold out to Chin. Mike then bought a large home on U.S. 60 West and turned it into the Shady Rest Tourist Home. (He later became a rural mail carrier on Rural Rt. 2 in Rowan County and retired in that capacity). Therefore, Mr. Clayton then had the sole responsibility as owner-manager, and business started to increase as the depression eased and people were working again. He also began to get involved in other business interests, such as the local dealer for Frigidaire appliances. With the Eagles Nest open 7 days a week, Mr. Clayton soon realized he had to have some help, and began to look for another partner.

Enter Austin Riddle

In 1937, Mr. Clayton approached local resident, Austin Riddle, about a job managing the Eagles Nest. Austin (named for the capital of Texas had a sister also named for another Texas city, Loredo), was a former star athlete and graduate of Morehead College. He was employed as teacher, coach and principal at Haldeman High School. Since he had a good job, he refused Mr. Clayton's offer. However, when offered a chance for a partnership, he accepted. Mr. Riddle's wife Mabel said, at that time she became a restaurant widow, because for 30 years her husband worked every weekend, and seldom was away from his work at any time. However, she did say, that "the last 5 years he managed the Eagles Nest, he was off every other weekend."

Austin Riddle and his wife Mabel (Murphy) Riddle, married while in college. They have two children, Larry and Jerry. Mabel is active, alert, and living in a personal care home in Ashland. She enjoys life, and maintains a very positive outlook on life. She has a marvelous sense of humor, and is a meticulous dresser. She is active in her church and club work, and enjoys her children, grand-children and great-grand children. Although she has lived at the home for 20 years, her memories of Morehead and the Eagles Nest remain clear and happy. Although her vision is poor, her mind is sharp, and sense of humor keen.

Mabel recalled those afternoons when many of the wives in Morehead dressed up and came to the Eagles Nest for coffee and gossip. She recalled among those who attended that afternoon ritual of coffee and gossip were Edith Crosley, Mary Jo Blair, Mary Duncan, Edith Marsh, Hazel Daugherty, Frances Laughlin, Elsie Corentte, Lona Fraley, plus many, many more.

The early Eagles Nest was the place for formal dining in Morehead. It was a place where hotel guests, tourists, and local residents came for fine good, service and atmosphere. (Lexington via old U.S. 60 was a long way to go for dinner.) Although there was never a formal dress code, customers in blue jeans, t-shirts, and sandals would have felt out of place.

SAILORS "SAIL" TO THE EAGLES NEST

During the 1940s when the sailors stationed on campus got liberty, many would put on their dress blues or whites, and sail to the Eagles Nest for dinner. Their favorite food was french fries and fried oysters. They especially enjoyed the food and attractive waitresses and were generous tippers.

The Eagles Nest advertised extensively throughout the region on roadside barns. Also, the restaurant advertised in college publications, but did little advertising in local media. Local word of mouth and advertising by traveling men and tourists traveling through Morehead helped make the Eagles Nest famous. Also those sailors stationed here made the name "Eagles Nest" known far and wide.

Wherever Moreheadians may travel even to this day and people find out you're from Morehead, they ask if the Eagles Nest is still in business. This writer and his wife were at St. Simons Island off the coast of Georgia last year, and when the hotel clerk saw we were from Morehead, asked about the Eagles Nest. He could still remember the delicious meal he had eaten there 50 years ago. Also the same thing happened to us on the same trip on down in Florida.

CELEBRITIES STOPPED AT EAGLES NEST

There have been many celebrities that have stopped at the Eagles Nest over the years. In the 1960s, there was a man in a white suit and black string bow tie with distinguished white hair, mustache, and goatee. He was not the world-wide celebrity that he later became, but he was known to the waitresses as Colonel Saunders.

He was trying to sell Mr. Riddle a franchise for Kentucky Fried Chicken, which Mr. Riddle turned down. But he did eat there and the waitresses were arguing over who would serve him, expecting a big tip. But they didn't know the Colonel very well. He left them a nickel tip (they should have framed it). Lewis Satch Armstrong, the black musician and blues singer, ate at the Eagles Nest with all of his band. They really enjoyed the country ham and red-eye gravy, and did leave a generous tip (unlike Colonel Saunders).

END OF AN ERA OF FOOD SERVICE

Before the death of Mr. Clayton, they were offered $100,000 for the business. Mabel Riddle urged her husband to sell, but they decided against selling. However, with the death of Chin Clayton and the retirement of Austin Riddle, the Eagles Nest was purchased by Phil Lewis, C. Roger Lewis, Paul Blair, and William Whitaker. In 1973, Bill Davis, local baker and restauranteur bought the Eagles Nest and tried to revive the business again. However, by that time, I-64 had replaced U.S. 60, and all the fast food companies had discoveredMorehead. Therefore, with all the quick competition, and everyone in a hurry, Mr. Davis sold the Eagles Nest in 1980. But the Eagles Nest never came back. The building was last used for a restaurant called the Chinese Wok, which only lasted a few years. But for 55 years the Eagles Nest of Morehead was a vital part of this community, and remains a Morehead Memory of good food, fellowship, and good coffee.

MIDLAND BAKING COMPANY

BOYS, BICYCLES, AND BREAD WRAPPERS

"Man shall not live by bread alone" (Matt. 4:4)

Hidden beneath a brown wooden weatherbeaten, windowless building located on Morehead's East Main Street is a long narrow brown brick and tile building. It once had steel screened casement windows that cranked open to receive the cool breeze blowing down Evans Branch (now College Lake). It was the air conditioning of that era. Also, there were two large display windows in the front. An alley came off of Main Street on the west side to a loading dock in the rear. The building was built by Morehead's E.E. Maggard and was a prime business location. (It now houses Pathways, Inc. but once contained Morehead's first bakery.)

FLOOD BRINGS BAKERY TO MOREHEAD

In 1934 Olive Hill, Kentucky, a town 20 miles east of Morehead, suffered a flood that devastated their business district. One of the businesses ruined by the flood was a bakery owned by Mr. J.M. Powell. When the waters receded, it left a one-foot deep covering of brown sticky mud throughout the bakery. After surveying the damage Mr. Powell elected not to rebuild in the flood plain of Olive Hill, but moved to Morehead where there was a better business climate and a lesser chance of flooding.

In the depression year of 1934, Mr. J.M. Powell, with his young son Jack, made the move to Morehead. They opened their bakery in a brown brick building on East Main Street (now part of Pathways Programs and next door to the Chevrolet Garage). The name of the new bakery was the Midland Baking Company. Many Moreheadians remember it as the place they bought their first delicious doughnuts, hot rolls and warm bread. Locally baked (store bought) sliced bread had arrived in Morehead. It was known as "That famous delicious Mary Jane and Jumbo Bread."

BAKING BREAD BRINGS DELIGHTFUL AROMA

Both brands of bread were wrapped and sealed in wax paper. The Mary Jane Breadhad a picture of a blond pigtailed six-year-old girl hugging a loaf of bread. The cost of a loaf was 9 cents.

Jumbo Bread was a larger, thinner loaf of "sandwich bread" with a prominent picture of an elephant on the outside. The cost of a loaf of Jumbo bread was 10 cents. They also baked delicious doughnuts, cakes, and cinnamon rolls. There is nothing as appealing as the fragrance of bread baking in the oven. This wonderful aroma wafted gently on the breezes over Morehead, and you hoped you were down wind. Psychologists say that the sense of smell is a strong memory stimulant. Every time I am near a bakery, I remember the Midland Bakery and that delightful aroma.

BUSINESS IMPROVES

Although Jack and Mr. Powell worked long hours, it was soon apparent they had to have more help. That was true especially when they got the bread contract to supply the local CCC Camp that housed 400 hungry men. Also they provided bread for Morehead State College. Mr. Powell hired two local men, Mr. June Justice and Mr. Ed Davis. These men were taught the skills needed to operate the bakery. But as the business grew, they became route men, delivering bakery products to Rowan and all the surrounding counties. Also, there was a demand for the bakery to sell retail across the counter. Mr. Powell then employed a lovely local teenager, Miss Mary Woods. She waited on customers at the front of the building, while helping in the baking process. Therefore, when you came in the front door for service, you might have to wait until Mary came from the rear to wait on you.

MOUSE LOST IN BAKERY

Local resident, Lindsay Caudill (who later became this writer's father-in-law), often stopped in to buy a loaf of that warm delicious 9-cent Mary Jane Bread. He wanted it right out of the oven. One day while waiting for Miss Mary to bring his hot loaf of bread, he looked down and saw a mouse running across the floor. Lindsay quickly grabbed the mouse by the tail thinking he would sling its head against the top of the glass counter, and toss it outside. He made his move quickly. But his plan didn't work. He ended up with nothing but the mouses tail in his hand. The mouse had disappeared. It was nowhere to be found in the retail area. But about 25 ft. behind the counter in the front part of the bakery was a huge, open stainless steel mixer tank in the process of mixing dough. Therefore, since he never found the mouse, he always assumed someone opened up a loaf of bread and received quite a surprise.

The old Red Rose Dairy was directly behind the bakery. It was only natural that a barter system develop between the Dairy and the Bakery. While helping my Dad in his job at the Dairy, I was always the "Gofer." They would send me to the bakery with 2 quarts of cold pasteurized milk (with the cream risen to the top) to exchange for a dozen hotdoughnuts. This barter system always worked well and everybody "gained" by it.

CONTEST FOR BICYCLE ANNOUNCED

On one "gofer" trip to the bakery (when I was 9 years old) I was fascinated to see two shiny new red bicycles with balloon white wall tires and a kickstand on display in the window. There was one boy's and one girl's bicycle. The sign announced each bicycle would be given to the boy and girl who collected the most Mary Jane and/or Jumbo Bread wrappers in the next 8 weeks. At age 9, I had only dreamed but never owned a bicycle. In fact, during those depression days, none of my friends owned bicycles. But now, I began to think, maybe, it might be just possible that I could win that contest. My mother was always a positive person, and she encouraged me to "go for it."

My mother, Dorothy Ellis, was a school teacher of the "old school." She was unemployed at the time and could not afford me a bicycle. But she always taught me to believe in myself and that a

positive self-image was as important as knowledge. Her motto was:
"Can't is not in our vocabulary." As
an only child, I had this precept
strongly imbedded in my mind, so
with dreams in my heart, stars in
my eyes, and believing in myself, I
became the youngest one to enter
the contest. The race was on! It was
a marathon race that ended two
months later.

DREAMS OF A NEW BICYCLE

Believing the race goes to the
swiftest, I got busy that very day,

Bicycle reproduction won in bread wrapper contest, 1936. Jack Ellis, Jean Hill.

and knocked on doors all over Morehead, explaining that I was in
a contest to try and win a bicycle. I asked that they save their Mary
Jane and Jumbo Bread wrappers for me. Many, many Morehead
citizens saved their bread wrappers for me. That was the first time
I remembered meeting eight-year old Miss Janis Caudill, who later
became my lifetime companion. (She saved bread wrappers for me.)
I had a regular route that I worked once a week, picking up their
wrappers. As my collection began to grow, I would walk by the
bakery every afternoon after school (summer school at Breckinridge)
and look longingly at that beautiful bicycle. I dreamed of flying,
swiftly down College Boulevard, out Second Street, and down the
Saints Church Hill on that shiny red bicycle. In my mind's eye, I
would be able to play bicycle tag with the older boys.

BREAD WRAPPER COLLECTION GROWS

My dreams of winning the bicycle grew in proportion to the
growing number of bread wrappers in my house. I worked even

harder. I kept a pretty close check on the local competition; however, the contest covered several counties, and no one knew exactly who the leaders were in the other counties. As the end of the contest neared, the "rumor" was thatprobably Teddy Hamm of nearby Clearfield or little Jackie Ellis of Morehead had the most bread wrappers in Rowan County. But the contestants from other counties were a mystery. Rumors were rampant. One rumor was that a boy in Bath County had 1,000 bread wrappers. My heart went cold as I heard that rumor. A plan was devised. With our mothers acting as our agents, Teddy and I agreed to met on July 2, the day before the contest ended. It would be a fight to the finish. A "shoot out" and the one that brought the most bread wrappers to the battle would win. Therefore, the one with the most bread wrappers would get the other's collection. It was a fight to the finish, a no-holds-barred bread wrapper battle. The winner would walk away with the other's collection. We were determined that whoever won the bicycle, it would remain in Rowan County.

BREAD WRAPPER BATTLE FIELD

We agreed to meet at home plate at the old Clearfield baseball field at noon on July 2, 1936. That day is remembered as the day of the great Rowan County Bread Wrapper Battle to this day. At the appointed hour, we met on the baseball battlefield. Teddy and I approached each other from opposite ends of the field, each eyeing the other suspiciously. We were both heavily armed with "coffee" sacks loaded with bread wrappers. Our mothers walked beside us as our agents, and several friends surrounded us as our seconds, each one making sure there was no "shenanigan" pulled. Teddy carried his bag to first base and dumped the contents on the ground. I carried mine down to third base and emptied the contents of my "coffee" sack. The tension was so thick you could cut it with a dull knife. As our agents (our mothers) counted both bread wrapper collections, my heart was pounding and my palms sweating. However, I had over 800, and Teddy had only 600, I had won the bread wrapper battle, and my friends cheered at the final count. My total count was now over 1,400 bread wrappers. But the contest was not over yet. There were four other counties to be heard from. Who knows, maybe some boy had pulled the same trick in the next county. Therefore, as July 3 arrived, I had to endure another heart pounding, palm sweating session before knowing the final outcome of the contest. But joy of joys, I won the bicycle. Also, my cousin, Alameda McKinney, won the girl's bike. It was a clean bicycle sweep for Rowan County.

There was a great deal of interest in Morehead's Midland Bakery products. Their business grew as they expanded products and people. Their route men, June Justice and Ed Davis, were kept busy delivering to stores and restaurants in the region. Young Jack Powell and Miss Mary Woods fell in love and married and became lifetime partners. Among others that were employed as the business grew was Joe McKinney, who did much of the baking.

When Mr. J.M. Powell moved to Morehead from Olive Hill after being flooded out, he almost settled in a building on First Street. Of course, First Street was devastated in the 1939 Morehead flood. But the bakery was not damaged on Main Street. It would have been ironic had he been ruined by another flood.

WINNING NEW BICYCLE A HAPPY DAY

The day I won that shiny red bicycle with balloon whitewall tires and a kickstand was the happiest day of my 9-year life. Riding proudly down the streets of Morehead made me feel like a celebrity. But the shiny red bicycle came to a quick and violent end the following October.

My cousin Adrian McKinney who was four years older than me had an old "dilapidated" bike in very poor condition. The gears in the "new departure" rear hub constantly slipped. Sometimes you could pedal vigorously and not move. Both our mechanical skills were limited, so one sunny afternoon we decided to take his old bicycle to Volney Skaggs in Clearfield, who was a skilled bicycle mechanic. I accompanied him on my bicycle, and Volney succeeded in repairing Adrian's bike, and we started back home.

NEW BICYCLE CRUSHED BY CAR

Since I wanted to see if his bike was really repaired, we exchanged bicycles on the return trip home. I rode about 100 feet in front of him along the left side of the limestone gravel road from Clearfield. About half way home I heard a car coming behind us. (There was never very much traffic on that road.) Glancing over my shoulder I saw the car on the wrong side of the road hit Adrian on my shiny red bicycle. He went flying through the air over the handle bars with the car actually missing running over him. But it did run over my bike. The car barely missed me and never stopped. But I memorized the license number.

Quickly neighbors and cars came to help. Adrian was unconscious. Someone loaded him in their car and took him to Dr. Homer Nickel, a local doctor. Someone with a truck loaded me, the good bike and my crushed bike in a truck and delivered us home. There I told my parents the sad news, and they rushed to the doctor's office to find out my cousin's condition. (We had no telephone.) After regaining consciousness, Adrian was sent home (no hospital here then).

HIT AND RUN DRIVER ARRESTED

I felt very important when our easy going, deep voiced Sheriff Bill Carter, came to my house the day of the accident to question me. When he asked me to describe the car, I said, "It was just an old black car, but I got his license number." Everyone seemed to be amazed at that revelation. But I honestly don't know if my memory was motivated more by the loss of my bike, or cousinly concern for Adrian's condition. However, as soon as I gave the sheriff the car's license number, he made the arrest at the man's house, and he was in jailbefore dark. (He was charged with drunk driving and leaving the scene of an accident.) Adrian recovered without any ill effects, but my bicycle was a different story.

Crushed Bicycle Replaced with Deluxe Model

After walking the two miles to school for several days, I was contacted by the drunken driver's attorney. He told me his client would pay for any new bicycle I wanted. (He also agreed to pay all of my cousin's medical expenses.) After looking at what was available, I learned that an older boy (Harry Caudill) had a souped-up super deluxe, slightly used bike he wanted to sell. After looking it over and taking a trial ride, I decided that was the one I wanted. It was the Cadillac of bicycles. It had everything on it. In addition to what my other bike had, this one was equipped with a basket in front, and a luggage carrier in the rear. Also, it was equipped with a horn, light, siren, wide steerhorn handle bars with special rubber hand grips and colorful streamers that blew in the breeze. It also had mud flaps on the front and rear fenders with reflectors that glowed in the dark. I now had the fanciest wheels in town.

It was then, at age 9, that I learned a valuable lesson. That some good can come out of bad, and every cloud has a silver lining. Because just when I thought everything was lost, and that shiny red bicycle I had worked so hard to win was crushed beneath that car, and my transportation life was ended, a new era opened up. A more promising and brighter era than I had even imagined. That bicycle was my main wheels for many years. It enabled me to get a paper route and go into business for myself. It was my most prized possession. However, it was stolen off of my front porch four years later and I never saw it again. But it remains a cherished childhood memory.

The Midland Baking Company was in business for twenty years. It provided not only delicious bakery products for Morehead's citizens, but a delightful aroma which was equally delicious. In the early 1950s, the bakery was sold to the Kern Bakery in London, Kentucky. But it remains a Morehead Memory in the minds of those who were here during that time.

TOURISTS, TOURIST CAMPS, AND TOURISM

Morehead and Rowan County leaders are making a major effort to attract tourists to our community. There is even a Department of Tourism designed to entice visitors to our county. However, since the Midland Trail (U.S. 60) came through our county in 1925, there have been local leaders in our community who recognized the economic value of tourism.

DANIEL BOONE—FIRST KENTUCKY TOURIST

The word "tourism" is a relatively new word in our language. It comes from theFrench word "tour," referring to a journey for "business, pleasure, or education, in which you return to your starting point." Americans have always been an adventurous people, migrating west looking for new opportunity. But they could not be called tourists. However, I suppose Daniel Boone could be called one of Kentucky's earliest tourists. Because on his first trip into Kentucky, I'm sure he was "educated", had fun, increased his fur trade, and returned home. That would qualify him to be called a "tourist," even though he later settled here.

EARLY SETTLERS NOT TOURISTS

In 1835 Washington Irving popularized the word "tour" in his book called *Tour on the Prairies.* It was an autobiographical narrative of his travels on the mid-western frontier. Although there were many settlers moving into Kentucky for the remainder of the 19th century, there were not many "tourists." Those traveling into Kentucky brought their own food, clothing, and shelter. Although those earliest travelers would sometimes knock on the door of a settler's cabin and offer to buy food, or a place to spend the night, they had no affect upon the economy.

TOURISM BEGAN WITH CARS AND ROADS

By the 1920's and the invention and manufacturing of automobiles, there came a demand in this country for better cars and better roads. With the "birth" of the touring car and the building of concrete roads, Americans began to travel for education, fun, or business and then returned home. The Age of Tourism was born in America early in the 20th century, along with a new creation called a "tourist." Along with the tourist came the need for food, lodging, and automobile service. Thus, a new industry was born called "tourism."

TOURIST CAMPS COME TO ROWAN COUNTY

In the 1920's as better roads were built across America, it brought with it an American phenomena called Tourist Homes and Tourist Camps. (They were called camps because prior to that time people traveling camped beside the road in tents.) Those places of lodging appeared throughout America along side the new highways. Therefore, tourism reached Morehead in 1925, with the construction of the Midland Trail (U.S. 60). It was a concrete ribbon that eventually ran from the Atlantic to the Pacific and came through the heart of Rowan County. It brought many travelers through Rowan County and inspired many local visionaries to see the value of tourism. Almost immediately, some of these local visionaries began to construct tourist homes and tourist camps

Mayflower Tourist Camp on Morehead's West Main Street owned by Mr. and Mrs. Clell Bruce, 1934-1946. Now owned by Mrs. O'Rear Caskey.

beside this ribbon of concrete called the "Midland Trail." Since there was no zoning restrictions in those days, anyone living along a highway could just put up a sign and they were in the tourist home business.

The tourist camps were more complex and included gas stations in the front, a restaurant inside the office, and small individual cabins at the rear. Tourist Camps were the motels of their day. (The word "motel" had not yet entered our language.)

Tourist homes were private residents with a sign indicating rooms were available to rent on a nightly basis. They were similar to today's bed and breakfast without the breakfast. There were many private tourist homes along U.S. 60 in Rowan County.

SHADY REST EARLY MOREHEAD TOURIST CAMP

The Shady Rest, located on W. Main and N. Blair Avenue in Morehead, was both a Tourist Home and a Tourist Camp. (It was on the site of the present Dairy Mart Convenient Store.) The service station sold gasoline, tires, batteries, and spare auto parts.

Woodie Hinton, local visionary and newspaper columnist, built the Shady Rest in the 1920's. In the early 1930's, Mike Flood, who was one of the original partners in the famous Eagles Nest Restaurant, sold his share to J.M. Clayton, and bought the Shady Rest. He operated it as a service station, restaurant, and tourist home. It also included separate cabins and was both a tourist camp and tourist home.

After Mike Flood went to work at the Post Office, he sold the Shady Rest to Chester Caskey, who operated the business until the 1950's. Beginning January 15, 1952, Mr. and Mrs. W.L. Keith and Leonard Davis leased the restaurant where the old restaurant and gas station used to be. They ran that restaurant until August, 1970, when the business closed. However, from 1952-1957, the restaurant was open 24 hours a day, seven days a week. (The first retail business in Morehead to offer such service.) The Dairy Mart on W. Main Street is presently located on the site of the old Shady Rest (wasn't that the name of the hotel in the old TV show Petticoat Junction?). Morehead's Shady Rest was in business fifty years before that TV show, and remains a Morehead Memory.

MOREHEAD'S MAYFLOWER ARRIVES

Soon tourist homes and tourist camps became quite a competitive business in Rowan County. There needed to be some "special attraction" to cause tourists to want to stop. Directly across the street from Morehead's Shady Rest was the Mayflower Tourist Camp. The Mayflower was a neat, well-maintained log cabin containing a restaurant with a large dance hall. Also, there were gas pumps and a grease pit outside for automobile service. A special attraction designed to get people to stop was a moonshine still. Although it had been captured by revenuers and rendered useless by punching thousands of holes in its copper cooking tank and condensing pipes, it looked very real. There were eight small individual log cabins for guests. The Mayflower served meals, and with the large dance hall in the rear of the restaurant, was a popular local night spot for Moreheadians to go for food and dancing. (But if you went into the dance hall area there was a 5-cent cover charge.)

The Mayflower opened in 1935 and was owned and operated by visionaries Clell and Sylvia Bruce. It was quite a successful business, because it was well advertised on road signs east and west of Morehead, "Log Cabins and Moonshine Still." Who could resist passing through Kentucky without sleeping in a log cabin, or seeing a moonshine still? (Two things closely connected to Kentucky's stereotype.)

This writer's best childhood friend, Meredith Mynhier, was the step-son of Clell Bruce. Meredith grew up in the living quarters behind the business. It was family operated, and he helped by washing dishes and cleaning cabins. Having spent the night with him many times and helping him with his chores, I knew it was hard work.

During WW II, Clell Bruce had to be away working in defense plants and on September 18, 1945, sold the Mayflower to Earl Maddox. Later owners of the Mayflower were Jack West and Alfred Caskey.

MR. AND MRS. O'REAR CASKEY PURCHASE THE MAYFLOWER

In 1947, the Mayflower was purchased by O'Rear and Velma Caskey. From 1947-1969, it was both a tourist camp and taxi stand. (They operated 6 taxis.) After the death of Mr. Caskey, Velma closed the tourist camp. Velma still owns the property on W. Main Street, which over the years had been a doughnut shop, dry cleaners, photo shop, and taxi business. Today, her son Ron has his classic car business on the property. Even though it burned down once, it has been restored to excellent condition and remains a Morehead

Memory. Allen Lake and his son did much of the restoration of the log cabin following a destructive fire.

MOREHEAD CAMP OPENED

Another early entrepreneur who saw a future in the touring trade in Rowan County was James Archie Williams. In 1935 when Mr. Williams, from Morgan County, married May Waggoner, from Carter County, they formed a lifetime partnership in the tourist camp business. Shortly after their marriage, they opened a tourist camp and restaurant on U.S. 60 in Farmers. After five years, they sold their business in Farmers and purchased property on U.S. 60, $1^1/_2$ miles east of Morehead. It was there they opened the Morehead (Tourist) Camp. The Camp contained a restaurant, gas pumps, and 12 separate rental cabins. Each unit contained a bathroom, potbellied stove with coal heat, bed and dresser.

Shortly after opening in 1941, Archie added a second floor above the restaurant for family living quarters. There they reared their children: Candy, Jim, and Sharon. (All now live away from Morehead, but return often.)

SPECIALTY WAS FRIED CHICKEN

Archie advertised on roadside signs east and west of Morehead as the "Morehead Camp: Home cooked food, specializing in fried chicken and steak." They also served country ham, home-made yeast rolls, and home baked pies. The food was delicious and it was a popular eating place for many Moreheadians. (This writer and his wife Janis during their dating years used to eat there on special occasions.) It was also a place where many Moreheadians would go for their Sunday dinners.

In talking with the genial May Williams in her retirement home on Knapp Avenue, she says that, "She cannot eat fried chicken to this day." Since their speciality was fried chicken, she was the one who

CHAPTER THREE • 165

fried the chicken. After Archie would go out into the country and buy the chickens alive, it was her job to kill them. But she also had to clean out their entrails and pick the feathers off, singe the remaining tiny feathers, and cut them up before they could be fried. She would prepare a dozen chickens at one time. Next she would soak them in boiling water, partially fry them in lard in a big black iron skillet. After that she would next refrigerate them until they were ordered. Then, she would re-fry them in that big black iron skillet as ordered by the customers. (No wonder she can't eat fried chicken today.)

MOREHEAD CAMP OWNER SPECIALIZED IN DEMOCRATS

May laughingly said another of her specialities was "Democrats." Long active in the state and county Democrat Party, she has served as county chairman and on many political committees. Following the death of her beloved Archie, she closed the Morehead Camp. Although she still owns the land (the building has been torn down), the Morehead Camp remains a Morehead Memory to many.

HOME-LIKE TOURIST CAMP OPENED IN 1930

In 1930, Morehead's Millard Moore was another local visionary who saw a future in tourism. That was the year Mr. Moore, his wife, and sister, Miss Bertilee Moore, opened the "Homelike Tourist Camp." It was located on U.S. 60, 2 miles east of Morehead. Mr. and Mrs. Moore were previously in the mercantile business on Christy Creek and were the parents of three children: Hilda, Gladys, and Wilbur, all now deceased.

In 1925, Mr. Moore moved to Morehead and purchased a Chevrolet dealership. He also became involved in politics and ran an unsuccessful campaign for sheriff in 1929. Following his defeat, he sold his auto dealership, as he recognized the future of tourism in Rowan County. Therefore, in November 1930, he opened his Tourist Camp in Rowan County. (Mr. Moore also owned a Tourist Camp in Wisconsin.) The new Midland Trail Highway was less than five years old and the future looked bright for the tourist trade. The new tourist camp was advertised as the "Brightest spot in Rowan County," and emphasizedhome-like treatment, and real Kentucky hospitality. Since Rowan County was a "wet" county then, everything to eat or drink was available. That included whiskey, wine, brandy and cold beer. Also available were complete meals, sandwiches, candies, cigars, cigarettes, tobacco, tires, gas and oil. All supplies were available for both the tourist and his car. The Homelike Tourist Camp offered state of the art clean, modern well-furnish cabins, as well as "the best barbecue in Eastern Kentucky."

The business closed long before Mr. Moore's death in 1972, and the buildings have all been torn down. However, Mr. Moore's grandchildren still own some of the site of the Homelike Tourist Home, which remains a Morehead Memory.

OTHER EARLY TOURIST CAMPS

Among other tourist camps in Rowan County during that era was "Joe's Place" on east U.S. 60 (across the highway from the entrance to the University golf Course). Joe specialized in hot dogs and barbeque sandwiches. In an attempt to attract families to stop, he constructed a small home-made children's play ground with swings, merry-go-round and sliding board. Also there were picnic tables. Joe's closed during WW II.

The "Trocadero" was located at the entrance of Cincinnati Branch and U.S. 60 west. It was a well-known night spot during the time Rowan county was "wet." But when the county was voted dry, it went out of business. Also another Tourist Camp was the "Mountain View" Camp in Farmers. One of the owners was Mort May, former sheriff of Rowan County. All of these tourist camps remain a Morehead Memory.

Looking at the tourist trade through the telescope of time, you immediately recognize the importance of U.S. 60 crossing the county. It brought opportunity and prosperity as people began crossing the county. Alert local entrepreneurs saw "gold in them thar cars," and worked hard to "mine" their share. Thus, forming the foundation for today's gigantic tourism efforts in Rowan County.

RED ROSE DAIRY (PHONE 217)

"You can whip our cream but you can't beat our milk".

In the 1930's many Morehead residents were awakened around daybreak each morning by the sound of glass as it rubs against steel. It was the sound of the Red Rose Dairy milkman as he delivered fresh pasteurized milk on their doorstep. The milk was bottled in glass bottles and hauled in heavy wire cases in the back of a red and white paneled truck. But no matter how quiet the delivery man would try to be, the sleeping residents could still hear the noise. This was especially true in warm weather, becausetheir screened windows and doors were kept open to capture the natural air conditioning– which was a cool breeze blowing down Evans Branch (where the College Lake is now located) or Oxley Branch (now North

Red Rose Dairy in Morehead 1930-1950.
Thomas Flannery, owner's son.

Wilson Ave.). But no one ever complained, because they were thankful to get the fresh pasteurized milk delivered to their door.

You will notice that I am emphasizing "pasteurized," because in those days there were people in Rowan County who would deliver raw un-pasteurized milk to your door. Indeed, many Morehead residents kept cows in their back yard, or in a small field adjoining their home. So home delivery of pasteurized milk in the little red and white truck was a luxury, and a welcome and familiar sight in town.

Morehead's dominant dairy in the 1930s and 1940s was the Red Rose Dairy. It was located in a low stone building on East Second Street that currently houses a child care center. The dairy's proud motto was:

"You can whip our cream but you can't beat our milk."

How It All Began

The dairy originated in the late 1920, on the Flannery family farm near Bluestone, now owned by Rufus Flannery. Ray and Delmer Flannery were attending old Morehead High School, and when they came to school each day, they began bringing jugs of raw milk and selling them to homes and businesses. The business grew and Ray and Delmer continued to bottle and deliver raw milk into Morehead after graduating from high school.

Ray Flannery's Vision

It was then that Ray Flannery saw great potential in the dairy business and about 1930, he bought Delmer's share of the business, and built a stone building with concrete floors and many drains on East Second Street. Here he built a modern dairy where raw milk was pasteurized, bottled in glass bottles, and stored. There was a walk-in cooler where the temperature was kept a constant 40 degrees and the milk was stored in preparation for delivery the next day. (The room was cooled in the early days with 100-pound blocks of ice.) Ray Flannery usually had four or five employees. The men that worked inside the dairy wore rubber boots and aprons and the inside was kept spotless. One employee would drive a truck and pick up the raw milk from area farmers. It would be picked up in 5-gallon or 10-gallon cans and brought into the dairy. The milk was poured directly into the pasteurizer, heated to a temperature of 180 degrees for 30 minutes, and then bottled in $1/2$ pint, pint, and quart glass bottles and sealed with paraffin coated caps that customers could pull off and lick the cream from under the cap. Then thebottles would be placed in cases and stored in the cooler for delivery the next day. Coffee cream and whipping cream were made by separating the cream from the whole milk thus leaving skim milk. In those days, the skim milk was given away to anyone who came to the dairy with their own container, or the skim milk was poured down the sewer. I used to think what a waste this must be. But few people in those days would drink skim milk.

Lon Ellis (this writer's father) was a milkman, and at various times other employees included Harold Ellington, Woodrow Hall, and several members of the Flannery Family. Many times I would help my dad as he ran his route. He had to be at work at 4 a.m., 7 days a week and load the red and white paneled milk truck. After loading, he began home delivery. Each customer on the milk route received daily delivery of milk at their front door. You would also pick up the glass bottles from the previous delivery. The empty milk bottles also served as a means of communication. Many times notes would be placed inside the empty bottles requesting extra milk or a bottle of buttermilk or whipped cream. Also at the end of the month, the bills would be left with the milk, and the checks would be placed inside the empty bottles the next day.

Recycling in the Truest Form

The empty bottles would be taken back to the dairy to be washed on rotating brushes and then sterilized. This was true recycling in its purest form. The milk that was delivered was pasteurized but not homogenized. This meant that the cream would come to the top and was clearly visible in the glass bottles. You could shake the cream up in the bottle before drinking it, or you could pour the cream off and use it for coffee cream.

While there were people in Morehead that milked their own cows, most people in town were on the milk delivery route. In the summer heat, the milk had to be left on the coolest part of the porch in an insulated metal box. In winter, the milk would sometimes freeze before being taken into the house, and the cream on top would pop up 2 or 3 inches above the top of the milk bottle. But it was still good to eat like ice cream.

After the home delivery was finished, usually by 7 a.m., the driver would eat breakfast and go back to the dairy and re-load for commercial deliveries. First, there would be the college deliveries, which would include three or four hundred   pint glass bottles for the cafeteria. The college cafeteria was then located in the basement of what is now Allie Young Hall, and delivery was made from the rear of the building (Ward Oates Drive), and taken down on an elevator. Also there would be several dozen quart bottles of whole milk and buttermilk for cooking. This was heavy work. After delivering to the college, milk was delivered to the local restaurants, such as "The Amos & Andy," "The Welcome Inn" and the "Eagles Nest." Also, stores such as Allen's Meat Market on Main Street and Sam Allen's on First Street, Clint Jones' Store on W. Main and Regal Store on South Wilson Avenue. The Midland Trail Hotel and the Morehead Camp (East U.S. 60)were other places on the milk route.

NO SCHOOL LUNCHROOMS

There were no schools on the milk route because all students at Breckinridge and the Morehead Public either brought their lunch to school, went home for lunch, or went to a restaurant for lunch. SCHOOLS HAD NO LUNCHROOMS!

MILK DELIVERY SERVICE EXPANDED

Two days a week milk delivery was extended to Clearfield, Farmers, Haldeman and Soldier. These deliveries were mostly to the businesses of these towns. To look at these communities now, one cannot realize how busy and alive they were in the 1930s and 1940s. At both Haldeman and Soldier, you could park the milk truck in one spot and deliver many cases of glass half-pints of milk to eight separate restaurants and stores without moving your truck. Business was good in those quiet days in Morehead.

The red and white paneled milk truck, with a bottle of milk painted on the side and a red rose on the bottle was a familiar sight to all the people of Morehead for 25 years. Yes, "You could whip their cream but you couldn't beat their milk."

Ray Flannery, owner of the Red Rose Dairy, died in 1950, and the business was sold to R.C. Pennington and William McClain. They operated the business as the Red Rose Dairy until 1955 when it was sold to Aubrey Kautz, owner of the new modern Spring Grove Dairy. The Red Rose Dairy remains a Morehead Memory in the minds of those who lived here at that time.

MCBRAYER STORE (PHONE 180)

The street sign on the corner said Fairbanks Avenue, and in the mid 1930s it was a busy street. (Now the street sign says South Wilson Avenue.) There is not much traffic now, but then it was an extremely busy thoroughfare connecting the established business district including banks, depot, hotels and freight station located on Railroad Street (now First Street) and the more recent businesses and post office on Main Street.

ECONOMY STORE OPENS

It was November 1, 1934, when J. Earl McBrayer opened a new store on Fairbanks Avenue (now South Wilson). It was called the "Economy Store," and consisted of 25 feet on the side of a building operated by the Farmers Produce Exchange. It opened with an inventory of about $150 in odds and ends of shoes, dry goods, and clothing. The first day total sales were two 5-cent handker-chiefs.

McBrayers Economy Store, 1934.

ECONOMY STORE EXPANDS

But business improved and Mr. McBrayer expanded to include all of the building. In 1936 the Economy Store added additional inventory to include seeds, fertilizer, light farm tools, furniture and appliances. In order to expand, Mr. McBrayer said he had to go into debt to the extent it would "even scare him today." Even though the business was growing and the work was demanding, Earl and his wife Martha operated the business with one part-time employee. Later, others were added as business increased.

THE FLOOD CAME

Then on the night of July 4, 1939, a date that will forever remain in the minds of Moreheadians who were living here then, a devastating flash flood hit the city. Twenty-five people in Rowan County lost their lives in the roaring flood waters of rampaging Triplett Creek, and Moreheadians have never been the same. Now every time the thunder rolls and the lightening flashes, older residents cast a wary eye at the sky and look for the high ground.

With so much carnage and loss of property and life in the flood, Mr. McBrayer even hesitated to mention what it cost him. But it appeared that he was ruined financially. He had just bought $15,000 (a fortune then) worth of merchandise (all on credit) when the flood roared down Railroad Street and Fairbanks Avenue. The water was 10 feet deep in his store, and everything was lost. But grateful that he and his family survived, he was determined to rebuild his business. Together with Martha, they slowly rebuilt their business on Fairbanks Avenue. They paid off every single dollar they owed as a result of the flood. Many people would have taken the bankruptcy law, but not Earl and Martha McBrayer. In 1942 they moved the furniture part of the business to Main Street. (Higher ground.)

Earl Enters WW II

In 1944, in spite of having six children, Earl McBrayer was drafted into the military service. Martha continued to operate the business as well as care for the children while her husband was in the Army Air Corps. When Earl returned, he bought Frank Haven's portion of the 5-and 10-cent store, and he and Dwight Pierce operated the business until 1962 when Earl bought Dwight Pierce's half of the business. Earl alsofounded Forest Lawn Memorial Gardens and operated that business after his retirement from the store.

Early Entrepreneur

Earl was an early entrepreneur in Morehead. He was one of the founders of Radio Station W.M.O.R. and served as radio announcer and host of the original W.M.O.R. Swapshop for several years. In addition to managing his furniture and appliance store, he also was in the 5&10 cent store business. Later, he was a partner in the Stucky Funeral Home on W. Main Street, and he also was a successful farmer.

Earl and Martha McBrayer were successful in spite of flood, war, and the depression. They helped this community grow from a small village to a thriving metropolitan area. They were successful through hard work, prayer, and determination. Two of their children, Jack McBrayer and Pauline Ellington, continued operating McBrayers Store until February 1997 when it fell victim to the "outlanders" chain stores, with a bigger is better syndrome." BUT THERE WAS A MCBRAYERS STORE IN MOREHEAD FOR 63 YEARS. (November, 1934 – February 1997.)

REGAL STORE (PHONE 25)

Lytle's Regal Store, 1936.

The memory of Fairbanks Avenue is fast fading from Moreheadians memories. (It is now South Wilson Avenue.) Yet in the 1930s and 40s it was a busy street connecting the business districts of Railroad Street now First Street) and Main Street. But in 1936 the Regal Store was located on Fairbanks Avenue, and it was that same year that Ray Lytle moved his family from Bracken County, and, along with silent partner E.B. Hancock, bought the Regal Store.

OPENING DAY SALE

After some minor remodeling, they held an "Open Under New Management Sale" and advertised: 24 lb. bag of Snow Goose flour, .87; 5 lb. bag of pinto beans, .38; 100 lb. bag of potatoes, .95. Although these prices seem small in today's economy, it must be remembered also that Lexington tobacco market paid an average of $19.20 per hundred for tobacco. (Hardly paid the shipping.) School teachers were paid an average of $67 per month. (The principal made $100 per month.) For 5 cents you could see a new movie at the Cozy Theater starring Buster Crabbe (1932 Olympic Champion) in *"Hold on Yale."*

REGAL—A RURAL ROWAN COUNTY STORE TOO

The Regal Store sold groceries, meats, feeds and seeds at competitive prices. The Regal Store was a popular place for people from rural Rowan County to shop–especially on Saturdays, and court days. It also served as the station where you met your ride back to the country after shopping in town. Although in 1936 there were some automobiles in Morehead, many people from rural Rowan County came to town on horseback and in wagons. It was a common sight in 1936 to see wagons and teams of mules lined up in front of the Regal Store. They were being loaded with food for cattle, hogs, sheep, chickens and people. BUT THERE WAS NO PET FOOD. What did the pets eat in those days? Why they ate people food! It is quite different today when many people eat pet food.

ADVERTISING HELPED BUSINESS GROW

The Regal Store grew as Mr. Lytle pursued an aggressive marketing policy of advertising sales and specials in the *Morehead Independent* (one of Morehead's newspapers at that time). Also, it was about that time, that Ray bought Mr. Hancock's share of the business, and hired a young man by the name of Ralph Ellis as his assistant, along with Philley Howard. Philley and Ralph were loyal employees for almost 20 years.

As business increased, Ray's wife, Novenda, began to help in the store. She was kept busy from early morning until late at night in the dual responsibility of rearing a family of four children plus working in the store. But she accomplished this dual role quite successfully.

THE FLOOD BROUGHT LOSS AND GAIN

The great flood of July 4, 1939, did much damage to the Regal Store. It was a devastating financial blow to Ray Lytle's business. But they were able to salvage the canned goods, and some other merchandise, and continue operating the business.

Since the Regal Store had just expanded their meat department, Ray was planning to buy a new meat block. "Low and behold," the devastating flood that did so much damage, brought him a new meat block. Yes, a meat block was part of the debris that washed up behind his store. Try as he would, he could not find the owner, so he cleaned the meat block up and put it to good use in his new meat department. The old saying "one man's loss is another man's gain" was certainly true in this instance.

NEW MARKETING STRATEGY: SELF-SERVICE

It was shortly after the flood that the Regal Store began using a new marketingtechnique. It was called "self-service." Up to that time you went to the store and told the storekeeper what you wanted, or gave him a list, and he filled your order. With this new self-service, the merchandise was placed pre-priced, pre-packaged, and pre-wrapped on shelving accessible to the customer, who made the selection and paid on the way out. THIS WAS A WHOLE NEW CONCEPT IN SALES. Many people thought that much of the merchandise would "walk out" in baggy overall pockets without paying. But this was not the case, and it did provide faster more efficient service to the customer. But many people then as now, were resistant to change, and for a while Mr. Lytle would fill the orders in the "old fashioned way."

SELF-SERVICE CARRIED TOO FAR

Self-service did work and was here to stay, and the Regal Store was credited with being the first store in Morehead to introduce this service. However, one local "character" in Morehead took self-service one step too far. It was on a Saturday night about closing time when one of the local drunks felt he needed some money for more whiskey. He slipped in behind the counter at the store and started serving himself a hearty helping of cash from the register. When Ray tried to stop him, the man pulled a knife. Mrs. Lytle screamed, "Stop Him!" About that time Charles Ellis, who happened to be in the store, picked up a 12 oz. bottle of Ale 8 and broke it over the man's head, knocking him to the floor. Stunned and quickly subdued, the man's only comment was, as he tasted the Ale 8 pouring down over his lips, "I wish you had broken a beer bottle on my head instead of that stuff, it would have sure tasted better." Ray did not even have the man arrested, but sent him home, because he was just one who had taken self-service a little too far. The men remained life-time friends.

NAME CHANGED AND STORE MOVED

In 1948, the Regal Store moved to a new location on West Main Street. The name was changed to Lytle's Self-Service Grocery, and Ray continued to operate the store until his death in 1976. The business was operated by his family until 1982 when it was sold. It is now known as Mullin's Food Market.

Ray Lytle was an active church, civic, and community leader in Morehead. His success in business seemed to be because of his early anticipation of what the public wanted. He also believed in advertising his store and products. Also, he believed hard work, prayer, and perseverence were keys to being successful. Ray Lytle was one who helped to make Morehead move forward, and the Regal Store remains a Morehead Memory.

STOCK MARKET

Morehead once had its own active and viable stock market. It was the center for buying and selling stock in this region of Kentucky. No, it was not blue chip stock listed on the Dow, but it was listed each week in the MOREHEAD INDEPENDENT as the stock report, eg:

Stock Report: August 22, 1944

Morehead Stock Yards: The sales report for the sale of Tuesday, August 22, at the Morehead Stock Yards are as follows:

HOGS: Packers $14; Mediums $13.85; Shoats (small hogs) $1.10 to $3.50.

CATTLE: Steers, $13.50 down; Heifers, $8.90 to $10.00; Cows $4.10 to $6.70.

COWS and CALVES: $58.00 to $133.00; Stock Cattle, $14.00 to $45.00; Bulls, $7.10 down.

CALVES: Top Veals, $15.05; Medium, $13.50; Common and Large, $6.20 to $12.50.

HORSES & MULES: market was considered fair ranging from $20.00 to $120.00.

STOCKYARDS OPENED IN 1941

The opening of the stockyards was called a red letter day and was referred to as one of the biggest days in Morehead's business history. Local farmers watched the stock prices as carefully as today's stock exchange. The stockyards grand opening day sale was February 26, 1941. On that day, Moreheadians were awakened

Photo: Roger and Marie Barbour

Morehead Stockyard, Dam, and Rail Yards, 1942.

by cattle bawling, pigs squealing, and mules braying. Also, there was a strong barn odor in the air. In 1941, the economy of Rowan and the surrounding counties had a strong agricultural base, so there was a lot of truck traffic in town that day.

BIG DAY IN MOREHEAD BUSINESS HISTORY

The yards and dropping pens (where you unloaded before being weighed) were located at the end of Bridge Street opposite the college power plant on the banks of Triplett Creek. Over 2,000 people attended the opening day sale, including Agriculture Commissioner Wallin Harris, and over 100 buyers from the major packing companies. The first sale day was extremely successful with 360 head of livestock sold at prices competitive with the Cincinnati market. A survey of both sellers and buyers reported everyone was pleased with the sale.

The original officers of the Stock Company were Chevrolet Dealer, W.L. Jayne, President; Sheriff William Carter, Vice President; and businessman, J.R. Wendel, Secretary-Treasurer. The Board of directors were Glennis Fraley, Ray Lytle, William Sample, V.H.Wolford, C.Z. Bruce, W.H. Layne, and J. Earl McBrayer. This group of public-spirited citizens put their capital where their mouth was by promoting the sale of livestock in our area. Capital stock in this new company was listed at $10,000.

FINDING STOCK WORKERS DIFFICULT

The yards opened for business under the able management of J.R. Wendel. Mr. Wendel hoped to profit by the mistakes of other yards, because before construction began, he visited other yards and asked what they would have done differently. Then he supervised and planned the construction of the Morehead yards. Also getting workers was a problem; you did not just employ anyone to work in a stockyard. The workers had to be assigned by the Department of Agriculture. Therefore, on opening day, Mr. J.M. Clarke of Mt. Sterling was assigned as a starter. (A starter was someone who knew the value of the stock and would start the bidding at a price he, himself, would be willing to pay for the animals, thus speeding up the sale.) Also, Mr. Sam W. Hill, Hillsboro, was assigned as auctioneer. There were also two weighmen. All weighmen had to be fully bonded. Their names had to be posted on large red and white signs beside the scales. Scales had to be tested regularly, with the date tested displayed prominently. Failure to do so could result in fines of $100-$500.

STOCK DAY BROUGHT "PEN HOOKERS" TO TOWN

The stockyards conducted a sale in Morehead every Tuesday. Stock day was always a big business, and heavy traffic day in Morehead. In addition to those that came to buy, sell, trade, or just watch, there were the "pen hookers." The "pen hookers" were men who came up to a truck waiting to unload live stock and make an offer to buy from the owner before the animals were unloaded and weighed. A good pen hooker would climb up on the side of a truck, poke a stick through the wood paneled truck, estimate the grade and weight of the animal, and make an offer to the owner. He was betting the owner that his offer was better than what he would get at auction, and he would not have to wait until the sale ended. The pen hooker would then either sell the livestock that day, take them to another market, or keep them hoping prices would increase next week.

One of the best pen hookers in the area was Clint Jones. Clint ran a grocery store and meat market at the corner of U.S. 60 and 519. He also operated the last retail slaughter house to go out of business in Rowan County. Mr. Jones could look at a cow, poke it a couple of times with a stick, and estimate the quality and quantity (weight) of the animal. He could do that with un-canny accuracy, and was proud of his skill. Clint rarely lost money on an animal he bought. But when he did, he would talk about it for a week because he wanted the word to get around that if you sold your livestock to him, he would probably pay you more than you could get at the auction.

Rowan, Morgan, Bath and Menifee counties had a lot more rich fertile farmland in 1940 than they now have, because the thousands of acres now covered by Cave Run Lake was then rich river-bottom farmland. The Morehead Stockyards was the closest market for all of the surrounding counties. Farmers soon realized they could increase their profits by eliminating the time and expense of hauling stock to distant markets in Maysville, Mt. Sterling, or Huntington.

EASTERN KENTUCKY HATCHERY OPENED IN 1940

In 1940, another agriculture based business opened in Morehead. It was that year that Mr. Jesse Ashlock opened the Eastern Kentucky Hatchery (poultry, not fish) on Fairbanks (South Wilson) Avenue. That hatchery was set up to assist, meet the needs and promote poultry and egg production throughout this region. They took orders and shipped baby chicks throughout Kentucky.

The baby chicks were shipped via parcel post, and when you entered the Morehead Post office, you could not only smell them, but could hear them "peeping". The mail handlers hated to have to ship chickens via parcel post, but they did.

WHICH CAME FIRST—THE CHICKEN OR THE EGG?

The hatchery shipped not only baby chicks, but specially fertilized eggs of special breeds of chickens, such as Leghorns and Rhode Island Reds. Those special fertilized eggs were for those who wanted to hatch their own. Many times the eggs became chicks between the time the eggs were shipped and they arrived at their destination. (This explains which came first the chicken or the egg.) As a result of the Eastern Kentucky Hatchery, poultry and egg production increased dramatically. The initial cost for someone getting into the poultry business was small; however, the profits were also small. Many local farmers entered the poultry business, but few were successful. Disease, cost of food, and the low egg prices drew most farmers out of the poultry business after two or three years. The Eastern Kentucky Hatchery went out of business at the end of World War II, but remains a Morehead Memory for those who made an attempt to get into the poultry production business.

AGRICULTURE COURSES ENTER HIGH SCHOOL CURRICULA

With the arrival of the stockyards and the hatchery, there was a demand for additional agriculture in the high school curriculum. The federal government began subsidizing high school agriculture teachers salaries. This brought Mr. Carl Wade to old Morehead High School to teach agriculture. (Later on he was replaced by Mr. Charles Hughes.)

Mr. Wade's courses in hog, cattle, sheep and crop production became very popular among the boys at Morehead High School.

Morehead High School Future Farmers Club, 1940. **Bottom:** *Mr. Carl Wade, Billy Stidom, Pete Kessler, Dof Marshall, Pete Brown, Maurice Hall, Bill Stewart, Joe Evans, Ivan Reed, Glen Poston.* **Second:** *Vernon Christian, Alvin Gulley, Earl Boggess, Charles Reeves, Glen Gilkerson, Charles McKenzie, Hanson Carey, Bill Joe Peed, Jack McKenzie, Elmo Epperheart.* **Top:** *Paul Dowdy, Lloyd Pierce, Claude Pierce, Billy Turner, Rodney Johnson, Paul McBrayer, Charles Roe, Allie Hunt, Emerson Lewis, Ed Carpenter, Adrian McKinny, Rufus Flannery.*

In order to take one of his courses, you had to have a "project." That meant you had to grow a field crop or farm animals for profit. The course required the boys to keep meticulous records of the cost of bringing the animal or crop to market. The goal of the course was to determine the profitability of the project.

Since there were few sheep grown in this county, one enterprising young boy by the name of Charles McKenzie decided he would raise sheep for his project. Charles (his nickname was "Nuke") lived on a farm in the upper Licking River section of Rowan County. His project served as a model for every project. He listed the cost of 10 ewes $100.00; and food, dipping, and marketing $23.75. After selling the wool and marketing the lambs, he received a total of $253.90 and a profit of $120.15. While Charles realized a profit on his project, sheep were never a profitable business in this area because there were so many dogs that were running loose, and they killed the sheep.

"TOWNIES" COULD NOT TAKE AGRICULTURE

Boys living in town had problems getting into these courses. J.D. Hicks, one of the "townies" tried to get into an agriculture course but his advisor, Coach Telford Gevedon, said what do you know about farming? He refused to allow him to take the course. J.D. entered the military service the next year. Following his service in WW II, he never returned to Morehead (except to marry his high school sweetheart, Frankie Messer.) J.D. and his brother, Warren, settled in the rich California farming country. They began buying farmland and farming commercially. The boy who could not get into the high school agriculture class told this writer on one occasion, "One out of every three tomatoes that the Campbell Soup Company uses is from my farm." So much for counseling!

FUTURE FARMERS CLUB POPULAR

The agriculture students all belonged to an exclusive club called the Future Farmers of America. That was a national organization with local chapters. The name was descriptive of their purpose, but the club involved so much more. The boys learned parliamentary procedure, public speaking, writing and business. The club encouraged social interaction, broadened their experiences by going on trips to state meetings. It gave them confidence and helped to improve their self-image. Many of the quiet, shy, self-conscious farm boys became more outgoing and self-assured through the Future Farmers of America. Just as all boys who became farmers were not in that club, so all who were active club members did not become farmers. But most who were members of the Future Farmers of America found it a very worthwhile experience.

The Stock Market, Eastern Kentucky Hatchery, and the Future Farmers of America are all a part of Morehead's history. They are all a part of Morehead Memories.

MONARCH SUPPLY STORE (PHONE 76)

In 1945, at the end of World War II, when this nation's industry converted back to peace time production, two of Morehead's early entrepreneurs entered into a partnership to establish a new business in Morehead. Those two visionaries realized that with the men returning from military service, there would be a demand for land and housing as the GIs married and started their families. They recognized also there would soon be a need for building materials and farm equipment, and they established a business to meet that need. Those two men were Glennis Fraley and Roy Cornette, and the business was called The Monarch Supply Store. It was, as the name implied, The <u>Monarch</u> of Morehead's hardware, farm, and building supplies for over 37 years.

Monarch Supply Store employees and onlookers with newly arrived farm equipment, 1947.
(Photo: Art Stewart). L-R: Jim Brammer, Glennis Fraley, Jr. Kelsey, Violet Hardin, Harvey
Lambert, Murvel Crosley, Danny Skaggs, Art Bumgardner, Roy Cornette, Bill Messer, Dudley
Caudill, Dave Gevedon, Alfred Jones, Noah Fugate, Lyle Tackett (on tractor) and Sherman Arnett.

Both men were native Rowan Countians and were successful in their own field before starting the Monarch. Glennis, a former school teacher and owner of Fraley's IGA Store, was married to Lona Cooper, and they had one son, John. Roy, a former school teacher, principal and superintendent of Rowan County Schools, was married to Elsie Hogge, and they had one daughter, Margaret. In January 1946, Roy resigned as school superintendent and Glennis sold his IGA store. Glennis had his share of the capital needed; however, in order for Roy to raise his share, he sold his farm on Route 32 near Hickory Pointe to Robert "Bob" Bishop for $1,750. "Bob" still owns that farm, and he laughed as he said, "That was the best investment I ever made."

"THUNDER MUGS ARRIVE"

The Monarch Supply Store opened in September, 1946, in one section of the Alf Caskey Building in downtown Morehead. (Near Arby's east parking lot.) Because of war time shortages, it was difficult at first to get the merchandise you needed for their store. Roy would take a truck to the Huntington, (West Virginia) Wholesale Hardware Supply Company and buy just about whatever was available. He returned from Huntington on one occasion with a truckload of "thunder mugs." For the uninitiated, those most necessary items, were also called "slop jars." They were what you used at night before there was indoor plumbing. The "thunder mugs" sold out quickly because homes with indoor plumbing were in the minority in 1946.

SELDOM HEARD "SORRY, WE DON'T HAVE IT"

As the store grew, it prided itself on handling nothing but quality, top grade merchandise. All the hand tools (saws, hammers, pliers, etc.) were Bluegrass Brand manufactured by Beknap Hardware Company of Louisville, Kentucky. Also the growingbusiness sold sawmill supplies, electrical appliances (Westinghouse), lawn mowers, plumbing and heating supplies, seed, fertilizers, housewares, hunting and fishing equipment. The store stocked every size, shape and form of nuts, bolts, screws and washers. They usually had in stock whatever size screw, nut or bolt you needed. You seldom heard the phrase "Sorry, we don't have it" or "We can order it for you" at the Monarch.

EXPANSION FROM HARDWARE TO FARM EQUIPMENT

In 1951, Roy and Glennis bought the old Federated Store Building next door (east) of their present site. Plans were made to increase staff and expand their merchandise. Among those employed at the Monarch during that era included Herb Bradley, Newt Porter, Danny Skaggs, Bud Bumgardner, Louise Black, Phyllis Black, Gene Hamm, Dorsie Hardin, Sr., Milton Tackett, Bill Messer, Herb Whitt, Vertner Tackett and Violet Hardin. In the fall of 1951, the business moved into their newly remodeled quarters next door. The new quarters provided much more display area, and the business changed to a self-service style of merchandising. The Monarch had the first Ford tractor Dealership in Rowan County after World War II. Along with the tractor dealership came a major farm implement dealership, including plows, harrows, rakes, and mowing machines. In 1948, Lon Ellis (this writer's father) bought a new Ford tractor, rake, and mowing machine. He then went up to Kenneth Lewis' garage on east Main Street and bought one of the first International string tie automatic hay bailers in Rowan County (after the War). The hay bailing business was brisk for a couple of years before there was very much competition. However, Mr. Ellis soon sold his hay bailer because it was difficult to get spare parts.

With the addition of the line of Ford tractors and major farm implements, the Monarch established a service center and maintenance shop. It was located at the rear of the building off Sun Street, and included spare parts, welding, tractor tire service, and tune ups. The shop manager was Danny Skaggs.

FARMERS EAGER FOR NEW FARM EQUIPMENT

In an attempt to increase the farm business, Glennis would travel throughout a five-county area, talking to farmers as he demonstrated the latest in farming technology. Since there had been no new farm equipment manufactured during the War years, there was a ready market available. Glennis sold about everything they could get, and the farm implement division of the Monarch became very successful.

DORSEY HARDIN SR. "MR. OUTSIDE"

In January 1952, Dorsey Hardin, Sr. former maintenance supervisor for the RowanCounty Schools, went to work at the Monarch. He was called "Mr. Outside" and was responsible for all electrical, plumbing and re-modeling work. He was also responsible for installing equipment, appliances, pumps and machines. Dorsey loved his work, and he had a keen sense of humor, and was constantly getting into difficult but humorous situations, e.g Roscoe Pennington at Sharkey, purchased a new electric pump to bring water from his farm pond into is house. Dorsey was out in the middle of the pond as he worked diligently trying to get it installed. He suddenly yelled loudly for Mrs. Pennington to come out on the porch and said, "Don't be worried, Mrs. Pennington, but I'm stuck here in the middle of the pond." She went to the field to get her husband and they had to throw Dorsey a rope and pull him out of the knee-deep mud in the pond with a tractor.

One other occasion Dorsey was installing an new pump and water lines in the home of Willie Frank Thomas on East U.S. 60. While he was under the floor, their dog decided he was some kind of "varmint" and wouldn't let him out from under the floor. He had to stay there until someone came home to chain the dog.

Many years ago this writer and his wife decided to buy ourselves our first automatic dishwasher for a Christmas present. We found the one we wanted at the Monarch. However, after Dorsey came up and measured where it had to be installed, he said there's not enough room. His measurement showed the space was an inch too small for the dishwasher. I measured it, and found that to be true. But Dorsey said if I would help him he thought we could make it work. I helped him and we made it work even though the measurements said it wouldn't. Dorsey said many people use "wall stretchers" to make furniture fit; we used cabinet stretchers to make the dishwasher fit.

MONARCH BECAME A SOCIAL CENTER

The Monarch became a central gathering place for farmers, contractors, businessmen and politicians. They would loaf, swap lies, tell stories, discuss crops, news, politics and the economy. Therefore, it became a social center for many of the men in the community. But the main Morehead social center and loafing place was at the Eagles Nest Restaurant, located a few doors down the street.

EAGLES NEST—PUBLIC RELATION CENTER

Many of the Morehead businessmen would met each morning at 10 for coffee. Although Glennis Fraley seldom sat in on those sessions, Roy Cornette was always there. He said he was the public relations man for the Monarch and much of his "public relations" was done at the Eagles Nest. One morning a very impressive group of local businessmen were having their morning coffee. Among them was Roy Cornette, President of the Kentucky Hardware Association; Bill Sample, President of the Kentucky Lumbermen'sAssociation; Claude Clayton, President of the Kentucky Postmasters Association; and Glenn Lane, President of the Kentucky Bankers Association. Looking over the group, Bill Sample said, "Gentlemen, we are up to our wazoos in presidents this morning."

"JUST SAY CHARGE IT"

The Monarch's business multiplied as they added more merchandise, services, and employees. At one time they had 12 full-time employees. It was surprising that the business was so profitable because they provided credit to almost everyone. However, contrary to all laws of sound business management they seldom ever sent out bills to customers, and they never levied any finance charges on outstanding bills. That was unheard of at that time. The Monarch customers would walk in, buy what they needed, (many times hundreds of dollars' worth), sign the ticket and walk out with the merchandise. It was understood that farmers would pay when they sold their tobacco, cattle or other produce. It was also understood that contractors would pay on completion of their contract. It was further understood that regular wage earners would pay a regular payment on their account each month. But no one ever signed an agreement, it was all understood and usually everyone paid as they agreed.

POSTING OF ACCOUNTS ALWAYS AND ADVENTURE

Violet Hardin, one of the bookkeepers, said it was always an adventure posting the accounts at the end of the day. That was because Mr. Fraley was always very poor at remembering names, and would never asked anyone their name. He was known to charge hundreds of dollars to a customer, write the ticket up, and leave the name blank. But he would always write some kind of identifying message in very small letters at the bottom of the ticket, eg. "lives second house up Rock Fork," or "works as a meat cutter at Allen's IGA," or "lives on the top of Clearfield Hill." The late Mr. Elmer Anderson was a steady customer, and Glennis could never remember his name. But he would always write on the bottom of the ticket in small letters, "has only one arm." That worked well as along as they had only one one-armed customer. Even when

Glennis got the correct name, it was sometimes a challenge to identify the item, e.g. on one ticket, Glennis had written "1 ZUD 2.95." The next day, Roy brought the ticket to Glennis and said, "Glennis, what's this item on the ticket?" Glennis said, "It's 1 ZUD." Roy said, "There's no such thing as a "ZUD." With that, Glennis walked over to a counter and produced a product called Zesty Unadulterated Detergent. Glennis had simply used his own shorthand and abbreviated the product.

SOME BILLS PAID WITH BARTER SYSTEM

In the early days of the Monarch, Roy and Glennis were known to accept farm produce as payment on an account. Roy's daughter, Margaret Morris, recalled Roy bringinghome three bushels of green beans, 100 pounds of potatoes, and one dozen live chicken as payment on one account, and they had to do a lot of "stringing, peeling and plucking."

When customers did not pay on their account for several months, then the store would somewhat apologetically send them a bill. One woman after receiving one of those late notices was very irate. She came in and told Glennis, "You 'dun-ned' me! I have not been able to buy groceries and you 'dun-ned' me." Glennis apologized and said, "We can wait a little longer if you're in a hard place." But the woman paid the bill as she protested being "dun-ned".

MONARCH—THE END OF AN ERA

The Monarch Supply Store was a staple in Morehead's business community for 37 years. But with the opening of I-64, and a new shopping center, the Monarch Store, like so many other small local businesses, could not compete with the chain stores. Ray Bailey purchased the Monarch in 1976, but was unable to make a success of the business. It closed in 1983 and ended an era of early entrepreneurship in Morehead. But Monarch's memory remains in the minds of those who were here during that era.

Morehead Main Street business district. 1940s

White building on the corner of Main Street and N. Hargis Avenue was Morehead's first hospital in 1917. Photo taken in the 1930s.

CHAPTER FOUR

Medical Men (and Women):
Treating The Sick

If medicine is considered to be the art and science of the prevention and treatment of disease, then medical practitioners are those individuals that are concerned with the treatment and prevention of disease. Every culture throughout history has had their medical practitioners. From the earliest archaeological discoveries throughout written history, people have "practiced" medicine. Wherever there were people who became sick, there was usually someone there to treat that "patient."

KENTUCKY EXPLORED BY DR. WALKER

When America was settled and the early pioneers pushed westward, there were medical men who led the way west. Some were both doctors and explorers, and one such pioneer physician–explorer was Dr. Thomas Walker. Dr. Walker was born on January 25, 1725, in King and Queen County, Virginia. He studied medicine at William and Mary College in Virginia and practiced medicine in Fredericksburg, Virginia. It was there he also became involved in business and helped organize a land speculation company called the "Loyal Land Company." Dr. Walker then organized the first English expedition through what he named "Cumberland

Gap." That first expedition into what is now Kentucky, started from Albermarle County, Virginia, in 1750, with a charter to explore 800,000 acres. The group consisted of Ambrose Powell, William Tomlinson, Colby Chew, Henry Loveless, John Hughes, and Dr. Thomas Walker.

Dr. Walker kept very detailed records, and the group was known to explore the headwaters of the Licking River, and moving down the Licking, they explored some of its tributaries. Although it definitely cannot be proven true, there was a good chance that the group may have come down the Licking and explored Triplett Valley. Therefore, in 1750, there was a very good chance that the first Englishman to arrive in what is now Rowan County, was a doctor. But it would be over 100 years before a record of another doctor arriving in Rowan County. But they have been arriving ever since.

1881 LAST BEAR KILLED AS RAILROAD ARRIVES

1881 was a banner year in the history of Morehead and Rowan County. It was the year that the last wild bear was killed in Rowan County. It was killed by W.T. McKenzie on the head of Ramey's Creek, near "Pretty Ridge" in Southern Rowan County. Mr. McKenzie tracked the bear after it had killed one of his calves, and his dogs treed the bear up in a big persimmon tree. 1881 was also the year that the (E.L. and E.K.), Elizabethtown, Lexington, and Eastern Kentucky Railroad was extended from Mt. Sterling to Grayson, Kentucky, where it connected with the Big Sandy Railroad. (B.S.R.) The isolated small town of Morehead had become a railroad town, connected to the outside world.

ROWAN – VIOLENT BUT SCENIC

On November 17, 1881, THE ASHLAND INDEPENDENT sent an adventurous reporter to Morehead to report on four murder trials being tried in Rowan County at the fall meeting of the Circuit Court. At that session the court tried Matt Lightfoot for the murder of Joseph McDermont in Crossroads (Farmers). Also, on the court docket was James Rayburn for waylaying and killing Josiah Hyatt near Morehead; Thomas Hargis for killing Elijah Fraley; John and Hiram Cornette and Garfield Williams, jointly for killing Hezekiah Jones. The last two killings grew out of an old feud. (Also, keep in mind this war was six years <u>before</u> the Rowan County Feud began.)

On November 17, 1881, that roving rail riding reporter from *The Ashland Independent* arrived in Morehead after a train ride of 36 hours. He changed trains twice between Morehead and Ashland; once at South Portsmouth, and again at Grayson, Kentucky (there he remained overnight). The reporter said he learned on that trip that "man proposes, and God disposes of unavoidable train delays." The train headed west on the newly laid track into Rowan County's primeval forests. It appeared that a tree had never been cut except for an occasional clearing that contained a small log cabin, and a hillside patch of corn. It appeared as if Rowan County had only recently been settled.

EARLY PHYSICIANS AND DENTISTS

When that unknown reporter reached Morehead at 4 p.m. (36 hours after leaving Ashland), he found a busy, bustling village of 800 citizens, with 4 hotels. They were owned by H. Clay Powers, H.T. Hamilton, G. Gorman, and Judge Carey. There were also two general stores, one owned by H.M. Logan the other owned by Warren Alderson. He listed the resident physicians of Morehead as Drs. C.M. Martin, H.S. Logan, and T.W. Banfield. (However, there was a Dr. Carter located in Farmers at that time.)

That unknown reporter stayed at the Carey Hotel on Railroad Street (First Street). It was owned by Judge Carey and operated by his daughter who was married to Morehead's Mayor Brains. Even in those days traveling reporters were interested in the food, and he reported that Mrs. Brains served the best coffee and corn muffins he had ever eaten.

In 1881 Morehead with a reported population of 800 was a wild west frontier town. With the new railroad came new saloons, moonshine whiskey, knife fights, drunken brawls and murders. There was very little law, and the fact that there were four murder trials at one session of the Circuit Court was evidence of the violent community of Morehead. Before Morehead residents could get through those violent times, they had to live through those times. So wherever there was pain, injury, sickness and suffering, there were doctors to help those in need. Morehead has had a long history of good medical care beginning around the Civil War years, and continuing down to this very day.

FIRST PHYSICIAN, DR. H.S. LOGAN

1864 was the earliest record of a physician to practice medicine in Morehead, and he was still here in 1881. His name was Dr. H.S. Logan. Dr. Logan was born March 2, 1818, in Nicholas County and died March 13, 1888, in Rowan County. He was thought to have attended the old medical school at Transylvania, and he moved to Morehead during the Civil War in 1864. Dr. Logan also operated a log cabin general store with a thatched roof across from the Courthouse in Morehead. Pioneer physicians had to have some other skill or trade (farming, shopkeeper, etc.) to further provide for their families.

FIRST DENTISTS ARRIVE

In the early days of medicine, doctors also pulled teeth. However, in the later 1800s, dentistry began as a recognized speciality. The record shows that before 1900 there were 13 doctors and 2 dentists that had hung up their shingles and announced their intention to practice their profession in Rowan County (some for just a short time, others were here a lifetime). But they were not all here at the same time. T.W. Banfield was the next physician to locate in Rowan County. He moved to Morehead in 1875 from Virginia and seemed to have a profitable medical practice, and did not find it necessary to engage in another vocation. His son, L.W. Banfield, joined his father in his practice in 1900. The name of Banfield was well recognized, remembered, and revered by several generations of Rowan County patients.

In 1891 Dr. Jeremiah Wilson (Dr. Don Blair and Paul Blair's great-grandfather) moved to Morehead after practicing his profession in Farmers and Elliottville. Dr. Wilson also ran a general store in Elliottville, but when he moved to Morehead, he seemed to have a successful medical practice and did not have to engage in another vocation.

FARMERS PHYSICIANS - CARTER, EVANS, MCCLEESE

Dr. F.M. Carter was an early resident of Farmers who practiced medicine in this region for many years. He went into partnership with Dr. Evans and later retired there.

Many of Rowan's early physicians first settled in Farmers and later moved their practice to Morehead. That was because the economy of Farmers was strong and more diversified than Morehead. They later moved their medical practice to Morehead as the town grew. That was the case with Drs. Jeremiah Wilson, T.A.E. Evans, and Allen W. McCleese. Dr. McCleese began his medical practice in Farmers in 1897 and kept meticulous records. From the appearance of his ledger books from 1897-1922, he had a difficult time in his first year of practice. He reported in his 1897 ledger book, $1,030.25 total on the books for that year. Only $114.50 was collected by cash, $110.75 was collected by merchandise (including one straw hat at $1.25), $59.40 was collected in work (including $ .25 in credit to a colored patient for replacing one shoe on his horse), and $21.07 was paid in produce that year. Total value collected in 1897 was $305.72, with $729.53 outstanding on the books that year. But he later became successful and treated many of Rowan County's leading citizens. Numbered among his patients were Mr. Hartley Battson ($2.00 for 2 office visits); Judge Arthur Hogge (office visits); and Alf Caskey, 3 office visits, treated burns on his face $10.00, $5.00, and $2.50. Also, James Clay ($1.50 office visit). Other patients treated included Ed Maggard, Lottie Stewart, George McDaniel, Clint Tolliver, Harve Alfrey, and Johnny Jones. Mr. A.E. Martin was listed as having an operation on his back. (Charge $1.00)

Rowan County's second "hospital" located at Haldeman. Small white building (right) dwarfed by brick factory No. 2, 1928. Staffed by Nurse Lacy Kegley.

DR. MCCLEESE MOVED TO MOREHEAD

Dr. McCleese moved to Morehead in 1922. Before becoming a doctor, he was a railroad detective on the C&O. After moving to Morehead, Dr. McCleese was appointed Rowan County Health Officer in 1922. (That was the office that preceded the office of Rowan County Health Director established in 1931). When Dr. McCleese began his medical practice in Farmers in 1897, at that time his account books showed a charge of .75 for an office visit and $1.50 for a house call. By 1915, Dr. McCleese charged $1.00 for an office visit and $2.50 for a house call. The ledger book showed that year a Mr. Moore's family in Farmers seemed to have three months of illnesses. However, the month of September showed Mrs. Moore growing progressively worse, eg.

Patient Given "Electrical Treatment."

September

1	Visit-wife	2.50
2	Visit-wife	2.50
3	Visit-wife	1.00
6	Visit-wife	1.00
9	Visit-wife	2.50
10	Wife-electrical treatment	1.50
11	Visit-wife	1.00
13	Visit-wife	2.50
15	Wife-electrical treatment	1.50
16	Wife-electrical treatment	1.50

Those records showed that Mrs. Moore was very sick. Evidently she was not responding to "conventional" treatment, and was coming into Dr. McCleese's office for "electrical treatment." That treatment must have consisted of some type of electrical shock that Dr. McCleese believed would help. It is not known whether Mrs. Moore survived or not, after having two consecutive days of "electrical treatment." However, because of the abrupt ending of all treatment, perhaps she did not survive.

PATIENT REFUSED SURGERY

In one ledger account, Dr. McCleese showed that one woman patient came to his office and was diagnosed with appendicitis.

His notes said "She refused an operation, and in the fulness of time, she died." Dr. McCleese dispensed his own prescriptions, suppositories, massages, and electrical treatments. He was involved with Morehead's first "Hospital" in 1917. Dr. McCleese died of cancer in 1927, and is buried in the Carey Cemetery in Farmers.

"HOSPITALS" APPEARED THROUGHOUT EASTERN KENTUCKY

Around the end of the 19th century and the beginning of the 20th century, "hospitals" began to appear in many of the small towns in Eastern Kentucky. Of course, the term "hospital" had an entirely different connotation than it has today. It was usually a place where patients come to die or have a baby. There was, of course, no ambulance service, and transportation was by wagon, buggy, or train. During that era there was a Presbyterian Hospital in Frenchburg and Dr. Claypool's hospital in Salt Lick. Dr. Claypool's hospital was a large two-story red brick house adjacent to the railroad tracks and across the street from the main business district. (This writer's great-great grandfather and early Morehead resident, Warren Alderson, died in Dr. Claypool's hospital in 1903). However, by being located next to the depot, sick patients could be transferred more easily on a train to Lexington. The hospital closed around 1912 and became a private residence. Over the years it has served as a private residence for the Byrd Perry, Sr., Lee Casper, and Bill Davis families. (The building was recently torn down.)

There was another hospital located in this region in the early 1900s. It was in a large white two-story wooden building on the main street in West Liberty. (Dr. Pat Serey has a painting of that hospital in his office at the Cave Run Clinic.) Grayson, Kentucky, also had the Stovall Hospital during that era. But Morehead was a little slow establishing their "first hospital."

FIRST MOREHEAD "HOSPITAL" OPENED 1915

Morehead's first "hospital" was opened in 1915 by Drs. Laban Rollins (or Robbins), Allen M. McCleese, and I.H. Rollins (or Robbins). It was located in a large white wooden two-story house with a screened-in porch on two sides. The house sat on the corner of Hargis Avenue and Main Street. (Present site of the First Federal Savings Bank). That hospital closed about 1920 and was bought by John Cecil. Mr. Cecil started a hotel in the old white building and it was used as a hotel until he built the new brick Midland Trail Hotel next door. After the new hotel was built, Mr. and Mrs. Cecil used the building as a private residence until they built another residence, and then it was used as a rooming house upstairs. Downstairs consisted of various businesses over the years including Frosty's Barber Shop, and Elwood Allen's book and magazine shop.

SECOND "HOSPITAL" OPENED AT HALDEMAN

The next hospital to appear in Rowan County was started in 1927. It was a small white wooden one-story building that looked lonely, where it was located in Haldeman, beneath the shadow of the giant smokestack of Brick Factory Number 2. (It is fondly remembered by old time Haldeman residents as the "Little Hospital". It was staffed by Nurse Lacy Kegley.) Nurse Kegley was employed as the company nurse by L.P. Haldeman who believed in providing medical are for his 300 employees and their families. The medical care provided by Nurse Kegley was free, not only to the Haldeman workers and their families, but also to the total community. ("Shades of socialized medicine".) Mr. Haldeman, owner of the brick yard, was described as a great humanitarian who was concerned about the welfare of his employees as well as the community.

Chris Barker recounted that when her grandfather died in Haldeman, her dad was the oldest boy in a large family. Of course there was no welfare then, and Mr. Haldeman, knowing the situation, gave her dad a job when he was about 13-years-old. He had a stool made for him to stand on to do his work, and the money that 13 year old boy earned was all the family had. He was loyal to the company and was one of the last employees to leave after the factory closed. He worked his entire working life at the Haldeman Plant, as did many other loyal employees.

Nurse Lacy Kegley delivered babies, set broken bones, gave shots, bandaged wounds, made house calls, and dispensed medicine to the citizens of Haldeman. The "Little Hospital" served that community well, and after it closed, Nurse Kegley was employed for many years by Dr. E.D. Blair in Morehead.

LATER DOCTORS AND HOSPITALS

Two early physicians that prominently prescribed medical treatment for early Rowan Contains were Drs. G.C. and H.L. Nickell. G.C. (Grover) Nickell was born at Yale, Kentucky, in 1884, and died in Morehead in 1943. His first wife's name was Ottie (Lawrene) Nickell, who died early in their marriage. His second wife's name was Mabel, and Grover had no children by either wife.

H.L. Nickell was born at Yale, Kentucky in 1887, and died in Morehead in 1943. He was married to Florence (Francis) Nickell for 33 years before divorcing. They had two sons: David and John Paul. David graduated from the University of Louisville School of Medicine. He also studied at the Mayo Clinic. John Paul studied at the University of Louisville and in North Carolina. He taught at the University of North Carolina. Neither brother returned to Rowan County.

Homer and Grover Nickell grew up on a farm near Yale, Kentucky. Their father farmed the rich river bottom land along the Licking, adjacent to the John Ellis farm (this writer's grandfather). Many times as the two farmers would cultivate their corn crops down along the river bank, they would talk to each other while resting their horses under the shade of a giant elm tree. Mr. Nickell would say very proudly, "The corn grown in that river bottom field was what put my boys through the University of Louisville Medical School." (Grover graduated in 1908 and Homer graduated in 1912.) Homer completed further study at the University of Chicago. Both doctors began practice in the Yale vicinity of Bath County. Yale

Dapper Dr. G.C. Nickell stands in front of his "hospital" located on Morehead's Main Street, 1934.

was a busy timber town, with a railroad that hauled the lumber and logs to market. It was also located near the confluence of Beaver Creek and Licking River. That brought more logs and timber to Yale, increasing the economy.

DOCTORS NEEDED HIGH SWIMMING HORSES

Both doctors were kept busy caring for the families of timber workers, and farmers in the tri-county area of Bath, Menifee and Rowan. However, there was no bridge over Licking River (not even at Farmers) in those days. Therefore, making house calls back and forth across the dangerous river became difficult for the doctors-- especially on horseback. That was because some horses can swim better than others. John Ellis, a friend and neighbor of the Nickells, said many times he would get up and go to the barn to feed his horses and find another horse in the stall where his horse should be. He always knew that Dr. G.C. Nickell had traded horses because he had to cross Licking River. Dr. Nickell always said he could cross the river on Mr. Ellis's horse and never even get his feet wet—because that horse was such a strong swimmer, and swam high in the water. Mr. Ellis said he told Dr. Nickell he was always welcome to make the switch when he needed to cross the river. When WW I began in 1917, Dr. Homer Nickell was called into the military service. He entered World War I as a 1st Lt. in the U.S. MedicalCorp. He served as a field surgeon in Europe during the entire war. He always said he was fortunate to have worked in an Army Field Hospital in France under the renowned Lexington Surgeon, Dr. W.O. Bullick. Dr. Bullick operated on this writer's mother in 1930 removing one third of her large intestines. He must have done it right because she lived another 65 years. When WW I ended, Dr. Homor Nickell practiced in Pikeville one year before returning to Morehead.

Drs. Nickell Open Morehead "Hospital"

In 1929, Drs. Homer and Grover Nickell opened their "hospital" on Morehead's Main Street at the present site of the University Cinema and the Wentz Building. Their one-story red brick duplex was connected by an open breezeway. The living quarters were on one side and the "hospital" was on the other side. Since Dr. Homer Nickell and his wife were divorced, it was the intention of the brothers to live on one side of the duplex and maintain their "hospital" on the other side. However, they did not get along very well and soon split up their practice. Homer moved out and set up his office on West Main Street (corner of Main Street and Fleming Avenue). He was later elected as State Representative for Rowan and Bath Counties. Dr. Grover Nickell continued to practice and operated the "hospital" until a broken hip and health problems forced him to close in 1942. During their twilight years, the two doctor brothers were reconciled and lived together caring for each other's health needs. On November 9, 1943, Dr. Homer Nickell died unexpected in his sleep. He was living with his brother and treating him for a broken hip and pneumonia. Dr. Grover Nickell died four months later.

NICKELL'S HOSPITAL – PAINFUL EXPERIENCE

In 1936, at 9 years of age, this writer was coming home from school at Breck, and stepped in a drainage tile in front of Morehead State College's Button Auditorium. The skin on my left shin bone was peeled back revealing the bone. (The scar on my leg can still be seen.) While lying on the ground writhing in pain, MSC Coach Downing came over to investigate. He saw the leg and immediately picked up that 9-year-old boy and carried him in his arms to Main Street to Dr. Nickell's hospital. There, the gruff-speaking rough treating physician asked Coach Downing and the nurse to hold that scared 9 year old patient on the table while he slapped red iodine like antiseptic into the wound (without anesthetic). Next, he pulled the skin back down over the shin bone and sewed it (without anesthetic). That was this writer's very unpleasant and painful experience with that early Morehead "hospital."

In 1933 Dr. Isadore Monroe Garred moved his medical practice from Ashland to Morehead. His office and home were located in a brick cape cod style house, at the corner of 2nd Street and College Blvd. (Across the street from MSU's Lappin Building, and is now owned by MSU). His wife Martha was his nurse. She was extremely efficient and always dressed in a white starched uniform. They had one daughter, Kay. Dr. Garred was an avid hunter and fisherman. He often went on extended hunting and fishing trips and was famous for his trophy fish.

RABIES RAMPANT IN ROWAN

During the summer of 1937, rabies were rampant in Rowan County. The deadly disease had spread from foxes to dogs to farm animals. That summer, little Margaret Sue Cornette and Janis Ruth Caudill became exposed to rabies while playing with the family pet bird dog. Th dog later developed rabies and had to be destroyed. The two girls were taken to Dr. Garred who immediately ordered the anti-rabies vaccine. The treatment required that the two girls get one anti-rabies shot every day for 14 days. (Those shots were considered dangerous at that time.) Dr. Garred gave those scared young girls and their families the assurance they needed that he would bring them through that traumatic time in their lives. Dr. Garred was one of Morehead's early medical men who provided quality health care for Rowan countians for 30 years.

DR. E.D. BLAIR BEGINS MOREHEAD PRACTICE

Dr. Everette D. Blair, physician and surgeon, was another early Morehead medical man. Dr. Blair was a graduate of the University of Michigan and a native of Morehead. Dr. Blair returned from Michigan and established his practice in 1935. He was married to a Morehead school teacher, Mary Jo (Wilson) Blair, and they had two sons who are local residents: Dr. Donald Blair and Attorney Paul Blair.

Dr. Blair began practicing medicine in a white wooden combination residence and office on East Main Street. He later built a new home on College Street, but maintained his office at the same location throughout his lifetime. His son, Dr. Donald Blair's office, remains in that very same building today.

DR. BLAIR TREATS TRAUMA VICTIM

Dr. E.D. Blair dispensed medicine, set broken bones, delivered babies, and provided quality medical and surgical care to Rowan countians for over 40 years. On a Saturday afternoon, this writer was struck by an automobile in front of his house on west U.S. 60.

Dr. Blair had sent my mother to the hospital in Lexington earlier in the week for major surgery. My father was there at the hospital with her at the time of my accident. (The man driving the car that struck me and knocked me about 30 feet was the principal of Breckinridge, Chiles Van Anthwerp.) I was knocked unconscious, and the Red Rose Dairy Milk truck driver, Woody Hall, stopped and loaded me into the back of the milktruck and delivered that unconscious boy to Dr. Everette Blair's office. I returned to consciousness in his office while he was examining me. It was not my time to die, and the only injury I sustained was a twisted knee, and I had to walk on crutches for six weeks. (Needless to say I transferred from Breckinridge to Morehead High School the next school year.) Since my parents were out of town at the time of the accident, I stayed in the Midland Trail Hotel while recuperating and the Dr. Blair monitored me closely every day for a week. My aunt and uncle, Peaches and Jack Cecil, owners of the Hotel, cared for me.

MORE MOREHEAD DOCTORS ARRIVE

Dr. Samuel Reynolds, a Morehead native, graduated from the University of Cincinnati Medical School. He received his training under the Navy V12 program, which was a program to prepare doctors for military service during WW II.

Dr. Reynolds began his medical practice in Morehead in 1946. He was married to Ruth (Williams). They had three children: Lisa, Terry, and Kim. Dr. Reynolds helped provide much needed medical care for Rowan residents during his 40 plus years of service. Dr. Reynolds died in 1989, and there is a marker in his memory in the Caudill Cemetery.

There was a shortage of doctors during WW II, and even though he had a severe physical handicap, which left him stooped over from the waist, Dr. Joseph E. McKinney, son of a local businessman, A.B. McKinney, decided to leave the political arena in Rowan

*Dr. C. Louise Caudill and Nurse Susie Halbleib make
a house call in rugged Rowan County, 1954.*

County and go to medical school. Joe was married to Amy Duley, daughter of Mr. and Mrs. C.P. Duley, and they had no children.

Dr. Joseph E. McKinney was the circuit court clerk of Rowan County from 1934-1944. After serving successfully in the political arena, he elected, at a mature age, to enter the University of Louisville Medical School, graduating in 1947. He returned to Morehead in 1948 and registered his intent to practice medicine in the Rowan County Medical Register. However, another young doctor and good friend, C. Louise Caudill, had just opened her medical practice in Morehead, and Joe McKinney decided to move to Maysville. There he established an extremely successful practice for the next 30 years.

DRS. CAUDILL AND PROUDFOOT AND ST. CLAIRE HOSPITAL

Probably one of Morehead's best-known and loved physicians was Dr. Claire Louise Caudill. She practiced family medicine in

Rowan County for over fifty years. Her legacy looms large throughout the hills of Eastern Kentucky. Claire Louise Caudill was born in Rowan County, and was the daughter of Judge D. B. and Etta (Proctor)Caudill. She attended the Morehead Public Schools and graduated from old Morehead High School in 1930. Early in her childhood, as she played with her friends, she dreamed of becoming a doctor. But when she went off to college at The Ohio State University in Columbus, she seemed to let those dreams die when she graduated in 1934 with a degree in Physical Education.

MOREHEAD COLLEGE PROFESSOR

Louise Caudill returned to her beloved Morehead in 1934 and taught physical education and coached the swimming and tennis teams at Morehead State Teachers College. She remained in that position until 1943. However, she took time out to complete a Masters Degree in Education at Columbia University in New York City in 1936. Although Louise enjoyed teaching, her childhood dream of becoming a doctor kept creeping back into her conscious mind.

During the WW II years, with a shortage of doctors and a shortage of men, Louise discussed the idea of her becoming a doctor with her parents. She always said her mother was opposed to her becoming a physician, because it wasn't "lady like." Her mother believed that young ladies should dress up prim and proper, wear hats, high heels, and act sophisticated. However, her dad urged her to follow her dream, "and go for it," telling her she could be anything she wanted to be. Claire Louise Caudill became "Dr. Caudill" when she was one of two women in a class of 100 that graduated from the University of Louisville Medical School in 1946.

RECEIVED ADVANCED TRAINING

Although she had received her medical degree, Dr. Caudill decided she needed more advanced training and practical experience. Dr. Caudill then completed a rotating residency at Women's Medical College in Philadelphia. (Now called Hahnemann School of Medicine). Following her residency, she wanted to gain some practical experience in a rural hospital; therefore, she joined the staff of the hospital at Oneida in southeastern Kentucky. It was there she met a young nurse by the name of Miss Susie Halbleib. Nurse Halbleib had just graduated from the Nazareth School of Nursing in Louisville, and had also gone to Oneida to join the staff at the Oneida Maternity Hospital. After they completed their advanced training, Dr. Caudill persuaded Nurse Halbleib to give Morehead a try for at least one year, and help her establish a medical practice. (That one year extended to a lifetime.)

It is always difficult for a professional practitioner to return to their small hometown to practice their profession. In Dr. Caudill's case there was the question of whether a woman doctor would also be accepted in her old hometown. But against the advice of what Dr. Louise called "some of the best friends she ever had", she returned to her beloved Morehead to begin her medical practice. In 1948, Dr. Louise and Susie opened their office on the second floor of a plain brick building on Morehead's Main Street. (Above Pat McGarey's Pool Room, and Kenneth Bays' Jewelry Store.) Access to the office was up a steep staircase from Main Street next door to the Jewelry Store. (The building was razed in 1999 and is now a city parking lot.)

LOUISE AND SUSIE SOON ACCEPTED

The upstairs waiting room was always crowded. Often, there would be patients standing in line up the stairs. The office was hot in the summer with no air conditioning. But it was there that the two health care professionals became whole-heartedly accepted by their patients as "Dr. Louise" and "Susie Needle." Dr. Caudill's close friends called her "Weezer."

"GOLDEN AGE OF MEDICINE"

Dr. Louise began her practice at a time when a doctor could treat a patient without much interference from government agencies. It was a time when a doctor could admit a patient into a hospital for whatever treatment they believed was best for that patient. They could run whatever tests they deemed necessary, and could keep the patient in the hospital as long as they believed was necessary for the good of the patient. Those days seem to be gone forever, and now hospital admittance, length of stay in the hospital, and treatment, are largely prescribed by government regulations. However, Morehead had no hospital, and one was urgently needed.

CLINIC OPENED

Dr. Caudill's practice soon outgrew the offices on the second floor above the Pool Room and Jewelry Store. She then opened her new modern clinic on East Main Street in 1957. With the opening of the new clinic, she did not have to make so many house calls

Northeast Kentucky Hospital Foundation, 1960. They were instrumental in establishing St. Claire Hospital in Morehead. ***Front****: L-R: Adron Doran, W.E. Crutcher, Mosigner Towell, C.P. Caudill, Dr. Louise Caudill, Elijah M. Hogge, and Glen Lane.* ***Back****, L-R: William C. Caudill, Adrian Razor, Otto Carr, Eleanor Queen, J.M. Clayton, John M. Palmer, Don Caudill, and Curt Bruce.*

throughout the isolated region. Most house calls were to deliver babies, and with the new clinic, the mothers were brought there for delivery. However, her practice grew rapidly because of the baby boom that resulted from all of the post-war marriages and men coming home from WW II. Dr. Caudill and Susie were working day and night, and patients were coming from the surrounding counties. There were times that in order to see the doctor at her office, you had to go there early in the morning and sign the register, and sometimes wait for hours. However, when you did get in to see Dr. Caudill, she made you think you were the only patient she had. She listened to your problems, empathized with your pain, and many times would say, "Yes, I've got that same problem." Her bedside manner was professional, sympathetic and understanding, and she always made your feel better by just talking to you. She was ahead of her time, because she not only treated the disease, but believed in treating the whole person.

A BRIDGE BETWEEN ERAS OF MEDICINE

Every one of Dr. Louise's patients had their own story about her, and it is not the intention of this article to write her biography. So much has been written about her in books, magazines, newspapers, and plays that her story has been told in many ways. She has received so many accolades and awards, and every one richly deserved. But she was unique! She was one of a kind! However, in examining her medical contributions in an historical context, one of her greatest accomplishments was to found a hospital named for her. But in addition to that, she successfully bridged the gap from an era of the primitive general practice of medicine to an era of specialization. She successfully moved from a time when there were few drugs, little technology, and an isolated practice to an era of the latest in modern technology, research, multiple drugs, cooperation, and specialization in diagnosing and treating diseases.

She served as a bridge over troubled medical waters from the past to the future.

Dr. Louise continued a life-long study of medicine. She always checked out audio tapes of the latest medical treatment from the Medical Library. She would listen to those tapes in her car as she traveled to Lexington. She was never one to waste time. She always scanned the medical materials for the latest research findings in her field. She once told this writer, "There is so much being published in medicine (much is junk, and some is excellent) that by the time you determine what is worth reading, it is obsolete." But she was always searching the medical literature for what would help her better treat her patients.

HILLS WERE HOME

Dr. Louise never had any desire to live anywhere else except Morehead. Although she and Susie were world travelers during their vacation periods, they were always glad to get "home to the hills." Dr. Louise once told this writer after he had moved to Florida for several years, "Shoot, why would I ever want to live anywhere else? Morehead is my home, I would never be happy anywhere else, except here among my lifelong friends." She also considered the hills her friends and was the happiest when she could look unto those familiar hills she could see from her office windows.

TREATED THE WHOLE PERSON

Dr. Caudill was not the typical physician. She was humble and self-deprecating. In the dialect of her beloved hill folk, "she never put on airs." If she did not know something, she was quick to tell you she didn't know, but she would try and find the answer. In fact, she was quick to say, "Honey, it's surprising how little we know." (About medicine.) But Dr. Caudill knew much about people. She understood their anxieties and their fears. She knew her patients and the impact of depression, worry, and emotional distress upon the physical condition of the body. She treated the physical, emotional, and spiritual condition of the patient.

TRIED NON-TRADITIONAL MEDICINE

In 1952, this writer's mother-in-law, the late Myrtle Caudill, was one of Dr. Louise's patients. She suddenly became afflicted with a terribly painful, crippling, debilitating case of rheumatoid arthritis. Dr. Louise sent her to various specialists throughout the country. But no treatment seemed to help. Dr. Louise even called specialists, studied the latest research, and tried every treatment known at that time including steroids and gold shots. She even tried non-traditional treatments of copper bracelets on the arms, and drinking that stinking sulphur water. She said, "It can't hurt anything." (We would go down the Lower Licking Road to a sulphur spring and get the water.) But her disease grew more progressively painful and crippling. Although Myrtle Caudill lived another 16 years (mostly in a wheelchair), Dr. Louise helped ease the pain and made her life a little more bearable. Dr. Louise and Susie would always make house calls as they treated Mrs. Caudill. Dr. Louise was with her when she died. She cared for her until the very end--as she did so many of her patients.

MOREHEAD'S MEDICAL SAINT

Many doctors of that era did not keep up on the latest advances in medicine, and the explosion of research in their field, as well as the many great drugs that were discovered. However, Dr. Louise was determined not to fall behind and she never stopped learning. She was an outstanding diagnostician. Dr. Louise's contributions to major medical care for Rowan residents is beyond measure. Dr. Louise died December 31, 1998, in the University of Kentucky Medical Center. She was laid to rest in the Caudill Cemetery in the community where she spent her entire life. But her memory will live through the St. Claire Medical Center, her patients, and the 8,000 babies she delivered. She was Morehead's Medical "Saint" before St. Claire Medical Center came to Morehead.

MEMORIAL TO BETTER HEALTH CARE

Following her death, many of her former patients felt uncomfortable seeing another doctor in her office. They somehow felt "disloyal" to Dr. Louise and that her office was a special shrine. But knowing Dr. Louise as we all did, she would probably say, "Take care of your medical problems, and the best way you can remember me is toget good medical care. That's what Susie and I devoted our life to."

The new Women's Health Care Center on the fourth floor of the hospital named in her honor is a fitting memorial to her tireless lifelong determination to bring better health care to the hills of Eastern Kentucky.

BIOGRAPHICAL DATA
CLAIRE LOUISE CAUDILL (1912-1999)

EDUCATION

1930	High School Diploma, Morehead High School
1934	Bachelors Degree, Ohio State University (Columbus)
1936	Masters Degree, Colombia University (New York City)
1946	M.D. Degree, University of Louisville (Kentucky)

EXPERIENCE

1943-1946 Physical Education Teacher, Swimming and Tennis Coach
Morehead State Teachers College

1948-1999 Family Medical Practice, Morehead, Kentucky

HONORS, AWARDS, AND ACHIEVEMENTS

1955   Rowan County Lions Club Woman of the Year

1963   Along with the Catholic Order of Sisters of Notre Dame, Founded St. Claire Medical Center in Morehead, Named in her honor

1972   Kentucky Council on Higher Education Member

1974   Academy of Family Practice Doctor of the Year

1979   Ky. Federation of Business and Professional Women's Woman of the Year

1981   Northeastern Kentucky Health Care Delivery Corporation Service Award

1981   Morehead State University Honorary Doctorate

1994   Country Doctor Museum, North Carolina, Country Doctor of the Year

WARREN H. PROUDFOOT, M.D. (1921-1991)

PHYSICIAN, SURGEON, EDUCATOR

A native of West Virginia, Dr. Warren Proudfoot moved his family to Morehead in 1963, when he became Chief of Surgery at St. Claire Medical Center. During the early years of the hospital, Dr. Proudfoot worked night and day to provide surgical care for his patients. He seemed to take a personal interest in each of his patients and always inspired hope to his patients, no matter how hopeless the case.

ACTIVE IN MEDICAL AND EDUCATIONAL COMMUNITY

A graduate of the prestigious Harvard Medical School, Dr. Proudfoot's skill as a surgeon was greatly admired by his colleagues, and deeply respected by his patients. He enjoyed teaching and working with young doctors, and served as Clinical Professor of Surgery at the University of Kentucky Medical School. His interest in young people was much broader than just in the field of medicine. Dr. Proudfoot was a member of the Rowan County School Board for 20 years, and served as chairman for 18 years. In that role, he provided the leadership needed to get the Rowan County Schools accredited by the Southern Association of Schools. Dr. Proudfoot recognized that a good school system was necessary in order to attract doctors as well as industry to this area. Vitally interested in public education, he served as a member of the Kentucky School Building Authority, and was chairman of the Kentucky School Board Association. He also served as a member of the Nominating Committee, and the Leadership Committee of the National School Board Association.

LIFE SAVING SKILLS USED AT EDUCATIONAL MEETING

During this writer's "library life," before retirement, I was at the American Library Association meeting in Dallas, Texas. During a dinner meeting, I sat across the table from the Library Director from Louisiana Tech. When he discovered I was from Morehead, he became very excited and said, "Do you know Dr. Proudfoot?" After I assured him I knew Dr. Proudfoot through my role as a volunteer chaplain at the hospital where he was Chief of Surgery, he told me this story.

He said, "I am a school board member in my local school district and two years ago, I attended the National School Board meeting in New Orleans. During one of the general sessions, I suffered a heart attack. They called for a doctor, and Dr. Proudfoot was the first to respond. Although I was unconscious, he gave me CPR and got my heart started. He rode with me to the hospital assuring me I would be all right. I owe my life to him. Tell him that, and tell him I asked about him." I did tell Dr. Proudfoot about meeting a man whose life he had saved, and he seemed pleased to hear from him. Many Moreheadians today can say the same thing about Dr. Proudfoot--they are alive because of his skill.

COMPASSIONATE PHYSICIAN AND EDUCATOR

Dr. Proudfoot was a compassionate healer and community leader. He received many medical and community honors. He was active in his church and community. He served as Chairman of the Board of the Markey Cancer Center in Lexington, Medical Director of the Kentucky State Health Education Council, member of the American Medical Association, and the American College of Surgeons, and the Rowan County Medical Association. Dr. Proudfoot also was awarded honorary doctorate degrees from Morehead State University and the University of Kentucky.

In almost 30 years of outstanding service to the medical and educational community of Rowan County, Dr. Proudfoot was a healer and leader. This community has a higher level of medical care and education effort because of his dedicated leadership. His unselfish service to this community will continue through the St. Claire Hospital and the Rowan County Schools.

MEDICAL PRACTITIONERS (1864-1950)

MEDICINE
Date Registered

1864	H.S. Logan
1875	T.W. Banfield
1881	C.M. Martin
1881	F.M. Carter
1888	Jeremiah Wilson
1894	B.J. Cox

Photo: Art Stewart

T.A.E. Evans, M.D. Physician, Banker, County Judge, and first Director of County health Department. Practiced medicine in Rowan County 1900-1950.

MEDICINE
Date Registered

1894	M.C. Cash
1894	Patrick Rogers
1896	L.P.V. Williams
1897	A.W. McCleese
1898	Charles Saulsbury
1898	T.A.E. Evans
1900	S.J. Porter
1900	L.W. Banfield
1901	I.H. Robbins
1901	Laban F. Robbins
1901	B.F. Fulks

1904	A.L. Blair
1905	A.J. Davis
1906	Grover C. Nickell
1906	Alexander Skaggs
1907	E.D. Frank
1908	Farris L. Allen
1908	John M. Logan
1910	Jeff D. Kiser
1916	James B. Messer
1917	John W. Moss
1918	Homer Nickell
1921	John H. Cavins
1923	G.S. McDonald
1924	Asa W. Adkins
1928	Elijah H. Maggard
1933	Isadore M. Garred
1935	John L. Clay
1935	Everette D. Blair
1946	Samuel E. Reynolds
1948	Claire Louise Caudill
1948	Joseph E. McKinney

DENTISTS

1895	G.F. Gray
1898	James Woodward
1900	Edward Bertram
1906	James Malone
1907	Homer Wilson
1908	E. McKay Miller
1914	William Mann
1914	F.G. Davis
1916	John Lester

1917	Ollie M. Lyons
1925	John A. Dorton
1926	Delbert L. Sparks
1927	Garman P. Salyers
1941	Audrey Ellington
1941	Harold L. Blair
1942	Maurice, F. Herbst
1945	Charles M. Caudill
1947	Harold E. Holbrook
1947	R.A. Weir

CHIROPRACTORS

1924	Charles McGuire
1931	N.C. Marsh
1947	O. Boone Morgan

OPTOMETRISTS

1927	Frank Pearlman
1935	George S. Burkett
1935	L.A. Wise

VETERINARIANS

1907	William Levi Hughes
1913	Joseph Jamison

HEALTH DEPARTMENT AND EPIDEMICS

One of Morehead's early medical men was Dr. Evans. Many Rowan residents remember him as the gruff country doctor who came to their school once a year to give them "shots" that sometimes really hurt. But he was much more than that. Thomas Asa Edward Evans was born August 27, 1873, in Fleming County, Kentucky, and died March 27, 1956, in Rowan County. He married Peachy Evans and they had three children: Vivian, Catherine, and T.A.E. Evans, Jr. Dr. Evans had one son (Deward) by a previous marriage. His first wife died in childbirth.

Thomas A.E. Evans graduated from the Cincinnati Eclectic College of Medicine in 1895, and was invited by an elderly Dr. Carter in Farmers to come there and practice medicine with him. Dr. Carter died a year later and Dr. Evans assumed full responsibility for the medical practice. Farmers, called "Crossroads" in the early years of Rowan County, was a busy trading center. Timber, stone cutting, and farming formed the basis of the local economy. The railroad and Licking River provided the means of transporting products to market. (Farmers shipped more railroad tonnage in the early 1900s than any other town between Louisville and Ashland.)

When Dr. Evans took over Dr. Carter's practice, Morehead physician T.W. Banfield questioned Dr. Evans' medical credentials. Therefore, Dr. Evans completed a course of study at the University of Louisville Medical College, in order to fully complywith Kentucky medical requirements.

MEDICAL MEN MIXED OWN MEDICINE

Medicine was primitive, and most medical treatment was done in the home. By the time a doctor was contacted, the patient was too sick to travel to his office. Therefore, Dr. Evans would make his way across streams, over hills and up hollows to treat the sick. He seldom wrote prescriptions because it would take a day to get to a drugstore. He would simply mix his own medicine out of his "doctor bag."

Dr. Evans' daughter, Vivian Young Lewis, recalled being in Battson's Drugstore, and Druggist Battson showing her a row of shelves filled with medicine bottles for local doctors. (He kept the medicines generally used by each doctor together on a shelf.) He said, "This is Dr. Evans' medicine shelf." Vivian said, "Most bottles were marked poison." Doc Battson said, "That's why it is important to get the prescription filled correctly."

PAYMENT MADE WITH FARM PRODUCE

Dr. Evans' office was in his home, and the children were never allowed near the office for fear of catching a disease. Vivian recalled that her dad was gone most of the time on house calls. He would often sit up all night with a sick patient or remain day and night waiting on a baby to be born. He delivered thousands of babies during his practice (several were named Asa after him). Many times he would not even be paid or be paid with chickens, ham, eggs, or other produce. Vivian recalled they never had much money but always had plenty to eat. Vivian also remembered her dad swam the river one cold winter day to reach a sick patient. He arrived at the home with his clothes frozen to his body. Almost every practicing physician in the early history of Rowan County had to have another job to support a family. Dr. Evans was no exception. As the economy of the Farmers area began to decline, Dr. Evans' practice began to decline. Therefore, in 1926, he ran and was elected as County Judge.

MIXING MEDICINE AND POLITICS

It could be said that Dr. Evans ran for County Judge because he saw in that position an opportunity to improve medical care in Rowan County. As Rowan County Judge, he witnessed the creation of county health departments throughout Kentucky. As a physician, he had experienced the difficulty and even futility of treating such diseases as smallpox, diphtheria, scarlett fever, typhoid, and yes, infantile paralysis (later called polio). Also, the high rate of infant and mother mortality during childbirth was a major medical problem. Dr. Evans believed that the future of better medical care was in education and prevention of disease. Also, he viewed the county health department as the vehicle to accomplishing those goals.

In the fall of 1930, a new County Judge, J.H. Johnson, was elected in Rowan County. When Judge Johnson, a resident of the Mt. Hope section of southern Rowan County, was elected, he had several small children. After the election one of the children came to his mother and asked, "Mammy, are we all little judges?" She replied, "No, honey, just me and your Pappy." Before being elected judge, Mr. Johnson was known as "Preacher Johnson." He was the preacher that married this writer's mother and father, Lon and Dot Ellis. They were married under a giant oak tree near the Mt. Hope Church. That union lasted 66 years. But Judge Johnson did something that lasted even longer than that, because it was under his administration the Rowan County Health Department was established.

ROWAN HEALTH DEPARTMENT ESTABLISHED

On July 20, 1931, new County Judge Johnson and the fiscal court adopted a resolution declaring that Rowan County establish and maintain a County Department of Health to be supported by state and local taxes. With that financial support, a County Board of Health was established. This board included one lay member, three local physicians approved by the State Board of Health, and by virtue of his position, the County Judge.

The first action taken by the new Rowan County Board of Health was to employ T.A.E. Evans, M.D. as the first Director and Evelyn West as the first nurse. When Dr. Evans and Nurse West were hired in 1931, such diseases as smallpox, diphtheria and typhoid fever were common diseases throughout Kentucky. (In 1930, 20 deaths from diphtheria alone were reported.) Dr. Evans immediately began a major effort of vaccinating county children. Also, there was a major state and national effort to educate parents and children on the vital importance of personal hygiene, physical fitness, disease prevention, and a healthy lifestyle.

On May 1, 1931, Public Health established a National Blue Ribbon committee to encourage better fitness and health care for children. This committee established a National Blue Ribbon Day. Therefore, every May 1, children throughout this nation that had received all of their immunizations and had been examined by their doctor and received a clean bill of health were declared to be Blue Ribbon Children. They were recognized in their school and on May 1 and were given a blue ribbon, which they wore proudly.

BLUE RIBBON CHILDREN IDENTIFIED

In 1935 a total of 289 Rowan County school children were awarded blue ribbons signifying perfect health by the Rowan County Department of Health. Breckinridge Training School led all schools in the county with 108. Among those listed as Blue Ribbon Children in the first three grades at Breck were:

> First Graders - Jimmy Bradley, Helen Tackett, Dickie Scraggins, Jean Sorrell, Lois Mousberger, Jimmy Leach, Roy Graves, Franklin Fraley, Jean Flannery, Claude Christian, Ralph Christian, Fred Bays, George Black, Betty Gillespie, Billy Gillespie, JimmyClayton, and Janis Ruth Caudill (this writer's future wife).
> Second Graders - Jo Ann Cecil, Zane Young, Allie White, Jr., Bernice Wells, Deforest Tackett, Ruth Roberts, Betty Jo Evans, Lois Cheek, Frances Burns, Helen Mae Black, and Merl Fair.
> Third Graders - Ruth Fair, Elmer Kelly, Delphia Fisher, Eugene Barker, Katherine Pruitt, and Jane Young.
> Morehead Grade School had a total of seven Blue Ribbon Children. Those were Almeda Joy, Lucille Crawford, Homer Carol, Hattie Caudill, Tyre Black and, James Butcher.

Clearfield School Blue Ribbon Children were Paul Hall, Carl Fugate, Faye Mynhier, Maxine Early, Virginia Blair, Susie Sergeant Lawman Caskey, Zona Mynhier, Ralph Early, Jessie Blair, Luther Rogers, and Elijah Dickerson.

CHILDREN CELEBRATE AWARDS DAY

On May 1, 1931, all of the Blue Ribbon Children came to town to receive their blue ribbons and to participate in an annual May Day celebration. This celebration consisted of the young girls in their yellow dresses and the young boys in their white shirts dancing around the May Pole. The dance was performed in front of the college's Button Auditorium. Then there were game and athletic events at Jayne Stadium.

During the 1930s and 40s, Dr. Evans and his nurse continued to emphasize public health programs of preventive medicine. They visited the schools in an attempt to educate and immunize every school child in Rowan County. The first day that Dr. Evans came to the school was a "wild and crazy day." It began with the sound of the old Model A Ford chugging up the road. Many times mothers brought their pre-school children for their shots. So babies were crying and the students groaning as they looked out the window.

FEARFUL CHILDREN VACCINATED

When the doctor and nurse came in and opened up their boxes of needles and serum, there was the strong stench of rubbing alcohol in the air. There was also the deep seated fear of the pain of those needles as they entered your arm. There was also the trauma of watching those in front of you get their shots. However, usually the bravest boys would step forward and rolled up their sleeve to receive the needle first. Those needles always looked bigger than needles look now but maybe that was because the children were smaller. Also, contrary to popular opinion, they did <u>not</u> use the same needle for everyone. Many of the children who wanted to look brave at the beginning, looked for an exit and ran for the door. Others even jumped out the window. One girl ran screaming out the door and her older brother ran after her and brought her back screaming and kicking. He physically held her as the nurse gave her the shot. (He later said he regretted doing that because she always had a morbid fear of doctors all her life.) Dr. Evans' nurse, Rosemary Stokes, always told the children that the shot would not hurt so much if they blew hard on it. Therefore, by blowing on it while the shot was being given they couldn't cry. After the first trip when the doctor came to the school and children understood what to expect, they were better prepared for his visits. Therefore, the situation improved. But the doctors first visit to a school was usually chaotic.

EPIDEMIC DISEASES CLOSE SCHOOLS

During the 1930s, such diseases as typhoid, diphtheria, small pox, and scarlett fever were prevalent throughout the county. It was not uncommon for schools to be closed and patients quarantined. In 1936, there were two cases of scarlett fever in the county, but the schools were not closed. However, little Miss Janis Ruth Caudill was one of those patients, and she was quarantined in her home for three weeks.

In 1938, there was a smallpox epidemic in Rowan County. There were thirty cases reported in two different schools. There were 25 cases in the Haldeman School, and 5 cases in the small Pine Grove School. (Many of the cases were severe.) Those schools were closed immediately and placed under a strict quarantine to prevent the disease from spreading. According to Dr. Evans, numerous children had been exposed, and there was no way of knowing just how far the exposure or contagion extended. He also urged everyone exposed who had not been vaccinated to do so when he arrived in that community. The following Tuesday, Dr. Evans and Mrs. Raymond (his new nurse) vaccinated over 300 residents of that community. He further advised every citizen of the county who had not been vaccinated to do so immediately. During the next week, about 160 people each day came to the Health Department Office on Railroad Street to be immunized. The epidemic was contained and the schools re-opened after three weeks.

CHEST X-RAYS BEGIN

On June 12, 1936, the first clinic to take x-rays and chest examinations for the purpose of diagnosing TB was conducted by the Rowan County Health Department. They were assisted by a field unit from the State Department of health in Frankfort. Even though the incidence of tuberculosis was dropping by this time, several cases were discovered. This method of screening for TB became an annual event in Rowan County for many years.

In the 1940s polio became more prevalent. During the summers there was a great fear of that disease. Parents refused to let their children be in crowds, go swimming, or be in hot stuffy rooms. In 1944, there was the worst outbreak of polio in the history of Kentucky. In January 1945, Dr. Evans asked Mrs. Marvin Wilson, Sr. (who was confined to a wheelchair), to serve as the Chairman of Rowan County's first polio fund drive. Dr.Evans emphasized the urgent need for funds to assist in rehabilitation of polio victims. Mrs. Wilson was assisted by Miss Lacy Kegley, a nurse for Dr. Everett Blair.

Dr. Evans was not only a fine physician, but also an able administrator and communicator. He began the Health Department in a building on Railroad Street. Later the office moved to the Martindale Building on Main Street. In 1957, a new building was built on West Sun Street, and still houses the Morehead/Rowan County Health Department. The new building was the result of

Dr. Evans' vision for a community health center. (Although he did not live to see it built.)

FAITH IN THE FUTURE

Dr. Evans was the first president of Morehead's Citizens Bank, and remained a member of their board of directors throughout his lifetime. When plans were made in 1955 to build a new Citizens Bank building, Dr. Evans attended the meeting. He was very feeble and had to be brought in a wheelchair by his son Deward. But his comment at that meeting was, "We are building for the future and to help make Rowan County a better place to live." He had that very same zealous belief in the future of a health department for Rowan County. He believed that it would make Rowan County a better, healthier place for our children.

Dr. Evans always gave credit to those members of his staff for their efforts in eradicating many of those dreaded diseases from Rowan County. Among those early pioneer diseases fighters were Gladda Florence, Evelyn West, Nina Blair, Mollie Raymond, Francis Reed, Rosemary Stokes, Maude Clay, Mary Kincer, Jo Ann Needham, and many others. Rosemary Stokes remembers Dr. Evans as a kindly country doctor who told her she was driving too fast as they would visit schools. Also, he insisted she blow her car horn going through the Paragon Tunnel.

GALEN BROWN NEW ADMINISTRATOR

Before Dr. Evans retired, he employed Mr. Galen Brown as County Sanitarian. Mr. Brown, a graduate of Morehead State University, was assigned the responsibility for new duties recently assumed by the Health Department. Among these were inspecting food establishments, garbage dumps, milk producers, drinking water, and private premises to insure proper sanitation (septic tank) procedures were followed.

Dr. Evans retired in 1952, and Galen Brown was appointed Heath Administrator, because the position no longer required an M.D. degree. Private physicians provided most of the medical care for Rowan residents. The county Health Department concentrated on environmental, health and welfare and many other issues.

Galen Brown, working with County Judge Bill McClain, succeeded in getting funds to build the new building on West Sun Street. During 1956, Rowan's centennial year, Judge McClain and Galen went to Frankfort to lobby the legislature for funds for a building. Judge McClain had grown a heavy beard for the Rowan County centennial. At that time full beards were very rare, and Judge McClain's beard got everyone's attention. He believed that because of his beard, the legislators listened to him, and Rowan County received funding for a new health center. Both Galen and Judge McClain always believed that the attention given to Judge McClain's beard helped get the funds to construct the building. The existing building has had one major expansion to allow for additional services and personnel.

In 1999, there are nine full-time and four part-time employees in the Morehead/Rowan County Health Center. The Board of Health includes Chair, Dr. Ralph Derrickson; Vice-Chair, Dr. Ted Pass; Dr. George Barber; Dr. James VanSant; Dr. Nancy Henley; Dr. Karen Shay; Dr. Thomas McHugh; County Judge Clyde Thomas; Nancy Flippin; Bernadette Stansbury; Glenn Boodry; and Bobby Ratliff.

The Health Department is now organized under Kentucky's Gateway District Board of Health with James R. Ratliff, Health Director, and Greg Brewer, Administrative Director. The local health director is Anna Littleton. This writer lives across the street from the health department, and can testify that it is a busy place. They provide a broad range of health, social and environmental services to Rowan citizens.

1988 HEALTH CARE LIGHT YEARS AHEAD OF 1931

During the fiscal year ending June 30, 1998, Morehead/Rowan County Health Department staff had 10,385 patients - client contacts. Those contacts were in education programs, nutrition, family planning, child care, and maternity care. Also included were diabetic education care, treatment, and prevention of diseases. In addition there are school, children, and adult nursing programs. Social workers and environmental workers provide other valuable community health services.

Rowan Countians receive better health care today because of the sacrifice and hard work of those past health care workers. Dr. Evans' vision of better community health care for tomorrow is here today. He built upon a solid foundation, and his efforts continue to affect us today. But thousands of Rowan Countians remember Dr. Evans well, as the one who came to their school and gave them their "shots"--and maybe their arms ache just a little bit thinking about it.

Morehead-Rowan County Health Center. 2000

Morehead High School students. 1927

Top Row (L to R): Louise Caudill, Virginia Jennings, Bessie Turner, Marie Barber,
Pearl Hall, Margaret Calvert, Watt Prichard, Jr.

Middle Row (L to R): Arye Miller Cassity, Elsie Lee Hogge, Docia Caudill, Blanch "Pud" Hardin,
Audra Thorne, Mary Alice Calvert, Drinda McClung.

Bottom Row (L to R): Roy Cassity, Ted Crosthwaite, Fred Cassity, Hendrix Tolliver,
George M. Calvert, Eldon "Tick" Evans, Robert Bishop.

CHAPTER FIVE

School Superintendents:
Leaders in Education

Historically, the economy of Kentucky, like other states in the Southeast, was based upon agriculture. As a result, education has suffered throughout the South. Also, the southern states suffered economically from the ravages of the Civil War. Although Rowan County lost its courthouse when it was burned in 1863, there was little damage to the economy as a result of the Civil War.

GROWTH STUNTED BY FEUD

As Rowan County began to grow following the Civil War, there was a major feud known as the Rowan County War from 1884-1887. This infamous feud did much to slow Rowan's progress. (Because it occurred just as the school system was beginning.) Following the final battle of the feud on June 22, 1887, Sam E. Hill, Adjutant General of Kentucky, was ordered by Governor Knott to investigate the "Rowan County Trouble." After a year-long investigation, his report concluded:

1. Rowan was a county without courts, laws, schools, or churches from 1884-1887.
2. The death toll from August, 1884, till June 22, 1887, was 23.
3. Many law-abiding citizens were forced to flee for their lives to other counties.

4. Both sides were responsible for the killing of 23 men during the three years of conflict. But the good people of Rowan outnumbered the bad people 80 percent to 20 percent.

5. Rowan County should be abolished and its land, courts, and officials be absorbed into other counties.

CITIZENS FIGHT TO KEEP THEIR COUNTY

But the local citizens were determined to keep their county. Therefore, on January 16, 1888, those 80 percent of Rowan Countians who were good, law-abiding citizens met in the courthouse. Their purpose was to fight to keep Rowan as a county and to counteract the Attorney General's report. The meeting was chaired by J.T. Hazelrigg, andA.J. Thurber was appointed secretary. Fiery speeches were made by polished orators D.B. Logan, James E. Clark, and G.W. Saulsberry. They implored the local citizens not to stand by idly and allow their county to be dismembered. Recommendations made by this citizens group were published in all of the surrounding newspapers, eg. Owingsville, Mt.Sterling, Flemingsburg, and Lexington. Among those recommendations were:

I. Resolved: Whisky was a major cause of the feud, and more control would be placed on the sale of whisky in the future.

II. Resolved: Rowan would determine to be as famous in the future for peace, law, and order, as it was been in the past for rioting and disorder. We do hereby pledge ourself to do all in our power to accomplish this goal.

III. Resolved: That we will urge our legislators to not divest our county out of its existence by an act of the Kentucky General Assembly.

IV. <u>Resolved</u>: The people of Rowan County have learned their lesson, and will do everything in their power to preserve peace and tranquility throughout the county in the future.

Although a bill was introduced in the 1890 Kentucky General Assembly to abolish Rowan County and return it to the counties from whence it came (Fleming and Morgan). The bill did not pass and Rowan was saved as a county.

FEUDING HELPED EDUCATION

Rowan County was not the only famous feuding county in Kentucky. The Pike County Hatfield and McCoy feud was much more famous than the Rowan affair. Also, Carter County and Breathitt County, among others, were involved in feuding. So Kentucky's image to the rest of the world was not too good. Therefore, in this writer's opinion, just as the Rowan County War brought the Normal School to Morehead, it also may have motivated the legislature to improve education throughout the state. The Rowan County War and Kentucky's feuding families were some of the reasons for providing for a system of common schools in the new constitution of 1894. It was believed an educated citizenry would be a more peaceful citizenry.

In examining any institution from an historical perspective, it is necessary to examine the political, geographical, social, cultural and economic forces that influenced its development. Certainly, every aspect of Rowan County's history has been greatly influenced by the Rowan County War. Therefore, in examining the history of public education in Rowan County, it was necessary to briefly examine the Rowan County War.

As a result of this feud, Rowan had an image problem. Its old image was world famous for rioting, killing, looting, lawlessness and illiteracy. In addition to state papers, the New York Times and the London England Times regularly printed stories of Rowan's feud. Therefore, if Rowan was to make any progress or even survive as a county, a new image had to be established. When the Rowan Feud ended in 1887, the local citizens began an odyssey to end the backward, illiterate and illicit image of Rowan county. (An odyssey that continues to some extent even today.)

Common School System Established

In February 16, 1838, by act of the legislature, Kentucky established a system of common schools. On February 10, 1838, the Governor signed the bill into law and appointed Reverend Joseph Bullock the first State Superintendent of Public Instruction. The legislature further provided $1,000,000 as the foundation of a permanent school fund. The wording of the original legislation stated: "The purpose of this act is to provide a good common school education for every child in the Commonwealth." This was a worthy purpose and is still being pursued 160 years later.

Various means of taxation was attempted to support the common schools in Kentucky. In addition to a property tax, there was a poll tax (people tax) and a dog tax. The dog tax required residents to register the number of dogs they owned. Bonafide Kentucky residents were permitted a "dogstead" (not homestead) exemption for their first two dogs. Above that number, they were required to pay $1 per dog per year. Also, each owner was liable for all of his "dog damages." Knowing the love Kentuckians have for their dogs, this tax would have produced significant revenues had they been able to collect it all. The dog tax was soon rescinded after an outcry of righteous indignation from dog owners.

Schools Arrive in Rowan

Although public education began in the major cities of the Commonwealth in the 1840s, public education in rural Kentucky was practically non-existent until the late 1800s. The first public school

Hiram Bradley, Rowan's first school superintendent, 1894-1902.

established in Morehead was a two-room log school built in 1882 at the corner of Sun Street and Hargis Avenue. It closed during the Rowan County War, but reopened in 1887. However, there was a Methodist Episcopal Church supported school in the Cranston-Rock Fork area of Rowan County in 1846. Fleming County court records show that in 1846, six acres of land was sold by Robert Triplett to the Methodist Episcopal Church for use as a school, church, and cemetery. A two story log school, about 24' x 24', was constructed on that site. (The teacher lived upstairs and conducted classes downstairs.) These classes were usually available by subscription and only then to the wealthy in the community, especially Methodists. This school survived until 1885. It was closed during the era of the Rowan County War and did not reopen. The cemetery remains and is one of the oldest in the county. But the two-story log schoolhouse and church were later dismantled and moved to an adjoining farm. Therefore, in 1846 the first organized school in what is now Rowan County opened on Rock Fork. It was a private church school.

In 1887, when the school in Morehead reopened, there was very little interest in education. Those that attended were unruly, undisciplined, and unsuccessful. They hardly remained long enough to learn to sign their name. Education had not yet come of age and most parents believed that young people were needed to help work on the farm more than they needed an education. There was a great tragedy in those unlearned lessons. The teachers were poorly trained, mostly men who were selected because they could maintain discipline.

SUPERINTENDENT HIRAM BRADLEY ERA (1894-1902)

Changes in Kentucky education came again in the 1890s when a new Kentucky constitution was adopted in 1891. It stated: "The General Assembly shall provide for an efficient system of common schools throughout the Commonwealth." It appeared that public education had made its entrance into Kentucky's conscience again. Although the constitution made provision for a public school system, it provided little financial support. However by 1894, the state tax was increased to provide only modest support for public education in the counties. Also enacted was legislation to provide for a State Board of Public Instruction. It also provided for county superintendents and county trustees. The county superintendent was elected by popular vote. Also, five county trustees were elected by popular vote from districts within each county. These trustees approve school buildings, budgets, and expenditures.

The first Rowan County School Superintendent was Hiram Bradley. He served from 1894-1902. Mr. Bradley was a lifelong resident of Morehead who believed passionately in the future of Rowan County. He was married to Miss Mackie Wollum on May 26, 1892. To this union were born five children: Bertie, Arthur, Kirby, Frank and Fred. Mr. Bradley was an active member of the Commercial Club of Morehead and also active in community affairs. The Commercial Club was a group of business and professional men working to improve the local economy. Hiram Bradley believed that education was the essential element in attracting industry to the area and growth to the community. That was true 100 years ago and is still true today. Although the Morehead Normal School was well established in 1894, Mr. Bradley understood that a "feeder" system of preparatory education was necessary to prepare students to enter the Normal School, as well as enter life.

The 1894 Kentucky Legislature established a state tax for a common school fund to support education. According to eminent Kentucky historian, Dr. Thomas D. Clark, it was "too little too late." But it served as a modest beginning for Kentucky's public schools. The legislation also provided that each county be divided into geographical districts and a local school trustee appointed for each school district. That meant that there were five county trustees in each county and one local trustee for each local school district. The local school trustee was recommended by the county superintendent and approved by the county trustees. The teachers were recommended by the local schooltrustee to the superintendent and approved by the county trustees. This system provided for excellent local control but proved difficult to administer.

ONE ROOM SCHOOLS CONSTRUCTED

In 1894, Superintendent Bradley began an ambitious building program. By 1900 the future appeared bright for education in Rowan County. By 1900 schools were constructed in the Farmers, Elliottville, Rodburn, Morehead, Haldeman, Cogswell, North Fork, Sharkey and other areas of the county. The average cost of a one-room school was $250 and bids were taken from local builders. It was the task of the local school trustee to establish school district boundaries, register and count all of the school age children. (Local trustees were paid 5 cents for each child registered.) Early board records showed local trustees were paid an average of $3 each year out of the school levee to register children. (This meant there were about 60 children in each district.) State funds were allocated based upon the number of school age children registered in the county. By 1900 there were 58 teachers, 38 local districts, 2,290 white students, and 23 black students.

Rowan's local trustees were the ones that recommended the appointment of a teacher for their local school. Next, the County Superintendent and County Trustees hired the teachers. Also, the local trustees insured that the building and outdoor toilets were maintained and that fuel (wood or coal) was delivered to the school in winter. Also in some cases they provided a shed for the horse ridden to school by the teacher. Some students rode horses, but there was no barn provided for them.

TEACHERS POORLY PREPARED

The early teachers were poorly prepared, requiring only a eighth-grade education. But quickly this began to change. Usually two years of high school or normal school was required to teach. By now there was state funds for support, and an administrative and political structure to administer public education in Rowan County. Basic education had begun. The question was then would it last? Was it going to be worth it? Questions asked today: Will it be replaced by private schools, computers, home schools, or something yet unknown?

A school is more than "a pupil sitting on one end of a log, and Mark Hopkins on the other end." But good teachers are the foundation of education. Superintendent Bradley was well aware of this and by 1900 had employed 58 teachers in the Rowan County School system. Among the Rowan County teachers employed before 1900 were Nick Fraley, Bertie Hamm, Dr. Banfield (M.D.), Ed Hyatt, Emory Evans, Paph Julian, Principal Charlie Bishop (founded Bishop's Drug Store), Hiram Bradley, Maggie Goodan, Betty Riley, Tina Nickel, Emma Nickel, Maggie Pack, Cora Wilson, Kate Clark, Annie Easton, Mary Dailey, Annie Bradley, Sara Bradley, Lena Tyree, Mary Patton, Dale Clark, Henry Caudill, William Caudill, Brother Wright (Methodist Pastor), Jim Harris, Roy Hogge, and William Hyatt.

MARGARET PARK LOVED TEACHING

One of Rowan County's earliest pioneer teachers was Miss Margaret Park. She was born September 18, 1866, in Virginia. Miss Park moved with her parents to Grayson Kentucky in 1870. She later moved to Lexington and attended the public schools there, and received her teacher training at the East Kentucky Normal School in Richmond.

Miss Margaret Park began her teaching career at Morehead in 1887 in a one-room log school located about what is now the corner of North Hargis and Sun Street. (The Rowan County War had ended in June of the year she began teaching.) She was a stern teacher, yet well respected by her students. Good classroom discipline was a requisite in those days, and Miss Margaret was a strong disciplinarian. In addition to teaching at Morehead, she also taught at Farmers, Moore, Carey, Brady, Bluestone, Freestone and many other schools. Her teaching career in Rowan County spanned four decades . She was a very dedicated teacher and rarely missed a day of school. At one time in her career, she lived in Morehead and taught in Farmers. Even though she owned a horse, she always walked the 8 miles one way, from Morehead to Farmers every day. (Today's teachers read and rejoice!) It was believed that she taught almost every student in Rowan County. In all probability, Cora Wilson was one of her pupils some time during her career. Miss Park was a talented musician, and deeply religious. She began each school day with prayer and group singing. Miss Margaret moved her piano each year into what ever school that she taught, and gave free music lessons to those who wanted to learn. Many of her students came to learn and appreciate music under her tutelage.

Miss Margaret Parks was a very devout person. She was a lifelong member of the Morehead Methodist Church. But in each community where she taught she would also teach Bible classes. The schools she taught became known not only as centers of learning, but as worship centers also. Miss Margaret left a large legacy for today's teachers. Her devotion and dedication to teaching formed a firm foundation for the future of education in Rowan County.

Miss Margaret Parks passed peacefully away in Lexington, Kentucky, February 21, 1956. She was a credit to her Christ she loved so much, and the career she followed so faithfully.

Looking back at the Rowan County School System through the telescope of time, you see clearly that during the last quarter of the 19th century, it grew from nothing to something. This was possible through the leadership of Mr. Hiram Bradley, Rowan's first county superintendent, and dedicated teachers such as Miss Margaret Parks, who gave her life to the children of Rowan County.

Taking her piano to every one-room school where she taught? That's dedication!!!

SUPERINTENDENT CORA WILSON STEWART ERA (1902-1906; 1910-1914)

MOONLIGHT YEARS

"Rowan children are priceless jewels, needing only to be refined."
(Cora Wilson Stewart)

Cora Wilson Stewart was a teacher in the Rowan County Schools. She was also Superintendent of Schools for two separate terms (1902-1906 and 1910-1914). She could be called one of Rowan County's citizens of the century. She was certainly the most famous. This writer has collected a bibliography of 65 books and materials both by and about Cora Wilson Stewart (only those written in English). Much was written about her and published internationally. She received numerous state, national, and international awards. Among the awards she received were first woman elected President of the Kentucky Educational Association and the first woman to be elected Superintendent of Schools in Kentucky. That was before women could vote. She was also Chairman of state, national, and international Commissions on Education. She frequently testified on education committees at Frankfort and Washington. She also advised other nations, including Russia, England and France. Also national awards included the Pictorial Review Award, Ella Flagg Young Medal, and the Clara Barton Medal. All were presented to her for her pioneering work in education.

Cora Wilson Stewart, Rowan school superintendent, 1902-1906; 1910-1914. Also founded the Moonlight Schools in 1911.

Photo: MSU Archives; painting by Sam McKinney

RECOGNIZED ON NATIONAL TV

Cora Wilson Stewart was given the highest award given by the General Federation of Women's Clubs for "her pioneering work in combating illiteracy around the world." She was recognized by governors, presidents, kings, queens and czars for her monumental efforts to eliminate illiteracy world-wide. At the Democratic National Convention in 1920 at San Francisco, her name was placed in nomination by the Kentucky Delegation for President of the U.S. That was only the second time a woman's name had been placed before the delegation. In 1957, Ralph Edwards of the old "This Is Your Life" TV program, chose her as the subject of a one-hour program. Although at that time she was just too ill to attend, they did show her delight at being selected at a pre-filmed portion of the program.

BORN IN RURAL ROWAN COUNTY

Cora Wilson was born January 17, 1875, on a farm in rural Rowan County, located about five miles up the Licking River from Crossroad (later called Farmers). She was the oldest of seven children born to Jeremiah and Anne Halley Wilson. Both her parents wereteachers. In those days doctors frequently had to have other employment to supplement their medical practice. Dr. Wilson was a farmer, teacher, and storekeeper at some time in his life. That allowed him to practice medicine.

In 1880, Jeremiah Wilson moved from the upper Licking River section of Rowan County to Farmers because he believed that a thriving community offered more opportunity for his children's education and his medical practice. Young Cora at the age of five displayed an inquisitive, intelligent mind. Her parents taught her to read and provided an early home atmosphere condusive to learning. Cora wrote in her autobiographical notes: "We had pictures on our walls and books and stories read to us. The difference between our lives and most of the other children was that our parents were educated." She read everything she could get her hands on, even her father's medical books. Also a neighbor, Mr. Sanford, subscribed to a published fiction magazine called THE OLD ARM-CHAIR. He was thought to be the only man in Rowan County that subscribed to a periodical. He would loan it to the Wilsons and Cora would read it regularly.

Cora Wilson began her education at Farmers, Kentucky, in a one-room school that was in session only three months a year. It was a one-room log cabin with dirt floors and cut out windows (no glass). Cora decided she wanted to be a teacher at a very early age. She would play school constantly with her friends. She was always the teacher and required her imaginary "students" to address her as Miss Cora.

FAMILY MOVED TO ELLIOTTVILLE

In 1884, Jeremiah moved from Farmers to Elliottville, where Dr. Wilson practiced medicine and ran a general store. It was during this period of time that Cora would sometimes accompany her father in his medical practice throughout the rural area. On one trip she was asked by an illiterate elderly woman to read a letter she had received several months earlier. It was from a son who was in the army fighting Indians in the West. As Cora read the letter she could see the woman's countenance change from distress to happiness. She was afraid the letter contained bad news and for three months there was no one there to read the letter. Cora determined then to do something about that problem.

ROWAN FEUD AFFECTED CORA

In 1884 while the Wilson family was living in Elliottille, the bloody Rowan County Feud erupted. Although her family was not directly involved in the feud, the violence that resulted had a deep effect upon young Cora. Although ill feelings had existed between the feuding families since the Civil War, it was during the years of 1884-1887 that the killing began in earnest. There were 22 men killed and 16 wounded.

Many times the wounded men would be brought bleeding and dying to her fatherfor treatment. Cora was greatly affected by the feud and the stories of the war remained with her throughout her lifetime. It was a significant event in the life of all Rowan County citizens of that time, and Cora Wilson would remember it the rest of her life.

That the feud affected her can be shown in the first magazine article she ever published. It appeared in 1902 in *The World Wide Magazine* and was entitled "The Rowan County War." She wrote it under the pseudonym "Edward T. Moran," which shows you just how sensitive a topic it was. As Cora witnessed the violence, feuding, illiteracy and human carnage upon the landscape of Rowan County, it made her more determined than ever to plant beauty where there had been blight.

WILSON FAMILY MOVED TO MOREHEAD

In 1888, following the Rowan County War, Jeremiah Wilson moved his family to Morehead. Morehead was growing. In 1880 the population was 400. But by 1890 with the feud ended, the town population grew to 800 and the county population was 6,129. The Normal School along with timber, stone, and agriculture were Rowan County's greatest assets. Also, with the new Normal School, there was a greater opportunity for the Wilson children to get an education and for Dr. Wilson to develop a successful medical practice. The family settled in a large two-story house at what is now the corner of Fifth Street and Wilson Avenue (Another landmark named for the Wilson family.) Cora attended the Morehead Normal School and began teaching at Little Brushy School at age 16. After teaching for three years she continued her education at the National Normal Institute in Lebanon, Ohio. After graduation she returned to Rowan County and taught at Seas Branch, Elliottville, and Carey. It was while at Carey that she met and married Grant Carey, a marriage that lasted less than two years. There were no children born to this union.

ELECTED SUPERINTENDENT OF SCHOOLS

In 1901, the Rowan County Democratic Party chose her to run for County School Superintendent. Although Rowan was traditionally a Republican County, she began her campaign on the Democrat ticket. Since no women had ever held the position, there was some doubt she could ever win. Also, her opponent was Emmit Martt, her sister's boyfriend. In spite of the personal and political obstacles, she campaigned vigorously on the slogan, "A Children's Friend." On November 5, 1901, Cora Wilson was elected by a substantial majority. On January 1, 1902, she assumed office as the first woman elected to a county office in Rowan County. (Since this was before women could vote, it was even more amazing.)

Perhaps because she was a woman in what was then a man's world, Cora was even more determined to be successful in her position. She set the standard for future school superintendents by

Moonlight School Teachers Connie Mauk and Reba Terrell commute to school, 1911.

going to work in her office every day in the courthouse. She visitedevery school every year, and since there were over fifty schools in the county and many could only be reached on horseback, it was a major effort. Also, it usually meant staying overnight in the home of one of the families in the community. She observed teachers and the physical conditions of the school. Cora encouraged teachers to be better prepared and the trustees to take better care of buildings.

By 1900, the county population was 8,277, and Morehead's population had reached 1,100, due in a large part to the growth of the Morehead Normal school. Also, the county was growing with more farm products, lumber, and stone quarries, spurring economic growth. Cora was perhaps one of the first to recognize the vital connection between education to economic growth. (In 1898, the

Commercial Club of Morehead only briefly mentioned the Normal School as they extolled the virtues of future economic growth.) But Cora knew that the county would not grow without a good school system. She lead the fight to awaken the people of Rowan County of the need for good schools.

ROWAN CHILDREN PRICELESS JEWELS

Cora Wilson, because of her teaching experience, and educational training, maintained that subject content and good teacher training were keys to improving education. She was convinced that the children of Rowan County possessed the native intelligence needed to learn. She often referred to Rowan's children as priceless, rough "Mountain Jewels," needing only to be shaped and polished through education. During her terms as school superintendent, she provided the dynamic leadership to accomplish that. Superintendent Wilson believed that schools should be vital parts of their community. She encouraged teachers to teach about such things as conservation of land through proper erosion control and crop rotation. Also, an emphasis was made to clean up filthy and unsanitary conditions and to promote better public health. She believed that the Lord made the earth clean and wholesome, and it was up to us to keep it that way. She was far ahead of her time in that respect.

Cora Wilson could by no means be called an environmentalist, but she believed you could balance the need for economic growth with the need to preserve the environment. She realized corporate mining and timber harvesting could, if not properly controlled, result in some damages. But she also realized the terrible plight of the poor people of Eastern Kentucky and the economic blight upon the region. She encouraged the commercial use of this region's resources.

MOONLIGHT MADNESS 1910-1914

After refusing to run for re-election for a second consecutive term as County Superintendent, Cora decided to run after a four-year absence. Cora who was married by this time, and in spite of her husband's objections, ran again for County Superintendent of Schools on the Republican Party. She ran against the strong Democratic incumbent, LydaMesser. However, Cora won by a very narrow margin, and in January, 1910, began a second term as School Superintendent. That was a task that made her world famous, but also resulted in her divorce from Alexander Stewart.

Early in her second term as County Superintendent (she did not serve consecutive terms), Cora Wilson Stewart was made acutely aware of the extent of adult illiteracy in Rowan County. One man confided in her that he would give twenty years of his life if he could read and write. Also, a young boy came to church one Sunday and sang a beautiful ballad. When Cora asked him for a copy of the song, he said he could neither read nor write, and that he had sung many other songs, but had forgotten the words before he could get anyone to write them down. Those instances, along with Miss Cora's early childhood experiences of being asked to read letters to families where no one could read, fired her passion to do something to help.

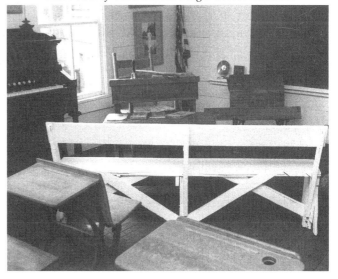

Inside view of Morehead Moonlight School Museum.

Cora realized her primary responsibility was to the children of Rowan County. Also, the fifty county schools were already over-crowded, and teachers were over worked. Adults also would be too embarrassed to come into the same learning environment with children or take time off from work to attend school. In addition, there were no funds to pay teachers. Neither were there appropriate teaching materials for adults. (The early primary textbooks, like *Dick and Jane Down the River Road*, just would not be appropriate.) It would seem to the casual observer that with all those negatives Cora would give up. But this was not the case, and she plunged headlong into the vast dark sea of illiteracy in Rowan County, trusting only that the ship of education would keep her afloat.

Photo: MSU Archives

Rowan Moonlight School Teachers on a free trip to Niagra Falls, New York 1912.

SCHOOLS OPEN

At the first teachers' meeting on September 1, 1911, Cora called for teachers to volunteer to teach adults at night, and every teacher in Rowan County agreed to serve without pay. She also gave them copies of a newspaper she published called *The Rowan County Messenger* to be used as a textbook. By using a newspaper she hoped to eliminate the humiliation of adults using the children's textbooks. On Monday, September 4, the teachers surveyed their district in an attempt to determine how many might attend the night classes. The survey indicated interest by 150 adults; and so the Moonlight Schools were born in Rowan County on September 5, 1911, at 7 p.m. Central Standard Time when over 1,200 men and women between the ages of 18 and 86 enrolled. They came walking across the green hills as moonlight flooded the countryside. Some carrying babies, lanterns, and yes, even guns; for Rowan County was still considered a dangerous place in the darkness. Everyone was delighted with the response, and it was only the beginning. Because after that first night, the Moonlight School movement to educate the uneducated under the silvery moon, spread like wildfire.

ADULTS MET ON MOONLIGHT NIGHTS

The name "Moonlight Schools" was given to that movement because classes were scheduled during the full phase of the moon. Also, it permitted better night vision and security in traveling over hills and hollows to those isolated schools. Aims of the program were to reduce illiteracy, increase school average daily attendance, and emphasize the need for better health, homes, farms, and roads for a better life. Each Moonlight School session ran from 7 to 9 p.m. (Rowan county was in the Central Time Zone then) four nights each month (when the moon was full) for six months.

PERFORMED DOUBLE DUTY

The second year of the Moonlight Schools was even more successful with over 1,500 enrolled. Cora Wilson Stewart was really performing two jobs–her duties as County Superintendent during the day and leader of the Moonlight Schools at night. Many times she would be at one school at 7 p.m. encouraging and challenging teachers and students. Then riding her horse to another school in time to do the same for that school. Many times she would not get home before 2 a.m. only to get up and go to her office that morning. Her family was worried about her health, and she was pushing herself too far. But her dedication and passion for fulfilling her dream of eliminating illiteracy in Rowan County kept her going.

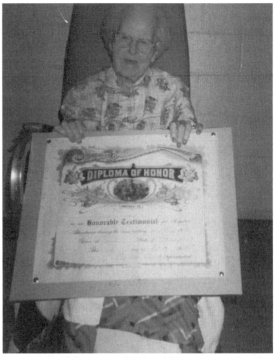

Mary Caudill, age 98, displayed her Diploma signed and presented to her by Cora Wilson Stewart in 1912.

The volunteer Moonlight School teachers were also teaching day and night. But morale was high because they believed their cause was just and the results worth the effort. They were called Rowan's "Earnest Teachers," and their motto was "one to everyone." Cora always gave credit to their dedication and unselfishness for the program's success. Since they were not paid, some teachers were rewarded with books, trips, and social events paid for many times out of Miss Cora's pocket. (Students were also rewarded for achievements with gifts.) In 1913, the community raised enough funds to send those "earnest" volunteer teachers on a trip to Niagra Falls.

The Moonlight Schools were not without their critics. Professional educators scoffed at her when she announced in 1913 that the 1,152 illiterate adults listed in the Rowan County had been reduced to twentythree. She silenced her critics by eventually getting the names of those 1,152 illiterate adults from the U.S. Census Bureau and providing proof they were now reading and writing. (Before the decade was over, she succeeded in obtaining the names of all 208,000 Kentuckians listed as illiterate in the 1910 U.S. Census.)

REFUSES TO RUN FOR RE-ELECTION

Cora Wilson Stewart did not run for re-election as County Superintendent in 1914, but instead plunged into the dark sea of illiteracy in her small boat named "The Moonlight School." After her last term as Rowan County Superintendent, she was in great demand as a speaker. She was an excellent speaker. Cora was articulate, knowledgeable andpersuasive. She spoke to many county, state, national, and international groups on the problems of illiteracy. Cora was an eloquent speaker, and wherever she spoke she told of the Rowan County success in overcoming illiteracy. As an advisor to other states, she insisted that they call their program "Moonlight Schools," and not "Night Schools." She said that night schools were a product of Northern States and urban areas. Cora believed the Moonlight Schools, born in Rowan County, were a southern rural effort very different from Night Schools.

PRIMARY BOOKS WRITTEN FOR ADULTS

Cora Wilson Stewart later wrote textbooks for adult illiterates, such as *The Country Life Reader*, published in 1916. It was written in a primary vocabulary but dealt with adult subjects such as farming, finance, personal and civic responsibility. Cora also authored other books such as *Mother's First Book*, and *Soldiers First Book*. When the U.S. entered WW I, 50,000 *Soldiers First Books* were purchased and sent to U.S. soldiers in France. *The Soldiers First Book*, written for the U.S. Army, was designed to teach soldiers basis skills of military life, such as marching, military courtesy and personal cleanliness.

In 1917, Cora's public statements that "30,000 Kentuckians who registered for the draft were unable to read and write," brought a storm of criticism from native Kentuckians. She was accused of emphasizing the ignorance of her native state, and, benefitting financially from that condition. She bitterly resented that accusation and repeated her burning desire to overcome illiteracy in Kentucky by 1920. Of course she did not accomplish that, but she did make a big dent in it. Perhaps she could have done even more had she not been so politically naive. Her continued statements throughout the nation about backward illiterate Kentuckians estranged even those local citizens and politicians who had initially supported her effort.

LEAVES ROWAN COUNTY

Although Cora Wilson Stewart went on to win many national and international awards, she became embittered against her native state and many of her colleagues. In 1936, she retired to North Carolina and spent her remaining years between Pine Bluff, Arkansas, and Tryon, North Carolina. (Cora Wilson Stewart died December 1, 1958 at Tryon, North Carolina.) She left a large legacy extending up to the present. Her early struggle as a woman in a male dominated society continues today. Also, her efforts to overcome illiteracy continues today. Not in rural moonlight schools, but in modern urban and suburban settings. Rowan County, the birth place of the Moonlight School effort to spread light through learning, should faithfully follow Cora's example.

ROWAN COUNTY MOONLIGHT SCHOOL TEACHERS (1911-1914) (A PARTIAL LIST)

J. M. Harris (Dry Creek); J.M. Butcher (Tabor Hill); Steve Caudill (Popular Grove); John Caudill (Seas Branch); Claude Crosthwaite (Alfrey); Bethel Hall (Upper Lick Fork); Amanda Hunt (Carey); Clella Porter (Elliottville); and Glenna Flannery DeHart (Rodburn).

Other teachers who also taught were Cleff Tussey, Henry Black, Willie Mabry, John Crisp, Farris Cook, Worley Hall, Herb Bradley, Mollie Skaggs, Claude Crosthwaite, and Boone Peyton. Also, other teachers were Pearl Bailey, Verda Surrott, F.E. Ellington, Audrey Ellington, Bethel McGlosson, Jasper Howard, Taylor Flemming, R.W. Cline, H.C. Black, Herbert Tackett, Flora Messer, H.C. Tackett, Conie Mauk, J.V. Harris, and Thomas Hogge.

The teachers were so dedicated and enthusiastic that one of them (in 1913) wrote a stirring song, dedicated to their leader, Cora Wilson Stewart. The "peppy" marching song was to be sung to the tune of "Onward Christian Soldiers," and is as follows:

ONWARD ROWAN COUNTY
by
Conie M. Mauk
(Tune, Onward Christian Soldiers)

I
Onward all ye teachers of Rowan
County schools,
Let's march into our school
rooms,
With the golden rule
Let us help one "LEADER:
Every bit we can.
To make the schools in Rowan
County,
The best in all the land.

CHORUS
Onward then ye teachers
Let us take the lead,
We must all be faithful
In every act and deed.

II
Like a mighty army
Moves this happy throng.
Other folks are joining us,
In this grand new song.
They help us swell the chorus
Make it loud and sweet,
they come into our county,
Which is learning's seat.

II
Onward then ye people,
Join us in the fight;
You can help the children
Win out for the right.
Glory, laud and honor,
To each little home
when all vice and ignorance
From ROWAN will be gone.

———————

This song is dedicated to "Our Leader,"
MRS. CORA WILSON STEWART

Lyda Messer Caudill, Rowan superintendent of schools 1906-1910; 1930-1934.
Posed with school children.

SUPERINTENDENT LYDA MESSER CAUDILL ERA 1906-1910; 1930-1934

ONE ROOM SCHOOL ERA

"Behold, thou hast instructed many!" (Job 4:3)

Lyda (Messer) Caudill was the third County Superintendent of Schools in Rowan County. She served two different terms. Her first term was 1906-1910. Her secondterm was from 1930-1934.

Lyda Messer was born in Rowan County, but the date of her birth is unknown. Those who knew her recalled that she would never tell her age. (She managed to keep it a secret to the very end of her life.) Lyda Messer was the daughter of William Sr. and Martha (Christian) Messer. She died April 22, 1958, in the Central Baptist Hospital in Lexington, Kentucky, and was buried in Morehead's Lee Cemetery.

CORA WILSON COLLEAGUE

Miss Messer attended Rowan County Public Schools and graduated in 1898 from Eastern Kentucky Normal School in Richmond, Kentucky. She received her teaching certificate that year and returned to Rowan County where she was employed by Rowan County's first Superintendent Hiram Bradley, and continued teaching when Cora (Wilson) Stewart was Superintendent (1902-1906). Lyda Messer and Cora (Wilson) Stewart were professional colleagues and close personal friends. When Cora Wilson decided not to run for County Superintendent in 1906, she personally picked Lyda Messer to run for that office. Although Lyda Messer did not have the charisma or oratorical skills of Cora Wilson, she agreed to campaign for Superintendent with the support of Cora (Wilson) Stewart.

Practically everyone in Rowan County was pleased with the former Superintendent (Cora Wilson). Local leaders believed that since Lyda Messer was a local teacher, a woman, and friend of Cora Wilson Stewart, she would capitalize on the previous superintendent's proficiency. She was elected by a substantial majority, even though women could not yet vote.

When Lyda Messer took office in 1906, the office was located in the Courthouse. Her County School Board was elected on a county-wide basis, not by districts. (They were called County School Trustees.) The members were W.A. Vinton, Secretary-Treasurer; S.E. Elliott; W.J. Fletcher; and Samuel B. Caudill. (This writer's wife's grandfather.) (The Superintendent served as chairman.) However, during Lyda Messer's first term of office, the law changed requiring the county be divided into four sub-districts. There was a County School Trustee elected from each sub-district (not county wide). Also, the new legislation in 1906 required that local school trustees within each sub-district be appointed by the County School Trustees. (One trustee for every one or two local schools.) This assured local control of the schools. However, that structure was cumbersome, and politically motivated. In 1910, the County Trustees appointed Dr. T.A.E. Evans, a physician in Farmers, Kentucky, to replace C.T. Flannery as the local Trustee in that sub-district. One was a Republican and the other was a Democrat.

TEACHER CONTRACTS SIGNED BY TRUSTEES

The County Trustees were powerful forces in the early education system of Rowan County; they were the ones who signed teacher contracts spelling out teacher duties and responsibilities.

A contract dated July 1, 1896, between teacher Festus Cash holding a first class teaching certificate, and County Trustees James Cassity, John Fanning, and Local Trustee Aaron Purvis (Dist. 16), stated:

"Teacher Festus Cash would have an enrollment of 68 children in his school. He was responsible for maintaining order, and was subject to supervision and correction by said trustees. He could be fired at anytime by said trustees. He also was responsible for oiling and sweeping the floor (oil and broom provided). The fires were to be made by said teacher with said trustees providing fuel. The teacher was to be paid $40 per month for five months."

TRUSTEES COUNT CHILDREN

In 1910 these were the local trustees appointed by the County School Trustees. These local Trustees were responsible for taking school census every year. They were paid 5 cents per student. The results of the year 1910 census was as follows:

Local District Members	Member of Local Trustees	Number of Registered Pupils
I	11	999
II	14	1,074
III	11	658
IV	13	785

Total Districts	Total Local Trustees	Total Reported School-age pupils
4	49	3,516

In 1910 the local trustees in Rowan Sub-District 2, and the number of pupils in their sub-district were Lee Craycraft (152), John Hyden (54), S.E. Elliott (97), Sam Swim (92), H.G. Alderson (87), J.J. Cook (110), Cyrus Alley (64), Turner Crosthwaite (43), Aaron Crosthwaite (69), Walter Thurman (72), Prestley Mavies (77), L.S. Armstrong(69), Turner Crosthwaite (46), and S.E. Elliott (42). (Total 14 Trustees and 1,074 pupils). Please note that some were appointed to more than one sub-district, also, that County Trustees also served as sub-district trustees.

Although there were a total of 3,516 school age children in Rowan County in 1910, only about 2,200 actually enrolled in school. A school year was for five months, extending from July through

December. There were no attendance laws and school attendance was voluntary; therefore, school attendance was about 60 percent of the children eligible to attend. The 40 percent who did not attend were usually the older children who already had learned to read a little, write less, and even figure less. Their parents used the older boys to work on the farm and the older girls to work at home. Education had not yet become a felt need among most Rowan County Citizens.

CONSTRUCTION COSTS VARY

Politics were rampant in awarding contracts for construction of new one-room schools. There were builders who would actually build schools without floors or windows. One contractor collected his money for building a school, and when it was inspected, there was no floor. It was an attempt to take advantage of a woman superintendent. Therefore, a trustee policy was developed that required at least one county trustee to inspect the building before payment as authorized. In 1908 the cost of a one-room wooden school house was between $300-$400. Usually the land was donated and the school named for the donor; e.g. Adams-Davis, Alfrey, Bradley, Gearhart, Johnson, McKenzie, etc. (There were philanthropists in Rowan County even then.)

The cost of the school building was just one aspect of the cost. There was a well to be dug ($50). Also, one outdoor toilet for both boys and girls ($25). But the toilet paper was pages from old Montgomery Ward catalogs. There was always plenty of reading material even in the outhouse. Also, when children needed to visit the outhouse, they would raise their hand, and then placed a book in front of the door, which indicated someone was out at that time. Only one student could leave at a time. If they stayed too long, the teacher would look at the name in the book and know which student was at the outside toilet.

Other expenses of school construction included fencing around the school and a shed for fuel (wood or coal). Items needed included a pot-bellied stove and water bucket, dipper, seats, blackboard and chalk, erasers, coal buckets, shovels and paper. All this was necessary before a school could open its doors to children.

However, during her first four-year term as Superintendent, Lyda Messer was building about two new buildings per year. There was also the problem of school maintenance. The maintenance of the school building was the responsibility of the teacher, local trustee, parents and students. Oiling the floors to keep down the dust, and daily sweeping was done by the teacher and pupils. Building fires during the cold months was usually done by one of the older boys who lived near the school and arrivedearly. He was paid a nickel a day by the teacher, and furnished his own pine knots for kindling.

The wooden siding on the building was usually "white washed." White wash was a solution of lime mixed with water, then applied to building and outhouse. Also, the trees in the school yard were "white washed" about 6 feet up the trunk to improve the appearance and help reduce insect damage.

CERTIFICATION CONNECTED TO SALARY

By 1910, more and better teachers were being prepared by the Normal School. Lyda Messer did not seem to emphasize the importance of teachers in the educational process as did her predecessor, Cora Wilson. Perhaps she took them for granted because the Morehead Normal School was improving the quality of teacher training and teachers were required to also pass an examination before being certified.

In 1906, Mrs. J. Pearl Browning from South Charleston, West Virginia, and a Morehead Normal School graduate, applied for a teaching position in Rowan County. Her "Official Statement of

Credit" (Transcripts) from the Morehead Normal School was signed by President F.C. Button. This allowed her to take the teacher exam.

Those teachers teaching in the early one-room schools in Rowan County taught all eight grades, but usually not all the same year. Although they taught the first three grades every year, they would usually alternate the upper five grades. That was possible by double promoting some students and holding other students back one year. Also, because by the fourth or fifth grade many stopped attending school. Also, many teachers would use those better upper-grade students to assist in teaching the lower grades. This motivated attendance and learning in grades 4-8 and was about the only way a teacher could handle fifty or sixty students in one room.

By the years of 1910-1915, teachers in Rowan County with a second-class certificate were paid $40 per month. Teachers with a first-class certificate were paid $45 per month. At that time it was enough to attract both men and women teachers into the program. During that period there were about 65 teachers employed.

EXPANDED ECONOMY BRINGS GROWTH

In 1900 the population of Rowan County was 8,277 and by 1910 it was 9,438. However, during that period Rowan County experienced significant commercial and industrial growth.

The Clearfield Lumber Company was established in 1907, moving here from Clearfield, Pennsylvania. Many workers with large families moved here to harvest the vast tracks of virgin timber. The timber was located in the Clearfield, Paragon, Bangor areas (southern part of the county). Also, timber companies were harvesting vast tracks of timber in the upper Licking River areas of Rowan, Morgan and Menifee Counties. Inorder to bring the timber to market, a railroad was built from Morehead to the Paragon, Wrigley area. This required building the Clack Mountain and Poppin Rock Tunnels.

Rowan County was growing rapidly. The timber from the Upper Licking Valley was rafted down the Licking to Farmers to market. The new surge in timber marketing resulted in a large influx of school age children in Rowan County in early 1900's. There were 3,516 school age children in Rowan County in 1910. (In 1999, that number is down to 3,100.)

AFTER 20 YEARS LYDA MESSER CAUDILL RE-ELECTED

Between her first and second term as Rowan School Superintendent, Lyda Messer married William T. Caudill. Mr. Caudill served as County Court Clerk from 1914-1930. He also was a widower with 8 children. They also had one daughter, Leola Margaret (Caudill) Hurst (now a retired teacher living in Lexington.) Also one step-daughter surviving, Hattie (Caudill) Maynard, age 100, living in Ashland, Ky.) Even with the responsibility of rearing such a large family, Mrs. Caudill continued her teaching career, and served as principal of the Morehead Grade School.

Her daughter, Leola Hurst, said her mother was devoted to her work, yet did not neglect her family. She recalled many happy days growing up in Morehead in such a large family. Her mother remained politically active during the 16 years between her first and second terms as Superintendent, and was re-elected for her last term in 1930. Lyda Messer Caudill was the last Rowan County Superintendent to be elected by popular vote. The Kentucky legislature changed the way superintendents were chosen in 1932, and when her term ended in 1934, she went back to teaching. She was a teacher, principal or Superintendent for over 50 years until she retired in 1952. Lyda Messer Caudill, Rowan County's second female Superintendent, died at the Central Baptist hospital in Lexington, April 22, 1958, and is buried in Morehead's Lee Cemetery.

Lyda Messer Caudill was one of Rowan's pioneer educators. She worked under many difficult primitive conditions. There were few roads, no utilities, no phones, and transportation was by horse and buggy. Yet she was very politically astute and worked well with trustees, county officials, parents and teachers. Her first term provided the foundation for the next few years of school expansion. She served well and did an outstanding job under difficult conditions.

ESTABLISHED FIRST "COLORED" SCHOOL

Lyda Messer Caudill's daughter, Leola Margaret, now retired and living in Lexington, was asked what her mother considered her greatest accomplishment as Superintendent. She replied, "Mother was always most proud that she established the first school for black children in Rowan County." That was during the ancient obsolete laws of "separate but equal" facilities in Kentucky.

In 1910 Mrs. Caudill went to the officials of the C&O Railroad and convinced them to rent her a box car. She then established the first (maybe in America) truly portable classroom. Next, she had it placed on a obsolete siding on the south side of the railroad tracks running through Morehead. That was near where the Black families lived. (However, there were black and white families living peacefully as neighbors along Raine Street in Morehead.) But the law did not allow the children to attend school together.

Superintendent Caudill equipped the boxcar with a pot bellied coal stove, desks, blackboards, broom, chalk, erasers, water bucket and dipper. She even had an outdoor toilet built in an adjoining field. Water was obtained from a neighbor's well. A teacher was hired to teach. Therefore in 1910, the first school for black children in Rowan County was in session. There are those who would argue that a box car on a railroad siding was not an equal educational facility. But that box car was as big as many one room schools. It had all of the equipment one room schools had, and was certainly located close to the neighborhood children. There was a much better teacher-pupil ratio. (Many one room schools had fifty children). So an argument could be made that at that time and place the education of blacks and whites were both poor.

In looking at the Rowan County Schools through the telescope of time, it can be said that just as Cora Wilson Stewart's legacy was the Moonlight Schools, Lyda Messer Caudill's legacy was establishing the first school to educate black children in Rowan County. Since she lived to see integration of schools come to Kentucky, she could be justly proud that her administration was a pioneer provider of education for black children long before integration in Kentucky.

SUPERINTENDENT J.H. POWERS ERA 1914-1930

TALE OF TWO HIGH SCHOOLS

"There is only one thing that costs more than education today, and that is the lack of it." (Unknown)

J.H. Powers was Superintendent of Rowan County Schools 1914-1930. It was an era of contracts, consolidation and construction. It was, as in the *Tale of Two Cities*, "The best of times and the worst of times," to be in the school business. The best of times because the economy was growing with new industry such as the Haldeman Fire Brick Company and the Lee Clay Tile Company. The worst of times because timber was running out and population shifts were moving people from one area of the county to another. That necessitated closing some schools and building others which put atremendous strain on the limited school budget. (There have been 81 schools in Rowan County's history–but not all at the same time.)

J.H. Powers was born November 10, 1884, in Rowan County, the son of John and Nannie (Carey) Powers. Mr. Powers died October 14, 1962. He was married to Janie (Harrison) Powers. To that union were born six children: Lottie, Norma, Catherine, Ernestine, Thomas and Harlan, Jr. Mr. Powers was one of Morehead's early attorneys, and was admitted to the bar in 1906. He practiced law in Morehead for 10 years before entering politics. In 1914 he ran for the office of Superintendent of Schools in Rowan County and was elected by popular vote. The superintendent by virtue of his po-

J.H. Powers, Rowan superintendent of schools 1914-1930.

sition was also chairman of County School Board of Trustees.

On January 15, 1914, Superintendent Powers called a meeting of the board. The meeting began at 10 a.m. and was held in the Superintendent's Office in the Courthouse. Those present were J.C. Stewart, J.M. McBrayer, and B.P. Hamm. One board member, W.C. Clay, was absent. The first item on the agenda was to set the salary of the superintendent at $150 per month. The next item on the agenda was to approve local trustee G.W. Bradley's recommendation to hire Grace Dehart to fill the vacancy created by Lona Porter's resignation. Also other teachers hired based upon the recommendation of local trustees were Mollie Skaggs, and C.L. Click.

LOCAL TRUSTEES CONTROVERSIAL

The last item on the agenda was to approve payment of claims, such as R.W. Cline 75 cents for fuel, Wilson Mabry $3 for hauling desks, Lexington Broom Works $36 for brooms, and E.W. Mart $5.98

for an out building. Mr. Powers' first board meeting was routine, but things changed as they built new schools and closed old schools.

There was a great deal of political pressure to be appointed local trustees. Also there were many controversies over where to build new schools, and what schools would close as a result of consolidation. School district boundaries were constantly changing to move more politically influential farmers' families from one district to another, e.g. "Be it ordered that the school boundary of District 1 be moved to include the farm of E.W. Brooks." At the January 12, 1916, board meeting, a letter was submitted to the board as follows: "We the undersigned request that Cooper Black be elected by the county board to serve as local trustee for the Little Brushy District, as we feel he is competent and qualified to hold said office." Signed: C.T. Taylor, C.T. Black, Jane Black, E. Roberts, Jordan Curtis, T.E. Harris, Sam Hargis, James Thompson." The board therefore elected Mr. Cooper Black as local trustee.

Mt. Hope School in Rowan County, 1937. Teacher: Dorothy Ellis.

INDUSTRIAL DEVELOPMENT COMES TO COUNTY

However by 1917, the county was growing and the Haldeman Brick Yard was established. Not only a new factory was built, but many homes were constructed for many of the 300 workers and their families. There was a company store, post office, and soon an over-crowded school. Also, General Refractories began mining clay on Christy Creek, and a railroad was constructed to those mines. Morehead resident, "Pa" Kessler, was their engineer for many years.

The Clearfield Lumber company, that began in 1907, was beginning to run out of timber, and the Lee Clay Tile Plant, a part of the Clearfield Lumber Company, began operation in 1926. It employed 300 men. Therefore, all of the economic growth in Rowan County dramatically impacted the school system. It required closing some rural schools and building new ones at other sites. (In 1917, Thomas Dillon was awarded the contract to build a new one-room school at the cost of $550.) The cost of school construction was increasing and the county school board was looking for ways to stretch the few tax dollars.

Morehead High School's first faculty, 1924. Fr. L-R: A.F. McGuire, ?, J.H. Powers. C. L-R: Roy Holbrook, Olive Day Caudill, Lyda M. Caudill. R. L-R: Warren Lappin, ?, Myrtle Cornette Caudill, ?.

CHILDREN CROSS LICKING RIVER

In 1921, at a time county boundaries were considered almost sacred, Mr. Powers entered into contracts with some of the adjacent counties that permitted rural students to cross county lines to attend school. Early board records showed that in 1921, Rowan and Menifee Counties, separated by the Licking River with no bridge, agreed, "That the families of Amos Donahue, George Donahue, Frank Hall, and Floyd Hall, now residing in Rowan County, be added to the Donahue district in Menifee County". Also, several miles down the Licking River another contract said, "Be it further agreed that the families of Ross Johnson, Green Johnson, and Jack Utterback now residing in the Buck Creek district in Menifee County be added the Charity District in Rowan County. Even though this meant that these children had to cross Licking River twice each day in a row boat, it helped reduce the need for each county to build another rural school.

The fact that the children had to cross the Licking River each day to attend school seems harsh today. But that was a common practice in those days. It was even practiced between states. This writer had a friend that lived in Lewis County, Kentucky, who had to cross the Ohio River (no bridge) each day to attend school in Southern Ohio. She said she had walked across the river on ice a few times.

MOREHEAD HIGH SCHOOL ESTABLISHED

In 1920, there was no public high school in Rowan County. Mr. J.H. Powers recognized the great need for education beyond the eight grade, and in 1922 established the first public high school in Rowan County. It was located in a white wooden structure located at the corner of Hargis Avenue, and Sun Street. (Later sold to Alex Patton for $3,000). The first high school freshmen were enrolled in the new building, and E.F. Brammel was the first principal. In 1922, only five students were enrolled in the ninth grade. They were Effie Hall, Mary P'Simer, Lionel Fannin, Jordan Caudill, and Nell M.Cassity. But the school was growing and a new building was urgently needed.

In 1922, the County School Board bought the land on Second Street for the proposed new 12-grade consolidated school. They paid Alex Patton $500 for the land. There was some criticism of that purchase because he had paid only $300 for the land six months earlier. Then the board sold the old school building and land on Sun Street to Mr. Patton for $3,000. He paid $500 down and gave the board a note for $2,500. The board promptly sold the $2,500 note to Drew Evans for $2,250 dollars. The board was severely criticized for this action, but they did nothing illegal in the transaction. The board then sold bonds in the amount of $30,000 to pay for the new 12 grade consolidated school, equipment, furniture, and four new rural schools. Superintendent Powers believed in getting things done quickly, and he did.

Rowan County School records show during the 1920s, there was the William Davis Trust Fund willed to the board. The original amount received in the trust was $6,580.14. It was administered by the Mt. Sterling National Bank. The trust was invested in bonds at six percent interest, and paid annually to the board. It could be spent as the Board saw fit. Some of these funds were used for equipment in the new high school.

WARREN LAPPIN MOVES TO COLLEGE

In 1922, Warren Lappin was appointed principal to replace Mr. Brammel. He taught every subject in high school that year including Latin, algebra, history, and English. Mr. Lappin was principal for four years before accepting a position at the new Morehead State College. There he served in many positions for over 40 years.

J.H. Powers was School Superintendent in Rowan County during the time the private Morehead Normal School became the Morehead State Normal School in 1923. He was a strong supporter of the new State College, and established a cooperative working relationship between the College and the public schools from the very beginning. Since the new college had no training school at that time, an agreement was reached between the College and the County School Board to allow the Morehead Consolidated Schools to serve as a training school for future teachers. School Board minutes, dated October 27, 1923, at 11:00 a.m. recorded the following action:

J.W. Cornette, Chairman; S.R. Rolston; and T.H. Caudill approved the following contract:

> *"This meeting called for the purpose of considering a plan for cooperation between Morehead State Normal and the Rowan County Board of Education for the purpose of establishing training schools in Rowan County under joint support. A proposition was submitted by C.D. Lewis, Dean of the Morehead State Normal and after full discussion it was ordered that J.H. Powers, superintendent and J.W. Cornette, Chairman, act for the board in preparing and entering into a contract with said Normal State College for the establishment of Training Schools in Rowan County.*
>
> *It was ordered by the board that no contract or agreement shall be made that would in any way affect the authority and control of that Board, in the Morehead Consolidated District."*

That contact made possible for future teachers enrolled at Morehead State Normal to receive supervised practical classroom teaching experience. Also, the contract reflected the excellent early cooperation between county and college, and stayed in effect until Breckinridge Training School was completed in 1931.

NEW MOREHEAD HIGH SCHOOL CONSTRUCTED

In 1923, bids were awarded for the construction of a new High School building. W.T. Jayne was awarded the bid for construction of the basement (cost $2,035.00) with a $500.00 bond. The I.A. Rhodes Company was awarded the contract to complete the construction for $20,262.00 with a $10,000 bond. The new high school building was completed on schedule and opened for classes in 1924.

In 1925, the first class to graduate in the new high school only completed a three-year program. They were Everett Amburgy, Mary Jo Wilson, Lucille Caudill, and Joe McKinney. That class finished the fourth year at the Morehead Normal School in 1926.

In 1927, there were eleven students in the first class to complete a four-year program at Morehead High School. Those students were Murvel Blair, Anna Jane Day, Vernon Dillon, Ernest Hogge, Catherine Powers, Henry Lee Pritchard, Austin Riddle, Gladys Riddle, Dixon Shouse, Inez Tussey, and Evelyn Hamm.

MOREHEAD HIGH SCHOOL PRINCIPALS LISTED

In 1922, Morehead High School began with one teacher and one grade (9th) and 5 students in an old wooden building on Sun Street. In 1924, it moved to a new building on Second Street (site of today's Board of Education Building). It was closed in 1962 when it became Rowan County High School and moved to a new building on West Sun Street. The principals of Morehead High School were: E.F. Brammel (1921-22), Warren Lappin (1922-26), Ebon Chapion (1926-27), Asa MCGuire (1927-30), Wurtz Jayne (1930-32), Amelia Duley (1932-33), Dennis Caudill (1933-36), Ethel Ellington (1936-46), Walter Price (1946-49), Lindsay Ellington (1949-50), J.C. Smallwood (1950-55), Calvin Hunt (1953-58), and Russell Boyd (1958-1961). Mr. Boyd was the last principal of Morehead High School and the first principal of Rowan County High School in 1962.

HALDEMAN HIGH SCHOOL

In the 1920s Morehead was not the only community in Rowan County to need a new high school. Haldeman, with its new brick manufacturing plant, was hiring workers, building homes and businesses. The school was overflowing with children of the new factory workers moving into the area. Mr. Haldeman and Mr.

Leadbetter urged the county to build a new high school, and School Superintendent Powers responded.

The June 7, 1924, minutes of the Rowan County School Board consisting of J.W. Cornette, presiding, and S. Ralston, Andy Williams, T.H. Caudill, and J.C. Stewart members, submitted the following resolution by S. Ralston and seconded by T.H. Caudill:

I.   Whereas the assessment of the Haldeman School District is $519,000 with no indebtedness, and

II. Whereas the Haldeman voters approved at the election on May 24, 1924, the issuance of bonds in the amount of $10,000.00 to build a new 12 grade school, and

III. Whereas the said election was given according to the Kentucky Statutes, Be it resolved that said bonds be issued and a new consolidated school be built.

The vote was unanimous and plans soon got underway to build a new building to house the growing enrollment. The Board did not let a contract for the building but hired J.R. Thorne to oversee the construction. Mr. Thorne employed carpenters, plasterers, and laborers by the hour. He hired brick layers to lay brick for $20.00 per thousand. Also, many parents donated their labor. This got the building completed in record time at a minimum expense. However, it later caused many problems with the auditors.

Mr. Roy E. "Pappy" Holbrook, an early Rowan County teacher, coach, and principal gives excellent insight into the beginning of Haldeman High School. In a letter written to Lloyd Dean on January 15, 1953, Mr. Holbrook writes, "I went to Haldeman on September 5, 1924 as a teacher and principal of a two-teacher, 8 grade school. Mrs. Amy (Nickell) Stinson taught the lower four grades. There were 51 students in the old school house on the west side of #2 brick plant at the mouth of the hollow. By January, the enrollment increased to 91, and a third teacher (Herb Bradley) was hired to take care of the overflow. He was housed in a cottage down the road by #2 plant."

First High School Year Added

In 1925, one year of high school was added to the school, along with two teachers, Ruth Cassity and Avonelle Bradley. Mr. Holbrook also was assigned to coach. By 1927, the new $10,000 red brick school building was completed and the move was made into the new facility. Also, three new teachers were added: Ollie Click, Lottie Powers, and Ewing Basford. (There were a total of 10 teachers in the 12-grade consolidated school when Mr. Holbrook was transferred to Morehead High School in 1929.)

Basketball "Bluebelles and Leopards"

While at Haldeman, Coach "Pappy" Holbrook wasted no time in organizing bothboys and girls basketball teams. Although the new high school had a small gymnasium on the second floor, many times they played their games on an outdoor court, to allow more fans to see the games. The brick company even put up lights and they played night games. In 1925, the school was admitted to the Kentucky High School Athletic Association. Both boys and girls basketball began that year. The girls uniforms consisted of middies, bloomers, and bandannas, and the team was competitive from the beginning. The girls team was called the "Blue-Belles" and the original team players were Linnie Cline, Lucy Cline, Emma Bowen, Olive Bowen, Beatrice Eldridge, Deloris Eldridge, Edith Vencill, and Evelyn Stinson.

During '27-'28 and '29, other outstanding players joined the team. Those girls included Gineva Adkins, Clonia Hicks, Bessie Cline, and Emma Hayes. During those three years the girls scheduled teams such as Mt. Sterling, Ashland, Georgetown, Maysville, and Mayslick. (Mayslick and Ashland were considered the best in the state.) The girls were district finalists for four years and regional finalists two years.

The boys team was known as the "Leopards." Their basketball team had fancy new modern uniforms. They included large blue blankets with "Haldeman" printed diagonally across them. (They were needed on the bench on the outdoor court at night.) These were used as "warm ups" as they sat on the bench. The same boys remained on the team for four years. They included John Harris, Willard Harris, Ora Cline, Curtis Stinson, John Eldridge, Harlan Bocook, Denver Eldridge, Willie Stamper and William Caudill. That team won the district championship four years and were defeated in the final game of the regional tournament three times (never by more than three points).

FACTORY FORMED ATHLETIC ASSOCIATION

Some of the reasons the early Haldeman basketball teams were so successful was that Roy Holbrook was a brilliant coach. Also, he had the support of Superintendent J.H. Powers and the community, including Mr. Haldeman and his brick plant. (Mr. Holbrook said that Mr. Haldeman was the greatest humanitarian he had ever known, and he supported all phases of education.) The 300 brick-plant employees formed the Haldeman Athletic Association and $1 monthly dues were deducted from their salary. (That was a well financed athletic program.) The dues allowed each family member free admission to all school athletics. The brick plant also had their own semi-pro baseball team supported by these dues. By paying dues, the families were also permitted free use of their park and recreational facilities, including tennis, horseshoes, marbles, and basketball. Haldeman was one of the leading centers for parks and recreation in this area.

The Haldeman High School Basketball team was the envy of all the schools in the region. It was a successful program, and in their first four years, the boys won 70 games and lost 25 games. The girls won 83 and lost 14. Coach Holbrook said that when he was transferred from Haldeman to Morehead High School in 1929, there was $3,100remaining in the Haldeman High School Athletic

Fund. Also, the school continued to be successful after he moved to Morehead.

FIRST MASTERS DEGREE

In September 1929, both Morehead and Haldeman consolidated (12 grade schools) opened with record enrollments. Morehead's total enrollment was 313. (79 in the H.S.) Haldeman totaled 283 (32 in the H.S.). Also, there was the assurance more students would enroll later. Morehead and Haldeman were then a fully accredited 4-year high school.

In 1929, Mr. A.F. McGuire was the principal of the Morehead High School, and Roy E. Holbrook returned to Morehead as principal of the elementary section. (Mr. Holbrook was also assigned as the high school coach.) There were 12 teachers assigned to the school.

Mr. H.W. Mobley was principal of the 12-grade Haldeman School. Also he was the first person to be hired in the Rowan County School System with a masters degree. He also taught mathematics. Mr. Roy E. Cornette was the assistant principal and taught history. There were a total of ten teachers in the school that year.

The Harlan Powers educational era (1914-1930) was both the best and the worst of times. The terrible teens (1914-1919) was a time of one and two room schools, shifting enrollment, and a narrow economic base. The decade of the 1920s was an era of consolidation, construction, and a broadening economic base. However, this increase in the economy did not provide a sufficient tax base to build schools, as well as support those already built. The rural schools suffered as a result of the new construction and consolidation.

TEACHERS PAY DELAYED

Teachers salaries suffered in spite of Mr. Powers struggle to maintain adequate salaries. Often times the sheriff could not collect taxes on time and get funds to the school board in time to pay teachers. The board sometimes could not even borrow money to pay teachers. This writer can remember his mother, a teacher during that time, having to "discount her check". That meant when the board did not pay her on time, she would go to the local bank and for a 50 cent fee, get the cash for her $60 monthly salary by signing her check over to the bank. (And people think this idea of check advance is something new.)

Mr. Powers was caught between the lack of funds to support schools and the needs of teachers and school. In 1929, he received an unfriendly audit by the Department of Education. He was not accused of doing anything wrong, but he paid theteachers their last month's check before they completed their record book for the year. That was a "no no" with the state, but Mr. Powers seemed to have compassion upon the teachers, and accepted them at their word. But sometimes they failed to get their record books in at all, which left Mr. Powers in an embarrassing position.

Although the two high schools built during Mr. Powers administration are now torn down, and there are no more one- or two-room schools, his influence remains. He worked tirelessly to provide a foundation for the future growth of education in Rowan County.

ROY E. CORNETTE ERA (1934-1946)

"Those who say there are no politics in education, would lie about other things also." Mark Twain

County school superintendents in Kentucky were elected by popular vote between 1892-1934. In 1934, the law was changed to permit each county's voters to elect four board members who then appointed a school superintendent. Also, in 1934, the law eliminated local school trustees and required teachers to be hired by the County School Board based upon their recommendation by the Superintendent. Recommendations were to be based upon education, experience and length of satisfactory service. No longer were local trustees involved in the process.

First Appointed Superintendent

Roy E. Cornette was the first Rowan School Superintendent appointed by a School Board in Rowan County. At the Rowan County School Board meeting on July 2, 1934, at 10:00 a.m., Roy E. Cornette, a teacher and principal at

Roy E. Cornette, Rowan County Superintendent 1934-1946.

Haldeman, presented his credentials to the school board and was unanimously voted a four-year contract at $150 per month. He then became the first Rowan County School Superintendent to be appointed by a school board. That school board consisted of D.B. Leadbetter, Chairman; and members I.E. Pelphrey, W.W. Hall, A.J. McKenzie, and J.L. Boggess. Mr. Boggess excused himself from voting because he was a relative of Mr. Cornette. (A practice that is now enforced by law.)

Roy Cornette was born in Carter County, but moved to Clearfield when he was five years old. He was the son of D.B. Cornette and Susan (Ward) Cornette. He attended the Rowan Public Schools, Morehead Normal School, and graduated from Morehead State College. He was a member of the first college football and baseball teams and was active in various campus clubs. He was married to Elsie Lee Hogge and they have one daughter, Margaret (Cornette) Morris. Mr. and Mrs. Cornette are buried in Lee Cemetery.

SCHOOLS CONSOLIDATED AND CLOSED

There have been 81 school buildings in the history of Rowan County. Not all 81 schools existed at the same time. However, school consolidation had decreased that number to 55 when Mr. Cornette was appointed. Spurred by the State Department of Education, he continued the predecessors' policy of school consolidation, which was as controversial then as it is now.

Rodburn in the late 1800s and early 1900s had a large sawmill, lumber and milling plant that employed 400 men. It was also a rail center for shipping timber products. Therefore, it had a four-room school at one time. But by 1935, after the timber was all gone, their school was closed. That was the case of many schools in 1935, and it was known as the year of the great Rowan County School consolidation. 1935 was Roy Cornette's first full year as Superintendent and he "hit the ground running" and wasted no time in consolidating schools.

The Rowan County School Board at their September 5, 1935, meeting, moved into territory where "angels feared to tread." They decreed that the following program be adopted:

1. That the Bluestone School be reduced to a two-teacher school and grades 7 and 8 be transported to Farmers School.
2. That Rodburn and Gayheart Schools be discontinued and the students transported to the Morehead Consolidated School.
3. That Glenwood School be discontinued and the students transported to Haldeman.
4. That Sharkey School be discontinued and children be transported to Little Brushy and Morehead.
5. That Bradley and Open Fork Schools be discontinued with children transported to Seas Branch and Elliottville.
6. That Sand Gap and Minor School be discontinued and

     students be transported to Elliottville.

7. That high schools at Farmers and Elliottville be discontinued and students transported to Morehead. (That did not happen for many years.)

8. That provisions be made for a temporary building at Perkins, and that temporary permits be secured to maintain all other emergency schools in the county.

9. Those closures saved $3,000 per year.

The above was the official policy for consolidation of Rowan County Schools in 1935. Many of those plans were not implemented for several years. But their plan was controversial and met with a great deal of opposition by parents (and teachers).

Farmers Consolidated School built by W.P.A. federal program, 1937.

PRINCIPAL DEFENDS CONSOLIDATION

     Mr. Frank Laughlin, principal of Haldeman Consolidated School, ably defended the Board's action to consolidate rural schools in a letter to the *"Morehead Independent"* on April 11, 1935, stating:

"School consolidation in some parts of the county has been met with disapproval of a few because they do not seem to grasp the advantages it offers a child. If you are not acquainted with it, I invite you to visit a county where this has taken place and you can readily see the advantage it offers. Any fair minded citizen can then see the advantages it offers." Also, he pointed out it would be much more cost effective and since that was during the dark days of the depression, money was really tight.

Certainly consolidation did save money, but in 1935, the school board finished the year in the red, and had to borrow $1,500 from the Peoples Bank in order to pay teachers their last month's check.

SCHOOLS CLOSE - TEACHERS HIRED

Closing local schools was hard to accept because the local school was the center of the entire social life of the community. It was used for political "speakings", religious revivals, pie suppers, farm and club meetings, and adult education centers. It was the hub of the rural communities, and when these schools were closed, the community lost its sense of identity. But the School Board and Superintendent believed they were doing what was best for the children. Also, state education officials refused to finance those schools except on an emergency basis.

On April 15, 1935, Superintendent Roy Cornette made his historic recommendations to employ the following teachers based upon their training, experience, and previous satisfactory service:

Morehead - Dennie D. Caudill, Principal; Grace Crosthwaite; Austin Riddle; Anna Jane Day; Buell Hogge; Marie Howard; Mabel Alfrey; Virginia Christian; Ella Mae Boggess; Mae Meadows; Mildred Blair; Norma Powers; Beulah Williams; and Clara Bruce.

Haldeman - Frank Laughlin, Principal; Nell Cassity; Hildreth Maggard; Mary Jo Blair; Ellen Hudgins; Lawrence Fraley; Mrs.

Lee Clark; Emogene Hogge; Margaret Stewart; Evelyn Stinson; Bessie Cline; and Mrs. John Kelley.

Farmers - Clarence Allen, Principal; Beulah Burrows; Christine Hall; Mrs. L.E. Blair; and Howell Howard.

Elliottville - John D. Caudill, Principal; Grace Lewis; Orville Caudill; and Mabel Hackney.

County Attendance Officer - Mr. Glenmore Hogge was appointed the first Attendance Officer in Rowan County at a salary of $100 per month.

Rural Schools - There were 64 teachers employed that year to staff the 55 rural schools.

MOREHEAD HIGH GRADUATES

In 1935, Morehead High School graduated 21 girls and 5 boys. It was their largest graduating class to date. Those graduates were: Madeline Alderman, Austin Alfrey, Opal Alfrey, Roger Barber, Bernice Barker, Clarcie Baire, Grace Branham, Lucy Brown, Virgil Caudill, Stella Crager, Miriam Conley, Thelma Fraley, Ivan Gregory, Dorothy Hill, Harold Jones, Vivian Lewis, Aileen McKenzie, Pearl Mocabee, Iva Lee Oakley, Lurline Penix, Mae Robinson, Matilda Roseberry, Edna Thomas, Dorothy Turner, Nancy Ward, and Anna Mae Young. Dorothy Turner was valedictorian and Thelma Fraley was salutatorian.

POLITICS RAMPANT

The 1934, school legislation required counties to eliminate local trustees and vote on county school board members. They would hire the superintendent and he would hire the teachers. That was designed to eliminate "politics in the schools." It did not. Superintendent Cornette was known to insist that teachers work to elect a school board member favorable to him. If a teacher did not support his school board members, they would usually find they had been assigned to the most isolated rural school in the county. (Banished to the Siberias of Rowan County.)

In 1936, Sam Caudill, W.H. Bradley, and William H. Layne were elected to the board. (All favorable to Mr. Cornette.) I. E. Pelphrey resigned, and O.J. Clay filled his position.

In 1937, W.H. Bradley resigned to take the position of custodian of Morehead High School at $65 per month.

In 1938, James Fraley and Hendrix Tolliver were elected to the board, and the next year Mr. Cornette's salary was increased to $200 per month.

FIRST WOMAN ELECTED

In 1941, Clyde White and Erna Crabtree were elected to the board. Although Rowan County had two female superintendents (Cora Wilson and Lyda Messer), Mrs. Crabtree was the first woman to be elected to the Rowan County School Board.

Mr. Cornette maintained strong board support throughout his tenure. He had to, especially during his early years in office, because of the many major consolidation and construction programs he initiated.

KERA "DE-JA-VU" ALL OVER AGAIN

A teacher today, struggling with KERA, might be happy to know that KERA is not new to Kentucky. The first KERA (Kentucky Emergency Recovery Act) was passed in 1932. It was referred to as K.E.R.A. and was the vehicle to assist in local economic recovery in Kentucky as a result of the Great Depression. KERA was an attempt to put people to work with money supplied from the state and federal government to build roads, bridges, buildings, and utilities. Also, a portion of that program permitted the hiring of teachers. From 1932-1935, over 1,400 unemployed teachers in Kentucky were put to work teaching adults and nursery school children. That program ended in December 1935, but was taken over by the W.P.A. (Works Progress Administration). Although at the time it was called "we piddle around," by many local people, it was a great help to many Rowan County citizens as well as helping

Morehead High School Sewing Class, 1941. Fr.: Aurola Kegley, Hazel Ellis, Anna L. Johnson, Dorothy Swim Deloris Lewis. R.: Clara McKinney, Lucille McKenzie, Lillian Hamilton, Juanita Maxey, and Olive Fouch.

schools. A sewing center was established in Rowan County that hired women to sew clothing for needy school children. Their goal was that every child in the county have clothing enough to attend school. A cannery under the direction of Mrs. W.H. Rice, was established on East U.S. 60. People could work in the cannery and can their own food. That helped to insure that the needy people might have food during the winter.

EDUCATION: DEPRESSION, FLOOD & WAR

"Education is an ornament in prosperity, and a refuge in adversity." (Aristotle)

School Superintendent Roy Cornette was quick to tap every source available to employ teachers, and build buildings. He hired teachers to teach adult education and kindergarten classes. Over 250 enrolled in 14 adult classes in 1935. The Adult Education Program was under the direction of Ted L. Crosthwaite. Such classes as journalism, typing, shorthand, automobile mechanics, dancing, (35 students enrolled in social and tap dancing taught by Marge

Thomas), literature and music. On September 28, Ira Caudill started an adult class in the church building near the Razor School. Seventeen adults were enrolled in Bible courses, music, and general education. Adult education in Rowan County schools, began under Cora Wilson Stewart, and continued under Roy Cornette, with financing through KERA (Kentucky Emergency Recovery Act).

BROAD COMMUNITY SUPPORT

By 1936, Mr. Cornette realized if he were to be successful in his planned program of closing, consolidating, and building schools, he had to have more community support. He visited every school, every year, talking to parents about their school. He established a "clean up" day in every school and encouraged parents and teachers to clean and beautify their schools. The program was so successful that Mr. Taylor Ellington, local photographer, visited many of those schools recording their progress on film.

SCHOOL NEWS PUBLISHED

Superintendent Cornette appointed a school advisory committee made up of the presidents of local clubs, and other civic, business and professional leaders from throughout the county. He also began a powerful public relations program by publishing a quarterly paper, *Rowan County School News*. It published local school news and encouraged pride of school and community. The paper was distributed to every school in the county.

In the December 3, 1936, edition of the *Rowan County School News*, Mr. Cornette wrote:

> "In the past two weeks I have visited the following schools: Sharkey, Little Brushy, Big Brushy, Lower Lick Fork, Upper Lick Fork, Perkins, Slab Camp, Wess Cox, Rosedale, Ditney, and Bratten Branch. In the whole I found these schools in good condition, and

attendance high. It is my aim to give the rural schools in this county every bit of help that our limited budget will allow." (Many of those schools were closed within two years, as a result of consolidation.)

In the 1930s, schools were urged to organize parent support groups--and the PTA was born in Rowan County during that era. Farmers PTA was organized October 31, 1936. Austin Riddle was the principal. Mrs. Joe Peed was elected President; Mary Alice Calvert, Treasurer; and Mrs. Lillie Ingram, Vice President. They wasted no time in scheduling a pie supper fundraiser for November 15. The refreshments committee was Mrs. Lillie Ingram, Mrs. Warren May and Mrs. Harold Pelphrey. This group was strong supporters of the coming consolidation.

BARRIERS TO CONSOLIDATION

The biggest barrier to closing rural schools was the poor road conditions. When Mr. Cornette began as superintendent, most of Rowan's roads were impassible in winter. Many roads followed creek beds, others were mud holes, mountain trails or had ruts three feet deep. However, with the aggressive road building of the CCC camps, and KERA (Kentucky Emergency Recovery Act), many roads were graded, widened, and covered with limestone gravel. That made the roads passable year round. It also made possible closing rural schools, and transporting pupils to larger schools with better facilities, equipment, materials, and teaching. (One teacher to each grade, rather than one teacher for 8 grades). It also made possible high school programs in Haldeman, Farmers, and Elliottville. (Morehead already had a high school program)

1930 INTENSIVE BUILDING

The federal programs of putting people to work (WPA) made it financially possible to build new schools in Rowan during the late 1930s.

Morehead High School Senior Trip to Carter Caves 1942.

During the next three years, three new modern buildings were built by the WPA at federal expense. These building were located at Haldeman, Elliottville, and Farmers. Each housed high school programs as well as eight grades. They were constructed of native stone from nearby quarries. The three buildings were of very similar size, style and construction. Each was about 168 feet long, 101 feet wide, and, with some exceptions, each had six classrooms, a basement, gymnasium, stage, dressing rooms, and equipment. (Each building still stands today although Farmers is the only one in use by the school board.) Those buildings served their purpose well by relieving a crowded school population, and providing a better educational program for students. The total cost of the three new schools was $145,000 with the federal government paying $100,000 of that expense.

RECORD ROWAN ENROLLMENT

In 1938, the Kentucky General Assembly enacted more stringent legislation regarding compulsory school attendance in the public schools. It held parents responsible for keeping their children between the ages of 7 and 16 in regular school attendance. The penalty was a $10 fine for the first offense, and $20 for each subsequent offense. (Many parents were fined during that era, and they got the message.) Therefore, with the new law in effect, and Mr. Glenmore Hogge, the new attendance officer, the schools began to overflow. In 1939, there were 5,225 students enrolled in the schools.

In October, 1939, an evaluation and survey of the Rowan County Schools was completed by Morehead State College's Dean W. H. Vaughn and Professor H.C. Haggan. The results were published by public relations director, Alton Payne. A summary of the results were:

1. Rowan County, encompassing 275 square miles and a population of 10,893, had an enrollment of 5,225 in the public schools. (That represented an increase of 100%, from 1931, when the enrollment was 2,424.) In 1939, there were 1,275 students in the four consolidated school, and 3,950 enrolled in rural schools.
2. A full-time home economics and agriculture teacher had been added, and a full-time music teacher dropped.
3. There was no full-time art or band teacher.
4. The average teacher had three years of college.
5. The bonded indebtedness of the board was $62,000, compared to 8 years ago when it was $97,000.
6. 625 students were being transported.
7. Rowan County's annual school budget in 1939 was $107,271.95.

The report congratulated Mr. Cornette and the school board for their excellent educational progress. Dean Vaughn concluded the report by saying:

"Rowan County and Morehead citizens have every right to be proud to their school system, which, for the size of the system, ranks second to none in their section of the state."

This report seemed to vindicate Superintendent Cornette's efforts at consolidation and rural school closing. He was given another four-year contract by the school board.

WAR YEARS 1941-1945

Between 1934 and 1940, county school board members were elected on at-large basis. However, in 1940, the law changed requiring counties to be divided into five districts with a board member elected from each district. That made the board members more representative of the total population.

In 1940, the nation's economy began a strong recovery from the depression years. Starting that year, many families moved away from Rowan County to Ohio, Indiana, and Illinois. That resulted in a decline in students, which continued for many years. That exodus from the county increased even more on December 7, 1941, as America went to war.

The war years (1941-1945) was a time of turmoil and trauma in the Rowan County Schools. Sixteen-year-old boys and girls could go north and get a job in a war plant making more money than teachers were paid. Seventeen and eighteen-year-old boys were drafted (or volunteered) into the military. Girls 16-18 went away to work in defense plants. In 1940, 140 freshmen enrolled in Morehead High School and only 22 graduated in 1944. Many teachers resigned to work in the war effort, or entered military service. Food, clothing, gasoline, electric, tires, and many other things were rationed. There was a shortage of paper, ink, and school supplies. There were no school newspapers or yearbooks printed. Clubs and other activities were curtailed. Very few school plays were produced. Boys basketball was the only sport that continued during most of those years. Many games were played in the afternoon and only 10 boys traveled in taxis to their away games (taxis could get gasoline.) The four cheerleaders were transported by parents who saved their gasoline stamps. There was very little record of any high school activities during those years. When boys who would have been playing high school sports were dying in battle, sports didn't seem that important in the total scheme of things. (This writer graduated from Morehead High School in 1944 and entered the Army Air Corps in July, 1944.) School didn't seem too important then.

WW II YEARS OF SHORTAGES

Superintendent Cornette who had provided leadership for the Rowan Schools throughout the depression years, was now called upon to lead them through the war years. But Mr. Cornette had learned during the depression years to do more with less. Therefore, he now had to do more and more with less and less during the years of shortages and sacrifices of W.W. II.

It was difficult to get enough teachers during those years. However, high schoolgraduates were issued emergency certificates to teach in Rowan Schools. Retired teachers and former teachers came back to the classroom. Each teacher accepted larger class sizes, and the schools were kept open.

Transportation was a problem then as it is now. But the problems were different. Then there was a shortage of buses (none were manufactured). Also there was a shortage of parts, gasoline, tires, and skilled mechanics. But the buses were kept running. Now the school transportation problems are icy roads, and the behavior of the students, or the threats of children's safety to and from school. However, problems in those days, were the shortages of coal needed to heat the schools, and getting that coal to the schools when it was needed. There was great interest shown by many people when the bids for the schools coal contracts were opened. It was one of the major school expenses every year, and many people attended those bid openings.

Roy Cornette was Rowan County superintendent for 12 years, through very few good times, and mostly bad times. He was a natural born leader who was friendly, out-going, and personable.

He had an excellent sense of humor, and always had a funny anec-
dote to illustrate the point he wanted to make. During part of his
tenure, "Hoss" Sorrell was the County Jailor. Hoss was a large man
who wore a size 48. He lived in the jail with his family. While he
was the jailor, Roy's office window looked out over Hoss' family
clothes lines. Many times Hoss's size 48 long handled red underwear would be hanging on the clothesline. Roy called him laughing one day and said, "Hoss at least when you hang your old
flanneled underwear on the line, button up the rear flap."

Mabel Alfrey, former teacher, principal, and attendance officer
in Rowan County, referred to Roy Cornette in her book, *The Hite
Place* said, "He had an innate quality without knowing it, to organize and promote an educational system that was the envy of surrounding counties." Mr. Troy Jennings, Rowan County Judge, one
said, "Roy's era as school superintendent was known as an era of
good feeling." Bob Bishop said, "Roy could get more done with
less than anyone I know. He was one of the best friends and one of
the best superintendents we ever had."

Roy received a new four-year contract in 1946, and promptly
resigned to go into business. He went out of office at the peak of
his career. He should be remembered as one who provided school
leadership during the great depression and the war years. Also, he
helped build a solid foundation for today's excellent Rowan County
School System.

Schools

1	Adams Davis	8	Brady
2	Alfrey	9	Bull Fork
3	Big Brushy	10	Carey
4	Blue Bank	11	Charity
5	Bluestone	12	Christy
6	Bradley	13	Clark
7	Bratton Branch	14	Cranston

15 Crix
16 Clearfield I *
17 Clearfield II *
18 Clearfield III *
19 Clearfork
20 Cogswell
21 Craney
22 Ditney
23 DryCreek
24 Elliottville I *
25 Elliottville II *
26 Elliottville III *
27 Farmers I *
28 Farmers II *
29 Farmers III *
30 Freestone
31 Gates
32 Gearhart
33 Glenwood
34 Haldeman I *
35 Haldeman II *
36 Haldeman III *
37 Haldeman High School *
38 Hardyman
39 Holly
40I sland Fork
41 Johnson
42 Little Brushy
43 Little Perry
44 Lower Lick Fork
45 McKenzie
46 Minor
47 Moore
48 Morehead I *

49 Morehead II *
50 Morehead III *
51 Morehead Middle School*
52 Morehead High School *
53 Morehead (Colored) *
54 Morehead Illiterate *
55 Mt. Hope
56 New Home
57 Oak Grove
58 Old House Creek
59 Open Fork
60 Perkins
61 Pine Grove
62 Pond Lick
63 Popular Grove
64 Ramey
65 Razor
66 Rock Fork
67 Rodburn I *
68 Rodburn II *
69 Rodburn III *
70 Rose Dale
71 Rowan County Senior High
72 Sand Gap
73 Seas Branch
74 Sharkey
75 Slab Camp
76 Tabor Hill
77 Tackett
78 Three Lick
79 Tilden Hogge
80 Upper Lick Fork
81 Waltz Wess Cox

*Separate generations of school buildings

"In a race, everyone runs but only one person gets first prize. So run your race to win. To win the contest you must deny yourself many things that would keep you from doing your best." **I Cor 9:24-25A**

CHAPTER SIX

High School History: Sports, Bands, Drama
"Sports Camels" in Educational Tents

There is an ancient Arabic legend about a man's camel that got his nose inside his tent. The man did not object because the desert nights were cold and the camel was help to him. The next night the camel got his neck in the tent, and although the tent was crowded, the man allowed the camel to stay. The third night the camel came completely inside and so dominated the tent, that there was little room for the man. The moral of the story seemed to be: Don't give too much to something designed to help you or it may dominate you. Many people believe that is what has happened to sports in America. The sports camel has gotten his nose into the educational tents, and now dominates our schools.

BASEBALL CAME FIRST

Sports and schools are closely connected in today's culture. But the close relationship of education and athletics is a relatively new phenomenon in Rowan County. When did this connection between sports and schools begin in our schools? How did it begin? Has it been positive or negative? Let's look at some of those questions. Baseball was the first sport to appear in the Rowan County schools. In the early history of Rowan rural schools, baseball was the first sports camel to get its nose into the schools. Usually the teacher would purchase a baseball (or students furnished a ball), and the older students would make a home-made bat. The rest of the equipment consisted of a face mask and catcher's mitt. Ball-gloves were rare, and consisted of a poorly padded piece of leather. Inter-squad games or one-eyed cat (a game with only 1 base and home plate and fewer than 9 players) were played during the lunch hour. (Many of the girls would also play.) Balls were seldom lost even in the rough brush around the playing area. If a ball was temporarily lost, the whole school would search until it was found. The ball would usually be taped several times until the yarn was completely un-ravelled around the core, and part of the cover was flapping loose around the ball. There was just no equipment available in those early days, but the children really enjoyed the game. Rocks were used for bases and the backstop was usually a "pig tail" (that was a sub-player who stood way behind the catcher and stopped the wild pitches).

TEACHERS COACHED AND UMPIRED

If the teachers happened to be sports minded, and, if the students had been on their best behavior, there would be an occasional inter-school game on Friday afternoon. The game was usually played in a pasture field half way between schools. In the early part of the 1900s in Rowan County, there were some games between schools such as Alfrey, McKenzie, Charity and Mt. Hope. Over the years, teachers in those schools included Dot Ellis, Davis Ellis, Aileen McKenzie, Asa B. Crosthwaite, Grace Crosthwaite, Loren Crosthwaite, and many others. Sometimes the intense competition resulted in heated arguments. But the teachers settled those arguments as they umpired from behind the pitchers mound. (This writer's mother, uncles, and aunts were teachers in some of those schools, and they said the children felt a sense of pride in their schools.) Although there were no cheerleaders, there was school spirit in players and spectators.

First sports team in Rowan County Schools. Clearfield Baseball Team of 7th and 8th graders, 1914. F. L-R: Lonnie McClanahan, Roy Cornette, Jesse Stewart, Henry Rogers. C. L-R: Cecil Bowls, Everett Abbott, Russell Bowls, Arthur Warren. R. L-R: Earl Cornette, Vernon Alfrey.

LEAGUE FORMED IN ELEMENTARY SCHOOLS

In 1914, Clearfield School had a well organized baseball team, and was the first school with a sports team in Rowan County. Not only did they have some equipment, such as bats, balls, gloves, catcher's mask and mitt, but they also had uniforms, including caps. In 1914, the Morehead and North Fork Railroad and the Clearfield Lumber Company made Clearfield a wealthy community. Many of Rowan County's more affluent citizens lived in Clearfield, and they supported their school baseball teams. Also, instead of just nine players, they had ten, which meant they had one substitute in case anyone was ineligible. Although none of those

7th and 8th graders ever went to the major leagues, many of them went on to play college and semi-pro baseball

By 1916, the more populated areas with 3 or 4 room elementary schools, organized, practiced, and formed what could loosely be called an inter-scholastic baseball league. Morehead, Clearfield, Farmers, Elliottville, and Haldeman were among those early teams. Even in those early days teachers used sports to improve grades, discipline, and attendance. Because any student who was having problems in those areas was not permitted to play in those Friday afternoon games. (That seemed to be the beginning of athletic eligibility requirements in Rowan County).

Like it or not, before WWI (1918), the "proverbial sports camel" had got his nose in the "educational tent" in the Rowan County schools. That "camel" slowly but surely increased its presence within the educational tent, until today it is difficult to determine where the "camel" ends and the educational tent begins. But those innocent early baseball games were only just the beginning of a "marriage" of academics and athletics in Rowan County schools.

BASKETBALL BEGINS

While baseball was the first sport played in Rowan's schools, it soon became less prominent because of the large amount of land and equipment needed to field a team. Also the men begin to play the sport of baseball and each community fielded an independent team. Therefore, baseball began to "die out" in county schools, only to be replaced by an even bigger "sports camel"-basketball. (Basketball did not require as many players, as much space or equipment.) At the time baseball was the sports "king" there were no public high schools in Rowan County. Therefore, baseball began in the elementary schools. But as high schools were built in Rowan County, basketball began in the high schools.

First Morehead High School Gym opened in 1929.

HIGH SCHOOL GYM PLANNED

In 1921, Morehead High School became the first public high school in Rowan County. It was located in a white frame elementary building near Sun Street and Hargis Avenue. There were five students enrolled in the ninth grade. There were three girls: Effie Hall, Mary P'Simer, and Nell M. Cassity. With only two boys enrolled, Lionel Fannin and Jordan Caudill, the future of athletics at Morehead High School did not look promising.

In 1922, Warren C. Lappin was appointed principal of MHS, and that year, the second year of high school was offered. Mr. Lappin was the principal and taught every high school class that year. In 1922, Morehead was a city high school, but it became so expensive to operate that the county took over the school in 1923. They immediately built a new high school building. (But no gymnasium). In 1925, the first graduating class of Morehead High School graduated after three years. That class completed the fourth year at the Normal School. Those three students were Mary Jo Wilson, Lucille Caudill, and Joe McKinney. In 1926, there were 8 students in the graduating class. By 1928, the high school enrollment had increased to 80 (including 32 boys). With a growing high school, a new building and increased interest in athletics, plans were made for a new high school gymnasium.

The school board appointed Superintendent Harlan Powers, *Rowan County News* editor Jack Wilson, and board member Flam Reid as the building committee to supervise the construction. After a successful fund raising drive to help pay the costs, and with the support of local citizens, the building was staked off early in February. The construction committee immediately hired a foreman to supervise the construction. That was necessary for sound construction and to direct much of the volunteer labor that was used during the construction.

BASKETBALL GYM A COMMUNITY PROJECT

Many local citizens, high school students, and Normal School students worked on the building. The boys (many who would later play in the gym) eagerly dug footers, shoveled sand, mixed concrete, drove nails, and pushed wheel barrows. (It was really aschool and community project with everyone working together.) After the foundation was finished there was an old fashioned "barn raisin" in which local citizens came together to put up the walls and roofing. By everyone working together on MHS's first gymnasium it developed a real sense of community pride (perhaps that was the reason it was revered over the years by so many people).

The school board, in an attempt to help the building pay for itself, established a rental policy for community functions. The new Morehead State College basketball team practiced and played some of their games in the new gym before the college gym was constructed. After the building was paid for, it was available rent-free for community activities. Morehead residents were in general agreement at that time, that the opening of the new gymnasium was one of the most important steps that had been taken to build up the school and the city. Therefore, it appeared that the sports camel was back in the local educational tent for good. Basketball was the name of that new sports camel!

First Morehead High School Building opened in 1923.

MHS BASKETBALL BEGAN ON CINDER COURT

When Morehead High School opened the new classroom building on Second Street in 1923, there was no provision for athletics in the school. It appeared that the sports camel had been evicted from the educational tent. However, there was a vacant lot beside the school with outdoor basketball goals set up on a cinder court. (Baseball was not even considered because there was not a large enough land area.) Therefore, the basketball program at MHS began on a cinder court in 1925. Bob Bishop recalled, that as a child, he watched the team play on that cinder court beside the school. Roy Holbrook was the coach for a few months before moving to Haldeman. Warren C. Lappin then stepped in as coach and principal before moving to the new State College. At first there was little interest in sports. However, as the school grew in enrollment to 80, they grew tired of just an intramural program, and began to schedule other schools. Soon it became evident that an indoor basketball court was a necessity.

*First Morehead High Basketball Team to play in the new gym were known as the "Black Cats"
1928. F. L-R: Fred Caudill, Mason Jayne, Graydon Hackney. R. L-R: June Evans, Watt
Pritchard, Jr., Peck Robinson, Roy Cassity, Earl Barbour*

Interest in athletics by the community grew rapidly when the Morehead Normal School became a state college in 1923. Baseball, basketball, and football were planned for the new state college, and this helped increase the interest in sports at the new Morehead High School. Therefore, the local citizens began to push the County School Board for an indoor basketball arena.

GYM FINALLY COMPLETED

The County School Board met on December 12, 1927, and voted unanimously to build a new gymnasium on the vacant lot, adjacent to but not connected to, the new high school. (Parallel to Tippett Avenue between Second and Third Streets.) The outsidedimensions were 100 ft. long by 80 ft. wide. The size of the basketball court was 80 ft. long and 60 ft. wide. At the time of construction, it was considered one of the largest high school courts in the state. (It was the Rupp Arena of its time.) It also served as a multi-purpose building with a stage at one end and seating for about 200 in bleachers on each side. The building was heated by four pot-bellied coal stoves (one in each corner).

Teams playing in the new gym had to be careful and not run into those pot-bellied stoves, because you could be badly burned as they were so close to the playing area.

There were team dressing rooms inside but no water in the gym. Therefore, there were no provisions for showering in the new gym. Later on dressing rooms and showers were added in the basement of the high school building. That made it necessary to dress in your basketball uniforms in the school building and come outside through snow, rain, and slush to get into the gym. But no one seemed to mind, because everyone was happy with the new facilities.

HOLBROOK RETURNS TO COACH BLACK CATS

In 1929, Roy Holbrook, the successful coach of the Haldeman boys and girls basketball teams, returned to Morehead High school and accepted the coaching duties as well as assistant principal. The fans and students were excited about having a new high school building and new gymnasium.

The opening of the new MHS gymnasium in 1929, brought a new era of sports into Rowan County. The boys had been playing on the outdoor cinder court for four years, and the team even had a name. No the first MHS athletic teams were not called Vikings, they were the "Black Cats". They were given the name of "Black Cats" for several reasons. (1) The Wildcats were already taken by U of K, and Owingsville High School; (2) The Tom Cats were already taken by Ashland High School; and (3) The team had played for four years on a black coal cinder based court, and believe me after playing a few minutes on that type of court with all the black coal dust and cinders, you were sweaty and black all over. This

First Morehead High School Girls Basketball Team known as the "Tabbies", 1931. F. L-R: Grace Evans, Mildred Caudill, Ruth Holbrook, Bertha Hall. C. L-R: Katherine Jackson, Edna McDaniels, Reba Caudill. R. L-R: Roy Holbrook, Coach, Altas Fraley, Maxine Elam, Nell Caudill, Athel Fraley, Lola Williams, Hildreth Maggard, Asst. Coach.

writer, as a child, used to play on Sonny Allens' cinder court in his back yard after school. (That's where Sonny developed much of his skills as a player). But we would all get black and sweaty playing on that cinder court that you could see why the first MHS team was called the "Black Cats". Although the first MHS boys team was known as the "Black Cats", however, the girls team was known as the "Tabbies".

GIRLS BASKETBALL POPULAR

The 1929 MHS girls basketball season opened on Friday, November 21, with a home game against Soldier in the new High School gym. Coach Roy E. Holbrook announced that sixteen Tabbies were attempting to make the squad. The competition for a

spot on the team was keen, because only 8 girls were to be selected. Those eight girls proved to be more than enough as they
trounced the girls from Soldier 22-12. That team went on to become one of the most successful teams in MHS history. (Girls sports
were stopped in the early 1930s because it was considered too
strenuous for the so called weaker sex.)

The 1929 MHS boys basketball season opened that same night
immediately following the girls game. There were 22 boys that had
tried out for the team, and only eight were selected by Coach
Holbrook . But those mighty eight were enough to soundly defeat
Soldier HS in their first game, and go into a very successful season.

There was standing room only at the opening game. Although
Soldier HS had several fans, the crowd was strongly supporting
the home team. Coach Holbrook thanked the fans for their support and asked them to continue to support the team. The admis-

*Morehead High School Basketball Team known as "Vikings", 1938. Front L-R: Junior Mutters,
Maurice Brown, Allie Rose, Charles Roe, Hobart Barbour. Rear L-R: Earl Bradley, Robert
Tackett, James Butcher, Ovel Johnson, Lloyd Brown, Clifford Barker.*

sion charged for that game was 25 cents for students and 35 cents for adults. That seems expensive for that time but basketball fever had struck Rowan County and both students and townspeople packed the new gym.

SPORTS CAMELS IN EDUCATION TENTS: FOOTBALL ARRIVES

"Rejoiceth as a strong man to run a race" (Ps. 19:5)

Morehead High School existed from 1922-1962. It was the first high school established in Rowan County. Other public high schools that later existed in Rowan County were Farmers, Elliottville, and Haldeman. As those high schools closed, Morehead remained the only public high school in the county. In 1962, the name Morehead High School was changed to Rowan County High School. This is the continuing history of sports at Morehead High School.

FIELD FIRST FOOTBALL TEAM

The year 1929 was the third year of competition for the MHS basketball Black Cats; however, it was the first year for the football Black Cats. The cost of fielding a football team was much more than the cost for a basketball team. Coach Holbrook saidthat the cost for basketball uniforms and equipment would be less than $100; but the cost of fielding a football team was estimated at $600. But the Morehead Squad was able to field a football team for $250 by purchasing second-hand equipment. However, it was still necessary to raise an additional $250 before a football team could take the field. Also, it was necessary to have a playing field. Their practice field was directly behind the High School and the teams dressed in the gymnasium. (Their games were played on the college field.)

Money was raised through the sale of season tickets. The cost of a season ticket was $1.50, while the cost of attending each individual home game totaled $2.50.

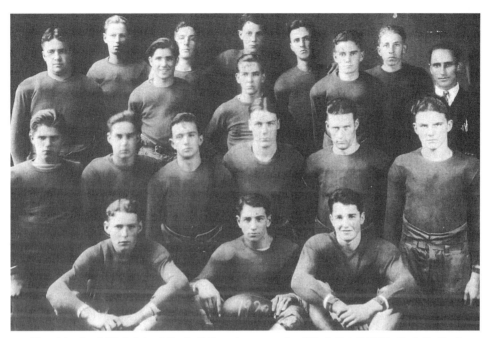

First Morehead High School Football Team known as the "Black Cats" 1929. Fr. L-R: Curt Caudill, Drew "June" Evans, Graydon Hackney. Second Row: "App" Honaker, Earl Barber, Fred Cassity, Alden "Peck" Robinson, Mason "Fuzzy" Jayne, Watt Pritchard Jr., Third Row: Dick Clay, Arch Cassidy, Earl Caskey, William Caudill, Roy "Pappy" Holbrook, Coach, Fourth Row: Eugene Miles, Roy Cassity, Arthur "Bub" Tatum, Arthur Barber, Clay Trumbo.

The 1929 schedule for the Morehead High School football Black Cats was: September 27, Grayson-away; October 5, open; October 12, Olive Hill-away; October 26, Grayson-home; November 2, Olive Hill-home; November 8, Boyd County-home; and November 16, Greenup County-home. All games were Friday afternoon games, and Coach Holbrook urged the local fans to support the Black Cats at home and away. Coach Holbrook announced that "although this was their first year, the team was practicing hard and were beginning to resemble a football machine." But they would be playing teams that had played football for several seasons and it would be difficult competing with experienced teams.

BLACK CATS PLAY FIRST GAME

On September 27, 1929, a large contingent of local fans followed the Black Cats east to Grayson on the newly opened Midland Trail (U.S. 60). They wanted to see the first football game ever played by Morehead High School. That historical first football team was both big and fast. But they were obviously in-experienced. Some of the boys that played in that game had never even seen a football game, let alone played in one. But players with such last names as: Barbour, Miles, Clay, Cassity, Honaker, Trumbo, Robinson, and Evans gave everything they had in a losing effort. They lost 14-0. They were determined to improve as the season progressed.

SCRIMMAGED MOREHEAD COLLEGE

One of the reasons the football team was unable to improve was the level of competition in practice. There were only 16 boys on the team, and they could not even scrimmage. However, that problem was remedied when a practice game was scheduled each Tuesday with the Morehead College Team. Fred Cassity, a running back on the High School team said: "The college would allow them to get close to the goal line, but would never allow the high school team to score. In one of those practice games, an official spotted a weakness in the college defense, and pointed it out to the high schoolteam. They immediately scored against the college. That touchdown lifted their confidence and the team improved.

Morehead won three games their first season. But the final game of the season (November 16) was a home game with Greenup. It was the green and white vs. the green and white. But the Morehead Black Cats overwhelmed the visitors by a score of 34-0. Therefore, it can be said that the "Football Camel" got its nose into the education tent in Rowan County in 1929.

SMALL ENROLLMENT LESS INTEREST

Throughout the early 1930s, interest in Morehead High School football began to wane. There were only a total of 50 boys enrolled in the High School and many of them had to work at home or on the farm. That did not allow much time for practice. This writer's uncle, Davis Ellis, who was a member of the high school football team, lived with us in town during the week and attended school. He would play a football game on Friday afternoon, and many times walk 13 miles to his home on Licking River to work on the farm during the weekend. (That was dedication.) Another reason interest in high school football slowed down was the competition presented by the new Morehead State College football program. Therefore, by 1934, football was almost dropped at MHS. Many players even turned in their uniforms thinking football was over at MHS. However, principal Denny Caudill, who was on leave attending Duke University, put those doubts to rest with the following letter dated August 15, 1935.

"MHS will continue football although greatly handicapped by small enrollment, lack of equipment, finances, competition for crowds and a playing field. Six games have been contracted, and two more will be added. We will continue football in hopes of building a team for the future, as well as give the boys who wish to do so, an opportunity to play the game. Also arrangements have been made to equip the team with new uniforms."

That decision was a landmark decision for sports at MHS. It provided the foundation for a solid sports program for the future.

BLACK CATS BECOME VIKINGS

By 1935, sports had gained a solid foothold at MHS, and the athletic teams were given a a new name. They became known as the "Vikings". That was a much stronger, bolder name than Black Cats. In addition to a new name, there was a new County Superintendent of Schools (Roy Cornette.) Also a new Principal, (Denny D. Caudill,) who believed in a strong athletic program. However, new coach (Coach Roy Holbrook had moved up to coach Breckinridge). Therefore, Austin Riddle was appointed MSH'sfirst Athletic Director. He also coached football and basketball, and was a graduate of MHS and MSC. Therefore with new faces in coaching and school administration, it appeared MHS was entering a new era of sports and education. But that did not prove to be the case.

FIRST CONFERENCE FORMED

In 1930, the Little Eight Conference was the first high school athletic conference organized in Eastern Kentucky. Charter members were Morehead High, Olive Hill, Prichard High (Grayson) Boyd County, Coles (Ashland), Raceland, Russell and Greenup. Although Greenup had a football team, it had no basketball team for several years. The conference allowed Haldeman to replace Greenup in basketball, since Haldeman did not field a football team. Later Coles withdrew, McKell became a probationary member, and Russell and Grayson dropped out of the conference. McKell later was suspended from the conference. Therefore, the first Athletic High School Conference in Eastern Kentucky was called "the Little Eight". However, it was soon succeeded by the "Little Six." MHS was a member of both conferences. Also, the Little Six Conference soon collapsed, and was replaced by another conference.

EAST KENTUCKY CONFERENCE FORMED

On September 12, 1935, representatives from high schools in Rowan, Carter, Boyd, Greenup and Lawrence Counties met at Ashland in the offices of the *Ashland Independent*. The purpose of that meeting was to form another High School Sports Conference. It was formed out of the collapse of the former Big 8 and Little 6 Conferences that never really were successful. They could have been considered conferences ahead of their time. Denny Caudill, MHS principal, was elected president, John McGlothin, principal of Ashland High School, was elected Vice President; and Brady Black, Sports Editor of the *Ashland Daily Independent* was elected secretary.

In order to become a charter member of that conference, the schools had to participate in football and basketball. (That eliminated the smaller schools.) Rules regarding scheduling, eligibility, number of players, officials, contracts and many more areas were established. Twelve high schools from five counties were charter members, (including MHS), of that first sports league. It was known as The Eastern Kentucky Conference (EKC). (The EKC is still alive and well in 1999).

TWO HIGH SCHOOLS IN MOREHEAD

Breckinridge (the College Demonstration School) declined the invitation to jointhe conference. At that time, Warren Lappin was on leave of absence attending the University of Chicago Graduate School. Coach Holbrook, speaking for him said, "Because of scheduling conflicts, uniqueness of our school, and the requirements of the conference, Breckinridge does not choose to join the EKC Conference". One of the main reasons that it was difficult to have a successful athletic program in Morehead during the 1930s was because there were two high schools. Both Rowan County and Breckinridge were small schools, with high school enrollments less than 100 students--half of which were boys. Also, only a few of those boys were interested in basketball. However, it was believed at that time, if the schools were combined, it could support a strong athletic program. But that would not happen for fifty years.

FIRST YEARBOOK PUBLISHED

By 1935, MHS was known for its sound and solid educational programs as well as athletics. A semi-weekly newspaper was published by the high school students. The name of that publication was *The Viking Voice*. Among those hard working students working to publish the school news were: Anna Mae Young, Dortha Hutchinson, Aileen McKenzie, Lurlene Penix, Hazel McKenney, Harvey Tackett, Della Crager, Monnie Fraley and Mary Alice Calvert. Excerpts from the 1935 *Viking Voice* listed the important events that year, eg.:

October 15	First MHS Alumni organized
October 29	First MHS P.T.A. organized
November 12	First MHS Library opened
December 10	New Library books received and a Christmas Program presented in the gymnasium
December 21	Christmas Vacation begins
January 14	Second Semester begins
February 11	Vikings get new uniforms
February 25	Vikings play Hitchins in District Tournament

SPORTS TEAMS HAD NO CHEERLEADERS

In 1935, MHS published its first school annual, and one issue has survived. The title of the annual was of course *The Viking*. That was the annual publication that was so cherished by graduating seniors. It included photographs of classes, clubs, faculty, and athletic teams. It was the 1935 *Viking* that published the earliest school song. Those words were designed to inspire and encourage both students as well as athletics. Although there was no evidence of cheerleaders in 1935, there must have been some that led the fans in singing that stirring song.

MOREHEAD HIGH SCHOOL "FIGHT SONG" 1935

We know you will fight, Morehead High,
We're green and white, Morehead High,
We'll back you to stand against the best in the land,
For we know you have sand, Morehead High, Rah! Rah!

Go crashing ahead, Morehead High,
Go smash that blockade, Morehead High,
Our team is our fame protector,
On, Boys, for we expect a victory from you, Morehead
High, Rah! Rah!

Fling out that dear old flag of green and white,
Lead on your sons and daughters, fighting for right,
Like men of age-old giants, placing reliance, shouting
defiance,
Oskey Wow-wow...

Amid the broad green plains that nourish our land,
For honest labor and for learning we stand,
And unto thee we'll pledge our heart and hand,
Dear alma mater, M.H.S.

MOREHEAD HIGH FOOTBALL WEAK

In 1935, the football teams of MHS and Breckinridge were not very successful. The MHS team consisted of names such as Whitt, Barbour, Hall, Tackett, Johnson, Carter, Justice, Calvert, Turner, Goodan, McKinney, Bowling, Reynolds, Calvert and Barker. (Only last names were listed in the line up). That team lost to Olive Hill 46-0. But the Breckinridge football team that year did poorly also.

The Breck Team consisted of: Tatum, Dillon, Young, Daugherty, Black, Allen, Long, Prichard, Elam, Johnson, Fraley, Caudill and Camp. Breck lost the same weekend in 1935 to Raceland 38-0. It was not a good year for football.

In 1936, Breck Coach Roy Holbrook, who had previously coached at MHS and Haldeman, returned to MHS as coach and math teacher. Breckinridge HS had ended their football program and was concentrating on basketball. Some of the football players atBreck transferred to MHS so they could continue playing football. (Paul J. Reynolds for one).

BASKETBALL GROWS STRONGER

Throughout the late 1930s, Coach Holbrook developed a strong basketball program. Although the team never reached the state tournament, they were regional runner-up. (Missed the state tournament by one game.)

The 1937-38 basketball team included: Jr. Mutters, Pete Brown, Allie Rose, Charles Roe, Hobert Barber, Earl Bradley, Robert Tacket, James Butcher, Oval Johnson, Lloyd Brown, and Clifford Barker. That squad won 14 games and lost 10. MHS lost to Breckinridge that year in the District Tournament. James Butcher was selected on the "all star" tournament team.

The B team that year was made up of Hubert Conley, Meredith Jones, Robert Kessler, Maxie Bowles, Bobby Holbrook, Homer Petitt, Jr. Mutters, Hobart Barber, and Claude Kessler. That team won 11 and lost 5. They also won the B Team tournament that year with three players selected for the all tournament teams: Barber, Kessler, and Holbrook. The future looked bright for MHS basketball.

1937 was a low point in MHS football. That team won one game and lost six, and only scored one touchdown all year. They beat Boyd County 7-0. Basketball began to grow stronger at MHS as football began to weaken. Lack of interest by players, fans, and competition from the outstanding college football teams would soon spell the end of an era in early football at MHS.

FOOTBALL DISCONTINUED

In 1939, football was discontinued at MHS because there were so few boys enrolled in school. Football would not reappear for over 20 years. Basketball then became the prime sports camel in the educational tent. But by 1940, something new appeared on the HS sports scene—cheerleaders. Three lovely young girls were elected to lead the crowd in yelling for their team. Those girls were Louise Adams, Rosa Caudill and Mildred McClurg. They rapidly became the "heart throbs" of all the boys at MHS. The strong support by students, fans, and cheerleaders, must have helped motivate the basketball team. That year, the team won 20 games and lost 7. However, they just could never make it to the State Tournament. The basketball team was defeated in the final game of the Regional Tournament several years. However, 1940 was considered one of MHS's best basketball teams. The leading scorers (total points scored) that year were: Clifford Barker (251); Bob Tackett (208), James Butcher (129), Charles Roe (121) and Bobby Holbrook (56).

In 1941, the last year of athletics at MHS before World War II, was one of school's best basketball teams. Their record that year was even better than the previous year. However, when it came tournament time, they were again defeated that year in the final game of the Regional Tournament by Catlettsburg in an overtime game. In that tournament, George Hill, one of the stars of the team, became too old the day before the final game, and was declared ineligible. Also, another outstanding player, Warren Hicks, was sick with the flu, and Bobby Holbrook, MHS's star guard, was sidelined much of that game with cramps. So once again MHS was destined to not make it to the state tournament.

WW II SLOWED SPORTS

December 7, 1941, the beginning of WW II, brought great change to America's sports scene. Not only colleges, but high school sports were greatly reduced. Boys were drafted into military service at age 18. There was also an urgent need for defense workers, and jobs were plentiful in the factories. Many boys knowing they would be taken into military service at age 18, dropped out of high school and worked in the defense plants until they were called into military service. However, high school basketball did continue during the war years.

SPORTS CAMELS IN EDUCATION TENTS
WW II YEARS

At the beginning of the decade of the 1940s, the future looked bright for MHS sports. Although football and girls basketball had been dropped as a sport, boys basketball was king in Kentucky. Also, it was the only "game in town" at MHS. Girls basketball had been dropped as a sport because it was considered too strenuous for young ladies. Also, there was no baseball, golf, soccer, tennis, track or any other inter-scholastic sport at MHS. It appeared that, except for basketball, the "sports camel" had just about been driven out of the educational tent in Rowan County.

WW II BROUGHT SHORTAGES

December 7, 1941, when this nation was attacked at Pearl Harbor, and WW II began, it was the beginning of basketball season. Immediately MHS boys at age 18 were eligible for the draft. Many did not wait to be drafted, but enlisted in the armed services. Many 16 and 17 year olds, knowing they would be entering the armed forces soon, dropped out of high school and went to work in northern defense plants. Girls also joined the exodus from high school to go to work, or enter the armed forces. Morehead High School enrollment was decimated during the years 1941-1945. (In 1940, 142 freshmen enrolled at MHS, but only 23 graduated in 1944, including only 7 boys.)   By 1942, it appeared that even basketball at MHS, might be dropped as an inter-scholastic sport. However, after Roy E. Holbrook, MHS's long time successful coach, resigned and took the coaching job at Catlettsburg, Kentucky, the school had difficulty finding a new coach. Most coaches were in the military service. Also there was rationing of food, gasoline, tires, shoes, and all means of transportation. All those sacrifices made basketball seem unimportant at the time. Also, the fact that young high school age boys were dying on the battlefields around the world, in an all out war, seemed to make basketball unimportant.

SPORTS IMPORTANT TO MORALE

As WW II continued, it was Superintendent Roy Cornette and Principal Ethel Ellington, that decided basketball was important to the morale of the students and athletes, and should be continued. In 1943, "Feets" Daugherty, an MSC graduate, and football player from Pennsylvania, was employed as principal at Farmers. He also served as basketball coach at MHS.

In the fall of 1942, some twenty-five boys showed up for the first basketball practice. Among them were Harold Holbrook, J.D. Hicks, Carl Christian, Ralph Christian, Quentin Hicks, Elman Riddle, Bill Bradley, Frank Burns, James Hall, and Jack Ellis. The cheerleaders were Thelma Roe, Ginny Amburgy, Bernice and Juanita Blair. During the war years, most home games were played in the afternoon. Travel to games at other schools was by taxi and private cars. (Because of the gasoline rationing, school buses could not be used.) During that school year, Coach Daugherty resigned for health reasons. He had a bad heart, and that is what had kept him out of the army. He died later that year. The school board then hired "Moose" Zachem, one of MSC's all time great football players, to finish out the season. Coach Zachem was from Mayfield, Kentucky, and he entered the military service as soon as the season ended.

BASKETBALL CONTINUED UNDER DIFFICULT CONDITIONS

In 1942-43, in spite of the change in coaches, the difficult playing conditions, and rationing, the basketball team had a fairly successful year. They won about 3/4s of their games that year. Among the highlights of that basketball season, was a win over the Jimmy Rose coached Olive Hill High School. (Their only loss that year until they were beaten in the semi-finals of the state tournament by eventual winner, Harlan County.) Also, that year, Harold Holbrook (Dr. Holbrook) scored 68 points against Soldier HighSchool. Harold was red hot that night and everyone fed him the ball. It seemed he couldn't miss. MHS won the game 122 to 29. Since it was played on their home court, there was almost a riot that night. Dr. Holbrook, in looking back on that game, said, "he was not really proud of what he did that night."

SCHOOL PUBLICATIONS CEASED

During the years of 1941-44, there was practically no press coverage of MHS sports. Also, there were no student publications, such as *The Viking* (yearbook) or *The Viking Voice* (semi-monthly) publications. *The Viking* and *The Viking Voice* were not published for almost a decade (1941-1950). Therefore, the only record of sports at MHS for those years was mostly team photographs.

In the 1943-44 school year, Telford Gevedon, MHS science teacher, was appointed the new coach of MHS. Among the players that year were: Bill Bradley, Frank Burns, James Hall, Jack Ellis, Berkley Cox, Quentin Hicks, Freeman Spencer, Clyde Day, Ralph Christian, Richard Maxey, and Roy Stewart. Bobby Stamper was the manager. The team that year had only modest success with a

12-8 record. The highlights of that year seemed we were happy to be number two. We were runner up to Ashland in the EKC tournament and runners up to Breckinridge in the District tournament.

In the spring of 1944, Coach Gevedon attempted to revive baseball as a sport at MHS. We practiced and played on the Clearfield mens baseball field. However, about the only teams we played that year were Breckinridge, Flemingsburg, and Olive Hill. The baseball team consisted of the basketball team plus Bobby Stamper, Tom Mobley, and others.

In 1946, Coach Gevedon's basketball Vikings, led by Berkley Cox, (who later starred at Murray State College) had a very successful year. That was the year Breckinridge won the State Tourney by blowing away all the competition. Breck was led by some of the greatest high school players Kentucky ever had. Sonny Allen, Frank Fraley, Marvin Mayhall, Don Battson, Bill Litton, Fred Bays, and Richard Scroggin. But that year Breckinridge barely made it out of the District tournament. That was at a time that only the District winners advanced, and they barely beat Morehead High School by 5 points in a hard fought game at Owingsville. However, Breckinridge went on to win the Kentucky High School State Tournament, and Morehead High School came home.

BOYS BASEBALL REVIVED

Although baseball had been dropped the second time after one year at MHS, in 1945, an ill fated attempt was made to revive the sport. In the spring of 1946, a group of MHS boys, led by Bobby Stamper and James "Ocky" Fielding, decided that the highschool should have a baseball team again. They began practice on the Clearfield mens baseball field. However, they had no coach, so Bobby Stamper, their star south paw pitcher, and catcher Berkley Cox, decided they would coach the team. They even scheduled games with surrounding high schools.

Morehead High School Basketball Vikings, 1945. L-R: Quentin Hicks,
Clyde Day, Richard Maxey, Berkley Cox, Telford Gevedon, Coach, Ralph Christian,
Roy Stewart, Claude Christian, Thomas Mobley, Bob Grey, manager.
Cheerleaders: L-R: Virginia Ellington, Margaret Cornette, Dorothy Swim, Oma Nell Cox.

The first game of the season was played at Flemingsburg. The day after the game when the boys returned to school, all ten boys were called to Principal Ethel Ellington's office. She asked the boys where they were the previous afternoon, and they said, "In Flemingsburg playing baseball. We had a game with their high school." A very irate Mrs. Ellington said, "Morehead High School does not have a baseball team", and she promptly expelled all ten boys, despite their insistence that they did have a baseball team. (They just didn't have a coach.) After a couple of days, Mrs. Ellington agreed if they would all come to the next chapel service at school, and sit on the stage, and apologize to the student body, she would lift the suspension. The boys all agreed, and apologized. They were then readmitted to school. However, they always believed they did have a high school baseball team, they just didn't have a coach.

OLD GYM CALLED RED BARN

In 1952, there was a new principal, C.C. Smallwood, but basketball was still the only sport at MHS. However, there were two coaches that year, Telford Gevedon was the head coach and assistant coach Roscoe Hutchinson, Jr. coached the "B" team. However, even with two coaches, their records were not impressive that year. The B team won 10 and lost 15, while the varsity won 11 and lost 16. But that team was one of the last teams to play in the "Old Red Barn", built in 1927. It was the first gymnasium in Rowan County. But one of the problems was there were no dressing room facilities, or water in the gym. Also, there was danger of the players running into one of the four pot-bellied coal stoves that heated the gym.

YEARBOOK RESUMES PUBLICATION

In 1952, the *Viking* Yearbook resumed publication after twelve years of silence. It contained comprehensive coverage of the school programs, people, and sports. It was paid for through the support of 25 local boosters, forty-nine businesses, and one church. That church was the First Church of God, M.L. Tate, minister, and George Ann Barker, music director. Also, of those 49 businesses that advertised in the 1952 *Viking*, only 6 are still in business. Those are: Big Store Furniture Company, White Lumber Company, Holbrook Pharmacy, Martin's Department Store, Citizens Bank, and Dixie Grill. Among those supporters that are no longer in business were: Pat's Pool Room, Buelah's Tailer Shop, Fraley Bus Line, Hudson Motor Sales & Service, Alfrey Pontiac, Lee Clay, CarrLumber, and Tacketts Service Station.

BASEBALL REVIVED AGAIN

In 1953, MHS had a new principal, Mr. Calvin Hunt. That year, the boys wanted to field a baseball team, and Mr. Hunt agreed. But they had no coach, so Mr. Hunt agreed to allow MHS alumnus,

Bobby Stamper, to serve as an unpaid volunteer coach. The players on that team were: Jack Cox, George Cox, Zane Collins, Oscar Lambert, Clifton "Tub" Baldridge, Don Hardin, Robert Hall, Bobby DeHart, Bill Joe Hall, and Jimmy Owens. The reason that they did not have a coach was that no one really believed in them, or would accept the responsibility of coaching them. So Bobby Stamper served as their coach. That 1953 team could have been called the original "unbelievables". They had no uniforms except what they could furnish themselves. The school did furnish balls and bats. They practiced and played their games at the Clearfield mens baseball field. But they had an unbelievably successful season.

TEAM WINS DISTRICT TITLE

The district tournament was played that year at Morehead College's Jayne Stadium. Morehead High had only one pitcher, Bobby DeHart. They beat Flemingsburg in a morning game, and Grayson in an afternoon game. Bobby DeHart pitched and won both games. The next day, the Vikings played Breckinridge, and with Bobby DeHart pitching, won the District. However, they lost in the Regional tournament to Wheelwright. But the unbelievables had made believers out of a lot of people--especially when they proudly accepted the District Tournament Championship Trophy before a home crowd at Jayne Stadium.

MOREHEAD HIGH SCHOOL BAND ERA

David and all of the house of Israel played before the Lord on all manner of instruments...even on harps...coronets and cymbals." (2 Sam. 6:5)

There is nothing as exhilarating and inspiring as the sight and sound of a marching band. The quick cadence of the drums, the sharp notes of the trumpets, the smooth sounds of the trombones, the soft sounds of the saxophones and the other instruments are sounds that serve to motivate and inspire the listener. Perhaps that is why bands always lead at military parades, political and patriotic rallies. Certainly that's why they always perform at school pep rallies, football games, and other sporting events. Music can both soothe the "savage beast" within, as well as inspire the "savage beast" within.

Morehead High School's modest move to motivate student interest in bands began with local music teacher Mrs. Emma Sample in 1943. Perhaps she was inspired by the sounds of the big bands of that era, or, perhaps she was inspired by the military marching bands seen in the movies. Certainly the navy base on the Morehead State College campus, and MSC's marching band may have played a part in Mrs. Sample's desire to begin a band at MHS. (Breckinridge High School students, if they were skilled enough, had long been permitted to be a part of the college band.) But MHS had no organized band until 1943.

BAND BEGAN IN 1943

There were perhaps a dozen students who answered the call by Mrs. Sample to form that first MHS band. Among those students who showed up at that first band practice were: Glen Poston, trumpet; Glen Gilkison, trumpet; Bobby Stamper, trumpet; Margaret Sue Cornette, clarinet; Clyde Day, trumpet; Sterling Johnson, trombone; Quentin Hicks, trumpet; Peggy Christian, clarinet; and Don "Herky" Riddle, drums. Those eager musicians had to rent or purchase their own instruments. There were no uniforms, no budget, and Mrs. Sample provided the music to be performed.

"PEP" BAND TO MARCHING BAND

At first, they were just a "pep" band, performing at the home basketball games. Some of the basketball players also played in the band. Quentin Hicks played the trumpet in the band, and was a substitute on the basketball team. Before the games, he did more warming up on stage blowing his trumpet than on the floor running, passing and shooting. Also at half-time he did not go into the locker room with the team, but went up on stage and played in the band wearing his basketball uniform. Also Bobby Stamper was the team manager, and he spent more time "tooting" his $25

Morehead High School Band members dressed in their new uniforms, 1954. L-R: Front Row: Virginia Anglin, Shirley Burns, Barbara Fraley, Marilyn Easterling, Brenda Gastineau, Barbara Reffett; Second Row: Betty Lou Hunt, Georgia Ellington, Margaret Sue Hall, Irene Sorrell, Kathyrn Worthington; Third Row: Richard Whitt, Carl Ross, Jackie Baldridge, John Ferguson, Clydia Carter; fourth row: Freddy Fraley, Ralph Greenhill.

trumpet than attending to the needs of the basketball team.

In 1945, the annual Rowan County School Fair resumed after being closed for the duration of World War II. That first band had improved considerably, and Mrs. Sample believed they were ready to march in the school parade. However, they had no uniforms, so they all wore white shirts and dark trousers or skirts. After getting the band started, Mrs. Sample soon resigned her position.

BAND DIRECTORS "FAIR"

One could truthfully say that the next two band leaders at MHS were "fair",because beginning in 1948, Morehead native and Morehead College graduate student, Miss Merl Fair, became the next band director. Merl, a former college band member, cheerleader, and Miss Rowan County, began working with the band in the small wooden band room at the rear of the old "Red Barn." (MHS Gym). Miss Fair (who later married her childhood sweetheart, John Sonny Allen) said it was always too cold or too hot in that room. Merl soon resigned the position to continue her graduate studies. Her younger sister, Nell Fair (Mahaney) took over where Merl left off. She continued the music program emphasizing the concert band more than the marching band. Nell also recalled the bitter cold mornings in the band room. She said the janitor would build a fire in the coal pot-bellied stove early in the morning. She would then come in before 7:30 a.m. and give free private instruction to any student who wanted special tutoring. Nell would also stay late in the afternoon and also give free tutoring.

The "fair" girls, by taking a personal interest in students with musical aptitude and interest, formed a firm foundation for future band members. It would be many of those students who would form the bases of future bands at MHS.

New Director Kept a Tight "Reign"

In 1951, Mr. Reign Shipley, a music major from MSC, was appointed the new Band Director. It could be said that he kept a tight "reign" on the students. Mr. Shipley was a stern disciplinarian, and demanded absolute perfection from his students. He approached the job of building a band like the drill sergeant he was, before entering college. He constantly challenged his students to achieve their best, and they rapidly responded.

Without a football team at MHS, the band had little motivation and no opportunity to perform on a regular basis. But they practiced regularly, and performed as the opportunities arose. Soon they were marching in such local events as the County School Fair, the Harvest Festival, and Fourth of July Parades. However, they had no uniforms and refused to compete in band competitions. But that changed as the quality and quantity of the band improved.

BOOSTERS CLUB BOOSTS GROWTH

Wherever you have a school band, you usually have a band boosters club. Those are parents, teachers, and students who organized to support the band in their fund raising and budget requests. Early in 1952 with the help of the band boosters and school board, the band was ready to purchase their first uniforms. The style, color, and fabric was selected by vote of the band members. Then, Home Economics teacher, Mrs. Virginia Rice, began measuring the student musicians for their new uniforms. However, it seemed like an eternity to the students before the uniforms arrived, but when those new bright green and white uniforms did arrive, there was an excited and happy group of band members at MHS.

By 1952, MHS's "budding" band was performing in surrounding counties and competitions. They marched in the first harvest festival in Morehead and the Rowan County School annual parade. Next they were invited to march in the Southern Ohio River Day festival at Portsmouth. The band then participated in the University of Kentucky's annual band competition. They won second place in the event. That group of early MHS band members came home proud of their performance, but determined to continue their quest to attain even greater musical heights. In 1953, Mr. Shipley resigned and was replaced by Mr. Fred Bland. Mr. Bland, contrary to his name, was not "bland". He was a red haired musician who just never seemed to get the band organized the way he believed they should be. (He resigned in less than a year.)

"LIVELY" BAND DIRECTOR APPOINTED

The quest for a bigger, better band got a lively jump start when Mr. Tony Allo was appointed band director in 1953. "Allo" is short for allegro, which the dictionary calls a lively musical composi-

Morehead High School Marching Band marched in President Eisenhower's second inaugural parade 1957.

tion. Mr. Allo began to motivate the MHS band to live up to his name. As they accepted his challenge, they began to improve. In a short time, the band outgrew the old band room attached to the rear of the old "Red Barn" Gym. They next moved into the "Red Barn" which was so poorly heated and cold in the winter time, that the students had to wear gloves to practice. In 1954, a new cafeteria was constructed at the rear of the high school. The band practiced there until the new gymnasium was build at Route 32 and West Sun Street. With the opening of the new gym, they had a place to practice, however, they had to walk out Second Street to the new gym to practice every day.

Jack Baldridge was a drummer in the band from 1953-1958. He began in the seventh grade and continued until he graduated in 1958. The reason he played drums was the school furnished the drums, but you had to rent or purchase the other instruments. He began in the concert band and moved up to the marching band as he improved. Jack became an accomplished drummer because he practiced at home. No, he did not have a drum set. But Mr. Allo showed him how to take a block of wood and stretch a piece of old inner tube tightly over the block and use it as a practice drum. Then, as you beat on that taut piece of rubber with your drum sticks, you got the same feel as actually beating on a drum. Jack recalled that he used to paint his drumsticks different colors for different events, such as green and white for school functions, or harvest colors for harvest festivals, etc. He painted his drum sticks red, white and blue when they marched in the presidential inaugural parade in Washington, D.C.

In 1956, during Rowan County's centennial celebration, there was a parade in Morehead every afternoon for a week. The Morehead High School Band led every one of those special parades, except the last day. That was declared college day, and the Morehead State College Band led that parade. Rowan County's centennial celebration was much more festive because of the Morehead High School Band.

BIG BAND ERA

Under Mr. Allo's direction, the marching band grew to over 100 members. They won about every competition they entered. Also, the band was receiving more invitations than they could afford to attend.

On October 6, 1956, Morehead High School's Band was invited to attend the band competition at the prestigious Daniel Boone Festival at Barbourville, Kentucky. The competition was strong that year. But the sharp marching cadence and rhythm of the green and white won first place, and they were given the honor of leading the parade. Also, they won $100 toward their expenses. Mr. Allo said "The competition was extremely tough, but our kids had worked so hard they were determined not to be denied that championship." They returned with the championship trophy.

BAND INVITED TO STATE FAIR

The quality and quantity of the MHS March Band continued to increase. In addition to a marching band, there was also a concert band and a dance band. In August, 1956, the marching band was invited to participate in the opening exercises of the newly renovated Kentucky State Fairgrounds in Louisville. It was an extremely hot summer, much like the summer of 1999, and some of the band members did not wish to interrupt their summer by going on a band trip and wearing those hot uniforms. But Mr. Allo said, "Any band member who did not attend (without a good excuse), would be dropped from the band." One of the drummers from Farmers did not attend, and his excuse was that their cow was ready to give birth, and his dad wanted him to be there to help in case he was needed. Mr. Allo excused him, however, later after Mr. Allo had left the school, he admitted they did not even own a cow.

INVITED TO WASHINGTON

The greatest honor to come to Morehead High School's marching band, came following Dwight D. Eisenhower's second presidential election in November 1956. The inaugural committee in Washington, D.C. invited two high school bands from each state to represent their state. Morehead High and Eastern High from Louisville were Kentucky's representatives. However, it was doubtful that Morehead would be able to attend because the band had only two months to raise enough money to pay for the trip. It appeared to be an impossible goal.

Many fund raising efforts were attempted during those next two months. One fund raising drive involved giving away bread. The new Kerns Bakery in London, Kentucky offered the band 10 cents for each home they visited in Rowan County. When they visited the home, they gave them a loaf of Kerns bread free, and in return got a slip of paper signed saying they received the bread.

The band was then given 10 cents for each signed slip they sent back to the bakery. Band member Jack Baldridge recalled, "We visited just about every home in Rowan County over the Thanksgiving holiday."

ROWAN RESIDENTS GIVE FREELY

Mr. Bill Wells, the first drum major at Morehead High School, recalled the strenuous practices in preparation for the Presidential inaugural parade. He said, "Every afternoon we marched and played all over the streets of Morehead, and while we were marching, people would come up to us and give us money to help pay for the trip." There was tremendous community pride in the band as they represented Kentucky in Washington.

Their most successful fund raiser was the Birthday Memorial and Anniversary Calendar for 1957. (Also on that calendar there were meetings, dates, and military dates.) Each person listed on the calendar paid $1 for each birthday, anniversary, or memorial (date of death). Upon examination of one of those calendars, now carefully and lovingly preserved by Jack Baldridge, there were 209 names just for July that year. Therefore, a conservative estimate would be 2,500 names included on that calendar. Also, many businesses, professional people, and politicians had their advertisements on the list of supporters. (This writer was not listed on that Birthday Calendar, however, my wife and two older children were listed.) That calendar fund raiser was what allowed the band to go to Washington. But a lot of work was done by band members and boosters, and they were on their way to Washington.

ON TO WASHINGTON

The happy hundred headed for Washington, D.C. on two chartered greyhound buses. They were all looking forward to the most memorable experience of their young lives. The group was well

Morehead High School Band director Randy Wells rehearsed with the last band before school changed to Rowan County High School, 1961.

chaperoned by teachers, parents, and friends. When they arrived in Washington, they were met by Kentucky's powerful democratic Congressman, Carl Perkins. He escorted them through the Capital and the White House. While there, they also visited the Smithsonian, Library of Congress, Washington and Lincoln Monuments, plus many more. (Those students from Morehead got to see things they had only read about.)

January 21, 1957, the day of the inauguration dawned cool and cloudy. But nothing could dampen or cool the enthusiasm of the green and white from Morehead. The parade was scheduled to last 2 1/2 hours, but the president was about a half hour late. Therefore, the parade started about one hour behind schedule. It consisted of a great display of military might, tuneful bands, pretty majorettes and flowery floats.

PARADING DOWN PENNSYLVANIA AVENUE

With over 750,000 spectators looking on (as well as live national TV), the Kentucky contingent came marching proudly down Pennsylvania Avenue. They were led by Democrat Governor, A.B.

"Happy" Chandler, riding in an open convertible. Next came two traditional Kentucky Colonels, closely followed by Morehead High School's Mighty Marching Band. As they approached the presidential reviewing stand, they played, "Hail to the Chief," then as "Happy" Chandler passed the presidential reviewing stand, he stood up in his convertible, smiled broadly at President Eisenhower and tipped his hat. President Eisenhower responded by standing and smiling just as broadly right back at "Happy" Chandler, and, folding his left hand behind his back and his right hand across his stomach, graciously bowed deeply several times. Clyda (Carter) Clark, a six year member of the Morehead High School Band, declared that the Washington trip was the high point of a Morehead High School Band.

ALLO RESIGNS - SHIPLEY RETURNS

In May, 1958, the marching members of the green and white were invited to the Holland, Michigan Tulip Festival. It was a national event and bands from all over the nation came to this tourist festival, bursting with beautiful colors. The band participated in that event despite a great deal of criticism that came from some other high school teachers that the band members were missing too many classes. (A charge usually leveled against athletics.) Some of the teachers threatened to fail the band members if they missed any more classes. Therefore, because of that criticism, the administration sharply reduced the number of band appearances each year. It was shortly afterwards, that Mr. Allo resigned his position and moved to Florida.

When Mr. Tony Allo resigned, former band director, Reign Shipley was reappointed the second time as band director. He had been supervisor of student teachers for Morehead State College. However, when Mr. Allo left, Mr. Shipley came back for the second time.

Mr. Shipley's second term as MHS band director was not as successful as his first. He had problems with the school administration over the band budget, band trips, and contests. Therefore, in 1960 Mr. Shipley resigned and accepted a job with a music publishing company in Louisville.

Randy Rejuvenates Band

In the fall of 1960, an enthusiastic, genial, multi-talented young Morehead graduate by the name of Randy Wells (singing Randy, not mail carrier Randy) was appointed the new MHS Band Director. Randy, (now Dr. Wells, retired MSU professor), dived into the band program that year with courage and vigor. He not only was the MHS band director, but was assigned to Clearfield, Elliottville, Farmers, and Haldeman schools. He was expected to organize and direct bands in each of those schools also. This allowed him only one period a day at MHS, plus after school practice. (That was spreading the new band director pretty thin.)

Band Forced to Turn Down Invitations

Mr. Wells continued, and even surpassed some of the previous band achievements, e.g. they won superior rating (highest possible) at the state music festival four out of five years. They marched in the Governor's inaugural parade and received prestigious invitations from such places as the New Year's Day Orange Bowl and Gator Bowl parades. However, they were not permitted to attend, because of a recently enacted school policy prohibiting out of state band trips. That policy sharply curtailed interest in the band.

During his tenure as band director, Mr. Wells promised the band new uniforms to replace the old ragged uniforms. However, there was no budget and the board refused to purchase new uniforms. Therefore, it was up to the students, parents and band boosters to privately raise money for the new uniforms.

Several different fund raisers were attempted over the year. There were chili suppers, ball games, bake sales, and candy sales.

One of the most successful fund raisers was selling candy door to door. But after one complaint they were not allowed to continue door to door sales. They had to sell the candy one bar at a time at school functions.

Former Morehead High School Band Directors: L-R: Nell Fair Mahaney, Merl Fair Allen, and Randy Wells.

NEW BAND UNIFORMS CONTAINED "R"

But the band members would not be denied. They were determined to buy new uniforms. Therefore, after many months of hard work, they achieved their goal of $6,500 for new uniforms. Those new uniforms had a "R" for Rowan County not an "M" for Morehead High School.

Dr. Randy Wells looked back on those years and remembered how hard he worked as he taught band in all the county consolidated schools, as well as the High Schools. But he established a "feeder" program from those small schools. Therefore, when students came to high school, they were prepared to move immediately into the High School Band and be productive. His comment was, "That was about the hardest job I ever had in teaching, but the most rewarding. Some of those students still come to me today and tell me they appreciated how much they learned about music during those years."

LAST MHS AND FIRST ROWAN COUNTY

Randy Wells was the last Band Director at MHS. But while there in 1960, the high school band led the parade in Morehead to celebrate the ground breaking for St. Claire Medical Center. It was a momentous day in the history of our county and the MHS band was proud to be a part of it. That was the last appearance of the MHS Band before becoming Rowan County High School. Dr. Wells was not only the last director at MHS, he was also the first band director at Rowan County High School. He helped establish the foundation for the present excellent band program at Rowan County. But the band began at MHS in 1943, closed in 1961. (However, it is alive and well at Rowan County Senior High School under the direction of Rex Payton.) Mr. Wells resigned in 1963 to become principal at Harrison County's West Side Elementary School.

Morehead High School existed from 1921-1961, before becoming Rowan County High School. Beginning in 1943, with their first band director, there were eight band directors before it became Rowan County High School. Those were:

 1943 Emma Sample
 1948 Merl Fair (Allen)
 1950 Nell Fair (Mahaney)
 1951 Reign Shipley
 1952 Fred Bland
 1953 Anthony Allo
 1958 Reign Shipley
 1960 Dr. Randy Wells

MOREHEAD HIGH SCHOOL DRAMA ERA

"A time to weep, and a time to laugh, a time to mourn and a time to dance." (Ecc. 3:4)

The roots of drama lie deep within the basic human instinct to imitate and mimic. That instinct to imitate appears in the early history of almost every culture. However, the ancient Greeks were the first to develop a higher form of drama. Out of that early drama grew the twin towers of comedy and tragedy. Therefore, out of those roots of classical Greek drama, there evolved the humor, poetry, plays, music, dance, speech and drama we know today as the dramatic arts in our schools.

EARLY CHRISTMAS PROGRAMS, MUSIC AND DRAMA

Plays, programs, pageants, and public speaking have long been an important part of Rowan County's Public Schools. Interested teachers, even in the small one-room rural elementary schools, would present plays and programs that were generally well attended by the community hungry for entertainment. Those were usually Christmas programs that involved the whole community. One of the parents would bring in a large cedar Christmas tree, and the children would then cover it with home-made decorations of bittersweet, holly berries, strings of popcorn, paper ornaments, and tinsel ice cycles. There was no electricity in those early rural school days, so there were no Christmas lights. Also, since there was no radio or television, school plays and programs were always well attended by parents and friends.

Miss Margaret Park, a teacher in Rowan County during the late 1800s and early 1900s, used drama and music extensively in her teaching. Miss Park, who was a deeply religious woman, and an accomplished musician, moved her piano with her to every school where she taught. She always had a Christmas pageant, complete with wise men, music, manger, animals, Joseph, Mary, and the baby Jesus. Her Christmas pageants were always eagerly awaited events, and well attended. The talented Miss Park taught in many Rowan County Schools for 50 years. During her tenure she enriched the lives of her students through drama and music. One of Morehead's earliest and most famous school plays was directed by Miss Margaret Park.

Park Presented Major Production

On April 19, 1907, Miss Park, a teacher in the Morehead Public school, presented a three act play that was a major production for that time. The cast consisted of children who later became Morehead's "movers and shakers." The title of the play was "At the Village Post Office", and it was estimated that about every one of the 400 to 500 souls living in Morehead at that time flocked to see the play that was described as a hilarious comedy. The play was an outdoor drama. It was given behind the school at the corner of Hargis and Sun Streets. The cast came in and out at the back door of the school as they received their cue, and the audience sat on the side of the hill beside the school.

The setting was in the present (of that day) and the plot revolved around the many eccentric characters who would meet at the post office and discuss their personal problems, as well as problems of the community and world.

Upon examination of the program for that early school play, it indicated that the cast of children later became successful business and professional people in and around Rowan County. The cast included Frank Havens, who later became the founder of the Big Store. He played the part of a "wolf" (ladies man), also known as the village "shirk." Jesse Boggess (who later was Morehead's leading general contractor who built such buildings as the College Swimming Pool and the City Hall), played three separate roles in

Morehead High School Senior Play, "Light and Lively", 1948. L-R: Goldie Kiser, Bobby Messer, Sis?, Allen J. Kazee, Virginia Ellington, Bernard Greer, Lucille Birchfield, Grace Crosthwaite, Teacher, Earl Alderman, Margaret Cornette, Billy R. Sargeant, Jewell Gulley, Carl Stewart.

the play. However, his main character was the Country Newspaper Editor. Charles Riley played the town's pessimist and Bart Tussey played the bumbling town constable. Phillip Banfield (who later became a doctor, left Morehead and moved to Washington, D.C.) played the part of a city dude who had moved to the country, and had trouble adjusting to the country culture.

Other characters in that early school play included Stanley Yount, Nell Tippitt, Fannie Barber, Myrtle Barber, Kash Strother, Elmer Maxey, Clarence Tussey, Mary Whitt, Nettie Blair, Victoria Ruley, Jane Skaggs, Rosie Royce and 6-year old Mary Caudill (She played the part of the spoiled brat. She died in 1999 at the age of 98.)

Miss Park, the pioneer producer of plays in Rowan County, died February 21, 1953, in Lexington's Good Samaritan Hospital. She was a devoted life long member of the Methodist Church. However, she could be considered the first pioneer play director in Rowan County's schools.

Many early Rowan County teachers used the dramatic arts to inspire, enrich, and improve the lives of their students. This writer's mother, a teacher in the Rowan County Schools in the 1930s, organized and directed school plays in her schools. At about the age of five (before school age), I remember she involved me in the McKenzie School Christmas play. I still recall how scared I was before a packed house for that Friday afternoon program. However, I managed to rush through the one line I had memorized (which I still remember to this day). It was a black faced comedy and I said, "O twould set my heart a swellen if Santa'd bring me a watermelon". Early school plays instilled self-confidence in students and support by parents.

DRAMA CLUB ORGANIZED

School plays were prevalent in the early history of Morehead High School. Beginning in 1935, there was a Dramatic Club organized at MHS with forty members. The officers in that first Dramatic Club were: Anna May Young, President; Rudolph Egan, Vice President; and Dortha Hutchinson, Secretary-treasurer. The faculty sponsor was Miss Anna Jane Day.

On March 25, 1935, the MHS Dramatic Club presented a play entitled, "Comic Characters Convention". It was of course a comedy where the students dressed up and portrayed comic strip characters of that era. Some of those old comic strip characters included: Maggie and Jiggs. Maggie and Jiggs were a married couple where Jiggs was always getting into trouble with Maggie, and she spent a great deal of time chasing him around the house with a frying pan or rolling pin. Another character in that play was "Snuffy" Smith. "Snuffy" was a hillbilly moonshiner who was always one step ahead of the "revenoors," and one step behind his wife who was constantly after him to improve himself and not be so lazy. Also, one of the characters was the consummate hero of those early comic strip characters. His name was "Smiling Jack," and he was a square jawed two-fisted, fearless fighter of the bad buys who always rescued the fair maidens in distress.

The year of 1935 was during the depth of the great depression. Those school plays always played to a packed house when they were performed on the stage of the old "Red Barn" Gym. (The old Cozy Theater was about the only entertainment in town). People were hungry for entertainment and comedy. Those depression day plays provided comic relief for families struggling to pay their debts and rear their families. Also, they provided valuable experience for those students to learn to speak in public and gain more self confidence.

ROYAL DRAMATIC CLUB FORMED

By 1938, the Dramatic Club had become the richer and more prestigious sounding "Royal Dramatic Club." The officers were Alpha Hutchinson, President; Kermit Tussey, Vice President; Mary Jane Peed, Secretary; James Butcher and Harold Prather, Sergeants at Arms. (They must have been a rowdy bunch to require two sergeants at arms.) The sponsor was Nelle T. (Cassity) Collins. Other members included: Virginia Alfrey, Lloyd Brown, Miriam Binion, Mildred Black, Clifford Barker, Roy Barber, Earl Bradley, Ova Bra-

Morehead High School Royal Drama Club 1954. Row One: Alene Estep Marietta Caudill, Joyce Hall, Lois Litton, Faye Gregory; Row Two: George Bowen, Arlene Cornette, Betty Gilkerson, Jack Parker, Glaspie Adkins, Roma Alderson; Row Three: James Lewis, James H. Caudill, Leroy Dye, Sanford Bentley, Bernard Stone, Mrs. H.C. Haggan.

dley, Vernita Bradley, Willard Calvert, Rosa Caudill, Hubert Conley, Bise Cox, Jewell Ellis, Mildred Haney, George Hill, Lee Roy Hill, Ova Johnson, Elmer Meyers, Harold Prather, Charles Roe, Allie Rose and Julia Stanley.

Black faced comedy was popular in those days, especially since the Amos and Andy Restaurant (named for a radio program of that era) was in Morehead. It was owned by Parnell and Elizabeth Martindale and they were one of the sponsors of the program. Therefore, those students delved into the dramatics of the Minstrel Show. Among the stars of that show were Alpha Hutchinson and Paul "Pot" Reynolds. Those students (with the traditional interlocutor moderating) presented a program of comedy, singing, and dancing. That show was well attended by both students and public. It brought welcome comedic diversion from the difficult economic conditions of that time. The cast of thatplay received a standing ovation as the curtain came down following the final act.

PRE WAR—POST WAR PLAYS PRESENTED

Senior plays at Morehead High School were always eagerly anticipated by both students and public. The senior play in 1938 was "Keep Off the Grass" by Charles George. It was a play about an absent minded inventor constantly coming up with weird inventions. It was similar to the "Absent Minded Professor" (in the Walt Disney film) about a professor who invented flubber. But the 1938 senior play and the Royal Dramatic Club fanned the flame of drama during the early days of Morehead High School.

During the World War II years, dramatic arts at MHS, like many other school programs, were sharply curtailed. There was rationing and shortages of food, fuel, and teachers. There was also a shortage of students because many boys entered the military service before high school graduation. Also, girls dropped out of school to work in the defense plants. Therefore, you could not count on the cast of a play to still be in high school at graduation. This writer graduated in 1944, and our class certainly did not have a senior play.

On May 12, 1947, the senior play as a part of the high school experience, returned with a major production. That year the class presented a comedy in three acts "Gabriel Blow Your Horn". The play was held in the Button auditorium at MSC, and was directed by Mrs. H.C. Haggan. The time was the present and the setting was near Ashville, N.C. at the summer cottage of wealthy society matron, Miss Thelma Smith. The plot involved Miss Smith trying to break up a romance between her niece and Herb Brown. But Mr. Brown gained access to a house party by donning a beard, using a funny accent, and using an alias. With that disguise, he was hired as the caretaker.

The cast included: Gabriel, Eldean Parker; Zerousia (his wife), Peggy Christian; and Daisy May (their daughter), VeeVee Rice. Other cast members included Maxine White, Ruby Flannery, Elizabeth Ingram, Mary Fisher, Roy Stewart, Wayne Cox, Bobby Stamper, Glen Crum, and Charles "Feets" Caudill.

One of the last senior plays of the 1940s was in 1948 with the production of a play entitled "Light and Lively". It was, of course, a comedy. (There were no senior plays that were tragedies.) Miss Grace Crosthwaite was the director and the play was presented in the old "Red Barn" MHS Gym. Earl Alderman, one of the cast members said, "he remembered he did not want to be in the play, but Miss Crosthwaite made him."

NEW ERA

By 1952, the Royal Dramatic Club of Morehead High School had become just the Dramatic Club (again). (That name did not sound nearly as impressive as "The RoyalDramatic Club). The name change indicated a reduction in either the prestige of the club, or, that they were unaware that there had previously been a group of students called the Royal Dramatic Club. But the newly revived Dramatic Club was determined to make their influence felt at MHS. Those officers were Robert Hall, President; Rodney Stewart, Vice President; Elmer Hall, Secretary; Victor White, Treasurer; Naomi Alderson, Reporter; Mrs. H.C. Haggan, Sponsor. The membership included: Iloma McClury, Barbara Swinnegan, Francis Dulin, James Earl Davis, Helen Barker, Geneva Harmon, Peggy Childers, Mary Ferguson, and Bobby Swinnegan.

Morehead High School "Mask-A-Raders" Club, 1957. Row One: L-R: Ray Dillon, George Ann Reeder, Phyllis Anderson, Sue Thomas, Dorothy Jones, Clydia Carter, James Earl Davis, Director. Row Two: Alan Parker, Jackie Vanhook, Margery Spencer, Ina Wagoner, Janis Porter. Row Three: Kenny Jones, Bobby Christian, Charlotte White, Jack Brooks, Janet McBrayer, Jo Ann Keeton, Jean Kidd, Hazel Kidd. Row Four: Marilyn Easterling, Barbara Caudill, Joyce Manning, Helen Thomas, Anna Eldridge, Ernestine Brown. Row Five: Margaret Messer, Delores Hall, Marcella Caudill, Rosemary Evans, Patsy Fugate, Garnett Hall, Susan Coyle, Janice Hamilton, Freda Campbell, Patty Williams.

In 1956, James Earl Davis, a Morehead High School graduate and former member of the Dramatic club, had finished college and returned to his alma mater to teach. That was the beginning of the James Earl Davis era of dramatic arts at MHS. It was an era that brought dramatic development in the growth of the drama department. The Dramatic Club became the "Mask-A-Raders," and that group expanded the dramatic arts to much more than the annual senior play.

ENTER MASK-A-RADERS

The Mask-A-Raders became the production unit of the dramatic arts classes at MHS. In March 1956, their entry in the Morehead Regional Festival, "Finders-Keepers," by George Kelly, was judged superior. Gary Eldridge played the leading role, and won the outstanding performance award. James E. Davis was chosen outstanding director of the festival.

On November 14 & 15, 1956, the Mask-A-Raders presented their first full length production, Mark Twain's "A Double Barrelled Detective Store". It was presented in the grade school gym auditorium, and the cast of fourteen did an excellent job in holding the audience in suspense throughout the play. Directed by James E. Davis, a brief synopsis of the play was:

Act I Early evening in the living room of a New England home in 1899.

Act II Late afternoon in the Hope Tavern in Hope Canyon, Colorado four years later.

Act III The Tavern two months later.

ENTER NATIONAL THESPIANS

The Mask-A-Raders, directed by James Earl Davis, brought a whole new dimension to dramatics at Morehead High School. In 1957, the Mask-A-Raders were accepted as an affiliate of the national Thespian Society, an honor society in the dramatic arts. They were honored by that group with special recognition for outstanding work in drama over a two year period.

The following Mask-a-Raders were considered eligible for national office and were installed at a very impressive ceremony in late December, 1957: Barbara Caudill, Clyda Carter, Ruth Mitchell, Lynn Crawford, Grace Hall, Jerry Marshall, Hazel Kidd, Rosemary Evans, Kenny Jones, Ernie Baldridge, Jackie Baldridge, Buddie Stidham, Janet McBrayer, Jo Anne Keeton, and J.B. Hall. That group continued the tradition of excellence in the dramatic arts at MHS.

PLAYS RUN FOR THREE NIGHTS

One of the groups next major productions was the old favorite "Lavender and Old Lace" by Rose Warner. Directed by James E. Davis, it was presented November 28, 29, 30, 1957, in the grade school gym auditorium. There was a full house for each production, as the 10 member cast gave a stellar performance. The entire action of the play took place in the sitting room of Mary Ainslie's home in a quaint New England Village. The time was the present, when it was presented. Act I was early April, Act III was three months later, and Act III was a late afternoon in August.

In 1958, the drama department expanded to speech, drama, poetry reading and debate. Among those who participated in the Morehead Regional Speech Festival that year were: Judy Parker, Kenny Jones, Buddie Stidham, Hazel Kidd, Bobby Combs, Margaret Debord, De Etta Lewis, Connie Fannin, and Grace Hall. That year the speech group spoke on the "Comparison of the Educational system of the U.S., Russia, Great Britain, and France."

The drama group that year presented the play, "A Man Called Peter" by Catherine Marshall. The play was directed by James E. Davis and included a cast of MHS seniors, as well as the Mask-A-Raders. It was performed in the Morehead Grade School Gym-auditorium on October 28, 29, 30, 1958. The play was a biography of Dr. Peter Marshall, who was the pastor of a Washington, D.C. church and U.S. Senate Chaplain. It included his rapid rise to prominence in the clergy, and his tragic death while the Chaplain of the U.S. Senate. Kenny Jones played Peter Marshall, Judy Parker was Catherine Marshall, and Larry Kegley portrayed Peter John Marshall. Those three were strongly supported by 12 other cast members.

"ICE BOUND" LAST PLAY AT MHS

On April 28, 29, 30, 1960, one of the last plays was presented by the Morehead High School Mask-A-Raders (before becoming Rowan County High School). The title of the play was "Icebound" by Owen Davis, and was directed by James Earl Davis. The play was presented on three separate nights in the Morehead Elementary Gym-Auditorium. The admission was 50 cents and they played to a packed house eachevening. (See Photo). That play was also presented at the Kentucky State Drama Festival in the Guignol Theater on the University of Kentucky campus, and won a superior rating.

That cast of "Icebound" continued the proud tradition of Morehead High School's Dramatic Arts. The membership of the Dramatic Club, Royal Dramatic Club, and the Mask-A-Raders throughout the history of the school were a credit to themselves, their school, and their community.

DRAMA FUTURE BRIGHT

It is a well established scientific fact that certain physical and intellectual traits are inherited, eg. Athletic ability, intelligence, musical ability, or the tendency toward contracting diseases such as cancer. However, if the research does not show that dramatic talent is inherited, then the empirical evidence does, e.g. Virginia (Ginny Beth) Lambert, Rowan County High School's extremely

Photo: Ward Williams

Morehead High School Play "Icebound". 1960. L-R: Roberta Hosack, Larry Kegley, Dickie Stidom, Ernestine Brown, Janet McBrayer Dulin, Bert McBrayer Jr., David Richardson, Sue Whitt, Marcella Caudill, Anna Eldridge, Ronald Caudill, Glen Buckner.

talented and successful speech and drama teacher, has led that school to winning first place in the state Speech and Drama Festival for many years. Most of that success is the result of good instruction and hard work. However, perhaps part of that success could be genetic, in that many of those present students are children and grandchildren of previous generations of speech and drama students at Morehead High School. The future looks bright as the Rowan County High School Speech and Drama Department begins a new millinieum of programs, pageants, and plays. Thanks to the gracious, generous gifts contributed by local philanthropist, Lucille Caudill Little, there is the promise of a new 1.8 million Fine Arts building, complete with auditorium. That will bring Rowan County High School physical facilities on par with their outstanding speech and drama program. (They will have a home for their programs and won't have to use other facilities.)

The new millinieum should offer a new dimension of the Arts at Rowan County High School. They have a long proud tradition of excellence to continue, as they remember the contributions of those who have preceded them.

Morehead High School Little 8 Champs.
F(L-R): Jane Evans, Roy Caudill, Earl Barber, Billie Caudill
R(L-R): Bub Tatum, Eugene Miles, Peck Robinson,
Graydon Hackney, Fred Caudill, William Caudill,
Roy Holbrook, coach.

CHAPTER SEVEN

Publishers and Printers:
The Paper Trail

Ever since Gutenberg invented the printing press newspapers have molded public opinion and influenced the history of western civilization. While the pen may be mightier than the sword, it takes time for the ink to influence individuals. In the latter part of the 1800s the "pen" (newspapers) in Morehead, would appear and disappear faster than banks appear and disappear today. Therefore, this researcher has found references <u>to</u>, but no surviving copies <u>of</u> several newspapers published in Morehead in the late 1800s. Among the ones with no surviving copies were: *The Morehead Sun, The Morehead Leader*, and *The Morehead Times*. *The Morehead Times* appeared briefly in the late 1880s, but disappeared with no known surviving copies in 1884.

Perhaps the reason *The Morehead Times* did not survive much longer than it took the ink to dry was because of the Rowan County War which began in 1884. The life span of *The Morehead Times* as well as the life span of 22 of Morehead's citizens was surely shortened by the trouble in the town. Since all the judges, officials, preachers, teachers, and many businessmen were forced to flee from Morehead, it was understandable that a newspaper editor might also flee. Very little is known of those early newspapers, and those who published them. But for a brief period of time they reported the events and people of their time. They instilled community pride and enhanced education. But not a single issue of these very early newspapers survived.

THE MOREHEAD ADVANCE 1895-1902 (WEEKLY)

The Morehead Advance, edited and published by William S. Schooler, was Morehead's first newspaper that survived long enough to make an impact upon the community. The printing office was located on Railroad Street (First Street) above the C.E. Bishop Drug Store and was financed by the Morehead State Bank. It was near the location of the Big Store. The paper was published weekly in pamphlet (tabloid) size. Very little was published of news outside Rowan County. There were no photographs. Advertising support came from wholesale companies mostly outside of Morehead, e.g.Hagan Wholesale Grocery Company, Huntington, W. Virginia (delivered every Thursday). Local advertisers included the City Drug Company, located on Railroad Street (now First Street), and Bradley Brothers at Brady (1 mile west of Morehead). Their claim was "we will show you how to turn your nickels, dimes, and dollars into Golden Eagles ($20.00 gold pieces) and at the same time live off the fat of the land." This was an implication of great savings at their store.

The printing was all hand set and printed on hand operated machines. Mrs. Schooler helped operate the machines, and Allen Fraley was the printer's devil (apprentice). When one examines a copy of *The Advance*, it is apparent that Mr. Schooler was a gifted writer. Also he was determined to change the image of Morehead from a feuding, fussing, lawless community to a law abiding peaceful place, with great potential for growth. His early passion was

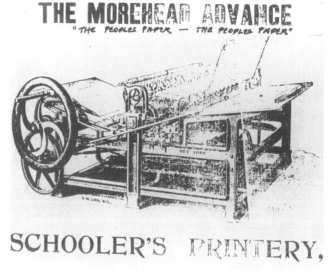

Earliest newspaper with a surviving issue was The Morehead Advance". Printed on a hand press, 1895-1902.

the positive promotion of Morehead as "The City of the Hills," a community with a future. However, he later began promoting some of his pet political projects, and later ran for political office. Before disappearing, *The Morehead Advance* did much to advance Morehead. It helped to unite the people, and to develop a sense of pride in our community because the pen was mightier than the sword, eg.

> "The object of this edition is to give the outside world some idea of what we have buried in the beautiful hills surrounding Morehead. Rowan County is rich in minerals and has some of the finest timber that grows (with) easy access, and some of the most fertile farms that the sun shines on." "Let the public know about Morehead in such a way that they will want to know more. If you want to make good money locate in Morehead. You can do no better than to invest in Rowan County land. Capital will do well if it will come our way."

> *The Morehead Advance,* July 1898

THE MOUNTAINEER, 1902-1917 (WEEKLY)

"Devoted to the Interests of Mountain People"

The Mountaineer arose out of the ashes of the failed *Morehead Advance*. Among early editors of this weekly publication (cost $1.00 per year or 60 cents for 6 months) were Oscar Swit and a Mr. Williams. The office was on the campus of the Normal School in Burgess Hall. The paper was printed on a Washington hand press. In examining these early editions you find a column called "Successful Mountaineers". This column presented detailed biographical information about a local citizen who provided devoted Christian service to the community, eg.

> "Mary Coffee, a girl who earned her own living, supported her widowed mother, and provided a home for an orphan child should be commended for her noble efforts."
>
> Local news such as the following item:
>
> "Mr. & Mrs. George Clayton and son, Morgan, returned from Florida Thursday morning. Uncle George left here with the intention of making the southland his future home, but that old saying, there's no place like home must have bothered him."
>
> *The Mountaineer*, July 18, 1914

George Clayton might have been the first to move from Morehead to Florida, and became disillusioned, but he certainly was not the last. This writer, moved to the Sunshine State in the late 1950s, but after 8 years decided there was no place like Morehead and returned.

On October 13, 1913 *The Mountaineer* was sold to the Christian Womens Business Group and Cora Wilson Stewart became the editor. Under her direction, *The Mountaineer* editorial policy changed to more emphases upon education. In the "Successful Mountaineer's" column she spotlighted outstanding teachers. She also gave much publicity to the Moonlight School, a program of adult education begun by Mrs. Stewart in 1911. e.g."One to every one was the 1913 slogan of Rowan's Earnest Teachers". (Evidently meaning one teacher was available to any one wanting to learn, regardless of age.)

The teachers with their rallying cry "one to every one" were urged to continue their heroic work with adults. Therefore, each teacher determined with missionary zeal to reach the last illiterate in the county. Their noble goal was to help those wanting to learn, to better enjoy life, and then they would be more productive citizen. (Still the goal of education today).

Cora Wilson Stewart, through her personal editing of *The Mountaineer*, succeeded in raising the educational conscience of our citizens. She helped them see the need for a better education. *The Mountaineer* was the tool that helped her launch the Moonlight School agenda that made her world famous. The "Pen" is a powerful tool in promoting an agenda, and Cora Wilson Stewart wielded it more effectively than a sword.

THE MOUNTAIN SCORCHER, 1927-1929 (WEEKLY)
"Stands for right and Condemns Wrong"

Several Issues Survive. (This paper began at the same time a daily paper in Ashland, called The *Ashland Times* began which did not last much longer than *The Mountain Scorcher*). Editor and Publisher: Sam S. Cassity

This paper was first printed in Mt. Sterling, and later moved to Morehead. It consisted of four pages, six columns wide. Sources of advertisements included blacksmiths, patent medicines and livestock sales. *The Mountain Scorcher* called itself "The Industrial Organ of Rowan County", and strongly proclaimed on its masthead: "Stands for the right and condemns the wrong". Sam Cassity was known to proclaim loudly his thoughts about people and places. Also, it billed itself as the only real newspaper in Rowan County. This was a deliberate "slam" against the *Rowan County News*, that had been published in Morehead since 1918. It is no wonder that for the brief time the Mountain Scorcher was published there was a politically motivated war of words between the two newspapers. Letters and editorials critical of political and social issues were published weekly by Editor Sam Cassity.

One example of this war of words was the controversy that arose over a road proposed between Fleming County and Elliott County. (now Route 32). Jack Wilson, *Rowan County News* Editor, wrote a burning editorial criticizing Governor Fields (Olive Hill native). He also questioned the integrity of the Highway Commissioner in not moving fast enough. He accused the Governor of giving preferences to a road between Carter County and Elliott County above the road through Rowan County.

Afraid that Jack Wilson would not publish his reply, the Governor replied to the *Rowan County News* editorial with a stinging letter to the *Mountain Scorcher*. He accused the Rowan County News editor of being <u>incompetent</u> and <u>untrustworthy</u>. Governor Fields further recommended that "The subscribers should cancel their subscription to the *Rowan County News*". Of course, "*The Mountain Scorcher*" loved the criticism of their competitor. They published the Governor's letter on the front page, and suggested the readers do what the Governor recommended.

The Scorcher carried a good balance between state and local news. (There were never any photographs published.) News of the local Kiwanis officials for 1927 was published. Among those were: President W.L. Jayne, Past President H. Van Antwerp, Program W.C. Lappin, Attendance H.C. Haggan, and T.F. Hogge. Other Kiwanians serving on various committee in 1927 were Harlan Powers, C.B. Lane, F.C. Button, D.M. Holbrook, C.E. Bishop, Robert Young, E.E. Maggard, and S.M. Bradley. It would appear that the Morehead Kiwanis Club was quite active in 1927.

The Mountain Scorcher lived up to its claim that it "Stands for the right and condemns the wrong". Whatever the Editor thought was right, he stood for, and whatever he thought was wrong he opposed. Sam Cassity had discovered the "Pen was mightier than the sword". He fought his political battles with words instead of bullets and he was a crack shot with his words. They usually found their target. But in any event it was words that were flying and not bullets as was the case in earlier years in Morehead.

Editor Sam Cassity died in 1929, and one of the most colorful chapter in Morehead's newspaper history died with him. But he had moved Morehead from battling with bullets to battling with words, and from wrestling with each other to wrestling with ideas. "The pen was mightier than the sword".

MOREHEAD INDEPENDENT - 1934-1945 (WEEKLY)
"Dedicated to the Advancement of Morehead and Rowan County"

Issues for 11 years Survive - Editor Charles E. Adams, Later W.J. Sample and W.E. Crutcher.

The first issue of the *Morehead Independent* was published on January 27, 1934. It was first located over the C.E. Bishop Drug Store on Railroad Street. (This was where the old *Morehead Advance* began in 1895). Later, the paper was moved to a brick building on Bishop Avenue (behind the Dixie Grill). The first editor was Charles Adams. The staff of the paper included: Vivian Caudill, Printer; Sam Meade, Linotype Operator; and a very young Miss

Lucille Caudill was listed as the Society Editor. W.J. Bill Sample, Editor of *The Independent* for 10 years also formed the Rowan County Lumber Company. He successfully continued that business after leaving the paper. This writer worked for Mr. Sample for a brief period of time in the lumber business. He was fair, friendly and honest, but a stern taskmaster. He would introduce me (age 17) as his "Partner" in the lumber business. I'm sure his staff of the Morehead Independent had a good working relationship with him.

George M. Calvert, a Morehead High School and University of Kentucky Alumnus, was a pioneer Kentucky newspaper man who devoted his life to the newspaper profession in several states. He worked on the *Rowan County News* from 1925-1930 and on *The Lexington Herald* from 1930-35, and on *The Morehead Independent* from 1936-37. Mr. Calvert is retired from the *Atlanta Constitution* where he worked for many years.

Mr. Calvert said, "*The Morehead Independent* began as a political competitor of *The Rowan County News*, but later became a good newspaper, always presenting both sides of an issue."

William Sample became the editor of *The Morehead Independent* in 1936. Together with Mr. George Calvert, they continued to improve both the circulation and the quality of the paper. It included local, state, and national issues from an unbiased viewpoint. For the first time in Morehead, photographs began to appear in the paper on a regular basis. It boasted that *The Independent* was an "all star paper" devoted to the betterment of the community. They printed news about the activities of local citizens such as:

> "Professor Henry Horton of MSC and the Foster Choral Club were heard over radio station WLW Cincinnati in a 25 minute broadcast Sunday morning."
> "One Act Operetta Presented" - The "Black Flamingo"

a dramatic performance by the Revelers Dramatic Club was invited to repeat their performance in Ashland and Grayson, but Miss Lucille Caudill said it was doubtful that the Revelers would be able to make both performances before Christmas."

Morehead Independent, Dec. 12, 1935

Advertising support for the paper now moved from livery stables and blacksmith shops to garages such as the Carr-Perry Motor Co. (Phone 7), and restaurant such as the Amos and Andy. This restaurant located on Main Street (close to the old City Hall) advertised hamburgers for .05 each. Parnell and Elizabeth Martindale (MSC graduates) were the owner/operators. Elizabeth reported to me that "When they sold hamburgers for .05 she could go to next door to the old Cut Rate Grocery and buy hamburger for 7 cents per lb. Other advertisers included Myrtle's Tea Room and Beer Garden (Phone 67) listing their menu of chicken & steak dinner with home cooked vegetables at reasonable prices. They urged you to "meet your friends at Myrtles".

Morehead was growing and becoming more sophisticated. The newspapers reporting the events and activities of its citizens began to reflect this growth and sophistication.

"This newspaper is dedicated to the advancement of Morehead and Rowan county and the well being of its people. Recording the happenings in business, and the doings of a live and prosperous community."

Morehead Independent (ct. 15, 1936)

But *The Morehead Independent* merged with *The Rowan County News* in 1946. However, it served a valuable role for 11 years as the competition for *The Rowan County News* which began publication in 1918. But for eleven years of that time the local citizens were given a choice of which weekly paper they preferred. Both the papers, and our history were better off because of the competition between the two papers. "The pen was mightier than the sword".

One Century (Plus) Of Morehead Newspapers

Title	Dates	Editor/Publisher
Morehead Times	1880s	
Morehead Sun	1880s	
Morehead Leader	1890s	
Morehead Advance	1895-1902	William Schooler
Mountaineer	1902-1917	Cora Wilson Stewart
Rowan County News	1918-1962	Wilson/Crutcher
Mountain Schorcher	1927-1929	Sam Cassity
Morehead Independent	1934-1945	William Sample
Rowan County School News	1935-1939	Roy Cornette
Morehead News	1962 -	Crutcher/Ron Caudill

Morehead College-University

??????????	1927	William Sample
More-Head-Light	1927-1929	William Sample
Trail Blazer	1929 -	Students

U.S. Navy Base At MSTC

Mountain Cruiser	1942-1945	Ensign P.R.

ROWAN COUNTY NEWS - 1918-1962 (WEEKLY)

THE JACK WILSON ERA, 1925-1945

Rowan County News - 1918-1962. Weekly. Published every Thursday at Morehead, Rowan County, Kentucky. Entered as second class matter at the post office at Morehead Kentucky, November 1, 1918. Subscription - $1.50 per year. (1918).

As we follow the paper trail through Morehead, we find that the early editors of *The Rowan County News* did not last long. (Although the paper itself has stood the test of time.) From 1918-1925 the editors included names like Frank Furham and Lee McGowhan. But it was not until August 13, 1925, when Jack Wilson and his sister, Grace Ford, moved to Morehead from Nebraska and bought the paper, that there was any kind of stability.

Jack Wilson, a devout Catholic, was a graduate of Wayne State College in Nebraska, and an officer in WWI. After his discharge from the Army he worked in the newspaper business in Oklahoma and Nebraska. It was rumored that he was forced to leave Nebraska because of his religious faith, and even in Morehead some of his neighbors felt he suffered some persecution. In 1925, there were very few Catholics here, and it was through the efforts of Jack Wilson and his sister that the first church was established in Morehead. The first Catholic Church started in Grace Ford's garage on Fourth Street. Their church now sits on almost the exact site where they began their worship services.

ROWAN COUNTY NEWS EXPANDED

With Jack Wilson's broad knowledge of the newspaper business, *The Rowan County News* began immediately to broaden and deepen its news coverage. There were thought provoking editorials on state and local issues. For the first time some national news began to appear. Also, greater in-depth reporting of Morehead sporting events began to appear. But very few photographs were printed. The technology to publish photographs was so expensive, that only the major newspapers could afford it.

Advertising support for the early *Rowan County News* included:

(1926) Cafeteria opened at Morehead State Teachers College offering meals for 15 cents.

(1938) Citizens Bank listing total assets $154,029.98.

(1943) Bruces 5 & 10 cent Store called themselves "Morehead's Toyland."

(1931) Goldes Department Store advertising dresses at $4.97 and up.

(1932) Carr-Perry Motor Co. listed 1932 Goodyear All Weather Tires beginning at $3.95

(1941) Morehead appliance Store listed Spiralator Washers at $79.95.

(1938) The London Flea Circus announced that Professor and Mrs. John Lynch and their trained flea circus would be in Morehead July 18 in a railroad car 150 feet long near the C&O Depot for 1 day only. There would be fleas on the high wire, fleas dancing to music, and fleas that push little carts. Also, there would be mama and papa flea fondly watching their new baby Elmer just able to crawl about. (I guess he had not learned to hop yet.) Also advertised was a 68 ton sea monster, a child born without arms or legs who could write, knit, and do many other things. (No- This writer did not attend this Flea Circus, maybe there are those still around that did.)

WILSON A RABID EAGLE FAN

The paper was a strong supporter of Morehead College and published a special section welcoming students to Morehead each fall.

"Morehead State Teachers College is the center of education in Eastern Kentucky. Its students are bettering conditions, and influencing progress throughout our region. So we welcome every student to Morehead this year, and invite you to come in and get acquainted with our community, and hope you will make yourself at home."

(Mr. Wilson was an avid Morehead Eagle fan who followed every game–and had no love for the UK wildcats).

COMIC SECTION FIRST APPEARED

For the first time cartoons such as "Pee Wee" (about two small boys), began to appear in a Morehead paper. Also, Will Rogers' humorous column poking fun at the politicians appeared. These did much to help Moreheadians to laugh, even though we were in the dark days of the depression. Jack Wilson appeared to have a good sense of humor and he helped us laugh.

Rowan County News, Sept. 19, 1929

WILSON A POLITICAL ACTIVIST

Mr. Wilson was determined to compete with *The Morehead Independent.* From 1934-1945 there was heated competition between papers. One was a strong, "democrat" supporter and the other strongly republican. Each paper pushed their own political agenda in local, state, and national elections. *Rowan County News* was considered a Republican paper, and *The Morehead Independent* supported the Democrat party. Of one of Democratic Senator Alben Barkley's U.S. Senate Campaigns, a *Rowan County News* article stated:

> "The Barkley Rally at Lexington was a disgrace to the State of Kentucky, and was nothing but a drunken brawl. The Barkley headquarters gave every W.P.A. employee in Louisville a dollar bill, a pint of whiskey, and a round trip ticket to attend the rally."

Rowan County News, July 14, 1938

People who say that negative political campaigning and critical media reporting are something new, have forgotten the "old days". Because the "mudslinging", and political "Shenanigens" were just as bitter and maybe even more intense then. The only difference was, they did not enter into critical political campaigning to sell papers. But it was something in which they sincerely believed, (maybe that's why those early newspapers were not basically successful) READ ON!

In a scathing editorial in the Rowan County News, Jack Wilson writes about Governor "Happy" Chandler's administration:

> "It is well known that the highway employees are being assessed "voluntary" contributions. The crop of weed cutters [in the highway department] has grown to such an extent that instead of there being a weed cutter for every weed, they now have two weed cutters for every weed. They now have so many weed cutters as to make traveling dangerous. As one Frenchburg man put it, they have to sow weed seeds in the early spring to prepare for the crop of weedcutters." (A weedcutter was a person, and not a mechanical device such as a "weedeater"). Also, in the same issue Editor Wilson writes:
>
> WHERE OH WHERE WERE THE WEED CUTTERS?
> It was also noticeable to motorists that weed cutters and state highway policemen were few and far between last Thursday. The reason: Governor Chandler was holding a rally in Bardstown. Also, prominent among those present was the Republican President of Morehead State Teachers College who has promised to deliver Rowan County into the hands of the enemy in exchange for his job.
>
> *Rowan County News*, July 14, 1938

WILSON DIES UNEXPECTEDLY

We will never know what the future would have held for *The Rowan County News* had Jack Wilson lived. However, the Thursday, October 29, 1942 edition of the paper contained this simple eulogy (no picture). Following are excerpts from the eulogy:

> "Jack is gone, there is not much more I can say. Friday night, October 16 he died suddenly. They say he had a blocked artery. He came here in 1925 and has seen the city grow and prosper and has had a big part in it all. He did much to help many people in the community. He has made a few enemies and many friends. He has supported every effort in the building of this community and never considered the cost. He liked politics but was no politician. He would never double cross a friend. His passing will leave a giant void in our community."
>
> *Rowan County News*, October 20, 1942

When you follow the legacy left by Jack Wilson along Morehead's paper trail it leads you through the roaring twenties when the economy was strong, and Rowan County was growing. With the Haldeman brick yard, the Clearfield Lumber Company, and the Clearfield Tile Plant, the future looked bright. But then the trail leads you through the depression years on into the beginning of WW II. (Jack Wilson died while awaiting a call to return to military service). Wilson's paper trail reported the events of these turbulent times, honestly, and fairly. But he also was passionately political and spoke out strongly for his beliefs, and for the candidates he supported. He left *The Rowan County News* a better paper than it was when he came. He had wielded well his pen, and found it "mightier than the sword."

SISTER SELLS PAPER

Grace Ford, Jack Wilson's sister, worked valiantly to keep the paper afloat after Jack's tragic death. Although she tried to continue his policies she was unsuccessful and in 1945 she sold the paper to W.E. "Snooks" Crutcher who had worked at *The Rowan County News* for several years. Mr. Crutcher also purchased *The Morehead Independent.* He now closed *The Morehead Independent,* and merged it into *The Rowan County News.* There was now only one paper in Morehead, *The Rowan County News,* and the Jack Wilson - Grace Ford paper trail in Morehead ended.

ROWAN COUNTY SCHOOL NEWS 1935-1939 (QUARTERLY)

This newspaper was published every two weeks in conjunction with *The Morehead Independent.* It was the official organ of the Rowan County Board of Education, and its purpose was "education and non-profit." The paper was published under the supervision of the Rowan County Board of Education and Superintendent Roy Cornette. It was printed by *The Morehead Independent.*

Roy Cornette was the first Superintendent of Schools in Rowan County to be appointed by a School Board. Prior to 1934, School Superintendents in Kentucky were elected by popular vote. This change in the law was intended to 'remove politics from Kentucky schools". It did <u>not</u>, in fact, it may have made it more "political". Teachers were expected to work for the school board candidate that supported the Superintendent. If they did not, they usually found themselves out of a job, or transferred to the most isolated rural school in Rowan County. So politics continued in the schools.

PAPER HELPED EASE THE PAIN OF SCHOOL CONSOLIDATION

Roy Cornette did a tremendous job during his tenure as super-intendent. (More will be written about his contribution when the history of the Rowan county Schools is written). He was the first to recognize the "power of the pen" and the importance of well-written information in school public relations. (There were no pictures in this early school newspaper.) In examining a copy of the August <u>1998</u> issue of Rowan County Schools paper, you find 91 photographs. This is one example of our moving from the printed page to the visual image. In 1935, each issue of *The Rowan County School News* printed a letter from the Superintendent to the people (not one photograph). He outlined the problems, plans, and progress of the school system. He explained budgetary problems, presented plans for the future, and promoted progress made in the schools. Believe me with 22 rural schools closed and consolidated under his administration there were problems.

Advertisement support for the paper came from many community businesses, eg.Cottage Café offered hot dogs and hamburgers for .05. The Leader Restaurant (Phone 277) next to the old City Hall offered clean wholesome food. Others included the Big Store, Sanitary Barber Shop, and J.W. Hogge's Grocery.

NEW COURSES, TEACHERS AND ACTIVITIES

The paper listed those pupils and schools with perfect attendance. It publicized new classes being offered such as a new journalism class offered at Morehead High School. It was taught by Sam Bradley, Jr. and was a part of the W.P.A. (Works Projects Administration). It was intended to teach students to read and write more critically. Also, a full study of journalism was offered. A new commercial class which included typing and shorthand was taught by Anna Lee Martin. Society news included marriages, deaths, and births as they related to school personnel.

The Rowan County School News included extra-curricular activities such as sports, dramatic presentations, P.T.A. meetings, and other club meetings. A special emphasis was placed on the importance of the Morehead Public (High) School library which proudly boasted of 1369 books in their collection. Miss Thelma Allen (aunt of "Sonny" Allen) Librarian, was determined to reach the goal of 1500 books that year.

RURAL SCHOOL NEWS PROMOTED PRIDE

This paper promoted pride in every school. Each school submitted news of their own activities at sometime throughout the year; e.g.: Adams-Davis School (10 miles out Rt. 377) reported the shades and curtains for the windows of Adams-Davis School were bought with proceeds from a pie supper. The teacher, Miss Dora Hutchinson, listed those students with perfect attendance: Homer Plank, Harrison Plank, Georgie Fraley, Chester Little, Guy Plank, Rosa Bell Little, Maxine Stone, Nadine Plank and Chester Stacy.

The Rowan County School News was <u>very successful</u> in helping people to see the importance of education. Those were depression days, many people were hurting, and this paper offered them hope, which is another way the "pen is mightier than the sword."

WORLD WAR II YEARS IN MOREHEAD

During the years of WW II much of the news dealt with the battle front and the home front. Such news as a letter from General George C. Marshall to Mrs. Effie Caudill attempting to console her on the death of her son Private First Class Mervel B. Caudill 35,429,571. He served in the infantry and was killed in action in the Southwest Pacific Area July 16, 1943.

War Bond drives, scrap drives, Red Cross drives, and rationing formed much of the home front news during the WW II years. "Rationing at a glance" was a weekly column on the front page of the paper, e.g.

Processed Foods - Blue stamps A8 through F5 in War Ration Books 4 are now good for 10 points each indefinitely.

Meats and fats - Red stamps A8 through Z8 and A-5 through C-5 in Book 4 are good for 10 points each indefinitely. (Who said life was much simpler in the "good old days"?)

This weekly column explained to the people in Morehead and Rowan County which ration stamps were valid, and for how much, and how long. Unless they grew their own food these ration stamps determined how well the people at home ate.

THE W.E. "SNOOKS" CRUTCHER ERA

THE ROWAN COUNTY NEWS - 1918 - 1962.
THE MOREHEAD NEWS - 1962-1976.

The late talented William "Snooks" Crutcher deserves all the credit for the present first class bi-weekly which the residents of Morehead now enjoy. "I consider myself fortunate to have 'Snooks' my friend," says George M. Calvert, newsman from the *Atlanta Constitution* who worked with Snooks in Morehead.

As we continue to follow the paper trail through Morehead and Rowan County, we come upon the untimely death of Jack Wilson in 1942. Following his death, his sister Grace Ford, struggled to keep the paper alive. It was during the years of WW II and she was not very successful. But with the competition of *The Morehead Independent* (1934-1945), and a war-time economy there was not enough business to support two papers.

MR. CRUTCHER COMES TO MOREHEAD

W.E. "Snooks" Crutcher was born in Louisa, Kentucky in 1912. he was given the nickname of "Snooks" as an infant, and it remained with him throughout his lifetime. Growing up in Louisa, Kentucky, on the banks of the Tug River, he worked for his uncle

Rowan County News publisher W.E. Crutcher stands in front of a new press, 1948.
L-R: Carl Messer, Crutcher, E.A Thompson.

in a grocery store after school. There was little to do in the small Eastern Kentucky town, but there was a movie theater across the river. However, there was no bridge, only a small ferry boat that charged 5 cents to cross, and, instead of paying the 5 cents fare, he would strip bare, seal his clothes in a water tight container, and swim across the river in the raw. He would then put his clothes on, go to the movies and repeat the process returning home.

In the late 1920s at the height of the depression Snooks came to Morehead to enroll at MSTC. He could only attend part time, and had to work to pay his way, and he got a job at *The Rowan County News*. Later, he also worked for a while at *The Morehead Independent*. About that time, he met Darlene Miller, another student at MSTC. Darlene was from South Shore in Greenup County, and they seemed to have much in common including growing up in a river town. They were soon married and he begin to work more, and attend MSTC less. Also, with the birth of their two daughters, Patricia (Pat) and Marilyn Sue (Mike), family responsibilities made it necessary for him to work full time. He began looking for another job.

Mr. Crutcher was appointed Postmaster at Morehead and served in that job for four years. He was never happy there, because he said he had printers ink in his blood. It was then he decided to get back into the newspaper business.

W.E. CRUTCHER PURCHASES TWO MOREHEAD PAPERS

With both local papers struggling financially during WW II, and several months before the war ended, W.E. Crutcher purchased *The Rowan County News* and *The Morehead Independent*. The masthead of the paper published January 11, 1945 read:

"*The Rowan County News* and *The Morehead Independent*".

Crutcher wrote on the front page of that edition:

"The original intention was to name the paper The Independent-News, but because the Rowan County News has a 62 year history we decided to retain that name."

W.E. "Snooks" Crutcher came to Morehead as a student at MSTC, and remained in Morehead first as Postmaster, then as the publisher of *The Rowan County News*. He loved and believed in the future of Morehead, and MSTC. His "pen" passionately promoted the people and places within this sphere. He was an eloquent spokesman for his areas of interest. He would sit down at his old manual typewriter, typing with two fingers, and smoking a cigarette at the same time as he pounded out interesting articles, and convincing editorials. Although he used two fingers, many times he was only using one, because he would use one hand to remove the cigarette from his lips and flip the ashes back over his shoulder on the floor. (He did not believe in ashtrays.) Consequently all of his shirts had burn marks on the back. Sometimes the ashes he flipped over his shoulder were still alive, and he would be so engrossed in writing he would have scars on his skin.

When the War ended in 1945, and the nation returned to a peace time economy, Crutcher, could see tremendous publishing possibilities. Indeed, W.E. Crutcher was a man of uncanny vision. He could see a brilliant future for Morehead, Rowan County, and Eastern Kentucky. But he decided the first thing he had to do was to increase the circulation of his paper. He succeeded in doubling the circulation in just a few months by conducting a contest, and giving away an automobile to the person who could sell the most subscriptions to *The Rowan County News.*

CONTEST WINNERS AWARDED NEW CARS

Analda Caudill won a new Ford by getting the most subscriptions in one of the contests. (Dorothy Ellis, this writer's mother, came in second place and received $250, and immediately used that money as a down payment on her own new Fairlane Ford.) A few years earlier, another contest was held and Lyda Carter was the winner of a new Hudson. These contests were extremely effective in increasing readership in *The Rowan County News.* Therefore, as a result of the increased circulation, Mr. Crutcher gained greater advertising support, and could charge more for advertising space.

PUBLISHING EMPIRE GROWS

W.E. Crutcher, with his deep faith in the future of Eastern Kentucky and in the publishing business, began to amass an Eastern Kentucky Publishing Empire. In the early 1950s he purchased *The Grayson Journal-Enquirer,* and *The Greenup News.* Next he purchased *The Olive Hill Times* and soon controlled the largest circulation of weekly newspapers in Kentucky. Also, he began to branch out into other publishing businesses, e.g. Birthday Calendar Company, and Morehead Printing Services, and all proved profitable.

As Crutcher's publishing empire grew, so did his influence in community, educational, and political affairs. He wielded well his publishers pen, by passionately promoting the people and programs in which he believed. His first priority was Morehead State College, and its new President Dr. Adron Doran. The dynamic Dr. Doran was an eloquent spokesman for the budget, building, and bonding needs of the college. (Soon to become a University). "Snooks" published those needs far and wide, not only through his papers, but through his substantial political influence. There was seldom an issue of a Crutcher paper that did not contain a positive article about Dr. Doran and Morehead State. Dr. Doran was certainly the greatest leader in Morehead State history. However, "Snooks" Crutcher did much to enhance that leadership with his positive publicity, and political support.

CRUTCHER GAINS POLITCIAL CLOUT

Mr. Crutcher combined the political arena with the publishing business. Although he never ran for public office, he was successful in helping elect local, state, and national politicians. He knew his way around Frankfort and Washington D.C. He was known by Governors, Congressmen, Senators, and Presidents. He rode on Air Force One with President Kennedy, and was asked by that President to come to Washington, and discuss the effect of specific legislation on Eastern Kentucky. On one occasion when he was scheduled to meet with President Kennedy, he packed his clothes, including a brownish tweed suite and headed for D.C. He asked his daughter "Pat" Skaggs to accompany him. "Snooks" was nearly blind as the result of an automobile accident many years earlier and needed help to get around. So daughter Patricia accompanied him on the trip. She recounted that in Washington they sent his suit to be pressed. It came back in just a few minutes before his scheduled appointment with the President. He dressed quickly and stopped by to ask his daughter if he looked presentable. To her horror, there was a 90 degree tear in the knee of his trousers. Pat tried desperately to find thread to sew it up and couldn't. She said dad you can't possibly go see the President with a tear in your trousers. He said, "If Adlai Stevenson can campaign for president with a hole in his shoe, I can meet with the President with a rip in the knee of my pants," and he did.

CAVE RUN DAM COMES TO LICKING RIVER

The controversial Cave Run Dam was another issue Mr. Crutcher strongly supported. (This writer is no stranger to the Cave Run Lake Controversy. It was in 1937 when he stood on his grandfather's farm and heard the Corps of Engineers discuss that the water would cover all his farm). Snooks believed the dam would enhance economic development in the region. But to those dozens of families displaced by the lake, whose lives were uprooted, it was a bitter fight. It was a fight between the "lakers" and the "landers" and almost came to bloodshed. (This writer was threatened to be planted six foot under one time.) But the "lakers" won the battle, but to those who were uprooted, it was agony. It was controversial but "progress" prevailed largely through the power of the publishers pen. In 1974 the 8,270 acre lake, built by the Army Corp of Engineers was completed, and the residents were displaced from their homes.

ST. CLAIRE HOSPITAL COMES TO MOREHEAD

Those who lived in Morehead before the St. Claire Hospital was here, are well aware of the critical need for such a facility. As the college, and community grew, the need became more acute. Of course, our own beloved Dr. Louise was more aware of the need for a hospital than anyone, and she began sowing the seed of need throughout our area. Her seed of need began to take root and grow.

It flourished rapidly, and in October, 1960, she presided over a meeting of 140 local leaders that resulted in The Morehead Kentucky Hospital Foundation becoming a legal entity. The Charter Board member officers were: C.P. Caudill, President; W.E. Crutcher, Secretary and Elijah M. Hogge, Treasurer. The Charter board of Directors were: Dr. C. Louise Caudill, Glenn W. Lane, William M. Caudill, Dr. Everett Blair, Adrian Razor, Otto P. Carr, J.M. Clayton, John M. Palmer, D.B. Caudill, Curt Bruce, and Dr. Adron Doran.

With W.E. Crutcher using his paper to promote the great need for a hospital, and keeping the people aware of the progress, the community soon raised $250,000. Therefore, with the help of a $500,000 grant from the Hill-Burton Act, and the Sisters of Notre Dame assuming responsibility for operation, ground was broken for the new hospital on September 19, 1961. The seed of need had flourished into fruition through Dr. Caudill's leadership and a determined community effort.

NEWS MR. CRUTCHER WOULD NOT PRINT

W.E. Snooks Crutcher deserves a great deal of credit for his continued publicity about the need for a hospital. His articles and editorials helped pave the way for an overwhelmingly Protestant community to graciously accept and warmly welcome the sisters of Notre Dame. Their presence has both exemplified and enriched our community as they cared for the sick, and, "Snooks" recognized the pen was mightier than the sword in molding public opinion, and overcoming prejudice. He wielded it well, and Morehead, Rowan County, and Eastern Kentucky are better off as a result of his efforts.

There was some local news that Mr. Crutcher refused to print. He always refused to print the "Courthouse News" which is a regular feature in our paper today. It includes arrests, divorces, court dockets, and motion hours. His thesis was these people were not guilty of anything yet, and he steadfastly refused to run this news in his papers. Mr. Crutcher would have trouble surviving in today's publishing world because it seems today this is what most people want to read.

NEW NAME—NEW IMAGE
MOREHEAD NEWS 1962

In 1962 *The Rowan County News* which began publishing in 1918 became *The Morehead News.* Mr. Crutcher believed it was time for a new image for the paper, and more people could identify with *The Morehead News.* Also, Morehead State College would soon become a University, therefore, the name of "Morehead" enhanced both the paper and the university.

Mr. Crutcher was a man ahead of his time because his was one of the very first newspapers in the state or nation to convert from hot metal to cold-type operation. When he installed a four unit offset press in April 1964, *The Morehead News* was only one of four such units in the state. Marvin Wilson Jr. was hired to change from hot type to cold. He then hired Helen Northcutt and Ron Caudill to make the change. But the technology was so new, no one had any experience but they finally worked through it. In 1965, "Snooks" spoke to the Kentucky Press Association, and said "By the end of this decade, two-thirds of the newspapers in Kentucky will be published on offset presses." He was ridiculed and laughed at for making such a statement, and promptly resigned his membership in the Kentucky Press Association. But by the end of the decade his statement proved more than prophetic, because three-fourths of the papers in Kentucky used off-set presses.

On September 15, 1969, *The Morehead News* moved to a new modern building at 722 West First Street where it continues to be published. In 1976 after building an Eastern Kentucky Publishing

Empire, he sold his holdings to Mt. Sterling attorney, William C. Clay and Morehead newspaperman, Ronald J. Caudill. Mr. Crutcher then retired and lived the remainder of his life in Florida.

LEAVES HIS LEGACY

W.E. Crutcher died in 1982 and is buried beside his beloved Darlene in Lee Cemetery. But he left a large legacy because of the power of his pen and his vision for the future. He prophesied so many times "That Morehead and Rowan County would become the educational, cultural, recreational, and medical center of Eastern Kentucky." Many people without his vision laughed when he continually used this phrase in his papers. But "he who laughs last laughs longest," and Snooks had the last laugh. If you don't believe this just drive around Cave Run Lake on any summer weekend, or try to fine a parking place on our University campus, or walk through the corridors of our beautiful, modern Medical Center. Also, if you take time to visit our Kentucky Folk Art Center, you must agree "Snooks" was right on target, and was one of the people who greatly influenced the building of Cave Run Lake and the Hospital. On the paper trail through Morehead, his "pen <u>was</u> mightier than the sword."

Ronald J. Caudill, editor, President of Morehead News worked at paper 1968-1998.

THE MOREHEAD NEWS 1962-1998 (BI-WEEKLY)

RONALD J. CAUDILL ERA

As we approach the end of the paper trail through Morehead, it becomes even more apparent of the unique role a local newspaper plays in the life of a community. It records our births and deaths, our successes, and failures, our weaknesses and strengths, our happy and sad events. It is one mirror that reflects who we are, where we have been and where we are going. It provides insight into the past, and offers hope for the future.

CRUTCHER HIRED CAUDILL

The paper trail–through Morehead's modern era leads us to the office of RonCaudill. He began his newspaper publishing career in 1963, with the late "Snooks" Crutcher as his mentor. Caudill readily admits it was "Snooks" who gave him his golden opportunity, and taught him the newspaper business. With a great deal of emotion Ron recalls his relationship with the late Mr. Crutcher: "He would call me into his office, take out a pad and pencil, and say, Mr. Caudill–(He always called Ron 'Mr. Caudill'). This is the way its going to be." Then he would write down two or three things he wanted done, and they would be done that way. Ron also traveled the state with Mr. Crutcher as his driver, because "Snooks" was practically blinded in an automobile accident and could not drive.

Ronald J. Caudill is a native Moreheadian. The son of Katherine and the late Nelson Caudill. He grew up in Morehead and is a proud product of our public schools. His experience with newspapers includes about all areas of publishing, such as printers devil, press man, production manager, director of advertising, general manager, and executive vice-president, and president.

MR. CLAY AND MR. CAUDILL PURCHASE PAPERS

In 1976, Mr. Caudill, along with William C. Clay, a Mt. Sterling attorney, purchased *The Morehead News* and the Kentucky Publishing Company including *The Morehead News, The Greenup News, The Grayson Journal-Enquirer*, and the *Olive Hill Times*. It also included the Birthday Calender Company, and the Morehead Printing Service. Ron, never content with the status quo, began to determine ways to expand the Kentucky Publishing Company.

In March 1977 he launched a regional publication called the "*Shopping News.*" Mr. Caudill recalled: "The original intention was to publish a paper with one page of news, and the rest regional advertising." The early editions of *The Shopping News* were delivered free to 21,160 homes. It was first published every two weeks, but it became so popular that they began publishing weekly.

Caudill recalled that nearby Menifee County did not have a weekly newspaper. Since it was in their *Shopping News* region, and in keeping with the Kentucky Publishing company's plans for expansion, The *Menifee County News* was born on December 21, 1977. In January 1980, the KPC purchased the *Greenup Sentinel*, and merged it with the *Greenup News*. This made the *Greenup News* one of the most circulated weekly papers in Kentucky.

Mr. Caudill recalls the extremely difficult task of starting a newspaper. You must first get a paid mailing list and submit it to the Post Office. Then you have to gather the advertising support for the paper. Next you must put together the sales, advertising, editorial, and technical staff needed to publish. The key to any successful organization is to surround yourself with a competent staff. Ron says he's been able to do just that and he gives credit to the staff for making the paper a success.

Another major expansion came in March 1980, when the KPC began publication of *The Montgomery News*. By now the Kentucky

Publishing company's seven newspapers had an astronomical circulation of 40,000 copies a week, or 2,080,000 copies a year. Mr. Caudill said it required about 600 tons of newsprint, 9,000 pounds of ink and hundreds of thousands of man hours (and woman hours) to publish those issues.

MOREHEAD NEWS MOVES TO NEW LOCATION

On September 13, 1969, *The Morehead News* moved to its present spacious site located on West First Street. Immediately plans were made to modernize and upgrade the equipment. On September 16, 1976, they installed a new five-unit Goss Community Press. Mr. Caudill recalled that on April 8, 1977, *The Morehead News* was the first weekly newspaper in Kentucky to print a full four-color picture. They had the capability to accomplish this because they could take the picture, develop the film, do the color separations, print the picture, and all done in-house. Also, *The Morehead News* was the first weekly newspaper in Kentucky with a 24 hour per day live *United Press International News Service*.

BI-WEEKLY PUBLICATION

In 1977, *The Morehead News* moved from publishing once a week to twice a week. This required more staff, and more delegation. Ron Caudill was president at that time, with Jeff Fannin and Joe Lamb as vice-presidents. These men, along with an outstanding staff, moved smoothly into publishing Tuesdays and Saturdays.

On June 12, 1987, Roy H. Park, chairman of Park Communications based in Ithaca, New York, purchased the twice weekly *Morehead News* and all of the other holdings of the Kentucky Publishing company. They also purchased three other Kentucky newspapers in South Central Kentucky owned by Mr. Al Smith, the personable host of the weekly KET television program, COMMENT ON KENTUCKY. This brought the Park Kentucky Newspaper holdings to 11. However, with the death of Mr. Roy Park, the newspapers were acquired by Park Acquisitions, who sold its holdings to Media General, a company with headquarters in Lexington, Kentucky. These new owners were primarily interested in the radio and television holdings. The new owner of the *Morehead News* was now a mega-media giant more interested in radio and television holdings than newspapers.

Under new ownership, it seemed the *Morehead News* would be lost in this media empire. But that was not the case because the company retained Ron Caudill to manage not only their Kentucky newspapers, but also newspapers in Virginia, Illinois, Indiana,and Arkansas. *The Morehead News* was autonomous, and encouraged to focus on news and features of local interest. This it did well under Ron Caudill's leadership.

The mega-media giant Park Communications, that owned *The Morehead News*, soon began to lose interest in the paper. *The Morehead News*, and all of the other 10 newspaper holdings in Kentucky were soon put up for sale. Ron Caudill and other backers made an offer but were out bid by Community Newspaper Holdings, a company with headquarters in Birmingham, Alabama, and financed by the Alabama Retirement system. Mr. Caudill was offered a lucrative position to manage their newspaper holdings, but he elected to retire. He was retained by the company as a special consultant for one or two days per week.

LONG CAUDILL LEGACY

Ronald J. Caudill left large footprints along the paper trail through 34 years of publishing *The Morehead News*. He kept the newspaper "flying" through some turbulent times. Like the pilot of a giant jet airliner, you may never see him, but rest assured he is there in control, keeping the plane flying on a steady course. Ron's vast knowledge and experience kept the *Morehead News* flying. Yes, without his technical knowledge, it may have crashed, but with Ron at the controls it continued to fly right on course.

It seems the paper trail in Morehead has come full circle. From the late 1800s when newspapers, because of financial problems, did not survive long, until 1988 with the same problem. Editor, William Schooler wrote in the *Morehead Advance* in 1898, "this newspaper is a business, and is dependent upon our advertisers and subscribers for survival. We can last only as long as we print factual news of local interest." This was prophetic 100 years ago, and it is equally prophetic as we face a new millennium.

It seems the old saying "What goes around, comes around" was true on the paper trail through Morehead. One hundred years ago, weekly newspaper owners had a limited longevity. Today that is equally true. One-hundred years ago, a weekly newspaper believed the way to survive was to print local news and features of local interest, (including local history). That is equally true today. Even though Moreheadians are bombarded with 24 hours per day television news reporting; even though we are saturated with television news, sports, weather, drama, comedy, and entertainment of all types, where is the news of local interest? Even though we have daily newspapers all around us, where is the news of local interest?

LOCAL NEWS NEEDED

There is a deep hunger in the hearts of Moreheadians for factual, meaningful local news. News and features to which they can relate. Local issues and concerns are the most meaningful. This is especially true for former Moreheadians, now living elsewhere. This writer lived in Florida for several years, and continued to subscribe to *The Morehead News* . It was almost like a letter from home, and everyone looked forward each week to its arrival. Also, those in the military, who were stationed in many far flung isolated areas of the world devoured every word in their hometown paper. It served as a connection to home and family, which were those things they missed most.

MOREHEAD A GLOBAL VILLAGE

A question in todays world is, how will we receive our local news throughout the next millennium? We read of a predicted paperless society. We now have the technology to read our newspapers on our television screens. We are drowning in information all around us. This is the information age. We are a global village as predicted by Marshall McCluhan in the 1960s. We now can know what's happening throughout the world even as it happens.

While we are a global village, what does the future hold for local news in the village of Morehead? There will always be a need to know what is happening here and now, and what has happened in the history of our community. As the Editor of the 1898 *Morehead Advance* predicted, "As long as we print factual news of local interest, there will be a market." Also, the pen (which now may mean a computer) remains "mightier than the sword."

CRACKER BARREL COMMENTS

"The Sage of Morehead"
"Then was our mouth filled with laughter." (Ps. 126:2)

Thomas Wood Hinton was born January 7, 1904, in Fleming County, Kentucky, and died April 26, 1949, in Rowan County. He was the son of John F. and Lula (Spradling) Hinton. Thomas Wood Hinton, "Woodie," as he was known, moved to Morehead in 1925, soon after the Midland Trail (US 60) was built through Rowan County. His nephew, Frank O. Hinton, said, "Woodie moved to Morehead because the new highway and Morehead State Teachers College offered more opportunities for the future than Fleming

County." Woodie soon opened up a service station and tourist camp and became a successful businessman.

Mr. Hinton met and married local beauty, Miss Lynn Sidney Evans, daughter of local lumber tycoon, Drew Evans. They had one son, Tommy. However, the marriage did not last long after Tommy was born, and they divorced.

COLUMN RAN FROM DEPRESSION THROUGH WW II

When the depression years (1929-1939) reached Morehead, many businesses failed. However, Woodie sold his businesses before the economic depression reached Morehead. He then began his next career, one that brought him in touch with almost every citizen of Rowan County. He began a career in journalism, and soon was writing a weekly column for *The Morehead Independent*, and *The Rowan County New*s. His column was headed by an artist's sketch of Woodie poking his head up through a cracker barrel. It was a welcome sight for his many readers each week. It was through his column that he became one of the best known columnist in Rowan County newspaper history. His widely read and frequently quoted column was always the first thing readers turned to when their paper arrived. This writer's mother would occasionally mail me a paper during my military service in WW II. It always helped raise my morale as I read about home folks. His comments were humorous, insightful, thought provoking and encouraging. He helped keep up the morale of many lonely homesick GIs from Rowan County during WW II. By doing that, he made a major contribution to the war effort. Woody's type of humor was ageless and timeless in his appeal. His column appeared in both *The Rowan County News* (now Morehead News) and *The Morehead Independent* for 20 years.

HELPED US LAUGH AT OURSELVES

Woodie Hinton was a poor man's Will Rogers and he made us laugh during the depth of the depression, and the weariness of war by helping us to laugh at ourselves and each other. He delighted in poking good natured fun at local citizens, politicians, business and professional men. It was always gentle humor and few people ever took offense. Except when Woody once wrote, "the only time C.B. Daugherty (President of the Citizens Bank) and his wife, Hazel, ever went out together was after the stove blew up." Cap Daugherty said, "that was not true, they went out once together before the stove blew up–it was only smoking."

SATIRE INCLUDED

Woody's insightful, humorous columns poked fun at issues, politics as well as local citizens. His analysis of the infamous MSC battle with the Southern Association of Colleges appears below in a reprint of his January 3, 1947 column:

SOUTHERN ASSOCIATION DROPS MSC

"I interviewed Lee Cochran yesterday to get the low-down on the school proposition. As you know, Lee is the night watchman at the college. His statement is as follows: "Instead of the Southern Association dropping us, we should have dropped them. I never did like that bunch...they're just a pack of rebels. My contention is to join the Western, Eastern or Northern Association.

"I run the college at night," Lee continued, "and I handle it right. I can see like a coon dog at night, and I don't care whether this college belongs to the Baptist Association or the Association of the Prevention of Cruelty to Animals, I am still for it. We have strived and we have struck: we have argued and we have fit. If any of them Southern rebels think they can run us out I am ready to meet them at the city gates."

"Credits," said Lee. "That is what is wrong with the country today. Everybody wants too much credit. Everyone should think more of learning and less about the credit (hours) they receive. And furthermore, the reason a dog has so many friends is because he wags his tail instead of his tongue."

Thank you, Mr. Cochran. I consider you a scholar and a gentleman.

MOREHEAD MUSTACHE CLUB

Woodie was ahead of his time, because in an era when very few men had facial hair, he proposed a Morehead Mustache Club. A portion of that column follows:

"I often wonder what has happened to all the mustaches. I'd like to see this town bust loose and the men folks grow some good ones. It's a great idea to stimulate business. Bob Bishop would buy some mustache combs and wax. Curt Bruce, 10 cent store owner, would order some cups. On the other hand there would be some strange sights. For instance, Jack Helwig–his would look like and be as coarse as an old mule's tail. I can't imagine Noah Kennard twisting the end of a "handle bar" mustache, or Murvell Crosley drinking buttermilk through his. Now a good bushy one would look good on Frank Havens, and the one that W.H. Rice would have would be what I would call a two-tone model, yellow on each side, and kinda sandy in the middle, for he is a constant pipe smoker. Professor Vaughn would look bad with a Hitler model. However, "Chinn" Clayton would welcome the idea. "Cliff" McClelland's mustache would be a complete fizzle, and Jim Clay, well its hard to tell what color his would be. I would not want to say. Well, boys, I am for the Morehead Mustache Club, but first lets ask the wives. We don't want to do anything that would get the ill feelings of the little women."

Woodie declared that Claude Brown, local auto dealer, weighed about as much as the car he drove. He also said of auto dealer W.L.

Jayne: "Mr. Jayne says you can buy one of his cars for a song, and Woodie said the song's title is "Over the Hill to the Poor House."

When Woodie didn't like something, he would offer some constructive criticism. For instance, Woodie had some constructive criticism about tattoo marks on the human body. (That is still a controversial topic even today.)

"TABOOD TATTOOS"

"There are four things I have found in life that I absolutely hate and I am confronted with the creeps and burst out in goose-pimples the moment I see them. The greatest fear I have is of snakes. I don't like even the pretty little garter snakes. I hate buttermilk, I have never tasted it in my life, but if I was told to drink a glass or jump from a two-hundred foot tower into the Ohio River, I would jump." "I hate infidels, and for ghost stories, I read Ingersoll, Pastor Russell, and have nightmares. I hate tatoo marks on anyone, yet I am not afraid of it. But if a man would ever come to me with a tatoo needle I would be gone in nothing flat. I like to read tatoo marks on people, and I know some very nice people have tatoo marks on them." "I always wonder just what frame of mind the people were in when they had them put on. It seems that it is coming back in now. I don't know why, and I don't care, but I can't resist asking a fellow why he had that done. You see so many with Social Security numbers on their arms. I know one man happily married, with a picture of a girl named Lillian on his chest, and she looks like a headhunter. He told me it was a girl he met in England during the war. I asked him if Lillian did not grow monotonous being so close to him all of the time. He said he would be very happy if she would leave." "I knew one fellow, engaged, with a picture on his arm, and before the marriage can take place it has to be removed. So far he has it down to a scar about the size of a dollar bill, that resembles a burn. Just give me vanilla!"

ROWAN COUNTY "SHAKERS" NEEDLED

Woodie got his "digs" in at local politicians at a time when personal contact was necessary to get elected. He was quick to point out that Morehead had a colony of Shakers in their community. He said, "Cliff Hamilton could shake lots of hands in one minute. But Arthur Hogge was the shakingest man I've ever known. He could shake more hands in one minute that your normal shaker can shake in 30 minutes. He's what I call a year round shaker. But Joe McKinney can shake hands without laughing out loud, while James Clay, esq. swells up like a bullfrog when he does his shaking."

Following the July 4, 1939 Flood, Woodie's column got serious. Three days after the flood he wrote: "No one can say that the people of Morehead and Rowan County can't take it on the chin. After a brief survey, and talking with several folks, I find them now in much better spirits. They are all working like "towheads" and are talking of building a bigger and better Morehead. They're saying, the fact is we can't stop, we have to go ahead." He also paid tribute to the many remarkable acts of kindness by so many people during the tragedy of the flood.

HATED HITLER

During WW II, Woodie, who was very patriotic, went to Louisville and got a job in a defense plant. He called it "the worst job he ever had," but he wanted to do his part for the good old U.S.A. He said "this was no time or feather bedding". His column continued as he described an incident with German Prisoners of War.

"On my way to Morehead, the train was stopped by the side of another train with seventeen coaches of German prisoners. They were fine looking chaps; all of them had a smile a yard long and one showed me a picture of his mother and sweetheart. They seemed so happy to be here. I could not understand what he was telling me, but his face really told me something. They are not the type of people we have them pictured. The boys I saw are the types that we would like to know and visit with us. They are all or most all big blondes with perfect teeth, and a perfect physique. It is one of the horrors of war to educate fellows like that, that they must kill to survive. I sincerely hope that this country, the country of countries, will not stop the war, until such people as Hitler will be singing in the deepest of Hells."

EVEN CHRISTMAS COMEDY INCLUDED

One of Woodie's last Cracker Barrel columns was a classic, as he poked fun at many of his friends over the Christmas gifts he did, and did not receive.

"Christmas has come and gone and I am about through with my exchanging. I have a trip to Lexington to make, but I am sort of afraid to get on the train with some of the ties I received. I got some shorts that if I put them on, minus my pants, and walked up the street people would ask: "Where is that barber pole going?" The $75 watch that Ezra Martt was going to give me didn't arrive. Something happened at the factory and production slowed down. The Parker pen that I was expecting from George Caudill had not come in. He was going to give me the "52" set instead of the Parker "51". Frank Laughlin gave me his good will and E.E. Elam sent me a picture of his goat. Ray White promised me a check for $3,399, but I found out that it was made to the Federal Revenue Department and has been endorsed and cashed by same. The Citizens Bank sent me a notice saying "Overdraft." I sometimes wonder if they have any blanks that say "Underdraft". I get so many drafts from that bank it is a wonder that I don't catch pneumonia. But Alpha Hutchinson, the assistant cashier, did give me a chew of tobacco.

"Snooks" Crutcher, the editor of this paper and my boss, was very generous this year. He sent me a Christmas card that had a name rubbed out on it. That lousy bum Clark Lane, the undertaker, had some beautiful cards this year, and the inscription read: "I'll be seeing you."

Woodie Hinton's Cracker Barrel Comments provided humor, help, and encouragement to a generation of Rowan Countians. It helped ease them through an economic depression, a tragic flood, and a weary war. Therefore, if laughter is the best medicine, Woodie was a fine physician. HE WAS A SPECIALIST IN HIS FIELD.

COLLEGE CAMPUS NEWSPAPERS

As we follow the paper trail through Morehead it leads us to the campus of Morehead State Normal School. It began in the spring of 1927 when half a dozen bright young students discussed the need <u>for</u> and possibility <u>of</u> a student newspaper. Their thesis was that the four year old Normal School and Teachers College had grown steadily from its beginning in 1922, and had reached the point where a student publication was a necessity.

Their statement was "Every school of any standing must have an organ through which it may make itself felt. It must not only reach the community in which it is established, but must also reach the entire region from which it draws its students". These early publishing pioneers believed strongly in both a need and demand for such a publication. They contacted some local businesses, and found many would support such a paper through advertisements.

Also, they contacted Jack Wilson, the new Editor of the *Rowan County News*, and found he would print such a publication. Also the faculty and administration strongly supported the idea. Therefore, these young idealistic journalistic hopefuls left campus that spring determined to return in the fall and establish a newspaper.

Before registration ended in September of 1927, a notice was placed on the bulletin board in Burgess Hall announcing a meeting of all students interested in a school newspaper. About a dozen showed up for the meeting and the newspaper "baby" was conceived and a staff was elected.

The first staff for the first student newspaper published on the campus of Morehead State normal School consisted of William J. Sample, Editor-in-Chief. (He later became the founding publisher of *The Morehead Independent*). The Associate Editor was John Ridgeway. News Editors were Marjorie Rayburn and A.D. Roberts. The sports Editor was Elwood Allen, (Uncle of John "Sonny" Allen). Reporters were Josephine Jeffers, Dorothy Hesson, and Willis Hankla.

EDITORIAL POLICY ESTABLISHED

The staff began rapidly writing the copy for the first edition. They gathered advertising support from local merchants. They established editorial policies such as "A paper to be a success must have ideals." Their ideals included promoting the school so that its influence will be felt throughout Kentucky and the nation. Also, they believed the paper needed goals. One goal was "that it be a paper published by students, about students (and faculty) and for students. Another goal was to aid the up-building of the school". Plans were also made to write a column in each issue about former students, and the ambition of the editor was "to give our fellow students a real 'newsy' school paper, one they will look forward to reading. BUT THE PAPER HAD NO NAME!

"NO NAME" PAPER PUBLISHED

On October 4, 1927, the "baby" was born with high hopes but no name. The first issue announced a contest to name the student newspaper. This was much the same way that the athletic team had been named the Bald Eagles, in a contest four years earlier. The student who named the athletic team the Bald Eagles was a freshman by the name of Peaches Ellis. (This writer's aunt). She won a prize of $25 for submitting the name. But alas, the prize for naming the school newspaper was only $5.

GROWTH EMPHASIZED

The first issue of The ??????? listed the progress the school had made since it opened in September 1923, with an enrollment of less than 100. But four years later (1927) the enrollment was:

First Term	308
Second Term	682
First Summer Term	486
Second Summer Term	172
Extension Dept.	400
Training School	105
Total Enrollment	2,153
Less Duplicates	875
Individual Enrollment	1278

The school now was accredited by the University of Kentucky as a class A Senior College. By 1927, it had graduated three Bachelors Degrees, 27 life certificates for teachers, eighty six elementary certificates, and 219 provisional elementary certificates.

SPORTS IMPORTANT

Also included in the ??????????? was the Bald Eagle Football schedule released by Coach Downing. The Football schedule for the 1927 fall semester was:

October 8	Morris Harvey
October 15	Kentucky Wesleyan
October 22	Rio Grande (Ohio)
November 6	Union College
November 13	Eastern Kentucky

Coach Downing said, "With only four lettermen returning from last year, Allen, Bates, Clayton, and Perry, we have our work cut out for us with this schedule." Also, included in the first edition of the school paper was a biographical sketch and picture of President Frank Button. The editor wrote about President Button: "Since 1887 our President has devoted his time and energy to the education of young people. He is loved by friends, loved and respected by all who know him, and he breathes good fellowship and faith to all our students." Appropriately enough, a history of the school was in the first edition. The new "baby" newspaper was well received, but it needed a name.

Finally the baby was named! The October 18, 1927 edition of the new student newspaper announced the winner of

First Morehead State College Newspaper was The More-head Light 1927.

the contest, and proudly proclaimed its identity on the masthead. The winning name, selected by a panel of students was submitted by Mrs. Pickett M. Snedegar from Mt. Sterling. The name of the newspaper was an obvious (and perhaps "corny") play on words. But it was intended to emphasize the need for more education and understanding. No, the name of the first Morehead College Student Newspaper was <u>not</u> *The Trail Blazer*, but was *The More-Head-Light*. The volume I number 2 edition of the Morehead College student newspaper was *The More-Head-Light* (the first edition was nameless). The headlines of that edition announced the football team's loss to Morris Harvey College in Barboursville, West Virginia by a crushing 81-0. Sports editor, Elwood Allen, put a positive spin on the game when he wrote, "Our boys completed three consecutive passes early in the game for a gain of 35 yards. But the fourth pass was intercepted and returned for a touchdown." Also, he wrote, "The score was 25-0 at the end of the third quarter, but during the final quarter our desperate passing attack backfired every time." It seems Morehead college had struggled to compete in football from its inception. But conversely, in this very same issue,

First Morehead College Trail Blazer staff, 1929.

there was an article by Mrs. Lillard Carter saying more pep and enthusiasm was needed to support the football team. She wrote, "Kicks, cuts, bruises, broken bones, and lacerations, are the daily lot of the football players. Yet they untiringly give of their best for their school whose welfare and good name they have at heart. They deserve our support."

FIRST NEWSPAPER EMPHASIZED COMMUNITY INVOLVEMENT

The newspaper also exhibited a social conscience when it printed, "We spend millions to advertise cigarettes, but only a few paltry dollars to tell the world about our school." Also, the editors recognized the importance of advertising support when they wrote, "We urge you to patronize those advertising in this paper. They are your friends, and you owe it to your school to patronize them ."

Another article on the front page emphasized that school spirit was better than "pep." The column emphasized that "pep" was something artificially created out of thin air. But enthusiasm for the team was solidly based upon support of the school, and appreciation for the effort made by our team. There was a photograph of the 1926 football team, however, they were not identified. (Perhaps, after the crushing defeat by Morris Harvey, they wished to remain anonymous).

CLUB NEWS AND SCHOOL CALENDAR PRINTED

Also, this edition carried a story of plans underway for the college to host the upcoming State YMCA convention December 2, 3, 4 1927. Colleges such as Centre, Georgetown, Transylvania, Eastern, and the University of Kentucky were expected to attend. The local planning committee included Dr. E.V. Hollis, Prof. H.C. Haggan, Mr. A.D. Roberts, and local "Y" President John Ridgeway. (Associate Editor of the Paper).

Also, that first edition announced the coming Lyceum program for the year. The program emphasized the theater and the arts. The schedule included, The Wood Bell Ringers on October 22, and The Musketeers November 5. Both expected a sell out crowd and tickets should be purchased in advance.

Also, the school calender for the year 1927-28 was printed in this first issue. Among the important dates listed on the 1927-28 school calendar were:

1. Christmas Holidays, December 22-January 2, Classes begin Jan. 3.
2. Registration for <u>second semester,</u> January 21.
3. Semester Exams, January 25-27. First Semester ends January 27.
4. Class work begins February 1
5. Senior Exams, April 25
6. Baccalaureate Sermon, May 27
7. Graduation Exercise, May 28

SCHOOL NEWSPAPER STRUGGLED DURING EARLY YEARS

The paper trail across the campus of the Morehead State Normal School, began with the???????, then changed to *The Morehead Light*. It was conceived by journalistic idealism when a small group of students on campus believed a student newspaper wasneeded. I'm sure the birth pains were severe, but the task of rearing such a child was extremely difficult. It involved covering expenses through local advertising. It involved getting faculty and student support. It involved getting people to volunteer their time and energy. But they did it, and now that the child is an adult, has it forgotten its roots? Does that child now called *The Trail Blazer* remember its heritage?

Hundreds of students have gained valuable real life experience in publishing a campus newspaper, a laboratory for Journalism. Many have gone into successful journalistic careers. Many have gone on to be successful in other fields of endeavor. But all have gained confidence to succeed in life as a result of their experience on the paper. Each generation of students, just as each generation of faculty, owes a debt of gratitude to the past. But *The More-Head-Light* might make a Morehead Memory for those reading *The Trail Blazer* today.

TRAIL BLAZER 1929-
(Irregular)

In 1929 the name of Morehead Normal School and Teachers College changed to just Morehead State Teachers College, dropping the Normal School from the official name. With a new name, a new president (Payne) and a new crop of students, many changes went into effect that year. There were many new faculty added also that year. With all these changes a new name for the student newspaper seemed to be in order. Therefore, the name *Trail Blazer* was selected, and is still published under that name seventy years later.

LIGHT GOES OUT

On October 12, 1929 the *Morehead Light* became the *Trail Blazer*. It was to be published every two weeks on the campus of Morehead State Teachers College. There were no photographs in the four page edition. Advertising support consisted of: The Cozy theater with a movie called "The Siren." Also, W.T. Baumstark Co. announcing a new line of dresses beginning at $4.95. Goldes Department Store also offered dresses at $4.95 and Blair Brothers offered Stetson Hats at reasonable prices. The Midland Trail Garage was selling Ford cars, and the Sanitary Barber Shop urged the students to look their best.

Student Staff Included:
Editor in Chief - Ernest White
Associate Editors - Catherine Friend and Robert Stewart
Sports Editor - James Maggard
News Editor - Josephine Daniel
Feature Editor - Hurbert Counts
Organizational Editor - Inez Foley
Exchange Editor - Anna VanHorn
Advertising Manager - Edgar Mcnabb
Circulation manager - Ira Caudill
Faculty Advisor - Rex L. Hoke

EDITORIAL POLICY ESTABLISHED

While the name was changed, and the staff was changed, the editorial policy of *The Trail Blazer* seemed even more idealistic than *The More-Head light*. Volume I, Number 1 was a four page paper that printed a stinging editorial chastising the students for doing only what was required of them. It urged them to go above and beyond what was asked of them in school, and in life. The following epigram stated: "he who never does any more than he gets paid for, never gets paid for any more than he does." Sound advice even for this generation of students.

The editorial portrayed students that are wrapped up in materialism as cynical and selfish, especially those who ask "What's in it for me when asked to volunteer for a job." Emphasizing that this did not bode well for the future by saying "The modern complex of expecting pay for any little service rendered does not speak well for the future of our community." Also, "The biggest things that we do are those things we do not get paid for, and "The bigger a person is, the more he is expected do, for which he does not get paid." What admirable thinking for young college students.

ARTS AND SPORTS PUBLICIZED

The calender of events listed in Volume 1, Number 1, 1929 edition of *The Trail Blazer* were:

Lyceum Events

November 5	Heidleburg Student Chorus
December 4	Garay sisters (Musical)
January 16	Gilbert Quartet
February 18	Take My Advice (Comedy)
March 7	Dr. Oneil (Lecturer)
April 15	Mardoni Company (Magician)

It was apparent that the arts were very important at MSTC in those early years. However, there was no radio (that could be received here), no television, few newspapers,no e-mail, web sites, or internet. Also, tickets were free to students. These Lyceum events then were indeed well attended.

Sports were displayed prominently in Vol. I, No. 1 of *The Trail Blazer* and the football schedule appeared just below *The Lyccum Schedule*.

1929 Football Schedule

October 7	Kentucky Weslyan
October 14	Transylvania
October 19	Campbellsville
October 26	Eastern
November 1	Salem College
November 9	Glenville College
November 16	New River State
November 23	Morris Harvey (Homecoming)
November 27	Sue Bennett

This represents the first really full football schedule for MSTC. Two years earlier the team was not very successful and lost to Morris Harvey by 81-0. But their football fortunes turned better in

1928, and they won over Easter 18-0. In 1929 they also beat Eastern 13-6. Anytime Morehead won over Eastern the season was considered a success. It was the battle for the "hawg rifle"; the symbol of victory in the game, and MSTC kept it in 1928-29.

FACULTY SURVEY PRINTED

Volume I, Number 1 of *The Trail Blazer* printed the results of a survey of faculty members' answers to the following question:

What would you do if you were 21? Following are some of the answers by faculty members:

Dr. Terrell - "I would propose to some little girl of sixteen. By-the-bye you think I am joking, but I am serious." (This was the same faulty member that had a car that the students wrote a song [Ee I Ee I O] about).

Professor Jayne - "I would give all my energy to understanding the needs of the country schools, and ways of meeting them. I would also try to see the funny things that happen, so I could pass them on." (Professor Jayne, the person Jayne Stadium is named after was a true gentleman, and great educator.)

Professor Graves - "I would vote four times for Herbert Hoover". (I wonder what he would say now after the way history has portrayed that president).

Professor Rex Hoke - "I would avoid the ensnarement of flirtatious women." (This was the chairman of the Psychology Department who drove his car to class one day, walked home for lunch and found his car missing from the garage, and reported it stolen.)

Dr. Black - "If I had time between dates, I would pick out a respectable paying profession and prepare to follow it." (Evidently Dr. Black was unhappy with his salary and fringe benefits.)

It would certainly be enlightening to conduct a survey of today's faculty at MSU asking the same question.

MSTC was not a suitcase college or a commuter college in 1929. There were few roads, no cars on campus by students, and transportation was limited to trains and buses. (Even in 1937 only two students had cars, and one student Roger Caudill, withdrew and went to UK. Therefore, if you didn't live on a railroad or bus route you seldom went home. But if you did go home you might get your name in the Personal Section of *The Trail Blazer*, e.g. Miss Chalma Thacker spent the week-end at home with her parents; or, Miss Gladys Gudgill spent the week-end at home with her parents in Owingsville. So when someone went home for the week-end it was news, but now it's almost news when someone stays on campus on weekends.

STUDENTS COMPOSE A SONG ABOUT A FACULTY MEMBER

Indeed a car on campus was a major event in 1929. No students, and very few faculty owned cars. Indeed when Dr. Russell Terrell, chairman, Department of Economics and Sociology, bought a Ford Model T, it was the inspiration for a song, that was published on the front page of Volume I, Number 1 of *The Trail Blazer*, called the latest hit song:

> Dr. Terrell bought a car
> Ee-I-Ee-I-O
> He takes the lassies for a ride
> Ee-I-Ee-I-O
> A blond head here, a dark head there,
> Here a lass-there a lass,
> Anywhere you chance to pass-
> Dr. Terrell bought a car
> Ee-I-Ee-I-O

LIBRARY PLANS ANNOUNCED

Volume I, Number 1 of *The Trail Blazer* in 1929 proudly announced plans to build a new Library on campus. (This was an article close to the heart of this writer). It announced the new library would replace Burgess Hall. It would cost $130,000 and would house 100,000 volumes and would be the most beautiful building on campus. Miss Ora Fuller was the Librarian, and Marguerite Bishop was her very capable assistant. (Miss Bishop was also this writer's assistant during part of his tenure as Library Director). Also, there were four student helpers: Misses Inez Foley, Gladys Snedegar, Florence Owings, and Hazel Mason. (When this writer retired as Library director of MSU in 1985, there had been 2 major additions to the Library, and over 500,000 volumes in the collection. Also, there were 42 full-time staff members, and over 100 student workers.) Also, it is still the most beautiful building on campus, and houses all forms of media including hundreds of computer terminals.

SIMILARITIES AND DIFFERENCES 1929-1998

After examining an issue of *The Trail Blazer* dated September 9, 1998, this writer is struck with how different it is, yet how much it remains the same. One of the similarities of Vol. I and Vol. 71 is that it is still a newspaper by the students and for the students. Although there are more students involved in the publication, eleven in volume 1 and 24 in volume 71. But the contents of the two volumes separated by 71 years of time was amazingly similar.

A survey of faculty members was printed in vol. 1, and a survey of students in Vol. 71. In vol. 1 there was an article chastising students for their lack of concern for others and their failure to volunteer to help on campus projects. In vol. 71 there was an editorial pointing out the need for consideration of others and emphasizing common courtesy.

Sports were emphasized in vol 1, page one, and in vol 71 sports were still emphasized, with a page of its own (back page). In vol. 1 there was a calendar of events for the whole year, in vol 71, there was a calendar of events for September. Vol 1 printed student club news such as Phi Deltas make a drive for new pledges, the Literary Club elected new members. Similarly vol. 71 announced Lamda Pi Eta was accepting members, and Delta Zeta loves their new member. Also advertising support for Vol. 1 consisted of ten local businesses and advertising support for Vol. 71 was consisted of twenty-four commercial interests including classifieds. Also, there were two inserts from a credit card company and AT&T Co. It appears that the more things change the more they stay the same.

While great similarities are evident in Vol. 1 and Vol. 71, the differences were also evident. Where the staff of each paper is listed on the inside of page one, in vol. 71, they list the room number, phone number, fax number, advertising number, e-mail number, and U.S. mail number. Also there is an affirmative action declaration. All of thesenumbers reflect a much more complex campus culture today. From two student cars on campus 50 years ago, to what seems like two cars per student on campus today. Morehead, like every large University in this nation, when discussing their biggest problem, parking always comes up first or second.

TECHNOLOGY IS OF COURSE BIGGEST CHANGE

Following the paper trail of *The Trail Blazer* across seventy plus years, one finds the biggest change is in the technology. There were no photographs in the early years. The printing was not very clear, and advertisers were few. But today's *Trail Blazer* because of the advancement in the technology of printing, has clear photographs, print and advertisements. With the exceptions of the investigative, and adversarial reporting, the content of the articles in Vol. 1 and vol. 71 are quite similar.

The 1998 staff of *The Trail Blazer* should never forget the responsibility they own to the future generations of students. That the present staff <u>are</u> *Trail Blazers*, charting a course that future students will follow. As was so well stated in Vol. 1, Number 2 in 1929: "A good school newspaper and a good athletic team does more to create a pride in your school than any other thing, and Morehead needs this more than any other thing". "The pen is mightier than the sword".

THE MOUNTAIN CRUISER, 1942-1945 (WEEKLY)

Following the paper trail across the campus of MSU we come upon a relative obscure, but nevertheless very important publication called *The Mountain Cruiser*. (A cruiser in Navy terminology is a small battleship in the 6,000 to 15,000 ton class.)

With our nation engaged in mortal combat during World War II, our colleges and universities were called upon to do their part. MSTC served proudly during those war years as a Navy Training Base. In March 1942, its service began as a Technical School for electricians in the U.S. Navy. The men were sent to Morehead from throughout the U.S. immediately following their basic training. After their arrival in Morehead, they were required to undergo an intensive 16 week course in basic electricity. The amount of time allotted for their training was less than two-thirds of the time required during peace time. Men successfully completing this course would then be prepared to go aboard any ship in the fleet with a rating of electrician Mate 3rd class, and immediately fit into their organization.

NAVY PAPER PUBLISHED

Before the first class graduated on August 21, 1942 a base newspaper was established. It was a weekly publication called *The Mountain Cruiser.* The staff included: Ensign P.R. Dougherty, managing

Editor; Yeoman 1st Class J.H. Hook, Associate Editor; Yeoman 3rd Class W.R. Ellis, Reporter; Seaman H.H. Selfer, Sports Editor. The stated purpose of *The Mountain Cruiser* was "Published by and for the men of the Naval Training School at M.S.T.C." It also contained general news of the war, editorials, sports and ships company news, along with an educational column that rated each section (class), against other sections. It was designed to motivate and inspire. Their office was located in Men (Mays) Hall, where the men were housed. Also men were housed in Thompson Hall.

Sailors arrived at Morehead College, 1942. The college trained naval electricians during WW II. They published their own newspaper called The Mountain Cruiser. (Photo: MSU Archives)

NAVAL TRAINING SCHOOL DEDICATED

The first issue of *The Mountain Cruiser* headlined the upcoming formal dedication of the Naval Training Station. It was to be dedicated to the Service of the United States and designed to build Navy men out of raw American material. The dedication was held August 21, 1942 in Jayne Stadium, and was a memorable Morehead Moment. It was a solemn moment of prayer and thanksgiving. Prayer for those already in battle, and for those men who would soon go into battle. Also, a day of thanksgiving that Moreheadians were able to do just a small part in that global conflict.

The dedication program included 200 sailors performing close order drill and marching in review before the review stand. (While only 200 sailors were here then, that number would eventually grow to over 600). Those in the reviewing stands included governor Keen Johnson, Senator Alben Barkley, Captain E.A. Lafquist (Assistant Commander of the Great Lakes navel Base), MSTC President William. Vaughn, Commander George Walker, (Base Commander) and many other dignitaries.

The next issue of *The Mountain Cruiser* announced that the first 200 members of the first graduating class of Electricians Mates 3rd class was held September 17, 1942. Each sailor then received orders for their next assignment, usually aboard a ship headed for combat.

USO SOON ESTABLISHED

The Mountain Cruiser helped build morale, motivate men, and move Moreheadians into a good relationship with the Navy. When 600 sailors were turned loose in a small community, there were bound to be some problems. But the Shore Patrol (Navy Police) kept a tight reign on the men when they were off base. The community responded by establishing a US0 (United Service Organization) in the Martindale Building on Main Street. It was a place for servicemen to go when they were off duty, listen to music, dance with the hostesses, and eat free food.

The Morehead USO was staffed and supported by volunteer ladies from local civic clubs. Surrounding towns such as Mt. Sterling, Owingsville, Flemingsburg, and Olive Hill, also helped to staff and support the club. On February 12, 1944, Olive Hill civic organizations sponsored a valentine dance at the Morehead USO. Home-made cookies and punch were served to approximately 500 sailors.

Those present were allowed to compete in a drawing for free telephone calls to their homes. The Morehead Junior Hostesses, the Olive Hill Hostesses, and the Navy wives organized the event, and served as hostesses. Miss Miriam Oppenheimer was the general chairman for the Olive Hill group, and Miss Mary Frank Wiley was the general Chairman for the Morehead Group. Those kinds of events helped to provide recreation, entertainment, and desirable social activities for the sailors stationed in Morehead.

COMMUNITY AND NAVY COOPERATE

Commander Walker was quoted as saying, "As is usual when a large number of service men are assembled, certain undesirable elements prey upon them. The best way to meet this problem is for the respectable citizens to provide social activities which will be more attractive to our normal American youths, than the dubious pleasures offered by these harpies." Commander Walker emphasized that Morehead's citizens had responded well, and he assured the community, it was not just a one way effort. But that the Navy recognized that "All work and no play makes Jack a dull boy", and they would do their part to provide recreational outlets on the Morehead Naval Base.

Commander Walker lived on East Second Street, and every morning at 7:30 a staff car, driven by his personal driver, would pick him up at home, and return him that afternoon. His chief lived across the street from this writer on Lyons Avenue. This same staff car would sometimes come by and pick him up and taken him to work. This writer was always very very impressed as this official staff car with the U.S. Navy insignia would turn in the driveway across the street.

Over the three years the naval Base was on the campus of MSTC, thousands of the best of America's young men came to our community. MSTC, Morehead, and many surrounding cities did their best to make them feel welcome and these men received excellent training in basic electricity.

Evidently by January, 1944 the navy need for electricians began to wane. By then many of the graduates were sent on to other schools for additional training in needed areas. Some were sent on to commando schools, others were sent to firemen schools. By then only those with top grades at Morehead were classified as Electricians Mates 3rdclass.

SAILORS MARRIED LOCAL GIRLS

Many of the sailors stationed in Morehead met and married local girls. Some returned to Morehead to live, others took their brides to other areas. This writer (and his wife) were driving through Boston one dark rainy night a few years ago, and became hopelessly lost. We stopped and asked directions at a service station, but received little help. Upon returning to the car, a women approached the car and said, I see you're from Morehead (Rowan County License Plate). When asked if she knew Morehead she said yes, I was in school there (from Elliot County), met a sailor and married. We have lived in Boston now for over fifty years. She had never returned, but asked many questions about Morehead. She not only directed us to a hotel, but led the way there. Also, about a month ago this writer received a call from a woman from Cleveland, Ohio who was in Morehead. She said her dad was stationed here during the war. She remembered coming to Morehead on the train and walking to where he was living on campus and was delighted when she was shown Thompson Hall, and remembered the building where her father had lived for 16 weeks.

Moreheadians have many memories of the Navy, the sailors, and the U.S.O. But there were also many men and their families throughout the world with fond memories of Morehead. Many of the sailors stationed in Morehead during WW II, left here, went into combat, and did not return, but those who did return carried the banner of Morehead throughout the war. During wartime it is necessary to use the "sword," but it always produces devastation and destruction. However, during the life of the publication called "The Mountain Cruiser" and the ending of WW II, the pen once again became "mightier than the sword."

Woody Hinton's "folksy Cracker Barrel Comments"
were published in two Morehead Newspapers for 20 years.
It was a combination of humorous anecdotes,
political satire and homespun philosophy.

Aerial view of Farmers, Rowan County Ky., seven miles West of Morehead, shows the devastation of the flash flood that struck Morehead July 4, 1939 drowning 25 people.

CHAPTER EIGHT

Federal Functions:
Post Office and CCC Camps

The hallowed hills and hollows of Rowan County are known for their scenic beauty, and the timber they produce. But in the early 1900s most of the old growth timber had been marketed and restoring the forests was hardly considered. However, by the 1930s, conservation began to enter our vocabulary, and thoughts began turning to ways of preserving forest land from fire and erosion.

When President Franklin D. Roosevelt was elected by a landslide on November 8, 1932 (he carried all but six states) his first priority under his "New Deal" was to get this nation's economy moving. Declaring, "all we have to fear is fear itself," he began formulating legislation designed to put poor people to work, instead of giving them monthly "relief checks." As Abraham Lincoln once said, "The Lord must surely love the poor people because he made so many of them." Although it was a government payroll, they were working and not rocking.

CCC AUTHORIZED BY CONGRESS

With conservation a key plank in his platform, President Roosevelt succeeded in getting Congress to pass his Emergency Conservation Act. On March 31, 1933, Congress authorized the

President to employ un-employed citizens to help restore the nation's depleted natural resources, and to establish an orderly work program of useful public work. Thus, the Civilian Conservation Corps under the administration of the U.S. Forest Service was born.

The CCC was a quasi-military organization, designed to give young boys the dignity of work, by building bridges, roads, trails, fire towers, and at the same time, conserving the forests. It also helped to reduce relief rolls, and provided a basic introduction into a disciplined military life. To join, you had to be at least 17 years old. Boys could enlist for six months, with an option of re-enlisting for another six months. They lived on base in a military barracks, and ate in the mess hall. They were not permitted off their base without a pass. Their housing, food, and clothes were all furnished and they were paid $30 a month, and $25 was sent home to their family, and the boys kept $5. (Later on the boys got to keep $8 dollars, and sent home $22.) Most said they felt rich every payday.

CCC CAMP ARRIVES IN ROWAN

On December 4, 1933, the federal CCC legislation reached Rowan County when Camp F 4, Company 578 was established at Clearfield, Kentucky. (It as located on what is now 519 just before you start up Clack Mountain.) However, the government began purchasing private land in 1930, and the Cumberland National Forest (now Daniel Boone) was growing. Also, the CCC Camp was beginning to outgrow the base on Morgan Fork.

Mrs. Chadima, a widow with several children had a small farm east of Morehead up Rodburn Hollow. In 1935, the federal government decided that was where they would build their new CCC Camp. After Mrs. Chadima turned down the government offer for their farm, she was sued, and the land was taken from her, under the law of eminent domain. (This writer had just joined the cub scouts and the scout master was her son, Joe Chadima.) When he told us he was leaving Morehead because the Government had taken his home, we could not understand a government like that--and were heart broken because he was leaving. (He later joined the CCCs, figuring if he could not "lick 'em, he'd join 'em.")

On November 19, 1936, CCC Camp F 4, Company 578 was

Triangle Fire Tower built near Morehead by the CCC, Civilian Conservation Corps 1935. Cost: $3,000.

moved from Morgan Fork to Rodburn Hollow. The number of boys in camp eventually grew to 470. This camp was responsible for maintaining the National Forest land in Rowan, Menifee, Morgan, Elliott, and portions of Fleming and Bath Counties. This amounted to a total of 281,507 acres of forest land.

FOREST FIRES FIRST PRIORITY

The first priority of the CCC was fighting forest fires. This area was once a great hardwood lumber center. When the government purchased the logged-out land from private landowners their goal was to protect the forests so that new stands of hardwood would grow, and a system of perpetual timber harvesting established. But forest fires were rampant in Rowan County in those days. Keeping the fire from destroying the timber was difficult and doubtful. In 1933 there were 3,000 acres burned in this region, compared to 610 acres in 1937. The CCC was making progress. Fires were mostly man made, either accidentally or on purpose. However, there were many mountaineers that would set a forest fire just to see the CCC boys work to fight it. A few were prosecuted, but not nearly enough.

BUILD FIRE TOWERS AND PHONE LINES

A key element in forest fire protection was the high forty-foot steel constructed fire towers at McCauley Ridge, Hickory Flats, Tater Knob and Triangle. The towerswere 14 ft. X 14 ft and contained 2 cots, a stove, table and stool. The one closest to Morehead was the Triangle Tower, on top of the mountain just off Dry Creek Road. Some of the towers were built in such isolated areas that the only way you could get materials there was by mule power. But the most famous one was the "Tater Knob" tower. It was located just across the Licking River near Yale, Kentucky in Bath County. Harvard Alfrey was a long time fire watcher and at one time he and his wife lived in the tower. (This was one of the times Harvard met Yale.) The Tater Knob tower has now been restored, and is worth the trip to visit. There you can see how it contributed to the safety of the forest. When it was first built, telephone lines were strung to the tower by CCC boys. The lines connected the tower to the camp, so that the fire alarm and site could be phoned in quickly to allow the CCC boys to get a head start on fire fighting. There were a total of 12 phones located in strategic areas and connected by 40 miles of line to speed up reporting the fires. A very important firefighting tool was the "alidade" or fire finder located in each tower. It used triangulation to pinpoint fires. When you stop to realize there were no phones in any rural areas in 1937, this was a monumental move forward in communications and firefighting.

HIKING TO TRIANGLE TOWER

The local Triangle Tower held a certain mysterious, yet romantic attraction for the young people growing up in Morehead during that era. It was an annual rite of spring for a class to hike up to that tower. To get there you crossed Triplett Creek at the dam, and walked up the hollow, climbed the mountain and then followed the ridge until you reached the tower. Then you climbed the rickety steps to the top of the swaying tower. Then you would walk around the outside platform, feeling like you were master of all you surveyed. The view was breathtaking. Almost every class at Breckinridge and Morehead Consolidated made the journey at least once. Hiking to Triangle Tower was considered one rite of passage to every child in Morehead. You had to or you were called "chicken" or even worse. On the trip you passed a huge rock overhang in which tobacco was sometimes hung for curing. One Breck student jumped out of that natural tobacco barn and broke his leg and had to be carried back.

578th CCC Company Camp F04 at Morehead, Kentucky, 1937.

LOCAL BOYS JOIN CCC

There was a maximum of 470 men in the Morehead CCC Camp in 1938. Many men from Rowan County joined for at least one six-month hitch. Some were stationed in Rowan County. Others joined and were sent to far off places. This writer's uncle, Norton Earley, joined on his 17th birthday and was sent to Montana where he spent a year clearing forests of dead trees, fighting forest fires, and building roads and bridges. Phil Hardin, another Rowan resident,

412 • Morehead Memories

joined thinking he would see the world (he lied about his age so he could join at age 16.) but instead, he was sent to Pike County and served his time there. Some fatherless children could join at age 16 under a special hardship ruling. Ralph Earley joined and spent two years in the CCCs and still was not old enough to enter military service.

While researching this chapter of Rowan County's history, the writer came across a copy of his father's discharge from the CCC Camp in Morehead. Lon Ellis serial number CC5-162897--was honorably discharged September 30, 1937 at the expiration of his enlistment.

Some married men with special skills were accepted and allowed to live off base. They received their clothing and were issued a weekly food supply to take home. We were very poor in those days and that food my dad brought home went a long way. (I can still taste those canned pears in syrup.)

IDENTIFYING AND NAMING PHYSICAL LANDMARKS

At one time one of his jobs was riding horseback over the county to identify and mark on a map the names of creeks, roads and hills. It was only then I found out where Wilson Hill was on Licking River although I was living right beside it. Dad was paid $30 a month plus $10 expenses for his horse.

Among other land marks on the map were Scotts Creek, Ramey's Creek, and Clay Lick, along with hundreds of others that were identified. Also at one time a part of his job was a fire watcher. It was then he spent some time in Tater Knob Tower. It was a lonely life on top of that mountain for several days at a time.

When the CCC boys were building the bridge over Licking River into Menifee County my father, Lon Ellis, was assigned as a night watchman to protect all the material and equipment on the construction site. He allowed me to come and spend a few nights with him there, and we did some night fishing.

CCC BOYS NOT ALWAYS ACCEPTED

Dr. Kenneth Jones, local retired Chiropractor, joined at Rodburn when he was age 17. He also hoped to see the wild west, but was sent to the mountains of Southern Kentucky at Camp Bledsoe. He said the CCC boys were taking all the local girls, thereby, making the local boys very unhappy. On one occasion while the CCC boys were working on a road, those mad mountaineers starting shooting at them from the brush. The men jumped in their truck and returned to camp and got their pistols from their barracks bag, returning to work and returning fire when fired upon. That camp was quickly closed, and the boys transferred to Junction City, Kentucky.

While the CCC camp was in Clearfield, there was lots of bad feelings between the local boys and the CCC boys. The Clearfield boys let it be known that the CCC boys were not allowed to cross Dry Creek. While the camp was in Clearfield the rule was strictly enforced. (Which may have been one reason the camp was moved to Rodburn Hollow.)

The Morehead Camp established a side camp at the mouth of Murder Branch in Menifee County. About 75 men were stationed there for three years before closing it and transferring the men back to Morehead (there were no murders there, the creek was named after an Indian Massacre of white settlers in the late 1700s.)

CCC CONTRIBUTED TO FUTURE OF ROWAN

Most of the young men joining the CCCs were unemployed, or eeking out an existence farming. (Rowan County had a 51 percent unemployment rate). The economic outlook was bleak and jobs were few. (You could get a discharge if you found employment or returned to school). But most families in Rowan County were too proud to go "on relief." That was a government handout, and they wanted no part of it. (The Rowan County brick and tile plants were operating at 50% capacity.) Most boys were hard working, poor people deserving of assistance. The CCC "permitted pride of purpose, keeping families from starving, giving gainful employment to the unemployed, AND CONTRIBUTING BEYOND ANYONE'S IMAGINATION TO THE FUTURE OF ROWAN COUNTY."

MANY ROADS AND BRIDGES BUILT BY CCC

By 1938, the CCCs had strung 40 miles of telephone lines, built 45 miles of year round (limestone gravel) roads. They had constructed fire towers, and bridges. They built all weather gravel roads to some of the most isolated and inaccessible areas of Rowan County. They built the road over Clack Mountain, and out Pretty Ridge, down Clay Lick to the Menifee County line. Also, they built the Lockege Road, that ran down to the old Cogswell Post Office, and Alfrey School. Also they constructed the CCC Trail from Clearfield to Elliottville, plus many other roads.

As a 10 year old boy this writer lived on Clay Lick Creek. Because of the depression, his father lost his job at the local Red Rose Dairy and his mother was not employed as a teacher that year, so we had to move back to the farm. I remember the talk of a road being built in front of our house and that summer I could hear the blasting and dozing as the road slowly inched toward out house. One day the bulldozer got closer and closer. Excitedly I sat out in the front yard waiting breathlessly for the first signs that progress was coming our way. Suddenly the first dozer came crashing out of the trees onthe side of the hill pushing a load of dirt in front of it. The dozer was driven by Gilbert Jones, and we were now on a gravel road to Morehead. (That road made it possible for this writer to continue school at Breckinridge.)

CCC HELPED EDUCATION AND ECONOMY

It is impossible to measure the economic, educational, social, and cultural impact the CCCs had upon this county and region. It should be noted the high correlation between the roads constructed by the CCC Camp and the increased enrollment at Morehead State College. CCC roads were also built in all the surrounding counties. Before these roads were built, there were many local people in Rowan County that wanted to attend college but could not. They could not afford to board in town, and the roads were impassable in winter. Also, this was the case in all the surrounding counties. The road from Morehead to Frenchburg, and the bridge across Licking River reduced the distance from Morehead to Frenchburg from 84 miles to 34 miles. Rural mail delivery was established as a result of these roads being built. Homes and schools began to appear along those gravel roads. Of course, the limestone dust was terrible during dry weather. Although people choked breathing the dust, they did <u>not</u> complain. (Some poured oil in front of their homes to reduce dust.) Morehead became much more of a business center, as well as an educational center with the establishment of these connecting, year round, gravel roads.

PREPARED BOYS FOR MILITARY SERVICE

The CCC Camp experience was also the means of preparing young boys for military service. The men in charge were all either officers in the R.O.T.C., regular Army or retired Army Engineers, recalled for this special duty. The engineers provided the skills needed for the construction of roads and bridges. Local physician, Dr. E.D. Blair was appointed their military surgeon and he was the one who helped keep the men healthy. (The surgeon reported each man averaged gaining 8 pounds while in the CCCs.) The discipline, drilling, working, eating, and sleeping was all according to military discipline. So, without realizing it, these boys were being prepared for their military service in WW II. Those who had experienced CCC Camp service adapted much quicker to military life when they were called into WW II

EDUCATION AVAILABLE

Educational opportunities were provided for these young men of the CCC. The W.P.A. (Work Progress Administration) provided employment for unemployed teachers. Those teachers conducted classes at the camp in such subjects as literature, reading, writing, leadership, journalism, forestry, typing, first aid, photography, personal development, cooking, baking and many others. In addition to education, recreation was an important part of camp life. Pool and ping pong tables, horseshoe pits, monopoly and many other games were a part of the recreation center on base. Also, the boys' religious faiths were considered, and church services were provided by local ministers. Each inductee was required to attend 3 hours per week in classes. The Educational Advisor was Earl C. May. Local teachers included Sam Johnson, Catherine Caudill, Mary Olive Boggess, Anna Lee Berry, Minnie Gastineau, and Bernice Barker. A cooking class was offered on the campus of Morehead State College, and 28 men from surrounding camps attended. (Good cooking was very important to camp morale.) The "Happy Days" magazine, the official publication of the national CCC Camps, published an article in their February 10, 1938 issue proclaiming the excellent educational opportunities at the Morehead Camp. The publication also commended the officers: Lt. Roy S. Williams, Commanding Officer, Dr. Everett Blair, Camp Surgeon, Bruce L. Vice Superintendent, and Earl May, Educational Advisor. It seems Morehead's camp was one of the nation's best.

ATTEMPT TO CLOSE CAMP REJECTED

On 1938 a move was made to close the Camp at Morehead. It brought on outcry heard from Morehead to Washington and back. A local committee was formed to combat the Camp closing. This committee included: Senator Alben W. Barkley (later Vice President), Congressman Fred M. Vinson (later Chief Justice of the Supreme Court), and local men: H.C. Haggan, Jack Wilson and W.E. Crutcher. The Camp was kept open, and the CCCs did not close until the beginning of WW II in 1941. But before closing the Civilian Conservation Corps had been of inestimable value to this county. Their roads and bridges had given outlets to people trapped in the most isolated regions of this county all winter. Black top highways now follow the trails they built. Forest fires almost became a thing of the past and the hills now grow timber again. Proper harvesting of timber was initiated.

The CCC Camp in Rowan County had a major impact upon the economic, educational, cultural, social, and recreational growth of this area. (It is only now being recognized as we examine it through the telescope of time.) Also, at the same time it helped hundreds of young men to believe in themselves and be better prepared for their personal involvement in the major world upheaval called World War II.

CCC SITE NOW BELONGS TO STATE

The site of the old CCC Camp of Rodburn Hollow now belongs to the State of Kentucky. It was obtained through a land exchange with the U.S. Government. It is now the local headquarters for the Kentucky Division of Forestry, and includes a well-maintained camp ground and lovely picnic area.

578TH COMPANY CCC CAMP F 4
Morehead, Kentucky
1933-1940
(Established December 4, 1933)

Some of the Rowan Countians Who Were Members of the CCC:

Harvard Alfrey
Charles Fraley
Earl Bradley
Virgil Caudill
Murvel E. Caudill
Joe Chadima
Virgil Conn
William Crum
Burl Crosthwaite
Thomas Early
Lon Ellis
Elmer Gulley
Perry Haney

Tip James
Robert Linville
John Litton
Merle Martin
John J. Mauk
Bert Puckett
Joe Rice
Ollie Roberts
Ray Stamper
John Swim
Clyde Tackett
Virgil Thompson

AND MANY MANY MORE

CCC PUBLISHED PAPER: "THE QUILL"
LISTED EDUCATIONAL PROGRAMS OCTOBER 1, 1937

Educational Program

Subject	Meetings per Week	Time	Enrolled	Instructor
ACADEMIC				
Arithmetic, Literacy	2	6:00-9:00	19	W.P.A.-Johnson
Reading, "	2	" "	"	" "
Spelling, "	2	" "	"	" "
Writing, "	2	" "	"	" "
Classes held for two hours between six and nine (staggered)				
English Literature	3	Correspondence	1	self and Advisor
VOCATIONAL				
Forestry	2	One man studying under the E.A.		
Journalism	1	7:00-8:00	15	Asst. E.A.
Typing	5	6:00-9:00	6	W.P.A. and E.A.
Job Finding	1	6:00-7:00	14	E.A.
INFORMAL				
Leather Craft	1	6:00-9:00	5	E.A.
First Aid	1	7:00-8:30	20	Camp Surgeon
Safety	1	6:00-7:00	all	Staff of Company

Lesson and study plans are made out by the W.P.A. teachers to cover the twelve week courses.

Classes are held at various times in the following subjects:

1. Nature Study
2. Metal Craft
3. Cooking and baking
4. Art Work
5. Music
6. Woodworking
7. Leadership
8. Discussion groups
9. Photography

The regular school year will start upon the enrollment of the new men in October. Three W.P.A. teachers will be on the staff. Classes in all advanced work demanded will be offered. A new photography and woodworking shop are near completion.

EARL C. MAY, Educational Advisor

GOVERNMENT AGENCIES: U.S. POST OFFICE

"Let such people understand that what we say by letter when absent, we do when present." (II Cor. 10:11)

Prior to the Revolutionary War, the early colonials had their own postal system, and they saw little reason to standardize the system. Therefore, there was a "hodge podge" of mail from one state to another. But on May 1, 1693, Andrew Hamilton was appointed by King William III of England "to receive and dispatch mail between the American Colonies and all parts of the civilized world". (The Colonies must not have been considered civilized then.) The Crown designated the Richard Fairbanks Tavern in Boston, as the center of postal exchange between England and the Colonies. But in any event, Andrew Hamilton could be considered the first Postmaster General in the new world. However, it was not until July 26, 1775, that the first Continental Congress meeting in Philadelphia, agreed that a Postmaster General be appointed at a salary of $1,000 per year.

MAIL DELIVERY SYSTEM BEGINS

The "modern" U.S. mail delivery system as we know it today began in 1836. It was then that Congress enacted legislation providing for "the business-like operation of the U.S. Postal System". President John Tyler recommended the appointment of Amos Kendall as the Postmaster General in 1845. It was at that point that the new Postal Service was born. Prior to that time, each state had their own mail delivery service and saw no reason to standardize the system. But that changed rapidly under the U.S. Mail System.

When gold was discovered in California in 1848, there was an urgent need for overland mail delivery to California. It was then that William Russell established the Pony Express. He advertised in the newspapers as follows: "Wanted: skinny, wiry fellows not over 18.

Must be expert riders willing to risk death daily. Orphans preferred." Thus, the Pony Express was established as a private enterprise. The Pony Express route covered 2,000 miles from St. Joseph, Missouri to California. The route was through wild un-explored territory, and many Pony Express riders were killed by Indians.

The first overland mail arrived in California in May, 1848. It required 10 $^1/_2$ days, and 75 horses to accomplish that spectacular feat. The fastest overland trip ever made by the Pony Express was 7 days and 17 hours. That was done in order to deliver President Abraham Lincoln's inaugural address in 1861. The Pony Express was a romantic part of the early mail delivery system in this country. It did much to unite this nation when the California settlers realized they could communicate across country in 10 days.

POST OFFICE ESTABLISHED BEFORE COUNTY

Rowan County's relationship to the U.S. Postal System began even before thecounty was formed. However, since its formation, there have been 44 post offices established throughout the almost

Morehead "new" Post Office, early construction phase, 1936. (Photo: Bob Fraley)

150 years of Rowan County history. Triplett was the first post office established in what is now Rowan County. However, in 1828,
what is now Morehead was called Triplett, and was then a part of
Fleming County. Early Morehead postmasters included: Henry L.
Powers (1828), John R. Powers (1835), F. Powers (1848), (In 1856,
the name was changed to Morehead when Rowan County was
formed) John Hargis (1857), James H. Hargis (1872), James W.
Johnson (1873), Harrison G. Burns (1873), and Cyrus Alley (1874).

On July 22, 1856 when Rowan County was formed, the name
Triplett was changed to Morehead, and John Hargis was the first postmaster at Morehead. It is interesting to note that the Morehead Post
Office was discontinued briefly June 20, 1873, when James W. Johnson
was postmaster. It was re-established just one month later on July 22,
1873 with Harrison G. Burns as the new postmaster. That break in
continuity was probably because of the change in postmasters.

MAIL ARRIVED BY STEAMBOAT AND STAGECOACH

There was very little mail arriving in Rowan County in those
early days. Therefore, the job of postmaster was very much a part
time job. There was very little mail and few people could even
read or write. In the early days of Rowan County, the mail was
slow, expensive and unreliable. In 1860 the population of Morehead
was about 200, and Rowan County's population was 2,282. Before
the railroad was built through Morehead in 1881, it was still an
isolated community with a population of 400. However, Rowan
County had a population of 4,420 in 1880. What little mail that
came to Morehead came via steamboat to Maysville, or by stage-
coach through Fleming County. Colonel Warren Alderson's freight
line brought the mail from Maysville and Fleming County to
Morehead before there was a railroad through Rowan County.

As the early pioneers pushed westward it was the U.S. Mail
that bound its people together. Without any other form of long

range communication (except maybe smoke signals) a letter from home was both rare and expensive. However, in the later 19th century, with the expansion of the railroads, mail became much more reliable and less expensive.

The first post offices in Rowan County was housed in grist mills, stores, or even homes of the Postmasters. Those were awarded politically as well as by bid. Morehead residents got their mail by going to the post office and asking for it. During the days before the railroad came through Rowan County, mail arrived here about twice a week. It was usually delivered by wagon from Maysville when it came by boat. (It was picked up by Warren Alderson's freight wagon and brought to Morehead.) Also, mail came on the stage coach that ran about once a week through Fleming County and Bath County. It wasthen delivered on horseback to Morehead.

RAILROAD ARRIVES IN ROWAN COUNTY

In 1881, the railroad opened through Rowan County. It brought a new era of reliable mail service. Morehead soon became a center for regional mail distribution to the surrounding counties with no railroads. Soon star routes (mail routes awarded to private bidders) were established to distribute mail to surrounding counties and post offices. The mail would come to Morehead and be sorted, and then delivered by star route carriers to the outlying regions. Morehead rapidly became a regional distribution center for mail and freight. The coming of the railroad put Colonel Alderson's freight line out of business.

The Postmaster usually held other jobs, such as store keeper, farmer, judge or sheriff. On October 1, 1913, Judge J.M. Carey resigned as the Morehead Postmaster. He was replaced by Rowan County's genial and popular Sheriff, J.D. Caudill. Mr. Caudill, the new Morehead postmaster, also exchanged property with the former postmaster. Judge Carey moved out to the farm of J.D.

Caudill, and Mr. Caudill moved into town so he could serve as postmaster. Although it was usually the husband that was appointed postmaster, in almost every case his wife took care of the postmaster duties so the husband could farm or work at other jobs. In 1925, the post office moved from its First Street location near the present Folk Art Center to the corner of Main Street and Carey Avenue. By that time, Morehead's main business section had shifted to Main Street. Mr. H.C. Lewis was the postmaster at the time of the move to Main Street.

FIRST WOMAN POSTMASTER APPOINTED

In 1930, Mattie Burns was appointed Morehead's first female postmaster. That year the post office moved to the Alf Caskey Building on Main street. (Present site of Arby's Parking Lot). That was the beginning of a new level of services by the Morehead post office. Lock boxes were installed, money order service began, and soon a village mail delivery route was established in town. Also, plans were made for a new post office building, and bids were accepted for a possible site for a new building site.

The bid submitted by Harlan Blair for 106 front feet on Main Street and South Hargis Avenue was accepted at the price of $50.00 per front foot or $5,300. However, the bid was later rejected as unsuitable and new bids were accepted. The successful new bidder was land owned by the Citizens Bank at the corner of North Wilson and Main Street. However, there was one small problem. The owners asked $7,500 and the government offered them $6,300. Condemnation proceedings were about to begin when local realtor James M. Clayton negotiated the compromise price or $7,250 (The Citizens Bank later bought the property from Harlen Blair and that is the present Citizens Banklocation). Dr. H. Van Antwert, Citizens Bank cashier said: "They had reached an agreement benefitting both parties." With the purchase of the land, bids were then received for construction of a new post office building.

CONSTRUCTION BEGINS ON NEW P.O. BUILDING

The successful bidder for the construction of the new post office was the DiBlasio Company of Canton, Ohio. Construction began on the new Morehead Post Office in August 1, 1936. Mr. W.G. Noll of Cinncinatti, Ohio was the architect for the new post office, and Mr. J.H. Parnell was the on-site construction engineer. At first, the work progressed slowly. Excavation for the basement was accomplished with two mules pulling a large two-man scoop. The excess dirt was hauled away in a Ford dump truck, and dumped along Triplett Creek at the end of Bridge (Union Street).

Work on the new post office moved rapidly during the fall of 1936. The weather was mild and workers were many. It was during the depth of the depression and there were many local skilled and un-skilled men who needed work badly. Also, some special skilled workers were brought into Morehead for the job. Work was completed, and the building accepted October 15, 1937, and plans were made to move the post office into the new building.

NEW P.O. BUILDING OCCUPIED

The new post office, located at Main and North Wilson Avenue, was occupied November 1, 1937. The move was made from the former post office on Sunday with no interruption of service. The new building was the ultimate in post office architecture. It was functional, attractive, and well constructed. It had a full basement and coal furnace with steam heat (no air conditioning). There was a covered loading dock at the rear, plenty of inside work space, and a well lit lobby. It was tastefully decorated with a mural in the lobby depicting family life in rural America. It was called WPA art. The mural in the 1937 Morehead Post Office is a study unto itself.

It was contro-
versial when it
was painted by
southern artist,
Frank Long, and
it is still contro-
versial today. It
was called de-
pression art,
and was the re-
sult of the
government's
attempt to hire

Morehead's "new" Post Office near completion, 1937.

Photo: Bob Fraley

un-employed starving artists to stamp their art into the depression era culture. There are those who question even calling it art.

Sue Beckham in her book, *Depression Post Office Murals*, L.S.U.
Press, 1988, calls it a "crude attempt to change the stereotypes of
southern culture." She says of the Morehead Mural (still located in
Morehead City Hall), that the artist Long, "celebrated positive as-
pects of contemporary mountain life–namely a close knit literate
family living in a well built house". He was trying to paint hard
working, earnest people,with little to celebrate.

MOREHEAD P.O. MURAL ONE OF MANY IN KENTUCKY

Frank Long, the artist and Berea College graduate, who painted
the Morehead Mural in 1937, died in January 1999. He was 92 years
of age. His murals were an attempt to decorate public buildings
during the depression era, and they now hang in Lexington, Louisville, Berea, Morehead and in public and private buildings in
many states.

The outside of the building had stone reliefs of a plane, ship,
and train. Those were moved to the Post Office on West First Street.

The lobby had 325 rental post office boxes. Also, there was a secret passage behind the work area where postal inspectors could spy on workers. They were the only ones with keys to that forbidden area, and you never could tell when you might be spied upon.

CITY MAIL ROUTE AND PARCEL DELIVERY ESTABLISHED

The mail arrived in Morehead on two trains going east, and two trains going west each day. The local Calvert Transfer Company had the contract to bring in-coming mail from the train to the post office and take the outgoing mail to the train. The post office was open 10 hours per weekday, and four hours Saturday. City mail was delivered mornings and afternoons each week day, and once on Saturday. Parcel Post was delivered 6 afternoons a week. Jack Lewis was Morehead's first city letter carrier, and he also began the first Parcel Post delivery service July 1, 1940. He delivered parcel post after delivering the first and second class mail. Parcel Post was delivered in town in a big two-wheel push cart furnished by the post office department. (Prior to the free city parcel post delivery service in Morehead, patrons were notified if there was a package for them at the post office and they had to come and pick it up.) Jack Lewis, a former college football and baseball player, had trouble controlling the cart going down Wilson Avenue, and pushing it back up Wilson Avenue. All pushing and breaking was by man power only.

DIFFERENT FROM "DOT COM" WORLD

In today's high tech "dot com", e-mail world, it is difficult to imagine the isolation of rural America in the latter 1800s. Rowan County, because of the terrain and lack of roads, was even more isolated than other communities. Roads were little more than twisted trails, creek beds, or deep rutted wagon roads. Travel from one small communityto another was a time consuming task of walking or riding horseback. It was in that setting that rural Rowan residents found themselves. Therefore, the only connection they had with the outside world was through their small community post office. Even then, they might delay picking up their mail for days, or even weeks because of the difficulty getting to a post office.

As the westward movement brought many more people to frontier America, the post offices moved west with the people. When Rowan County was established in 1856, it consisted of a population of 2,282.

MOREHEAD POST OFFICE FIRST CALLED TRIPLETT

Colonel John Hargis was the first postmaster at the time Morehead was selected as the county seat for newly formed Rowan County in 1856. The site of the first Morehead post office was at the corner of Main and University Boulevard. Colonel Hargis was required to furnish a building to house the post office. In order to meet that requirement, he contracted with William Nickell to build what became one of Morehead's most historical buildings--the Gault House. Under the terms of the contract, Mr. Nickell constructed the log building and roofed it. (His pay for that job was a team of young oxen.) Also, there was a small rough basement with dirt floor and walls under the heavy oak beams that formed the foundation for the log building. (It was under there that some of the shots were fired during the Rowan County Feud.) Those beams still remain under the present building (owned by Maude Clay), located at the corner of Main Street and University Boulevard. Therefore, the first site of the Morehead post office, after it was named Morehead, was in the Gault House. Also, Mr. John Hargis ran a tavern and general store as well as the post office in that building.

At the time the Triplett post office became the Morehead post office in 1856, there were three other post offices in Rowan County. Those were: Gills Mills, Farmers, and Blue Rock. However, by 1900, the county had grown to 8,277 residents, and twenty five more post offices.

MORE PEOPLE EQUAL MORE POST OFFICES

By 1928, Rowan, with a population of 10,893, had added fifteen more post offices within its borders. The last post office to be established in Rowan County was Hamm. It was founded in 1928, and named for a prominent family in the community. Therefore, throughout the history of Rowan County, there have been (according to postal records) 44 post offices. Over the years some were discontinued and then re-established.

Although many early Rowan post offices carried family names of prominent community residents, many did not. Others were named for geographical features, eg.Blue Rock, Blue Bank, Bluestone, and Dry Creek. However, early post office names indicated that whomever named them had a keen sense of humor. (Smile and Grin). They could have used a smiley face for their post mark.

BETTER ROADS EQUAL LESS POST OFFICES

In the 1930s as better roads were established in Rowan county (with the help of the CCC), there came a new mail service to this county. It was called Rural Free Delivery. The first RFD was established in Rowan County in 1936. That meant closing 6 small post offices. By 1940, Rowan, with a population of 12,734, had three RFD routes out of the Morehead post office. Also, that led to eventually closing many other small community post offices. The last post office to close in Rowan County was Haldeman. It closed in 1997. In 1999, there are only four post offices open in Rowan County. Those are: Morehead, Clearfield, Elliottville, and Farmers.

The following "fable" is a story using the names of all of Rowan County's Post Offices.

AN OLDE POST OFFICE FABLE

(All the letters in black capitals were, or are, names of Rowan County post offices.)

*Do some of you FARMERS want to go to MOREHEAD? First, hitch up your buckboard and grease its wheel COGSWELL, so you don't have a RODBURN out. Please remember that you can go either the LONGWAY, or the NEWAY. However, the most scenic route is across a DRY CREEK, beside a neat CLEARFIELD and through lovely VALE. As you look around you might think, this is really funny, and you would SMILE or even GRIN.

When lunch time comes, you can eat a HAMM sandwich. Following lunch, if you are thirsty, and even if you're a MINOR, you can get a drink out of PINESPRINGS. You stop at GILLS MILLS and buy a bag of meal before proceeding on through regal QUEEN CITY. There you cash your check at the new BLUEBANK. Suddenly you realize this is IBY (abbreviation for the international biological year) and, you wonder if the bank is IBY ready.

As you continue on your journey, you PEKIN the next CRIX you cross, and see little SHARKEY(s) swimming around. Your horse almost bolts as you cross noisy POPPIN HILL, and then you notice most of the BLUESTONE has washed off the road. When you reach the RAMEY house, you DEBORD (step down off of your buckboard), and ask them to get some FREESTONE on the road, before you reach CRANEY.

Waving at your old girlfriend HILDA, FRALEY, you feel like a PARAGON of virtue. Now that she's married, you congratulate her on her new TRIPLETT(s). Youthink you are lost when the

Hogtown community is now called ELLIOTTVILLE, and the North Fork of Licking community is called BANGOR.

You forgot that you were supposed to meet your Pa on the road, and you WALTZ right on by and MIZPAH.. You go back and get Pa and HALDEMAN on over to CLAYTON. As you enter into town, you're sorry you didn't bring your new girl friend, CHRISTY, but you just didn't want to have to WAGNER around. Also, you missed EADSTON, CRANSTON, and MUNSON, that cannot be included in this fable.

There have been 44 Post Offices in Rowan County's history, and in 1998, there were four: MOREHEAD, ELLIOTTVILLE, FARMERS, and CLEARFIELD. HALDEMAN, (established on February 12, 1907), was the last post office to be discontinued in Rowan County. It's doors were closed on January 2, 1997, and Avenelle Eldridge was the last postmaster. David Leadbetter was the first post master in 1907.

ROWAN COUNTY POST OFFICES 1828-1928
(LAST DATE OF A NEW POST OFFICE OPENING IN ROWAN COUNTY)

1. BANGOR - est. in Morgan County 06/22/1868. John J. Cassity; 03/01/1875, Christopher C. Hagemeyer.... (Into Rowan County on or before 06/28/1891); 06/28/1891, Sanford A. Day; 02/08/1906, William Martin.... W.D. Perry.
2. BLUEBANK - 11/01/1901, T.W. Razor, order rescinded 12/06/1901.
3. BLUE BANKE - 07/31/1871, John W. Morgan; Disc. 01/28/1874.
4. BLUE ROCK - 09/03/1861, William H.H. Garvin; Disc. 10/10/1863; re-established 02/09/1864 in Carter County; Disc. 11/30/1865.

5. CHRISTY - 04/05/1899, Malissie F. Bradley; 04/27/1999, Hiram H. Stamper....

6. CLAYTON - 06/04/1894, Aaron McRoberts; 02/02/1895, William M. Ball; Disc. 09/13/1895 (papers to Muses Mils, Fleming County).

7. CLEARFIELD - 08/04/1908, Blaine Fulton; 03/15/1918, Howard M. Turner; Anna Bowne, 1930; Bethel Hall, 1938; Gail Stamper, 1968.

8. COGSWELL - 07/22/1881, Fielding Alfrey, 01/20/1899, Boone L. Tabor. 01/04/1906, William P. Cogswell; 06/30/1906, Bert McKinney; 1909, Harve N. Alfrey; 1911, Anna Alfrey; 1933, Walter Ellis; 1934, Lloyd Walter Ellis; 1949,Charles Ellis; 1951, Nellie Alfrey McKenzie.

9. CRANEY - 02/20/1910, U.G. Blair; 03/29/1928, Willie A. Bishop.

10. CRANSTON - 07/17/1902, James A. Littleton, declined; 08/28/1902, Belford P. Ham; 12/11/1906, Nellie A Littleton....1934/ Leland and Margaret Hogge. Closed: 12/16/74

11. CRIX - 02/11/1899, Robert Arnold; 06/01/1903, Jesse H. Cornett, Disc. 03/20/1905, effective 04/15/1905 (mail to Wagner); Re-established 12/22/1906, Wesley Cox; 04/15/1914, Elijah K. Warren....

12. DEBORD (sic) - 04/02/1894, Joel H. DeBord (sic); 04/19/1899, Joseph C. Williams; 10/21/1899, Howard M. Turner; Disc. 10/03/1900, effective 10/15/1900 (papers to Morehead).

13. DRY CREEK - 07/27/1903, John M. Debord (sic), order rescinded 04/21/1904.

14. EADSTON - 10/23/1882, J. Stout; 11/09/1882, James H. Shumat....

15. ELLIOTTVILLE - 09/12/1876, John P. Huff; 04/24/1877, Will P. Ward...

16. FARMER'S - est. in Fleming County 08/28/1849, John B. Zimmerman; 01/22/185?, Thomas J. Thomas; (by now in Rowan County); 09/18/1857, Joshua M. Carey...(by now the post office had lost the apostrophe).

17. FRALEY - 01/26/1888, John M. Cornett; 10/17/1893, Benjamin F. McGill.... 10/03/1911, William McMillen; disc. 12/31/1913 (mail to Sideway).

18. FREESTONE - 04/16/1883, Henry f. Martin; 07/28/1897, Henry d. Myers; 12/17/1914, John w. Jones; name changed to BLUESTONE, 04/17/1920, John W. Jones.

19. GILLS MILLS - est. in Bath County on or before 09/11/1832, Thompson L. Parks; 11/21/1836, Harrison Gill; 05/11/1842, Marcus Gill.... 02/14/1855, William M. Ragland; Disc. 09/20/1850; Re-established 01/20/1860, Oliver P. Maxey; 05/30/1862, William M. Ragland; Disc. 07/31/1863; Re-established 09/23/1865, William M. Ragland; Re-established in Rowan County 04/02/1866, Charles P. Brown; 04/03/1867, Jonathan M. Lewis.... 01/05/1877, Newton Johnson; disc. 04/28/1881.

20. GRIN - 07/14/1920, John W. Barber; discontinued effective 11/15/1921, (mail to Morehead).

21. HALDEMAN - 02/12/1907, David Leadbetter; 07/16/1909, Henry K. Leighew; 1919, James E. Leighow; 1919, Ernest Fisher; 1946, Thomas Eldridge; 1954, Delbert Kegley; 1966, Avenelle Edlridge, 1967.

22. HAMM (sic) - 06/21/1928, Rushie Martt, Last post office established in Rowan County.

23 HILDA - 06/30/1897, Mattie M. Howard; 04/19/1899, John E. Johnson; ....

24. IBY - 10/05/1892, John Kelly; discontinued 06/21/1895 (no papers sent).

25. LONGWAY - 07/20/1916, William Wagoner; 07/16/1917, Russell Jones; Discontinued 09/29/1917 (mail to Sideway).

26. MINOR - 05/15/1890, William R. Wells; 11/28/1905, Green Wilson.

27. MIZPAH - 08/05/1897, William Patton; 05/15/1900, Henry R. Johnson;

06/21/1900, Rebecca J. Harris; discontinued 06/06/1905, effective 06/30/1905 (mail to Elliottville).

28. MOREHEAD - 07/22/1856, John Hargis; 09/08/1857, James H. Hargis;10/02/1872, James W. Johnson; 07/22/1873, Harrison G. Burns; 10/23/1874, Cyrus Alley.

29. MUNSON - 02/25/1888, Fantly R. Muse; 12/26/1889, Hiram d. Lyttleton (sic) .... 07/01/1912, Rosa E. Mullen; discontinued 11/30/1914 (mail to Cranston).

30. NEWWAY (sic) - 08/22/1919, Henry C. Caudill; discontinued effective 12/31/1925 (mail to Waltz).

31. PARAGON - 04/14/1882, David Myers, 03/13/1884, John H. Day...11/17/1884, William C. Brown; (in Morgan County about now); (back to Rowan County on or before 12/14/1908); 12/14/1908, John M. Phillips.

32. PEKIN - 05/27/1891, John g. Evans; 03/17/1892, Annie Plank; discontinued 07/15/1892.

33. PINE SPRINGS - 06/29/1869, L.b. Heflin; 11/28/1876, Fielding B. Ham (sic).... 11/11/1892, Daniel W. Clark; changed to Pinesprings, 02/28/1895, Wyman Blanton; 04/20/1895, James Henderson; Discontinued 09/01/1895 (mail to Munson).

34. POPPIN HILL - 04/30/1879, William w. Phillips; discontinued 07/20/1880.

35. QUEEN CITY - 04/11/1878, Delaney Bolling, 11/15/1882, William Fowles, Discontinued 05/28/1884 (papers to Morehead).

36. RAMEY - 10/14/1901, John H. Ramey; 12/29/1903, William f. Prater.

37. RODBOURN - 07/03/1888, Amos s. Hixson; 02/17/1894, Henry G. Vincil... 12/03/1909, Michael t. Dillon; Discontinued effective 01/31/1922 (mail to Eadston).

38. SHARKEY - est. in Fleming County 07/10/1913, Lewis H. Ratliff; 12/28/1921, Jennie L. Ratliff; discontinued effective 02/15/1927 (mail to Ringos Mills); Re-established 03/16/1928, Samuel N. Sorrell; (into Rowan County on or before 03/16/1928; 03/16/1928, Samuel N. Sorrell.

39. SMILE - 09/12/1913, Lydia J. Caudill; 11/03/1920 Maud Richardson.

40. TRIPLETT - est. in Fleming County on or before 11/08/1828, Henry L. Powers; 05/06/1835, John R. Powers... 08/22/1848, F. Powers; changed to Morehead (C.H.) When Rowan County established; 07/22/1856, John Hargis; 09/08/1857, James H. Hargis... 10/02/1872, James W. Johnson; discontinued 06/20/1873, re-established 07/23/1873, Harrison G. Burns; 10/23/1874, Cyrus Alley...

41. TRIPLET (sic) - 02/24/1880, fielding b. Ham; 07/05/1892, John W. Shumate...

42. VALE - 01/29/1903, George W. Bruce; 05/09/1911, Jesse Adams...

43. WAGNER - 04/02/1894, Samuel B. Caudill, 04/26/1898, Abel Caudill.

44. WALTZ - 12/26/1906, Dawson M. Waltz; 03/19/1907, George W. Waltz...

<u>Record of Appointment of Postmasters in Kentucky 1832-September 30, 1971.</u> (MICROFORM) USPO Archives.

PETITION FOR RURAL ROUTES I, II, III
ROUTE I ESTABLISHED

On January 1, 1936, a petition was filed with the Post Office Department to establish a rural route out of Morehead. The petition was approved and on October 10, 1936, and Rowan's first Rural Free Delivery Mail Route (Route 1) was established. Mr. Howard Spurlock was the first Rural mail Carrier. Route 1 went north on what is now Route 32, eliminating post offices at Hilda, Ringos Mills, Sharkey and Ramey. The route continued to Sharkey on Route 158. Then it continued across Tar Flat (Route 801) to the Licking River. From there, down Licking to the Fleming County line. Then back to U.S. 60 to Farmers and back east on U.S. 60 to Morehead. The route was 65 miles long and had 125 patrons on that first Rowan Rural Route. Except for State Road 32 and U.S. 60, the roads were mud and gravel. (Many times the mail carrier had to be pulled through the mud by mules across Tar Flat.) This writer's family lived on West U.S. 60 at that time, and was one of those 125 patrons.

There was a petition circulated opposing the route, because of the post offices it might eliminate, but it failed to get much support. The new mail route was overwhelmingly received because it meant better mail service to your home and mail box. It was not necessary to walk to the post office to get mail and stamps, or mail a letter. Mr. Howard Spurlock, the rural letter carrier, was to receive a "fair" salary and expenses for his work. (Mr. Spurlock remained as the letter carrier on Route 1 until he retired in 1966.)

ROUTE II AND III ESTABLISHED

RFD 1 was so successful that on July 1, 1940, Rural Routes 2, and 3 were established. Mike Flood, the former owner of the Eagles Nest, was employed as the first rural mail carrier on Route II. There were about 175 patrons on the 70 mile route that began on Cranston

Road (Rt. 377) and extended all the way to the Lewis County line. (It was a dusty gravel road all the way.) Then the route came back and ran up Holly Fork and back across Big Perry to U.S. 60. (Still a gravel road until U.S. 60) Then east on U.S. 60 to Carter County line and from there the route extended across to Haldeman and Brinegar, and back down U.S. 60 to Tolliver Addition and back to Morehead.

On July 1, 1940, RFD 3 was established with Mr. C.O. Leach as the first rural carrier. The route had about 160 patrons and covered 75 miles, beginning on (32 South) Christy Creek and extending to the Elliott County line. Then back across the CCC Trail from Elliottville to Clack Mountain. Then over Clack Mountain up the North Fork of Licking as far as the Morgan County line at Craney. Next, the route came back across Clack Mountain down Morgan Fork, through Clearfield, and back to Morehead. It was 75 miles of hard driving, and, except Route 32, it was all a limestone gravel road or worse. Many times the mail carriers would get stuck in mud and have to be pulled out.

The reason this writer can write of the details of those rural mail routes is because for seven years, I was a substitute carrier on those routes. (1948-1955). The pay was excellent for this region of the country. In fact, when Dr. Adron Doran was appointed President of Morehead College, he was paid $5,400 the first year. Those rural mail carriers used to make fun of me because I kept trying to finish college and they were paid more than the President of Morehead College in 1954.

The time came in 1955 when I had to either quit the post office or the bookmobile. Everyone in Morehead believed I had lost my mind when I elected to quit the post office for a career in library work. However, this writer has never had any regrets over that decision.

RURAL CARRIERS - THREE SEPARATE PERSONALITIES

Each of the three rural mail carriers had a different attitude toward serving their postal patrons. When the routes were first established, carriers were required to pick up un-stamped mail as long as it was accompanied by the money for the stamp. Later on, that policy was changed and the carriers were not required to pick up un-stamped mail.

Howard Spurlock, the RR 1 carrier, immediately implemented the new policy. He would never pick up un-stamped outgoing mail. Mike Flood, RR 2 carrier, was a little slower weaning his patrons away from the old policy. However, C.O. Leach never did implement the new policy. He continued to accept un-stamped outgoing mail as long as it was accompanied by enough money to cover the cost of the postage. Also, even if there was not enough money to cover the postage cost, he would pay the difference himself, and put a notice in their box that they owed him for previous postage. Mr. Leach wouldpick up groceries in town and deliver them to isolated patrons, sometimes carrying them in their house. He would also pick up some of his patrons doctors prescriptions, and get those prescriptions filled at the drug store. He would also wrap outgoing parcel post for his patrons. (C.O. Leach was considered a full service carrier if there ever was one.)

When this writer substituted on those routes in the late 1940s and early 1950s, I was expected to provide the same services in the same way as the regular carrier. That meant when I carried the Leach route, I spend a great deal of time licking ad pasting stamps, especially at Christmas time.

STRAY DOGS A PROBLEM IN CITY

Every Saturday, I delivered City Route 1. Jack Lewis was the regular carrier, and stray dogs were always a problem. If the patron had a dog running loose, Jack wouldn't deliver their mail.

Therefore , when I substituted on his route, I would not deliver the mail if there was a dog problem. However, Randall C. Wells, City Route 2 Carrier, said the dogs never stopped him, but he did have to take rabies' shots on three different occasions. (This writer never was bitten by a dog in seven years.)

EARLY EXPERIENCE WITH THE U.S. MAIL

This writer's earliest memory of the U.S. mail was when I was about 4 or 5 years old. At that time, we lived on a small farm next to "Doodle" Armstrong's mill and general store on Clay Lick (we moved back and forth from the farm to Morehead several times).

One day my mother wanted to bake a cake and had no sugar and no money. So she sent me to the hen house to gather eggs. When I had gathered a dozen, she sent me to Armstrong's store to exchange the eggs for sugar. (Eggs were about as expensive then as they are now). The road to the store was narrow, crooked and very close to the small creek. Suddenly the mail man, Ed Lowe, approached around a curve in the road in his horse and buggy. When he saw me he pulled back on the reins and yelled whoa! I tried to get out of the road, keep the eggs from breaking, and not fall into the creek at the same time. When the horse stopped right close to where I was crouched, it looked as big as an elephant to me. In a very small voice I said, "Don't run over me Ed Lowe, I'm on my way to the store to get mom some sugar". (In my child's mind I must have thought if he knew I was on a legitimate errand, and not just wondering around, I would be safe.)

MAILMAN MOVED FROM BUGGY TO AUTO

Ed Lowe had the star route (awarded by bid) to carry mail from Farmers, upLicking River to Cogswell and Bangor. He would also deliver the mail to the homes enroute. It was a distance of 18 miles round trip. During the 1930s, he used a horse and buggy and did not convert to an automobile until the late 1930s.

In 1942, Labe McKinney won the bid to carry that route to the two post offices (Cogswell and Bangor) and back to Farmers. The 18 mile round trip was over some pretty rough roads. My cousin, Adrian McKinney, was the carrier. I remember skipping school and riding with him on the mail route one day. We stopped at the old post office at Cogswell where Walter Ellis (another cousin) was postmaster. It was a dark and dingy place with two windows for light. There was no electricity and the store opened at daylight and closed at sundown. Walter Ellis was the postmaster at Cogswell until his death and the post office closed shortly afterwards.

After leaving Cogswell, the mail route continued up the Licking Valley and out by Mt. Hope School, and back down to the Bangor post office. W.D. Perry was the postmaster there for many years. He also ran a general store. There was a front porch at the post office that also served as a convenient place to mount and dismount from your horse and tie it to the hitching post. Following "Dee" Perry's death, his wife continued to operate the post office out of her home until it closed.

POST OFFICE ONLY CONNECTION TO FEDERAL GOVERNMENT

The early Rowan County post offices were centers for discussing politics (some times heated), crop conditions, religious revivals, and, was the only connection to the Federal Government. That was a time of no income tax, federal roads, federal farm subsidies, flood insurance, or tobacco allotments. Therefore, the U.S. post offices were the only connection to the U.S. Government and were a vital part in the lives of early Rowan Countians.

Morehead Post Office employees, 1960. They include: Bob Amburgey, Don Green, William Tomlinson, Bill Calvert, Bill Thomas, "Dub" Bellamy, "Fuzzy" Jayne, C.O. Leach, Randy Wells, Bruce Botts, Bob Grey, Bob Fraley, Henry Glover, Pete Armstrong, Ezra Adkins, Glen Vencil, Jack Carter and loyal dog "Zip Code".

EARLY MOREHEAD POSTAL WORKERS

In 1939, W.E. "Snooks" Crutcher was appointed postmaster at Morehead. By that time, Morehead was a busy mail center. In addition to city carrier, Jack N. Lewis, and rural carriers, Howard Spurlock, Mike Flood and C.O. Leach, there was assistant postmaster, Flora Cooper. Also clerks, Henry Glover, "Dub" Bellany, and Watt Pritchard. Robert Fraley also began work as a clerk there in 1942. Among others working at the post office during the war years (1941-1945) were Randall C. Wells, Marvin Wilson, Jr. and C.W. Bailey. Allie Manning and Ernest Flannery were the two custodians. Later on Pete Armstrong and William Tomlinson came to work.

In the fall of 1943, while a high school student, this writer began work as the special delivery carrier at the post office, replacing Harold Holbrook who had gone on to college. I was required to deliver those special delivery letters before school, at noon, and at 6:00 p.m. I would deliver them on my bicycle, and receive 10 cents for each letterdelivered, and was paid every two weeks. (I thought I was getting rich because some times my check was for over 12 dollars.) However, in 1944, like others working there, I soon answered the call of Uncle Sam, and went to work for him for 30 dollars a month (plus benefits).

WORLD WAR II CHALLENGED POSTAL SYSTEM

The years of WWII, 1941-1945, were the U.S. Mail's finest hour. Letters from family to their loved ones stationed in the far flung, remote areas around the world had to be delivered. Mail call was always the highlight of the service man's day. Their morale and fighting spirit depended upon "chow time", and mail from home. Therefore, a new slogan was introduced into our language, "As welcome as a letter from home". Also, on the home front, a letter from a son or husband from one of the remote places on the globe was anxiously awaited. When that letter did arrive from a battle zone announcing, "Mom, I'm doing OK so far", it brought both rejoicing and thanksgiving at home. The U.S. Mail and the U.S. Military combined to keep those important epistles of communication flowing between the home front and the war front.

One of the saddest times for service men was when they were on the move and their mail had not caught up to them yet. But when the mail did catch them, nothing was more welcome than a letter from home (unless it was a copy of the hometown newspaper).

V-MAIL HELPED SOLVE LOGISTICAL PROBLEM

Delivering world wide mail was a gigantic logistical problem, because the mail was going to many remote areas around the globe.

Also, because of censorship, servicemen outside the U.S. were assigned an A.P.O. (Army Post Office) number. Therefore, mail was addressed to the serviceman at an APO (Army Post Office) number at a U.S. port, e.g. APO San Francisco, California. Most mail was flown throughout the world by the military However, it soon became a "weighty" logistical problem. Hence the development of "V Mail" (Victory Mail). No, not <u>E</u>-mail, but <u>V</u> Mail!

V mail was the system of microfilming a letter from a service man (after it was censored) and then flying those reels of microfilm back to the states. Upon arrival in the U.S. the microfilm was then enlarged, printed, and then forwarded to the addressee. Using that system, 1 1/2 tons of paper mail could be reduced to 45 pounds of weight. That made mail delivery much more efficient and saved a lot of aviation fuel. Plans are now in effect for another type of V mail (vision mail). That's where messages could be received on a cell phone, but it's a far cry from the original V mail in WWII.

Packages from home to the servicemen usually took a lot longer to reach their destination. However, even packages were flown many times. In fact that's how Germany decided they had lost the war, many months before it ended. During the Battle of the Bulge in December, 1944, the German Army overran a U.S. Army post office behind the American lines. There, they found chocolate cake among the packages. It was then that German General Rommel said, "The war is already lost when the Americans can use aviation fuel to fly chocolate cakes across the Atlantic, we don't have a chance".

A LETTER WAS MANY TIMES THE LAST MESSAGE

The mail exchanged between home and servicemen during World War II, was also a very important morale builder at home. Those treasured letters from that father, husband or son may have been the last message they ever received from them. It certainly was for the 258,000 who never came back. Those "dog-eared", yellow faded letters, to this day are the greatest treasures those families have, because it was their last words to them. Even if their loved one returned home safely, those letters mailed during those days of that "great crusade" carried a very important emotional message, as well as a historical record of that era. Also, they were lovingly preserved as an important family record, as well as the last words from that loved one.

This writer, to this day, has preserved the last letter written to me from my cousin, Adrian McKenney, 371 Bomb Sqdn. 307 Bomb Group, APO 709, San Francisco, California. The letter was dated March 15, 1944. It is faded but still legible, and in his own handwriting. His last words began by saying, "Hello Jack, how's my old hunting partner". (He used to take me squirrel hunting). The letter continued by asking where some of his old high school buddies were stationed (James Butcher, June Flannery, Ted Williams, Oscar Calvert, Jack and Charles McKenzie). In his letter he also encouraged me to take more math in high school if I planned to enter the Air Cadets. He closed by saying, "Take care of every little thing in Morehead and we'll be knocking off more squirrels in a few months." His plane was shot down on his next mission, and he has been missing in action for 55 years. (My answer to that letter was among his personal effects returned to his family.) That experience can help understand how important the U.S. mail was in uniting America's war effort and home front together during an all out global conflict.

MOREHEAD POST OFFICE 50 YERAS AGO

After returning from the military service, I took the civil service exam for a post office job, and was one who was hired in 1948. C.G. Clayton and I were appointed substitute clerk carriers on December 1, 1948. Our starting pay was 60 cents per hour. We were both in college and tried to juggle the two responsibilities. It was the height ofthe Christmas season and we worked 14 hours a day. However, we took time off to go to class until the college closed for Christmas. As the job description said I was a substitute clerk-carrier, and I worked wherever I was most needed. Also, whenever a regular clerk or carrier was off, I filled in for them. I soon learned all of the jobs in the post office and served as a full-time substitute. After dropping out of college, I worked at the post office, and also, drove the School Bookmobile until 1955.

One of my post office jobs was "casing" the mail. That meant sorting and tying the mail in bundles according to the train that carried the mail to those post offices. (Prestonsburg was worked by a train going from Ashland to Praise). Praise was a small town on the Virginia border. To work that job meant learning about six hundred small post offices and which train transported their mail. Trains such as Ashland to Cincinnati, Lexington to Fleming, Ashland to Lexington. It was a difficult task to learn all of those post offices, and which trains handled their mail. (We were required to take a case examination and timed to see if we were efficient.)

U.S. MAIL MONEY MOVER

In the late 1940s, there was no armored car service to Morehead. All cash was sent through the U.S. mail to and from the Citizens and Peoples Banks to the federal deposit banks, usually in Cincinnati. The money was sealed in a small bag, and placed in a larger mail bag. Each bag was then registered. That meant each bag had a separate number, with the name, date, time and address. Both sending and receiving cash required checking and verifying that information by two postal clerks. Each had to write the date and time before signing. Close scrutiny was given by the postal clerks handling those shipments of cash, and as far as I know, none was ever lost, strayed, or stolen.

DELIVERING MAIL TO COLLEGE WAS VERY DIFFICULT

Another of my jobs while working at the Morehead Post Office was to deliver the mail to the College. During the 1948-1955 era, the College bookstore and post office, run by John Collis, was located in the basement of Rader Hall (Then the administration building). At that time there was no UPS, FED-EX or any other private parcel delivery company. Therefore, I had to carry on my back every textbook, library book, paper and letter to the College post office then located in the basement of Rader Hall. All College mail had to be carried from College Boulevard up the steps and down into the basement of Rader Hall (My back aches just thinking about it). However, I resigned my job at the post office in 1955 to go back to school and library work. While working in Florida, one of my jobs was the materials supervisor for Pinellas County Schools. During that time I had to establish daily intra-school mail and parcel delivery service to 80 county schoolpick up points. (My post office experience was very helpful in that responsibility.)

"How beautiful upon the mountains are the feet of him that brings good tidings." (Is. 52:7)

The latter half of the 20th century was an era of rapid growth of the Morehead post office. There was not much "junk mail", however, that changed rapidly. Under the new postal system it is no longer referred to as junk mail, but business mailings. That mail also pays its own way. In fact, Morehead postmaster, Donna Oldfield said, "The U.S. Postal Service is no longer subsidized by tax payers." With the exception of non-profit mailings, no tax payer money is provided to the post office department. Therefore today's postal service is operated in a business like manner with sufficient revenue received to cover their expenses. That new business approach to the post office department changed with approval of Congress in 1971.

POST OFFICE RE-ORGANIZED

In 1971, the post office was dramatically re-organized and became a quasi-governmental organization called the U.S. Postal Services. That occurred when President Nixon signed into law, PL91-375. It was the most comprehensive postal legislation in this nation's history. It did much to reduce political influence, by placing the post office under the operational authority of a Board of Governors. The law also made it a self sustaining business operation. That change allowed more career postal employees and employment was based more on ability than political influences. Also the employees are now allowed collective bargaining agents between management and unions. But they are prohibited from striking, much like the air controllers union.

Scotty Hicks, Morehead Rural Route 1 carrier who replaced Howard Spurlock, began work in the Morehead Post Office in 1959. He later went on to become president of the National Rural Letter Carriers Association, with over 100,000 members. He was elected to a national office 10 times, and spent 10 years in Washington D.C. working in various leadership positions in that organization. He is now retired and lives in Owingsville, Kentucky.

NEW TECHNOLOGY MOVES MOUNTAINS OF MAIL

On July 7, 1987, the Morehead post office moved to its location on West First Street. It is a new modern facility with state of the art bar coding equipment. Incomingmail arrives by truck twice daily and out going mail leaves Morehead by truck twice a day. In 50 years, the population of Rowan County has not increased 100% but the volume of mail has increased 1,000%. Today, in an average week, over 200,000 pieces of mail will be delivered to Morehead postal patrons. (Including 7,244 copies of *The Morehead News*.) Sixty-five percent of all mail arriving in Morehead is automatically sorted by the latest bar coding machine. It is first sorted by route, then it is further sorted by the way it is delivered on that route. Therefore, that saves a great deal of time by the carrier in preparing mail for delivery.

The machine also sorts the post office lock box mail according to box number so the mail can be placed in each post office box much more efficiently. All outgoing mail is sent to Lexington, where it is placed in an optical scanning machine that scans and prints a 9-digit barcode on the mail at the rate of 30,000 per hour. From there all of Morehead's mail is returned, then the local bar code reader sorts the mail according to route and delivery point on that route, based upon that 9-digit barcode. Without this modernization, the U.S. postal service could never deliver the 25 pieces of mail to each of the 130 million households in 50 states every week. The post office delivers 3.4 billion pieces of mail every week. Forty-one percent of all mail delivered in the world is delivered by the U.S. post office and Japan is second with 6%.

The Morehead post office is light years ahead of where it was 50 years ago when this writer worked at the post office. They now handle 10 times the volume of mail with about twice the number of employees. That is all done without any tax dollars (except for the supplement for delivering charitable mail). Today the post office is a self-sustaining business that pays its own way.

ROWAN MUCH MORE DENSELY POPULATED NOW

On November 26, 1999, there are a total of 36 employees in Morehead. That includes 10 rural routes and 4 city routes in the Morehead post office. (Today, the rural mail patrons receive their mail with a street address instead of a rural route number). Those rural routes average 70 miles per mail route, with an average of 506 boxes per route. Rural Route 1 that was the first established in 1936 with 125 boxes, now has 469 boxes, within the same number of miles. By 1940, there were three rural routes out of the Morehead post office with a total of 425 boxes. In 1999, there are ten routes with a total of 5,063 boxes.

In 1940, there was one city delivery route in Morehead with 450 delivery points. In 1999, there are four city routes with a total of 2,528 delivery points. (None of these include the University.) However, in 1940, city delivery was an all walking route, and today they are all mounted routes. In 1940, the Morehead post office had 325 post office boxes, and in 1999, there are 867 rented out of a total of 1,400 boxes available.

POST OFFICE Y2K READY

Today's post office is Y2K ready for the next millennium. But whatever happens, one thing is certain, that is, change will occur. Whatever the new technology brings to transmit messages between people, it will be far different in the future. In looking at the development of the Morehead post office for the past 100 plus years, the only thing that hasn't changed is the name Morehead. Who knows, in the next 100 years even that may change. (I hope so, I never did like the name MOREHEAD.)

MOREHEAD POSTMASTERS 1828-1998

(First called Triplett)

Yr. of Postmaster Appointment	Name
1828	Henry L. Powers
1835	John R. Powers
1848	F. Powers
1856	Triplett changed to Morehead
1856	John R. Hargis
1857	James H. Hargis
1872	James W. Johnson
1873	Harrison G. Burns
1874	Cyrus Alley
1888	J.M. Carey
1913	J.D. Caudill
1925	H.C. Lewis
1930	Mattie Burns
1939	W.E. Crutcher
1941	Allie Holbrook
1942	Claude Clayton
1970	Robert Fraley
1975	Norman Gross
1980	Charlie Johns
1990	Donna Oldfield

SEVEN LOCATIONS OF MOREHEAD POST OFFICES
(1828-1999)

(Earliest location that can be determined)

1828	1	Corner of South Wilson and First Street (across from present Folk Art Center)
1856	2	Gault House, (corner of University Blvd. & Main Street)
1888	3	First Street across from C&O Passenger Depot (Tourism Center)
1913	4	Corner of Main Street and Carey Avenue (Old Shouse Building)
1925	5	West Main Street in Alf Caskey Building (Present Arby's)
1937	6	Corner of Main Street and North Wilson Avenue (Present City Hall)
1987	7	West First Street and Normal Wells Lane

MOREHEAD POST OFFICE CHRONOLOGY
1828-1998

Nov. 8, 1828   Triplett post office established in what was then Fleming County (Fleming County established in 1798).

July 22, 1856   Rowan County Established. Triplett changed to Morehead. (Rowan population 2,282) Post office located in the Gault House.

Jan. 22, 1869   City of Morehead Incorporated.
(City population 200–County population 2,291).

Sept. 1881	Railroad opened through Rowan County. (County population 4,420–City population 600).
Jan. 1, 1888	Post office located on Fairbanks Avenue, (now South Wilson), across from Kentucky Folk Art Center.
Jan. 1913	Post Office moved west to corner of Main Street and Carey Avenue.
June, 1925	Post office moved to Alf Caskey Building on Main St. (Arby's Rest.)
July, 1927	Morehead postal business doubled from previous fiscal year. New post office fixtures bought .
Sept. 15, 1929	Plans began for a new post office in Morehead.
Oct. 1, 1930	First Village Mail Delivery established in Morehead. (Jack Lewis,city carrier) (also, Goldes Department Store opened for business next door to post office on Main Street.)
July 6, 1932	Postal rates raised.
Sept. 5, 1935	Site of new Post Office selected at the corner of S. Hargis and Main Street (Harlan Blair property, now Citizens Bank parking lot).
Jan. 15, 1936	Hargis Avenue post office site rejected as unsuitable.
Feb. 6, 1936	New post office site selected at the N.E. corner of Wilson and Main. (Present City Hall Building and Police Station.)

April 10, 1936   First Rural Route (I) established in Rowan County. Howard Spurlock was the first carrier.

Nov. 4, 1937   Moved into the new post office without any delay in service.

Dec. 31, 1937   Mural by artist Frank Lovy completed and hung in Morehead post office lobby.

July 1, 1940   Free parcel post delivery initiated in city limits. Jack Lewis delivered parcels in a two-wheel push cart.

July 1, 1940   City mail delivery Route I established in Morehead. (Jack Lewis, city carrier.)

July 1, 1941   Rural Route II established (Mike Flood, carrier).

July 1, 1941   Rural Route III established (C.O. Leach, carrier).

July, 1943   Postal zones established in city.

July 1, 1945   City Route II established and combined with parcel delivery (Randal C. Wells, carrier).

July 1, 1958   3-cent stamp for 1 oz. Letter increased to 4 cents.

July, 1963   Five digit zip codes established.

July 1, 1971   Postal Reorganization Act passed. Converted Post Office Department to executive branch. Post Office Department changed to U.S. Postal Service.

Oct. 1, 1983   Zip code plus 4 installed. Mail sorted more efficiently.

July 4, 1987 Moved to new Post Office on West First Street.

July, 1992 Mail barcode sorter began operation in Long Island, New York.

July, 1998 Sixty-five percent of Morehead's first class mail sorted by bar codes.

This Post Office mural by artist Frank Long was in the Morehead Post Office Lobby for 50 years (1937-1987). It was an example of W.P.A. art depicting strong southern family values during the depression. (Now located in the Morehead City Hall).

CHAPTER NINE

Flood and Fire: Deluge and Ashes

THE FLOOD (JULY 4, 1939)

During the past year (1998), an MSU Oral History class interviewed 32 individuals who were survivors of the 1939 flood, or who had memories of that tragic event. They did a thorough job, and even transcribed the interviews. (This writer and his wife were among those interviewed.) After reviewing the transcripts of many that were interviewed, I searched for more information. Also, I personally talked to 10 that were not interviewed, as well as relying upon my own memory. This account, on the 60th anniversary of that tragic night is presented as a memorial to the 25 Rowan residents who drowned in The Flood of 1939.

Ask most Moreheadians, alive at that time, where they were the night of July 4, 1939, and they will readily remember. Just as they remember where they were when Japan bombed Pearl Harbor on December 7, 1941, and where they were the day President Kennedy was killed, old-time Morehead residents remember sadly July 4, 1939. It was a night that will remain firmly imbedded in their psyche as long as they live. That was the night of The Flood. No, not the Biblical flood that Noah (and family) survived in their ark, but the flash flood that devastated Morehead and much of

Rowan County. It resulted in 25 deaths, and $2,000,000 in property damage. (Estimates ranged from $2,000,000-$5,000,000). That terrible tragedy ended a gala fourth of July celebration in Morehead that began July 2.

Morehead's new Trail Theater announced some very prophetic movie titles scheduled to be shown that week. Those titles included: Saturday: *Doomed at Sundown*, starring Bob Steele (25 citizens were doomed that night and never saw the dawn of another day); Thursday-Friday: *Water Rustlers,* Dorothy Page, (water not only "rustled" but roared down our valley that night); and Monday-Tuesday: They *Won't Forget*, starring Claude Rains (most Moreheadians "won't forget the rains that fell that fateful night). Those movie titles seemed to predice the approaching tragedy.

JULY 4TH CELEBRATION PLANNED

A gigantic gala celebration was planned the 4th of July, 1939 by the American Legion's Corbie Ellington Post 126. Dr. H.L. Nickell, local physician, Legion Post Commander, and WW I Veteran, said, "It would be the largest 4th of July celebration that Morehead had ever seen". As Moreheadians struggled to overcome the depression, the planned celebration had the full support of the Morehead business community. That included: The Lee Clay Tile Company, L.P. Haldeman Company, Economy Store, Big Store, C&O Café, Imperial Cleaners, Consolidated Hardware Store, Nehi BottlingCompany, Jack West, Perry Motor Company, and Midland Trail Garage.

The city was decorated with flags, bunting, and ribbons by professional decorators. The celebration officially got underway with a parade at 10 a.m. July 4th. The parade included an American Legion Honor Guard, two drum and bugle corps bands, floats, clowns, monkeys and other acts from the C.F. Sparks Carnival in town for the week-long celebration. The parade began at MSC's Jayne Sta-

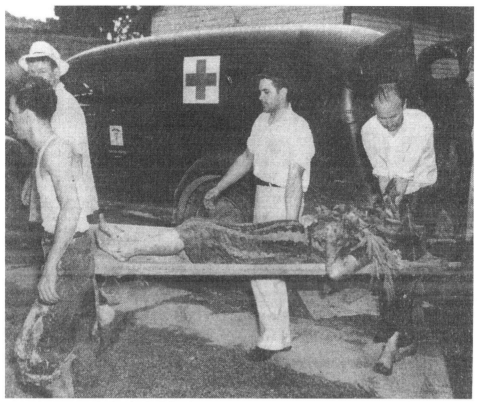

Searchers recover body of a flash flood victim. This young woman was one of 25 Rowan County victims of the July 4, 1939 flash flood.

dium, and marched west down Main Street, then south on Trumbo Avenue, west on First Street (Railroad), then North on South Wilson (Fairbanks) Avenue. Then the parade marched east on Main Street and back to Jayne Stadium.

Following the parade there were many events and contests scheduled including a cracker eating contest, hog calling contest, ugly man and beautiful woman contests, and a greasy pig contest. Local resident Clifford Barker caught the greasy pig, and won that contest. (The winners of the other contests are unknown). At 3 p.m., a special "drawing" was held by the merchants as they gave $50 to two individuals holding the lucky tickets. At 8 p.m., another drawing was held as the American Legion raffled off a new 1939 Chevrolet.

Looking out over Triplett Valley in the 1939 flood.

(Value $700.00). The lucky winner of the new car was Bath County resident, Mr. Lacy Parks. He had bought two 25 cent tickets and drove the new car home. At 9:30 that night fireworks were scheduled at Jayne Stadium. Also scheduled to appear were the famous country singers, the Carter Family, and also Miss America was scheduled to appear. (Sponsored by Lee Clay Tile Company.)

CARNIVAL BROUGHT BRIGHT LIGHTS

Small Town USA is a concept, an ideal, fondly revered and fondly remembered by most Americans who lived through at least half of the 20th century. In small town USA during the depression years, the arrival of a carnival in town was an exciting event. That was especially true in "small town" Morehead in the depression doldrums of the summer of 1939. However, on Sunday afternoon, July 2nd of that year, Morehead came alive with excitement as the trucks transporting the animals, rides, games, tents, and carnival people arrived in Morehead.

As they passed this writer's home on U.S. 60 west, I jumped on my bicycle and rode to my friend, Meredith Mynhier's home, and he, his younger sister, Janet, and I rode our bikes to what was known as the "Show Lot". It was an open field located at the end of South Hargis Avenue adjacent to the railroad tracks. (It was a dead end street then). That was where the carnival and circus shows set up at that time. My friend and I hoped to get a job helping "set up" the carnival, and get free passes for the rides. However, we were too young and too small, so we just watched excitedly and walked around. As we wandered around, Janet, Meredith's sister, got too close to the monkeys, and one of them jumped on her back and bit her on the shoulder. Unconcerned about her monkey bite, we left, trying to figure out how we could come up with the cash needed to get into the carnival when it opened the next night

EXCITEMENT BEGINS

The carnival that opened Monday, July 3, 1939, in Morehead was more than just a carnival. It was billed as the J.F. Sparks Shows, feathering six thrilling new rides, seven exciting shows, and band, free acts, concessions, and fireworks each night. Even a local couple was scheduled to be married in an open wedding on the midway July 5 (that never happened because the midway was no longer there on July 5).

The carnival, bright lights, rides and shows attracted not only local residents, but people streamed in from a five-county area. The rides included the tilt-a-whirl, loop-the loop, Farris wheel, merry-go-round, and many others. Games included ring toss (toss a small wooden hoop over a pin about 16 feet away), baseball toss (knocking down wooden milk bottles with baseball from a distance of 30 feet), and target shooting with 22 caliber rifles. Also, there were games of strength, eg: hitting a spring on the ground with a giant wooden mallet hard enough to drive a ball to the top of a 12 feet pole and ring a bell. Winning at any of these games brought you a kewpie doll, or small furry panda bear. There were never very many winners.

The carnival also offered stage shows, music, dancing girls, and animal acts, such as monkey's riding bicycles. Also for 5 cents you could get in to see what was billed as the world's largest snake, a 350 pound Python. It was no wonder that with the carnival in town, Morehead was ablaze with excitement during the July 4th, 1939 celebration.

BASEBALL GAME BEFORE RAIN

On the afternoon of July 4, 1939, this writer returned home on west U.S. 60, about five houses west of the Freewill Baptist Church. The parade was over, and I planned to play baseball with my friends in the vacant lot near the abandoned ironing board factory. It was located behind my house adjacent to the railroad tacks. About 3 p.m., 10 or 12 of us got a pickup game going. One of the boys was new to the neighborhood. He was 11 year old Leon (I didn't know his last name). He lived across the railroad and came over to play with us that day. (There was no organized baseball then, only choose up games.) I had the bat so I got to be one of the captains. In order to determine who got the first pick, I tossed the bat to the other captain who caught it in one hand, and then we put each hand on top of the other's and the one with his land on top of the bat got the first choice. We chose up sides and Leon was the last boy I selected.

We played until about 6 p.m. when our mothers called us to supper. I remember Leon walking slowly back across the railroad to his humble home right next to the tracks.

EARLY TO BED--EARLY TO RISE

I could not go to the carnival that night because my grandmother and cousin had arrived from Florida for a visit. It was a hot muggy night, and my cousin, BuddyThompson, and I made us a pallet on the floor of our screened in back porch. We went to sleep around 10:30 p.m. (Central Standard Time). Rowan County was the eastern most county in Kentucky in the Central Time Zone. Also, there was no such thing then as daylight savings time.

I was awakened about 2 a.m. by the continuous sounds of the shrill whistle of a freight train. Looking out my back porch I could see the engine had stopped after rounding Brady Curve. It was stopped almost adjacent to Leon's house, and its light was shining up the track toward Morehead.

My mother and dad came out on the back porch with a kerosene lamp because there was no electric power. They said there was a terrible flood and people were drowning. But at that time it did not seem to be raining extremely hard however, the lightening was flashing continuously so that you could see clearly out over the valley toward Clearfield.

SOUNDS, SIGHTS, AND SCREAMS OF TERROR

I remember clearly hearing the roar of the water, as it swept its deadly path down stream. I could also hear the pitiful anguished

Household items deposited by the raging waters in Morehead's flash flood, 1939.

cries of people in mortal terror. There were the high pitch sounds of women and the hoarse sounds of men as they screamed for help knowing they faced death at any moment. Some were in tree tops, some climbed on

Cars, homes, and businesses washed away during the flash flood, 1939.

top of box cars, some were on stacks of lumber and some had gotten on top of their roof before the house was swept away by the tremendous force of the strong current. Others were screaming for loved ones and children whom they could not locate. As the lightning flashed, I could see houses as they floated silently, smoothly and deadly, like giant ice burgs I have seen in the North Atlantic. As the lightning flashed, I saw one man on the roof top of a house floating downstream, holding on to the chimney that still protruded grotesquely above the roof top. Those who were on the housetops were fairly safe unless the house hit a bridge or tree and broke up. Many did and the people drowned unless they were fortunate enough to swim to safety.

The lightning continued flashing rapidly like you would experience when you turned your overhead light switch on and off as rapidly as you could. You could see the brown muddy water was from hill to hill, and was roaring like the rapids above Niagara Falls. During that night we knew something terrible had happened to our town, but we did not realize just how tragic it actually was. But the sounds, the sights, and the sadness remained with those who lived through The Flood throughout their lifetime.

ONE SURVIVAL STORY

Throughout the night of the Flood, my family was in no danger and the water just barely reached in to our backyard. But throughout that night we were worried about my aunt and uncle and their family. (Julia, Buster and Don Day). Their home was just acrossTriplett Creek from Brady curve. The water reached up in the attic of their home. They survived by first getting in the attic, then chopping a hole in their roof and there they survived the ordeal. The house was saved because of a giant elm tree just up stream in their yard, that split the force of the current. It enabled their house to stand when the others around them washed away.

The afternoon following the flood, after the waters had receded, search parties began searching through the mud and driftwood for bodies of those listed as missing. I followed along behind a group of CCC boys as they searched the area below Brady Curve near the old City Sewage Disposal Plant. There, they discovered a body lodged in a barbed wire fence and covered with mud and driftwood. It was Leon, the 11 year old boy I had on my pickup baseball team less than 24 hours earlier. (Then I was glad I had chosen him on my team.)

NEIGHBORS WARNED NEIGHBORS

There were many individual acts of heroism that night. Many unselfishly risked their own lives as they attempted to warn others of the rising waters. Maxie Arnett, his mother and brothers, Joe and Scott, lived across the railroad next door to the Jesse Boggess family on Raine Street. (Presently across the bypass from the Rowan Water Building). Maxie stated in his interview that "he was awakened by Jesse Boggess pounding on his door and yelling for them to get out of their house." He gave Mr. Boggess credit for saving their lives as they barely got out of their house before it washed away. He went on to say, "I've often wondered if Jesse Boggess's mother, who drowned, might have been saved if he had not taken the time to awaken us." Also, there were other people on that street who were awakened by Mr. Boggess, or they probably would have drowned.

BOGGESS INTERVIEWED

This writer contacted James Boggess, the only living child of the Boggess family to hear his account of The Flood. Jimmy, who was eleven years old at the time of the flood, is now a successful Commercial Real Estate Broker, living in Miami Beach, Florida. Here is the Boggess story: Jesse Lee Boggess married Ethel (Cornette) Boggess. They had five children: Harry, Earl Lee, Mary Olive, Ella Mae, and James. In 1939, they lived in a two story stately white house on Raine Street. It was located directly across the railroad track from the end of South Hargis Avenue. Jesse's mother lived two houses downstream from his house in a modest one story house. Mr. Boggess looked after his 77 year old mother. Mr. J.L. Boggess was a prominent member of the community and he was chairman of the School Board as well as a building contractor in Morehead.

July 4th, being a holiday, the Boggess family worked to put the finishing touches on a major remodeling of their home. That day they finished painting, papering, installingnew carpet, getting new furniture, and hanging new drapes. They finished mowing the lawn about dark. But the children managed to cross the railroad tracks to attend the carnival. But when it started raining they came home and went to bed about ll p.m. The phone rang about 12 midnight. It was Clark Lane, one of the local funeral directors, (who also operated the ambulance service), asking Jesse to come to Mrs. Wood's Boarding House next door and help load one of the guests into the ambulance. It seems the guest had a heart attack.

Mr. Boggess dressed and helped Mr. Lane load the victim into the ambulance. By the time he returned home, it was raining so hard he said you had to put your hand over your nose in order to breathe, and the air was literally saturated with water, leaving very little oxygen. Also, by the time he got home the water had risen to his front porch and the lightening was flashing continuously. Mr. Boggess ran into this house, and quickly he and Ethel got all the children out of bed. He told Ella Mae, his oldest daughter, to take their Packard touring car and drive it to higher ground. By the time they loaded in the car with a few belongings, the water was up to the running board of the car. Ella May drove the car to her Uncle Lindsay Caudill's house on Second Street where she woke them up saying there was a terrible flood, and they needed help.

UNABLE TO SAVE GRANDMOTHER

Soon after the car drove off, the water began rising rapidly and the electricity went off. Mr. Boggess sent his oldest son, eighteen-year-old Harry, to his mother's house two doors away to get her out, while he went around knocking on his neighbors doors screaming get up, get out, there's a flood coming! Before Harry could get to his grandmother's house, a four foot wall of water came roaring down the valley sweeping him off of his feet. He said one minute he was wading in water knee deep, and the next minute he was swimming for his life. Harry was an excellent swimmer, but because of the force of the current, he could never reach his grandmother's house. Soon another four foot wave came roaring down the valley. With Harry swimming for his life, he soon found refuge in the top of a tree where he spent the night. His grandmother's house was washed away like a row boat tossed about in a pounding surf. The house broke into small pieces and Mrs. Minerva Boggess became one of the 25 victims of The Flood. Harry Boggess survived the longest night of his life, and was rescued the next morning. The Boggess family home was washed about 25 feet from its foundation, but it survived. The water reached to the ceiling on the first floor and the yellow muck and mud was two feet deep in the house. However, the family spent several days living with friends and relatives. Then they rented a house on West Main Street for several months, but they eventually cleaned the mud out, and restored the house to a livable condition. They remained in that house for another five years, before moving to Grayson, Kentucky. (But they always kept one eye on the weather most of the time.)

In 1939, the disastrous floor waters on First Street reached a depth of 6 to 8 feet. There is a tiny brass plate on the N.W. corner of the Passenger Depot (Tourism Center), marking the depth reached by the water in that flood. The next time you drive east on First Street, stop and look at that marker. It will give you an idea where the water level was in that flood.

Calvert's Taxi washed away with houses and barns in the flash flood, 1939.

DEATH, DESTRUCTION, AND SURVIVAL

"Let not the water overflow me, neither let the deep swallow me up."
(Ps. 65:15)

As the sun arose brightly over Morehead the morning of July 5, 1939, many people were still walking around in a daze. There was a pall of sadness over the entire community as they began to realize the death and destruction that had struck their community. Entire families were trapped in their homes, and swept helplessly through the raging waters to their doom. Others had barely escaped the fingers of death and they knew it. The screams of the doomed still lingered in their ears. Cries of those separated - mother and child, husband and wife, young and old, all were drowned out by the noise of the roaring water.

Two fifteen year old boys, Wayne Amburgey and Norton Earley went to the carnival the night of July 4th. Norton planned to spend the night with his friend, Wayne. The two boys left the carnival around 11 p.m. when it first started to rain. They walked west one mile down the railroad track to Wayne's house, located between the railroad track and Triplett Creek near Brady Curve. The two boys slipped into the house and quietly went to bed so as not to awaken Wayne's mother and two sisters, ages 8 and 14.

The storm increased in intensity and because of the thunder and lightening, Norton could not go to sleep. He began to be concerned that his widowed mother would be worried about him. Therefore, he got up and dressed, and told Wayne he was going home to see about his mother. Norton said he walked the one-half mile across the valley to his home on Clearfield Hill, while the lightening flashed continuously. He said: "You could see as plain as day." The lightening illuminated his path home, and as soon as he arrived, he went to bed. But was awakened by the mournful shrill sound of the Clearfield Tile Plant whistle attempting to awaken the people in the flood's path. By that time the electricity was off, and Norton and his mother could hear the people screaming. He began to worry about his friend Wayne Amburgey.

SON SURVIVED--MOTHER AND TWO SISTERS DROWN

Wayne Amburgy was awakened by the splashing water, as his house began floating downstream in the rushing current. His mother and sisters were screaming as he broke the window in his bedroom and was swept away by the powerful current as he climbed out of the house. He could not help his mother or sisters because of the swift current. All Wayne could do was go where the water took him. He said he was carried effortlessly as the current took him directly and deposited him in the top of a tree near Rockwall Hollow. It was just below there that his house was swept into a high bank and broke apart. His mother and sisters' bodies were recovered just below where the house broke apart.

Wayne clung frantically to the top of the tree until daylight. He was then rescued by a boat. Years later he told his friend: "Norton if you had stayed all night that night, we might have saved my mother and sisters." Norton said: "Yes, and maybe we all would have drowned, and five lives would have been lost instead of three."

CHILDREN DROWN--PARENTS SURVIVE

Mr. and Mrs. Ted Sparkman and their four children, James Elmer (age 9), Paul Edwin (age 6), Thelma Lee (age 4), and Bobby Everett (age 7 months) lived in a one story white frame house across Triplett Creek behind the tobacco warehouse. It was near the point where Christy Creek empties into Triplett.

Nephew, Garrad Sparkman recalled that he had attended the carnival the night of July 4th and was spending the night with his grandfather, Tom Sparkman. Mr. Sparkman lived on East U.S. 60 near the present site of the Dairy Queen. Mr. Sparkman was awakened by the storm, and, worried about Ted and his family, he went down to the water edge. There he could hear Ted and his wife screaming for help above the roar of the water. Ted and his wife were in voice contact with each other and with Mr. Sparkman at the water edge. Ted and his wife were in separate trees. They yelled to each other during that long and tragic night. Ted's wife kept screaming are the children OK and Ted answered yes. They had left the house so quickly just as the water washed the house away and the current swept them away. Ted could not return to the house to help the children because of the force of the water. He was helpless and the fate of the children was hopeless. But after Ted and his wife were separated and found refuge in two different trees, he could not let his wife know that the children had already been swept from his grasp as he tried to hold them together in the tree top. However, he did not want his wife to know that, and he wanted to keep her spirits up during that long tragic night. When the dawn arrived, Ted and his wife were both rescued, but sadly the four children were lost. Three of the bodies were recovered the next day, but the 7-month-old baby was not found. A large casket was made and the three children were to be buried in one casket. But a few hours before the funeral was scheduled, the body of the baby was found in a small barn two miles downstream from where they lived. Plans for the funeral were delayed and the four children were all buried in one casket. It would seem that their loss was more than most could bear, but the parents survived the flood, but never the trauma and grief.

DAVIS FAMILY SURVIVED

Bill "Jinks" Davis and his wife, Odie (Padgett) Davis and their five children, Ralph, James Earl, Lovena, Betty and Wilma lived directly across Triplett Creek from the present Freight Station. (below Triplett View Apartments.) In order to reach their house you had to cross a high swinging bridge. Although there was the old bridge across the dam, there was no road down the south side of Triplett. Their next door neighbor was Mote Rose who owned three nearby rental houses. She had a telephone and someone called her and warned her to get out, but she would not leave her home. Although her house washed off of its foundation about 25 feet, she survived.

Ralph and his sister, Louvena recalled that terrible night of death and destruction. They had been to the carnival, Louvena recalled, she rode the then daring ride, "Loop-the-Loop." When the rain began around 11 p.m., they left and walked over the swinging bridge to their home, and went to bed. Ralph went to sleep on the porch, but was awakened by the continuous lightening, sheets of rain, and the roar of the water rushing through their front yard. Also, they heard people screaming for help as they were being swept away by the swiftly rising, muddy waters. By then, the family was awake and could see as the lightning flashed, that the swinging bridge was already washed away. Their only hope of survival was to reach the steep hill about 50 yards behind their house.

LIGHTNING GUIDED THEM

They recalled Mr. Davis trying to get a gasoline lantern lit as each member of the family hastily put their clothes on and headed out the backdoor, grabbing a few items of clothing as they ran toward the door. By that time there was no electricity, and Mr. Davis never did get the lantern lit. But the family could see clearly as the lightening flashed, that the muddy water was swirling through their back yard between them and the hill. Holding hands tightly, they waded through water above their knees to the safety of the hill behind their house. There they survived the night, praying, singing hymns, and hearing the mortal cries for help by those in trees, on house tops, or being swept away by the water.

LISTED AS MISSING

The Davis house washed downstream about 50 feet and lodged against a tree. It did not break up, and they later moved it back to its foundation. The Davis family was all listed as missing until late the next afternoon. It was then that Ralph and his dad scaled the side of the hill intending to cross into Morehead at the Clearfield Railroad Bridge (but it was washed out). However, they went on to the highway bridge (now 519 at Clearfield) and came back up U.S. 60 and reported their family safe.

HOLBROOK SAGA OF SURVIVAL

John Will Holbrook, Sr., his wife, Dorothy (Miller) Holbrook, and their 3 children: John Jr., Tommy and Nancy lived with their grandmother in a large two story white house directly across the railroad from the C&O Passenger Depot. (Today's Tourism Office). John Jr. recalled his father calling his uncle Luther and Leona Fraley who lived directly behind them on the banks of Triplett Creek, and warned them of the flood. He then woke up tenant worker, Bill Coleman. He told Bill, who lived in a small cottage behind the main house, to get up and come upstairs because the water was rising quickly. John Will, Sr. then quickly moved Bill and all the family with some of the furniture to the second floor. He then opened the windows of the first floor to allow the water to flow through the house. That relieved some of the pressure of the current and saved the house, otherwise it surely would have been washed away. The water was 5 feet deep in their first floor.

During that night the family listened to the roar of the water and the mournful cries of people stranded on house tops, in tree tops, or on top of boxcars. They could hear the loud prayers of Noah Bowling lodged in a tree top near their home. He was praying loudly, "Lord save old Noah from this flood as you did the first Noah. I'm as good as anyone." John Jr. recalled seeing his Uncle

Lon Fannin's house float right down the railroad track with a table lamp sitting straight up on the front porch. (His uncle's family had already evacuated). It floated on down the track for about one-half mile and hit a box car and broke up into pieces.

Mrs. Ramey Never Recovered

The eerie screams of Mrs. Custer Ramey (George Ann McBrayer's grandmother), could be heard all over Morehead. She lived in a small cottage near the present M.S.U. Power Plant. As the water rose quickly in her home she climbed into her attic, then the water got up in her attic, and she chopped a hole in the roof and climbed on top of her house. She remained on the roof all night long terror stricken, and screaming for help. A McKinney boy felt so sorry for her he risked his own life and swam to her house, and remained with her throughout that long and frightening night trying to comfort and calm her. Mrs. Ramey survived the flood but never did get over the post traumatic stress syndrome of that night. It remained with her as long as she lived.

Houses Never Found

The day after the flood, and the water subsided, John Jr. and his brother, Tommy, were walking on the railroad west of Morehead and saw their Uncle Luther Fraley walking along the tracks. John Jr. said, "Uncle Luther what are you doing?" His Uncle Luther said, "Oh, I'm just out looking for my house." All he ever found of his house was just a few pieces. But the Holbrook house survived even if it was covered with sticky, stinking muck and mud one foot deep over the first floor. However, the family continued to live in the upstairs part of the house even as they slowly cleaned up the first floor making it habitable again. It took several weeks of hard, dirty work but the house of Holbrook all survived that long night of terror.

The following poem expresses dramatic insight into the tragedy of The Flood of 1939:

ROWAN COUNTY FLOOD
By Edward Mabry

It was in the hills of old Kentucky, in the year of thirty-nine.
There was an awful flood, it was a distressful time.

You could see the lightning flashing, you could hear the thunder roar.
While the water it was splashing, through many a home and store.

There were many people walking on the streets of Morehead,
While others they were sleeping snugly in their beds.

It came all unexpected, many people had to die.
That was a terrible flood, that fell on the fourth of July.

The storm could not be conquered, for hours it did last.
Many people they were struggling, while the water was raising fast.

From the little town of Haldeman, through Morehead and Bluestone.
Many people they were suffering, and left without a home.

The storm in all its fury swept across the mountain tops.
It filled the valleys with water, and destroyed many crops.

It washed away many bodies, and covered them in the mud.
I'm tellin' all you people, that was a terrible flood.

25 DIE IN JULY 4TH FLASH FLOOD

The following names and ages were released by Rowan County Corner Lester Caskey as drowning victims in the Flash Flood that struck Morehead July 4-5, 1939:

	Name	Age
1.	Geneva Amburgey	47
2.	Margie Amburgey	14
3.	Oma Amburgey	5
4.	Minerva Boggess	77
5.	Junior Leon Bays	11
6.	Minnie Carter	38
7.	Lula Mae Collins	32
8.	Maggie Frances Collins	12
9.	Mrs. Walter McRoberts	24
10.	Ruby Gladys McRoberts	26
11.	Harrison McRoberts, Jr.	4
12.	Slyvia Lee Perry	16
13.	Albert Porter	5
14.	Nora Belle Porter	43
15.	Mabala Mae Ratliff	49
16.	Loren Ratliff	8
17.	Mary Francis Salyers	25
18.	Ivan Eugene Salyers	8
19.	Bobbie Carl Salyers	6
20.	Alberta Mae Salyers	3
21.	James Elmer Sparkman	9
22.	Bobbie Everette Sparkman	7 months
23.	Paul Edwin Sparkman	6
24.	Thelma Lee Sparkman	3
25.	Emma Tolliver	77

FLOOD AFTERMATH

"The rain descended and the floods came and the winds blew, and beat upon that house, and great was the fall of it." (Matt. 7:27)

Following what was the worst disaster in Morehead's history, the number one priority was to recover the bodies of flood victims and account for all those listed as missing. After two days, all bodies were recovered and the missing had been accounted for. But tragically, 25 souls had been swept into eternity by the raging water of the usually placid Triplett Creek. In retrospect, many asked why did so many die, and why wasn't more done to rescue those who were stranded. The answer was given by one local citizen.

EYE WITNESS EXPLANATION

Stanley Iverson, an eyewitness to the tragedy explained it very well when he said he was awakened at 1:45 a.m. by his landlady, Sue Fugate. He dressed quickly and ran down Wilson Avenue to the old Post Office steps. There he saw a helpless, stricken city. The rain was coming down so hard he could hardly see. But he could hear the screams for help four or five blocks away. He could also hear the raging torrent of water rushing down the valley. The water was waist deep in front of the Post Office.

They tried to locate boats to help in the rescue. Dr. Garrad's boat and Henry Haggin's boat were not here. The Hudgins brothers (Howard and Bill) soon arrived with their boat. But at first the current was so swift they could not even get across the street to rescue people on the other side of Main Street. However, by daylight, more boats were located and between 50 and 75 people were rescued from tree tops including Mr. & Mrs. Ted Sparkman, who lost their four children.

The fact that there was so much rain so fast (meteorologists estimated 3 inches in one hour) but it must have even been more than that. Another reason for the loss of life was the rain came while everyone slept, and the water rose so fast, and the current was so swift. Also the creek channel was so narrow that it was unable to hold that amount of water. All of these factors contributed to the drowning of the 25 victims. Those 25 victims, as a percentage of the population in 1939, compared to 1999, would be about 100 people today. It would be like waking up in the morning with the news that 100 people drowned last night. That gives one an idea of the magnitude of the disaster that struck this community sixty years ago July 4-5.

MASS FUNERALS CONDUCTED

The next tragic task was burying the dead. That resulted in many mass funeral services. (The City of Morehead should erect a modest plaque honoring those 25 souls drowned in the Flash Flood of 1939. It could be placed as you cross Triplett Creek in the park on the north side of the Wendell Ford Bridge.) Mass funeral services for six members of one family was conducted at Muses Mills in Fleming County on Friday, July 7, 1939, at 2 p.m. Those six from one family were Mrs. Mary Francis Salyers, and her three children, Ivan Eugene, Bobby Carl, and Alberta May. Also, Mrs. Salyers' mother, Mrs. Mahala Ratliff and son, Loren.

On Friday, Mr. & Mrs. Albert Porter were buried at Redwine, Morgan County. Also, Mrs. Lula Collins and daughter, Maggie Frances, and Mrs. Collins' sister, Miss Sylvia Lee Perry, were buried in Clearfield. Friday funerals also included Mrs. Minerva Boggess who was buried in Harrison County, and Mrs. Emma Tolliver, who was buried in Morehead's Caudill Cemetery. Friday funerals were also conducted at Waltz for Mrs. Minnie Carter, and her son, Junior Leon Bays. Funeral services were held Friday at 2 p.m. at Cranston for Mrs. Minnie McRoberts, her daughter-in-law, Mrs. Walter McRoberts, and son, Harrison. Funeral services were conducted Saturday for Mrs. Geneva Amburgey and her two daughters, Margie and Oma.

HEALTH AND SANITATION PROBLEMS

After burying the dead, the next task faced by the Health Department was to make sure the water supply was safe. The water was tested daily, and city water customers were urged to boil their water for several days. Those with wells were urged not to use their water until it had been tested, or pumped out. Dr. Evans, County Health Director, said that the county would be in a disease danger zone for a month and those who had not taken typhoid shots should do so. One refugee was heard to ask another, "Have you been embalmed for typhoid yet?"

Emergency electric power was restored by volunteer crews from Cynthania and Mt. Sterling, working round the clock. Route 32 to Flemingsburg was the only road open to Morehead. Trains were all rerouted through Maysville and back to Ashland because one mile of track had been washed away on each side of Morehead. Also one small railroad bridge was swept away. Telephone service was restored within 24 hours, but lost again after a short time. However, the local Red Cross representative, Rene Wells, was able to contact the state headquarters and Red Cross representatives were here within 24 hours.

RED CROSS ARRIVES

The American National Red Cross was made the official relief agency in Morehead by Mayor Warren C. Lappin. They set up their temporary headquarters in the City Hall. National representatives were Miss Helen Moses, Richard and Maurice Reddy, as well as dozens of other experienced workers. They were assigned to take charge of the disaster relief in Rowan County. The Red Cross began immediately by providing emergency help to refugee families that had lost their homes and possessions. They set up temporary shelters in the Morehead High School Gym, local churches, courthouse, and college dormitories. Blankets, cots, and bedding were brought in. A field kitchen was established in the High School Gym to provide free meals for the homeless. Morehead College housed 25 state highway patrolmen to help with security, and two doctors from the State Health Department to help with medical are. They also housed homeless families in the dormitories.

Mail service was resumed on Friday, and the George Washington Train at 6 p.m. was the first train to get through the rebuilt tracks. With the dead buried, the homeless cared for, and water, electricity, phone service, mail service, and train service restored, the dirty, messy job of cleaning up began in earnest. It was difficult to get the clean up started because of "gawkers."

Sightseers Interfere With Clean Up

On Sunday, the sightseers streamed into Morehead. It was called "guess," not "guest" day. The idea was to guess how many sightseers were in town that day. Stan Iverson guessed 2,000 and was nearly laughed out of town. Bill Sample and Roy Cornette guessed 25,000. That was considered more likely, when Jim Clay said 596 cars and two motorcycles passed his house on Route 32 in one hour. Also, airplanes were flying overhead photographing and viewing the destruction. Best estimates of the Sunday sightseers ranged from 25,000 to 50,000. This writer has no idea how many people were here that day, but there were "several" because I could hardly ride a bicycle to deliver my papers.

Those flood victims with something left to salvage, began cleaning away the messy, dirty, stinking mud from their damaged businesses, homes, furniture, and yards. The valiant volunteer firemen, and the Civilian Conservation Corps (CCC) who had helped in searching for bodies, now began to assist in the clean up. Those who had something left to restore were the fortunate ones. Many never even found one piece of their house, let along furniture. There were some instances of people finding their property and animals they thought they had lost. Jesse Caudill's hog swam out of the pen and was carried downstream to the site of the carnival. There Jesse's hog tried to join the carnival. He finally found his pig in the cab of one of the carnival trucks. He also found his cow grazing in a field in Farmers.

PYTHON FOUND DEAD

The carnival had a complete loss. They had a 350 lb. Python snake in its cage. When the water receded, the cage was turned over and the gigantic snake was not there. The company printed leaflets and distributed a warning all over town that the snake was loose. People panicked, but after turning the cage upright and cleaning out the driftwood, they found the snake downed in its cage. This writer did not see the dead snake, and I often wondered if that was told just to calm the people. But for the rest of that summer I watched for that snake whenever I was in the woods. However, the next year, I was not worried because I knew it could not survive our cold winters.

The Red Cross moved their headquarters to the second floor of the Peoples Bank on Railroad Street (First Street), and began the process of registering those people damaged by the flood. They announced that 700 people were eligible to receive Red Cross assistance. One young teenage girl came in for help. She was barefoot and needed some shoes, and she held up her mud caked foot to emphasize the need. There were five shiny bright red toenails showing through the caked mud on her foot. She got her shoes.

SEVERE FINANCIAL LOSSES

In addition to the 200 homes lost and 800 damaged, many Morehead and Rowan County businesses were devastated. Biggest business losses sustained were: J.F. Sparks Carnival, $38,000; Morehead and North Fork Railroad, $20,000 (steel bridge and one half mile of track); Union Grocery, $30,000; Big Store Company, $15,000; Big Store Furniture Company, $15,000; C&O Railroad, $22,000; City of Morehead, $10,000; Elam-Wheeler, $15,000; Morehead Lumber Company, $10,000; and the Economy Store, $15,000. Businesses with major damage but un-estimated included: the Lee Clay Tile Plant, the Imperial Cleaners, and the Rowan County News (they missed publishing one issue, awaiting a new part to arrive from Chicago).

Other firms less severely damaged included: W.S. Allen Beer Distributors, $1,500; Carr-Perry, $5,000; Morehead Independent, $5,000; J.A. Allen Grocery, $3,500; Eagles Nest Restaurant, $1,500; Standard Oil Company $5,000; and Kennard Hardware, $4,000.

Other businesses damaged but unestimated included: Calverts Garage, Model Laundry, Myrtle's Tea Room, Imperial Cleaners, People's Hotel, The Bargain Store, Brown Motor Company, The Regal Store, The Golden Rule Store, and Johnson Barber Shop. Of all those businesses damaged by The Flood, the only one still in business sixty-years later is The Big Store Furniture Company.

FARM CROPS AND ANIMALS LOST

Rowan County Agent, Goff, estimated that 900 of the 1,100 Rowan County farm homes were wrecked or damaged. The biggest loss was from erosion. Agent Goff estimated that 40 percent of the tobacco crop was lost, valued at $50,000. Also, destroyed according to his estimate were: 200 head of livestock; five to seven thousand acres of corn; three to four thousand chickens; three thousand acres of hay; 40,000 rods of fence; and many other farm crops and equipment. Agent Goff emphasized that it was still early enough to plant some crops eg. Buckwheat, millet and potatoes. The county qualified for special low interest loans to help rebuild.

Businessmen, companies, home owners, and farmers were determined to rebuild a bigger and better Morehead and Rowan County.

WASHINGTON SENDS HELP

A special bill was introduced in Congress by Joe Bates (and passed) to appropriate federal funds to help the flood victims of Rowan County. Many federal agencies provided some valuable help following the flood. But in most instances, clean up and salvage was accomplished by the blood, sweat and tears of the property owners themselves.

Mr. W.E. Taylor of Washington, D.C. and Mr. L.S. Castor of Cleveland, Ohio, arrived in Morehead July 10, 1939. They represented the Disaster Loan Corporation, authorized by Congress in January, 1937, to make appropriate and necessary loans to victims of floods, tornadoes, and other disasters. As soon as that office opened for business in Room 1 of the Morehead High School, they began immediately accepting applications for loans to assist in rebuilding, and replacing property damaged by The Flood.

REBUILDING BEGINS

Other federal agencies that assisted in the rebuilding included: WPA (Works Progress Administration); NYA (National Youth Authority), and the CCC (Civilian Conservation Corps). Also, volunteer firemen, electrical workers, construction workers, and equipment operators all rushed to Morehead to help in the flood aftermath. Also, embalmers from neighboring city funeral homes came in to assist with that necessary but unpleasant task.

Those that had homes and businesses covered by the water, but were salvageable, had the unpleasant task of cleaning away the one or two feet of sticky mud. Some buildings that washed to the middle of the street were torn down, others were moved back to their original site. One home owner "Ditty Bo" Ramey's house was washed several hundred feet down stream across the railroad track and landed in a vacant lot next door to Mrs. Miller. Mrs. Miller then sold the lot to "Ditty Bo" and he moved in and cleaned up his home on its new site. But many just rebuilt completely because "They allowed as how it would be easier to build another one than to clean that one up."

REBUILD A BETTER SAFER TOWN

Morehead citizens were determined to rebuild after THE FLOOD, even though very few of the losses were covered by insurance. Most people had to borrow money to start over again. But they did! Their recovery from the greatest disaster to ever strike Morehead was phenomenal. They rebuilt a bigger and better town and community. Many years later with the help of another federal agency, the Gateway Ad. District, grants were approved over the years to dredge and widen Triplett's channel. Also funds were received to build flood walls between the city and the creek. While those were under construction, many people questioned whether that was a wise expenditure of funds. But old time residents remembered and were thankful for those flood walls. Roger Russell, while working for the Gateway Ad. District, wrote several grants for those projects, amounting to millions of dollars. Those, along with other funds, received by Morehead and Rowan County, hopefully will prevent another tragedy like The Flood.

When heavy rains hit Morehead even today, there is still some flooding along First Street. But when residents drive along the new by-pass and look over at the high green flood wall or drive over to the Don Greenhill City Park, and look down stream at the wide Triplett Creek Channel, be thankful.

According to the Book of Genesis, God sent His rainbow to assure people he would never again destroy the world with water. Hopefully, the widening of the creek bed, and building of the flood walls, will mean that Morehead will never again suffer the death and destruction they suffered during The Flood of 1939.

FIRE AND FIREMEN
"We went through fire and through water, but you brought us out."
(Ps. 66:12)

Every city and town across this great land of ours has had many major fires and valiant firefighters. Morehead is no exception, and throughout its history has had a record of disastrous fires, and courageous firemen. Morehead, just as in every community, has tried to make proper preparation to combat those fires when they occurred.

During the late 1800s, most of the city's firefighting was done by friends and neighbors as they formed bucket brigades. By the early 1900s, not much had changed in the city's ability to extinguish those fires as they occurred. However, practically every fire was a lesson in fire fighting futility, because by the time help arrived, it was too late, and, about all that could be saved was a few pieces of furniture, and a few personal items. The reasons for that was the buildings were made of highly combustionable wood and the slow response time, as well as the shortage of available water.

FIRE PROMPTS PURCHASE
February 21, 1914, was a bitter cold night in Morehead. That was also the night that the new Morehead Power Plant was completely destroyed by fire. After connecting the city power lines to the Maggard and Bradley private power lines, the City Council decided more was needed to be done to improve the local firefighting capability. It was then the City Council voted to purchase a fire engine, and establish a fire department to be manned by volunteers.

The city immediately ordered its first fire engine from the American La France Fire Engine Company. (A company still in business today.) The new engine was a horse drawn engine, (but could also be pulled by a tractor), and had a hand pumper with a 300 gallon storage tank. The cost of that engine is unknown, but it

Morehead Volunteer Firemen demonstrate an old hand pumper, 1956.

took the city five years to pay for it. The last payment was made August 1, 1919. The new engine was housed in a wooden shed in the alley just off of Bishop Avenue, behind the present Dixie Grill. With the acquisition of the new fire engine, the local fire fighting success rate improved. But the volunteer firefighters consisted of those eager individuals who could get to the fire first after the alarm sounded. (Before the fire alarm was installed, the local church bells were used as a fire alarm.) But those that responded had very little or no training. However, they were willing and eager to learn, but more organization and structure was needed.

FIRST FIREMEN APPOINTED

On December 11, 1922, the City Council recognized that more was needed for avolunteer fire department than to just sound the alarm and see who responds. Therefore, they appointed Isaac Blair as the first fire chief. (He was local residents Don and Paul Blair's grandfather.) They also appointed the following men as the first members of the Morehead Volunteer Fire Department: V. Hunt, Leo Oppenheimer, Hartley Battson, Moody Alderman, Oliver

Caudill, Earl Young, Tom Hogge, J.B. Calvert Sr., Melvin Hamm, Alf Caskey, and D.C. Caudill. Those men formed the first structured Morehead Volunteer Fire Department. They were required to attend some meetings and have some training. Therefore, after the city acquired the new fire engine, and men to operate it, it was about to do something even more dramatic to improve local fire fighting.

WATER SYSTEM VOTED BY CITY

On July 10, 1922, the City Council proposed a referendum for a bond issue to establish a water system for Morehead. It was placed on the November, 1922 ballot, and the results were 298 for water, and 3 against. With the overwhelming majority for building the new water plant, the city moved rapidly. They immediately proposed for the sale of bonds to pay for the new system. On April 5, 1924, $25,000 in bonds were sold to Woody, Heimerdinger, and Watts of Cincinnati, Ohio, to pay for the new water filtration plant, and waterlines. Then by October 24, 1924, a local committee appointed by the City Council, staked off the location for the new water filtration plant. That site was near the present dam on Triplett Creek near the Wendell ford Bridge. The first water lines were laid in Morehead in 1925, which improved the local residents quality of life, as well as the quality of fire fighting.

In 1925, even after the new city water system was installed, there was another major fire. The Morehead Main Street Motor Sales Company was destroyed by fire. But it seemed the main reason the business was not saved was the old American La France Fire Engine failed to function properly. It seemed Morehead was having difficulty getting the right mix of manpower, machines, and water at the right time. Following that fire, the city Council authorized a committee to make a recommendation for a new fire engine. On February 9, 1926, the search committee requested that the city purchase a second fire engine. They recommended the vehicle be purchased from the Boyer Fire Apparatus Company of Logansport, Indiana. The new fire engine was "state of the art" first lineequipment, and consisted of a fire engine mounted on a Ford chassis and engine. The total cost was $2,700, which was expensive for that time.

CITY WATER LIMITED

1930 was the year of one of the greatest droughts in this region. Like the summer of 1999, it rained very little in the spring, and even less in the summer. The drought was so severe that the city rationed water to its customers. Finally, the water shortage became so critical that the water was turned off 20 of the 24 hours each day. If it had not been for the vision of the city fathers (and mothers) who made the decision in the 1960s to go to Licking River for Morehead's water supply, we would probably be at that stage today.

In 1960, it became apparent that if Morehead was to ever grow, it must have more water. The City Council consisted of George Hill, Paul J. Reynolds, Bobby Allen, Roger Caudill, Austin Riddle, and Wilburn Crager. Elden "Tic" Evans was the Mayor. Several studies indicated that the city faced a severe water shortage in the near future. Also, in order to attract industry, for the college to grow, and to ever get a hospital, more water was needed.

WOMEN FOR WATER

The City Council agreed something must be done. They disagreed on what to do. The choice was between expanding the present treatment plant, and using Eagle Lake as an additional source; or, to lay a pipeline to Licking river. The vote was tied. Mr. Hill, Reynolds and Allen voted to go to go to Licking River, and the other three voted against it. Mayor Eldon Evans untied the vote, and voted to go to Licking River. Later Mr. Caudill changed his vote and voted to go to the river. As a result of the vote, the future water supply to Morehead was assured if they could get the money for the pipeline. Although the vote resulted in a breach between the town and the college. Most citizens supported the vote. Many women in Morheead organized to support the vote, and help get financing for the pipeline. They were called women for water, and included: Lucille Evans, Mabel Reynolds, Agnes Williams, Jean Hill, Terry Caudill, Patty Smith, Lois Holley and many others. Therefore, that an organization called, "Women forWater" began a concentrated effort to get funds for the pipeline to Licking River. For months, they lobbied local residents, Frankfort, and Washington, D.C. They finally succeeded in getting a grant to help get the new pipeline and water plant for Morehead. The vision of those City Council members, and the determination of those hard working women should be commended. Today, without the rich resource of water from the Licking River, not only Rowan, but all of the surrounding counties would probably be in a severe water crisis.

The drought of 1930, and only four hours a day with water, caused many Moreheadians to uncover and clean out their wells. But by September most wells were dry, and every one was happy to have water four hours a day. During that drought, Lindsay and Myrtle Caudill (this writer's in-laws) lived in their home on East Second Street. They uncovered and cleaned out their well, and it never ran dry. During that drought, that spring-fed well supplied cool water for most of the neighborhood, and never failed. Since my wife still owns that old home place, and the well is still there, it may be necessary to open it up and clean it out again, should the drought of 1999 continue.

During that dreadful drought of 1930, there seemed to be some dissension develop within the volunteer fire department. Just as in any organization, especially in a group of volunteers, there were some dissidents and complainers. Most of the volunteers took their responsibility seriously, however, some did not. Therefore, the city Council once again decided some action should be taken to improve the morale and effectiveness of the firemen.

On October 27, 1931, the Council voted once again to establish a new volunteer Fire Department. Melvin Hamm was appointed Fire Chief and was instructed to select 11 men to serve as firemen. Those men were required to practice one night a week, (still a requirement) or they would be dropped from the group. Also, the firemen were to be paid $1.00 for each working fire. (Still a requirement today–except they are paid $10.00 for each fire). Most of the policies established for the training, improving the efficiency, and morale of the firemen, were initiated in 1931, and are still in effect today.

FIRE TRUCK WOULD NOT START--HOUSE BURNED

In January 1932, this writer lived with his parents near the corner of WilsonAvenue and main Street, behind the post office. Melvin Hamm had asked my father, and he had agreed, to serve as one of the volunteer firemen. After attending a couple of training sessions, he got his first fire call one below-zero bitter cold February night. He jumped up, put on his clothes and ran to the fire station. But he returned in an hour sweating profusely. They were unable to get the old fire truck started. The men had pushed the truck down Bishop Avenue, and Railroad Street, but it never did start. Unfortunately, the home of Mr. and Mrs. D.B. Cornette on Fifth Street

Peoples Hotel and Sam Allen's Store were destroyed by a fire in 1946. Both were historic landmarks in Morehead.

burned to the ground. (My father was so disgusted that he ended his firefighting career before it was started.) Therefore, on May 12, 1932, the City of Morehead purchased their third truck in 18 years. But not before it was badly needed.

FIRE AND FLOOD DELIVERED DOUBLE "WHAMMY"

On July 4, 1939, Morehead suffered the worst fire in its history. But on July 5, (the next night) a flash flood devastated Morehead and Rowan County. The flood destroyed 200 homes and businesses throughout the community, and resulted in the loss of 25 lives. However, because of all the lives that were lost in that flood, very few people ever knew of the fire. It started almost exactly 24 hours prior to the flash flood, and gave Morehead a double disaster "whammy".

BLIND MAN SAVES HOTEL GUESTS

The City Hotel, owned by Mr. Alf Caskey was a three-story, 32 room brick structure, located in the heart of Morehead's main business district. (Where Arby's Restaurant is now located). The carnival was in town and all the rooms were packed to capacity. Jim Day, (whose name was later changed to Jillson Setters) was a partially blind itinerant musician who was sleeping in the lobby that night. About 1:30 a.m., as smoke spread throughout the building, Jim's keen sense of smell awakened him. Alarmed, he "groped" his way to the owner Alf Caskey's apartment, and pounded on his door to awaken him. Mr. Caskey and his family rushed out, and he called the fire department and started down the halls awakening the guests.

Ten year old Billie Jean Caskey recalled the horror of that night. She and her father, Lester Caskey and step mother lived in an apartment on the second floor. "I was awakened by my grandfather (Alf Caskey) pounding on the door, and my father throwing a few items out the window. Then he grabbed my hand and we all ran from the burning inferno wearing only our night clothes. Later on that night, some of my family (Hubert and Beulah Pennington) came and took me home with them. It was a terrible night, but little did I realize that the next night would be even worse for so many people." (The Flood).

Hotel Filled With Carnival Workers

On that night of July 4, 1939, Morehead was preparing for a giant July 4th celebration. The great J.F. Sparks Carnival was in town. The hotel was filled with carnival workers and probably had many more guests in the rooms than had registered. (They were known to do that). Because on one occasion, this writer's father-in-law rented his small cabin to two of the carnival workers. Then late one night, as he accidentally walked behind the cabin, he caught two people climbing through a window. He went around to the front door and returned their money and told them to leave. There were eight people that left. But fortunately, thanks to the keen sense of smell by Blind Jim Day, there was no loss of life in that hotel blaze. But most of the guests who escaped were only wearing their night clothes. However, no one complained because they were all alive.

Firemen Respond Quickly

Morehead's firemen responded quickly to that fire call. As they arrived the whole block seemed to be ablaze. People were standing around dazed, in their night clothes, not knowing what to do. The firemen quickly moved the people back, and set up a barrier as they connected their hoses and started pouring water into the fiery inferno. Someone had called the Olive Hill Fire Department and soon they responded. Both fire crews valiantly battled the blaze until long after daylight, and at one time it appeared that the whole city block would burn.

Among those firemen who fought that major fire and flood on successive nights were: Chief Lionel Fannin, C.B. McCullough, Tag Calvert, Cecil Landreth, John Bays, Joe Mauk, Mason Jayne, Ernest Jayne, Luther Jayne, and many others. Those men helped to establish the high standard of courage and sacrifice for all of Morehead's future firefighters.

FAMILY FOUGHT FIRE

On July 4, 1939, young Hubert Allen lived above their family-owned business almost directly across the street from the hotel. He vividly recalled being awakened that night about 2:00 a.m. by the sirens, as the fire truck came dashing down the street. He and his family got up and went downstairs and out on the street. Hubert recalled, "The heat was so intense we had to move away from our building, and it seemed certain that the whole block would burn." Hubert said his job was to get on top of their roof with a shovel, and as the burning embers landed on their roof, he would shovel them over the side. However, their windows were all broken anyway, but their building survived even though all the eyewitnesses thought the whole city block would be destroyed. Also, those spectators said, except for the herculean effort by Morehead's valiant volunteer fire fighters, the whole block would have burned. Morehead Fire Chief Lionel Fannin said that the absence of any wind that night was the deciding factor in being able to contain the fire to one building, and those businesses located in that building.

Hubert Allen's sister, Bess, went to bed early the next night after being up all night fighting to keep their building from catching fire. She said before retiring for the night, "I'm so tired it will sure take more than a fire to get me up tonight." It did. A flood got her up again to try and keep the water out of the store.

BUSSES, BUSINESSES, BOURBON DESTROYED

In addition to the hotel, there were seven other businesses located in that building that were destroyed in that fire. Those businesses were: Caskey Tire Company, Caskey Taxi Cab Company, Trail Barber Shop, Morehead Real Estate Company, Parkers Pool Room, W.P.A. Packhorse Library, seven school busses owned by Alf Caskey and leased to the county, and the Snell and Wendell (S&W) Liquor Store.

In preparation for the 4th of July celebration, the S&W Liquor Store had just received a large shipment of bourbon and scotch whiskey. And all through the night as those bottles exploded by the intense heat, it sounded like gunfire. Also, that highly flammable alcohol added fuel to the flames. But the next day some of the local characters known for tipping the bottle, frantically searched through the blackened embers looking for an un-exploded bottle. Some were actually located un-exploded, under the fallen timbers.

Most of the surrounding buildings had some smoke and water damage, as well as broken windows. The Eagles Nest suffered $300.00 damage the night of the fire, and $500.00 the next night in the flood. Also, those displaced carnival people who barely escaped the fire with their life, would, the next night, barely escape the flash flood with their life. (I doubt if any of them ever returned to Morehead.) They had been hit with a double "whammy".

RECORDS SURVIVE FIRE AND FLOOD

Pucky Jayne Bradley, whose family was one family that was damaged by both the fire and the flood, recalled her experience the night of the fire. She recalled standing across the street, and watching the fire fighters as they tried to contain the blaze. She also recalled some of them praying for rain to help contain the blaze. (Little did they realize the flood would come the next night.)

Her dad, W.L. Jayne had a garage in an adjoining building, but was in the process of moving to their new site on East main Street. (Present site of Larry Fannin Chevrolet). However, the customer accounts were still in the building, so her dad sent someone into the building to get those papers. She said, "They were afraid that the building would burn also." Pucky said, "All those papers were brought home, and the next night the flood came and they had to be moved upstairs since water was about 5 feet deep on the first floor." One could say those records were permanent since they withstood both flood and fire.

LOSS OF PROPERTY--NO LOSS OF LIFE

Mr. Alf Caskey's loss in the fire was estimated at $75,000, none of which he saidwas covered by insurance. ($75,000 in 1939 dollars would be probably $1,000,000 today.) Most of the other businesses were covered by insurance. However, Mr. Caskey rebuilt his business even without insurance.

Morehead had suffered a major fire to its downtown business section. But the volunteer firemen were due great praise for their heroic efforts. They succeeded in saving many buildings because of their hard work. But their efforts were overlooked because of the tragic flood that came 24 hours later with such tragic loss of life. Those firemen had been up almost all night fighting fire, and the next night they were up almost all night fighting for their homes and lives. The fire chief, Lionel Fannin, lost everything he had in the flood, as did some of the other firemen. They were also called to help rescue flood victims, and search for bodies.

FIRE AND FLOOD BROUGHT MATURITY OF VOLUNTEER FIREMEN

Morehead's volunteer firemen came of age on those two nights. Like a military unit trained for combat, and when the battle came, they met the test of fire. Thus, with those two major crises, they responded successfully to those crises! From that time on, the firemen knew that they could succeed under almost any conditions. It instilled confidence and pride in their unit. There were other major fires, Peoples Hotel on Railroad Street, "Lil Abner" Restaurant on East main Street, and the C. Roger Lewis business and home on Main Street and others. But in each case the Morehead Volunteer Fire Department has responded with great courage and success. Today, they are second to none in Volunteer Fire Departments. Many of these volunteers go on to become professional firefighters on municipal fire departments such as Ashland, Louisville, Lexington, Georgetown, as well as in the State Fire Marshall's Office.

Morehead's very capable full-time fire chief, Dale Adkins, says the department now has 40 volunteer firemen. They have four fire trucks, one pumper, one tanker, one ladder truck, two brush trucks, and one air-lighting truck. Last year, the fire department responded to 475 calls. Hopefully you will never need them, but when you do, they will be there quickly, and know what to do.

During the past 100 years, Morehead has had sixteen very capable fire chiefs. Those men are:

1. Isaac C. Blair
2. Melvin Hamm
3. Norman Wells
4. Jack Cecil
5. Lionel Fannin
6. C.B. McCullough
7. Walter "Tag" Calvert
8. Joe Mauk
9. William Lee Helwig
10. Glenn Terrell
11. Harold Holbrook, Jr.
12. Raymond Adkins
13. William Hankinson
14. Ronnie Day
15. Randy Walker
16. Dale Adkins

CHAPTER TEN

Bookmobiles and Black History:
Literacy and Tolerance

The geography and topography of Eastern Kentucky have contributed to the isolation of this region. These also contributed to the lack of economic, educational, cultural, and social development of Eastern Kentucky. Lack of schools and reading material made illiteracy the norm instead of the exception 100 years ago in Rowan County. Many people could not read, and there were no books available.

BOOKS DELIVERED BY PREACHERS ON HORSEBACK

The circuit riding Methodist preachers traveling in Rowan County over 100 years ago were the first to bring books to the people of Rowan County. These usually consisted of Pilgrims Progress, a primer of reading, a Bible and simple Bible stories which they loaned to the people. Books were rare and expensive on the frontier. All Kentucky school children know the story of young Abe Lincoln who borrowed a book from a neighbor, and snow blew through the cracks in the log cabin ruining the book. Honest Abe walked several miles and returned the book and agreed to split rails to pay for the damaged book.

One hundred years ago as rural schools began to appear in Rowan County, each school made some effort to have 10 or 12 books

Packhorse Library Bookwomen (and men) head out on the trail to deliver books in Eastern Kentucky, 1935.

they called a "library." These books were usually old textbooks. It was not until the coming of the W.P.A. (Works Progress Administration), a federal program, that library books were first distributed in Rowan County. This program was established in the 1930s to help put unemployed teachers to work. The W.P.A. was a part of this nation's New Deal under President Franklin D. Roosevelt and succeeded in putting many people back to work during a decade ravaged by depression. The program also brought much needed reading material to rural Rowan County.

Using modern terminology, it can be said that the first software information delivery system in Rowan County was "old Dobbin," a packhorse. Librarians used the packhorse library as a means of circulating books into isolated rural areas. However, some drove Model A Fords over the rough rural roads. On the night of July 3, 1939, there was a major fire in downtown Morehead, destroying the Caskey Hotel on Main Street. Also, this fire destroyed the books for the packhorse library that were stored in a small room in the rear of the hotel. The fire ended that early library service program in Rowan County. World War II came along and for the next eleven years, darkness was over the land called Rowan because there was no library service to the people.

FIRST BOOKMOBILE ARRIVES

In October 1951, this writer was employed as the first Bookmobile driver/librarian in Rowan County. (The rest of this article will be written in the first person.) There were 37 public schools in Rowan County, and I was charged with the responsibility of providing bookmobile service to 36 of them. (Morehead High School had a very respectable school library, and an outstanding librarian by the name of Ward Williams.) The bookmobile books were stored in the basement of the old Morehead High School.

In October 1951, the only paved roads outside of Morehead were U.S. 60 from Carter County to Bath County, State Route 32 from Fleming County to Elliott County, and the road from U.S. 60 East to Haldeman. All other roads were limestone gravel, creek gravel, or no gravel. "Alice" (the green paneled bookmobile) was a 1951 Chevrolet with six ply tires, and a good heater. It had custom made three-tier shelves on the inside from front to rear with a very narrow isle, and low ceiling. (The taller students had to bend over). The shelving was tilted downward on a 25 degree angle to keep the books from sliding off the shelves while driving over the rough, curvy roads. The outside panels could be propped up exposing four rows of shelving set on a 25 degree angle. The primary books were shelved inside, and the more advanced juvenile books on the outside. When fully loaded, "Alice" would hold about 600 books. It had to be re-stocked each day on the first round of the schedule and during the first three weeks at the beginning of the school year. After the first scheduled visit to each school, there would always be over 2,000 books checked out at all times. The books would then just move from school to school.

First Hardware Delivery System

In 1951 when Mrs. Eunice Cecil was appointed Rowan County Superintendent of Schools, she was acutely aware of the need for some type of library service in Rowan County. Having served as school supervisor for many years, she knew the people and the need for books in the schools and was determined to do something about it. Working with Miss Margaret Willis, Director of the State Library Extension Division in Frankfort, she obtained a bookmobile for the County.

The first "mechanical" software information delivery system in Rowan County was a 1951 green Chevrolet solid panel truck adapted to hold books. It was donated to the Rowan County School system by Mary Belknap Gray (of the Belknap Hardware Company in Louisville). The total cost of the first bookmobile was $2,000 and was donated to Rowan County in honor of Mrs. Gray's mother, Alice Silliman Belknap. This first bookmobile was known affectionately throughout Rowan County as "Alice." Also, this first bookmobile was one of Kentucky's first demonstration bookmobiles purchased through private donations as an experiment to determine its effectiveness in providing library services.

Superintendent Cecil agreed to hire a teacher to serve as the Bookmobile

School children flocked to the first bookmobile in Rowan County as it stops at Bratton Branch School. Jack Ellis, Bookmobile Librarian, and Robert Needham, Teacher.

driver and librarian. Also, she agreed to maintain the bookmobile and the Kentucky Department of Libraries agreed to supply the books. Therefore "Alice," a green Chevrolet bookmobile, became hardware for the first software delivery system in Rowan County. It was made possible through the cooperative effort of the local school board, Kentucky Department of Libraries, and private donations.

JACK ELLIS BEGINS BOOKMOBILE SERVICE

Before beginning bookmobile service in 1951, I had to move the total collection of 3,000 books from the basement of Morehead High School to the basement of the Superintendent's Office at the corner of College Blvd. and Second Street. Next, a regular schedule was established that allowed the bookmobile to visit each school every three weeks. In the 36 schools, there were 79 classrooms when you included Morehead Elementary, Farmers, Haldeman, Clearfield and Elliottville consolidated schools. (Writing about it almost 45 years later I don't see how I did it all, but then I was about 45 years younger.) In addition to being the bookmobile librarian, I also worked at the Post Office part-time. (Perhaps the reason I got the bookmobile job was because I was a substitute rural carrier and knew the roads.) The teachers and children knew the day the bookmobile would come to their school. I would drive up close to the front door, get out and greet the excited children. The teachers and children were so appreciative of the bookmobile and the books. They took good care of the books, and were seldom late returning them. The first visit of the schools each year the children only checked books out. Each child was limited to one book, but they would exchange their books among themselves many times before I returned in three weeks. Some children would read eight or 10 books in the interim. Teachers would quiz the children to insure they actually read the books. The next trip each book would be returned, and the students checked out another. I would then place the books back on the shelves to be read at the next school. Thus we kept a revolving collection at all times.

BEFORE TV CHILDREN READ EXTENSIVELY

What a joy it was to bring children and books together in that era of time. There were very few distractions to keep children from reading - except their chores. There was no television, very few radio stations, and newspapers. Also certainly none of the students had cars to distract them.

Reading became a passion among many of the children. They read broadly and deeply. Biography was very popular. The Bobbes-Merrill "childhood of Famous American" series was a collection of about 75 famous people, including Clara Barton, George Carver, Sam Houston, Daniel Boone, Jane Addams, Zack Taylor and dozens ofothers.

The girls were interested in the Nancy Drew Mysteries and Louisa Mae Alcott books. They also read Laura Ingalls Wilders's "Little House" books. The boys were reading Jack London, the Cobly Books, and Nordoff and Hall books. "How to books" were also popular then as well as cookbooks. The smaller children were reading such books as the "Little Engine that Could" and one of the first Dr. Seuss books, "The Cat in the Hat." The Caldecott books (Best Illustrated) and the Newberry Award books (Best Literature) were never very popular among young children. I have always maintained these are awards given by adults for outstanding children's book represented what adults thought were interesting but were not as well liked by children as adults.

In 1952, with no TV to use up their time, the children in Rowan County read veraciously. They eagerly anticipated the day "Alice" (name of the bookmobile) came to their school. Many teachers told me there were very few absences the day "Alice" came. Each book might be read by ten or twelve children. Also many of the children would tell me the plot of their favorite book. Others would tell me how many books they had read since my last trip, and how many of the books their parents had read. (Accurate circulation statistics were kept on the number of books read.) Some would even select a book for their parents instead of one for themselves, because they were limited to one book. (Later when we got more books they could get a book for the parents.) Book circulation records "skyrocketed" during those early Bookmobile days. Reading levels increased dramatically, and test scores improved significantly. After careful evaluation by local teachers and State Department officials, Rowan County's demonstration (pioneer) bookmobile "Alice" was declared a resounding success.

ROAD CONDITIONS PRIMITIVE—SCHOOLS ISOLATED

Because of the very poor county road conditions, getting to some of the more isolated rural schools was an adventure. In order to get to Mt. Hope School (near what is now the high bridge to Menifee County), I had to follow a small creek for a quarter of a mile. The creek had a solid rock bottom and normally with water about one foot deep. But I always had to make sure there had not been a recent rain. Or, if it clouded up while I was there, I had to pack up an get out quickly lest I get stranded.

On one beautiful spring day in 1952, Superintendent Eunice Cecil decided to ride with me and visit the schools on the bookmobile schedule. We visited Dry Creek School and went over Clack Mountain, then down Lick Fork through the "Poppin Rock" tunnel past the old Paragon Post Office for about 3 miles to Craney School. There the dirt road came to a dead end. Before getting to the school the narrow road followed the side of the hill for a quarter of a mile about 50 ft. above the North Fork of Licking. While at the school, it clouded up quickly and the rain came down in torrents. We packed up quickly and about 3 p.m. started our return trip to Morehead. Much to our dismay when we arrived at the narrow portion of the road high above the stream there had been a hugerock slide. The road back to Morehead was completely blocked. We were trapped, and there was no way out. At that point, I was thankful for the "Survival Gear" I always carried hidden in the bookmobile. That included a loaded rifle, blankets, kerosene, matches, knife, and ax. Mrs. Cecil took the situation with her usual good humor and said, "We'll just have to wait until someone comes to find us." (There were no telephones anywhere in the area.)

TRAPPED AT TREACHEROUS CROSSING

I remembered that several years earlier I had hunted up Craney Creek, a hollow that opened on the road behind us. I remembered a gravel road on top of the ridge at the head of the hollow. Also, at one time there had been some semblance of a road there. With it still raining, we turned around and started up Craney Creek in the Bookmobile. It was pouring rain as we stopped at a small house and asked about a road that would get us out of there. The woman who came to the door said there had not been a car or truck up that road in 20 years. But we dauntlessly drove on and sure enough the road ended in a corn field. We drove through the cornfield and came to Craney Creek where the water was by this time running swiftly and was five or six feet deep.

There had been an old road there, and there were the remains of an old wooden bridge that had crossed the creek. There was no flooring on the bridge and only two heavy hand-hewn oak beams across the stream had survived. However, it appeared the beams were the same width as the bookmobile wheels.

With the rain still coming down Mrs. Cecil got out of the bookmobile and crawled on her hands and knees across one of the oak beams to the other side of the creek. She then directed me with hand signals as I inched the vehicle toward the creek. The wheel width matched exactly with the cross beams. Without knowing if they would support the weight of the truck, I moved forward on faith. The bookmobile crossed without incident. We continued on up the hollow, mostly through the woods, keeping to the high ground and occasionally having to cut a small tree with my ax, or clear out some brush from our path. But we made it up to the head of the hollow where there was a log road that brought us up to the top of the ridge between Clearfield and Elliottville. We made it back safely and Eunice used to laugh and say both of our reputations would have been ruined if we had stayed out all night in the bookmobile.

LUNCHTIME WAS PLAYTIME

There were some lunchrooms in the county rural schools, notably Johnson, where Mrs. Marie Ellington was the teacher. Depending on the schedule, I would usually eat at a lunchroom. When at Johnson, the children always wanted me to play softball with them. They would let me be the pitcher for both teams. On days when I would not be at a school with a lunchroom, I would "brown bag" it. At lunch time I would stop beside aclear stream or on top of a ridge with a scenic overlook for lunch. I did not read while eating but always enjoyed the scenes of nature surrounding me.

Many times when my schedule placed me at one of the consolidated schools at lunchtime, there would be a basketball game scheduled with one of the other county schools (usually at 12:30 p.m.). Since I was a registered basketball official, they would ask me to officiate. I kept in pretty good physical condition that way, especially since I was the only referee. Books, boys, and basketballs mixed well in Rowan County in the 1950s.

RED MULES SAVE THE DAY

One cold snowy day in January I was returning again from Craney. That time the road was covered with ice and snow. The bookmobile slipped into a ditch and could not get out. Soon a heavy log truck loaded with logs came by and hooked a chain up to the vehicle. Because of the ice, the truck could not budge the bookmobile. I rode with the truck driver down to the Paragon Post Office (I knew the Post Master, Fred Phillips, from delivering mail in the summers and at Christmas.) I told him the log truck could not pull me out. He proudly proclaimed he could get me out. He went out to the barn and harnessed his two big red mules, and we rode them in a snowstorm back to the stuck bookmobile. He hooked his trace chains around the front bumper and cracked his whip once; and with a loud "GET UP MULES," they dug their hooves into the ice and pulled the bookmobile out after the log truck had failed. These were some of the "adventures" I recounted on Radio Station WHAS in 1953, as Kentucky began their state-wide drive to get a bookmobile in every county.

LIBRARY CERTIFICATION

When I began the first bookmobile service in 1951, I had a teaching certificate with no library training. Also I worked part-time in the Post Office as a substitute clerk/carrier. My P.O. Clerk schedule was either 4-8 a.m. or 4-8 p.m. I worked Saturdays as a city carrier, and summers as a rural carrier. The bookmobile librarian position was nine months a year, so this schedule worked well for me. However, I had to take library science courses to keep the bookmobile job, and after one course I was "hooked on books." The late Ione Chapman and Clarica Williams, head librarians at Morehead State College and Breckinridge respectively, took me under their wing and guided me through their Library Science program. I shall be eternally grateful for their guidance and counseling during that time. With their help, I was able to complete my degree and certification. Becoming the first male to graduate from Morehead with certification in Library Science. (Twenty years later as Chairman and Professor of Library Science at M.S.U., I had to close that department as a result of a cut in funds.)

TELEVISION INCREASED—READING DECREASED

In 1952, television came to Morehead from WSAZ-TV in Huntington. Gradually, as TV antennas began to spring up throughout the county, library circulation decreased. The downward journey along the path from a print oriented society, toward an oral, visual society had begun. In today's computer literate society, children are having more difficulty reading because of the demand for moving images and a sound track. Also, the most computer literate student today is not necessarily the best reader. But reading is essential to understanding what is on the internet. There is a difference in being able to surf the net and understanding what is on the net.

Bookmobiles in Kentucky proved suitable for providing library services. They could reach remote rural areas with basic books and personal attention to reluctant readers. In 1953 as a result of the success of the demonstration bookmobiles in Bell, Bath, and Rowan and other counties, the Kentucky Friends of the Library began a statewide drive to raise $300,000 to purchase 95 new bookmobiles. These bookmobiles would be given to counties willing to operate them. A Fund Raising Committee was formed. The Kentucky bookmobile fund raising committee consisted of business and industrial leaders from throughout the Commonwealth. However they were mostly people from the Louisville area. Among those committee members were chairman Harry Schacter, president of Kaufman-Straus Company in Louisville, and Mrs. Mary I. Bingham, owner of the *Louisville Courier Journal*. Mrs. Bingham later became chairman of the committee after Mr. Schacter resigned and moved out of the state. Other members included the Kentucky Chamber of Commerce President, Lions Club President, Ashland Oil President and Mary Belknap Gray of the hardware company in Louisville, as well as many other prominent Kentuckians. As the bookmobile fund grew, the amount was published regularly in the Courier Journal.

NEW BOOKMOBILES PURCHASED

Thursday, September 16, 1954, was Governors Day at the state fair in Louisville. On that day I drove one of 95 new bookmobiles in a parade through Louisville out to the state fairgrounds. There were Federal, State, and County officials, as well as educators, librarians and seven thousand interested Kentuckians in the stands (many Rowan Countians). Those 95 new bookmobiles had been paid for entirely with private donations from throughout Kentucky. Since I had about worn out our original demonstration bookmobile, I had the honor of receiving a new one. It was taller, wider, roomier and held over twice as many books. It was white instead of green and more modern. The driver's seat would swival around permitting me to help the children with their books. I actually went up to Mansfield, Ohio, and drove our new bookmobile off the assembly line at the Gerstenslager Company. It was an exciting era for books and libraries in Kentucky. One Kentucky racing stable named a promising yearling "Bookmobile". (I don't know of any children named "bookmobile" but there were girls named "Alice" for Rowan's first bookmobile.) I never heard if the

Eunice Cecil, former School Superintendent stands beside new bookmobile named in her honor, 1970.

horse won a race, however, bookmobiles in Kentucky won the race against ignorance, illiteracy, and idleness of that era. THE FIRST ROWAN COUNTY BOOKMOBILE, KNOWN AS "ALICE," WAS ONE OF THE PIONEERS THAT PAVED THE WAY FOR ALL KENTUCKY COUNTIES TO RECEIVE A BOOKMOBILE. ALSO IT WAS THE BEGINNING OF THE EXCELLENT ROWAN COUNTY PUBLIC LIBRARY WHICH IS A CREDIT TO OUR COMMUNITY.

FIRST PUBLIC LIBRARY AND BOARD

By 1954 the bookmobile service to the schools had become very successful. That year the Library Extension Division in Frankfort insisted that some library service be provided to the general public. Since the Division provided the books, an attempt was made to accomplish this. To do this, the books were moved from the basement of the superintendent's Office to the rented building at the intersection of Flemingsburg Road and Fleming Avenue. There I was asked to keep the library open to the public three afternoons a week from 2 p.m. to 4 p.m. This became the first public library in Rowan County, even though it was supported by the school board. I served as the first public librarian until 1955. At that time I had to either work full time at the Post Office or resign. I resigned in order to continue library work at one half the salary of the Post Office. Also, at that time, Rosemary Stokes, an RN, who had been unable to get a nursing position, (no hospital here then) was appointed to keep the library open in the afternoons. She continued in that position until she became the County Health Department Nurse working with the late Dr. T.A. Evans.

In 1956 the Kentucky General Assembly passed the Library Services Act enabling a county public library board to be appointed. The first Rowan County Public Library Board consisted of Eunice Cecil, Ione Chapman, Randy Wells (mailman Randy), Ollie Barker, and Alpha Hutchinson. The Kentucky Library Services Act was strengthened in 1964 permitting counties to levy a library tax by petition of the voters. It was then, this dedicated group of public minded citizens began a lengthy effort to get enough signatures on a petition to establish a 2.9 mil tax on property for a Rowan County Public Library. Needless to say, there were many who fought hard against this library tax.

In 1955 the bookmobile collection was moved again into the basement of the Courthouse. I continued keeping the library open to the public three afternoons a week. A grant from the Kentucky Department of Libraries in Frankfort provided money to renovate the Courthouse basement room into suitable library quarters. Mr. Lindsay Caudill did all the renovation and built shelving and a circulation desk. The state sent us a basic collection of books for a public library and the public library expanded services in the basement of the old courthouse.

FIRST PUBLIC LIBRARIAN APPOINTED

In the fall of 1956, the state provided a grant to hire a part-time public librarian. Miss Inez Faith Humphrey, a recently retired English Professor from Morehead State00 College, was the new public librarian. This allowed me to devote more time to the bookmobile program in Rowan County. By the fall of 1956, Mrs. Eunice Cecil had been replaced by Mr. Clifford Cassady as school superintendent. It was during that time I began to realize that it was necessary for a man with a family to get a graduate degree in Library Science. After applying and receiving a leave of absence effective January 1, 1958, I attended Vanderbilt University's Graduate Library School. After receiving the degree, I went on to Florida before return to Kentucky in 1966.

The Bookmobile had been turned back in to the state and the public library closed for a period of time in the early 1960's. In 1972, a new bookmobile was obtained by the Library board to serve the citizens of Rowan County. The Bookmobile was named in honor of Eunice Cecil. In less than 25 years the bookmobile called "Alice" was changed to the bookmobile named "Eunice." As "Eunice" travels the new blacktop rural roads of Rowan, which are very different than the old muddy roads, it brings honor to Mrs. Eunice Cecil. She had the vision and determination to bring the first bookmobile to Rowan County, thereby influencing a generation of readers.

BLACK HISTORY
"God hath made of one blood all nations of men to dwell (together) upon the face of the earth" (Acts 17:24)

Historians writing about racial relations in this nation have repeatedly emphasized the cruel and violent acts perpetrated by the white race against Afro-Americans. Little has been written of the positive relationships that existed between the races, as was the case in Rowan County. The history of Rowan County shows that the two races have co-existed and always lived together in peaceful harmony. This was true even though the school census showed black children have always been about 1 percent of the school age children in Rowan County; e.g. in 1898, there were 2,290 white children and 23 black children. But in 1910, with 3,151 white students and 12 black students, Superintendent Lyda Messer Caudill established the first school for black children.

FIRST BLACK BORN IN ROWAN COUNTY
The reason there were so few black families in Rowan County was there were no large farms or plantation estates in this area. Neither were there factories here that might attract black settlers to the area. Consequently, the few black families living in Rowan County were timber workers, domestic workers or independent farm owners workingtheir our land. However, the record shows

that the first black born in Rowan County was Ulysses Grant Carey. He was born in 1869 (the year Morehead was incorporated into a town). He lived in the Farmers section of Rowan County and was the son of a former slave. His mother was a domestic worker who lived with Judge J.M. and Mary E. Carey. (Grandparents of Lena Wilson). Ulysses's mother died when he was very young and he was reared by the Carey family and given their name. They taught him to read and write and gave him a home and job. He worked for the Carey's in exchange for room, board, and wages, and was affectionately known as Uncle Sy. Following the death of Judge Carey, he moved into a small cottage behind their granddaughter Lena Wilson's home on East Second Street. He did garden work, grocery shopping and other household duties. He would go to the grocery carrying a large round bottom egg basket to assist him in bringing groceries home.

A MASTER GARDENER

Uncle "Sy" was a kind and friendly neighbor, who was known as Morehead's master gardener. He grew some of the finest vegetables in Morehead. That was at a time when the only fertilizer was the manure collected from farm animals. Since the Wilson's had no farm animals in town, Uncle "Sy" would take a small wheelbarrow around the courthouse on court day, shoveling up the horse manure for his garden. That helped keep the city clean and helped his garden grow real organic vegetables. That was Morehead's first attempt at recycling.

Uncle "Sy" lived with the Wilson's until his death in 1949 and was buried in the Wilson plot in the Lee Cemetery. He was loved and accepted by all of the Wilson family and Morehead residents. He was a well respected and contributing member of the community.

YOUNG BILL COLEMAN COMES TO MOREHEAD

In 1893, Anderson Miller was the C&O station agent in Morehead. A.L. and his wife, Hattie (Pope) Miller, lived with her family in a large house just across the tracks from his office. One day the railroad police brought in a young black hobo who had been taken off of a freight train as it passed through Morehead. He was brought to Mr. Miller to see what action should be taken. The kindly Christian, Mr. Miller, asked the boy his name. He discovered that his name was William C. Coleman and that he was 16 years old and had not eaten in two days. Mr. Miller took him home and fed him a good home cooked meal. Mr. Miller then asked him if he would like to stay with him for a few days and help him raise a garden and do some work around the house. "Bill" Coleman agreed and remained with the Miller family for 51 years until his death in 1944. During that time he had his own cottage on the Miller place, earning his room and board plus a small wage. He was buried in the Miller family plot in Morehead's Lee Cemetery.

A.L. and Hattie Miller were the parents of Dorothy (Miller) Holbrook. Dorothy's son, John Will Holbrook, Jr. said: "During the depression years they had to move back in with his grandparents, the Millers." During that time he got to know Bill Coleman well and said he was an integral part of their family. He had taken care of two generations of the Miller and Holbrook children. He was their caretaker, friend, and trusted employee. When Bill Coleman died in 1944, the family was devastated, because they felt they had lost a family member. Bill Coleman, who came to stay a few days in Morehead, remained 50 years. He proved the old saying "That if you ever take a drink of Triplett Creek water, you would never leave." Bill stayed and helped Morehead grow.

FIRST BLACK FAMILY MOVES TO MOREHEAD

Between 1908-1918, the Clearfield Lumber Company was established in Rowan County. Also the Morehead and North Fork Railroad was built, running from Morehead to Wrigley in Morgan County. There were many black families brought in to Rowan County to work on that railroad. However, it was at the time of the influenza epidemic. Many died and the rest left Rowan County. But in 1910, Luke and Lizzy France moved from Bath County to Morehead. In making that move, they became the first black family to establish a permanent residence in Rowan County. Luke worked for the C&O Railroad and his wife worked for Mrs. A.L. Miller and other Morehead families. Their home was located near Raine Street, south of the railroad tracks. Lizzie was loved by all the neighborhood children. She would often bake cookies and give them to the children as they walked down the railroad tracks in front of her house on their way home from school.

Luke and Lizzie France had four children: Lewis, Freddy, Helen and Aileen. They were friends and neighbors of Anderson and Hattie Miller, who had eight children: Nell, Edith, Vivian, Dorothy, Mary Sue, Walter, Ralph, and Earl. Also, the young black man, Bill Coleman, was considered a member of the family at that time.

BLACK TEENAGER KILLS WHITE TEENAGER

The Miller and the France families were not only neighbors but very friendly and charitable toward each other. Each helped the other in times of need. Although state law forbid the children from attending school together, they often played together. One day in 1914, Earl Miller and Freddy France were playing marbles behind the Miller home. The two 13 year old boys got into an argument over a marble game. The argument escalated into a fight and Freddie France stabbed Earl Miller to death with a pocket knife. That terrible tragedy rocked race relationships in the community.

Tempers flared. A black boy had killed a white boy. Thirteen-year old Freddy was arrested and jailed. In spite of his young age, there was even talk of a lynching. Rowan's fine record of race relations had suddenly deteriorated. Many wanted to run the black family out of town but theMillers intervened.

PARENTS OF VICTIM INTERCEDE

Even though they had lost a son and were crushed, broken hearted, and grief stricken, A.L. and Hattie Miller interceded on behalf of their son's killer. That great Christian family who loved their God and their fellow man had their faith tested by fire. But their faith survived the test and they interceded on behalf of their son's killer. In Christian love, they forgave Freddy France and pleaded to the Judge for leniency. Because of their intercession, Freddy received a probated sentence and grew up to live a normal life.

The Miller family (Dorothy Holbrook's parents), never blamed the France family. They remained lifetime friends, and their children grew up together without further incident. There was never the usual call for retribution that made Rowan famous as the home of feuding families. Freddy grew up and moved to Dayton, Ohio, where he married and had a family. One of his sons grew up to become a professional football player. Lewis France became a Pullman Porter on the luxurious George Washington train that ran between St. Louis and Washington, D.C., eventually working his way up to conductor.

Tom France, a distant relative of Luke France, was another member of Rowan County's Black community during the 1930s. He lived at Haldeman working in the brickyard to support his four children. They rode the train to Bath and Montgomery Counties for their education.

JOE HODGE MOVES TO HALDEMAN

In 1929, Joseph Hodge, Sr. and his wife, Margaret (Moore) Hodge moved from Bath County to Haldeman in Rowan County. Joseph Hodge, Jr. was six months old at that time. The children in the Hodge family were: Mary Elizabeth, Betty, Carolyn, Margaret, L.P., Russ, Tommy, George, Robert and Joe Jr. Six of the children were born in Haldeman. The senior Mr. Hodge was personally recruited to move with his family to Haldeman by factory owner, L.P. Haldeman. He wanted him to work as the chef in the Haldeman Clubhouse. (It was a kind of private country club but without a golf course.) The clubhouse was located at the crest of a beautiful green hill overlooking the town and was the social center for factory employees. (This writer used to help his father deliver Red Rose Dairy milk to that clubhouse.) Mr. Hodge continued as the clubhouse chef until 1935 when he was promoted to a job in the brick yard. Joe Hodge, Sr., enjoyed an excellent relationship with the factory owner, L.P. Haldeman, and named one of his sons, L.P. (Lunceford Pitt) for him. He continued to work for the company until 1947 when the brick plant closed.

CHILDREN ATTEND SCHOOL IN BATH COUNTY

By the time the Hodge children reached school age, education became a problem. Kentucky's "Jim Crow" law prohibited black and white children from attending school together. Also, the old Morehead Colored School had closed because there were few black children in the district at that time. Therefore, during elementary school, the Hodge children were sent to school in Bath County. They boarded the C&O train at 6:00 a.m., attending classes in Bath County, and returned on the 6:00 p.m. train. It made for a long school day, but the Hodge children made the best of a difficult situation. By the time they reached high school, the children had to go on to Mt. Sterling for their education.

COMMUNITY FIGHTS "JIM CROW" LAW

When asked his reaction to that arrangement, Joe Hodge, Jr. said, "It was the law." He also said: "Mr. L.P. Haldeman and the people of that town were extremely incensed with that unjust law." Mr. Haldeman organized two bus loads of people that descended on Frankfort to try to get the law changed in 1935. However, history showed they were unsuccessful, but the Hodge family was always grateful that their friends and neighbors cared enough to make such a dramatic effort for their civil rights. They considered it a valiant attempt to help them. That incident was additional evidence of the good relationship and Christian harmony that existed between the races in Rowan County. I asked Joe Hodge, Jr., if he felt much discrimination growing up in Haldeman in the 1930s. He said, "Not one bit. I always felt I was accepted as equal in that community."

Rowan's Board of Education paid all transportation and educational expenses of the Hodge family. They also paid the other counties for the cost of their education. At that time it seemed that was separate but equal. But looking back through the telescope of time, separate was inherently unequal.

LIFETIME LOCAL RESIDENT

Joe Hodge is married to Deloris (Botts) Hodge. Joe is retired, but Deloris still works at St. Claire Hospital. They have three children: Kermie, Timoli, and Lisa. The children have all moved away from Morehead. But Joe has refused to leave Morehead. He has remained a well-respected lifelong resident of Rowan County. After he graduated from High School, he worked for local businessman, Curt Bruce. He looked after and showed horses for Mr. Bruce, as well as working at the Bruce 5 and 10 cent Store. Later, he took care of LeGrand Jayne, a prominent local businessman, paralyzed by polio. LeGrand spent his life after polio in a wheelchair. Much of that time he was lovingly cared for by either Joe Sr., Joe Jr., or

L.P. Hodge. Joe Hodge, Jr., has spent much of his life as a care giver to many prominent people in our community. But he has also been a successful businessman and is now retired from the advertisement and promotion business.

Honored By Community

Joe, a lifelong resident of this county, has received many honors. He is on the Advisory Board of the Citizens Bank and a member of the Rowan County ASCS (Agriculture) Committee. He is also on the Board of the Kentucky Folk Art Center. Joe has been a Deacon in his church in Owingsville for 40 years. Also, he has been very active in the local Republican Party. Joe said, "I never wanted to live anywhere else, Morehead is my home." When this writer's mother died three years ago, Joe Hodge was the first to visit. He said she had called him and written to him for many years. He said her calls and letters were always encouraging, and they usually came at a time he was "down." Joe Hodge, Jr., is a respected member of the Morehead community and has helped the community grow.

Storey Family Moves to Morehead

In 1940, Lee and Grace Storey moved from Fleming County to Rowan County. They had three children: Mona Mae, Johnny, and Louise (named for Dr. Louise Caudill). They lived as neighbors to Luke and Lizzie France on Raine Street. Lee, a veteran of WWI, was a local trucker who hauled coal and scrap iron. Grace Storey was a domestic worker for many Morehead residents, including: Judge D.B. Caudill, Bob and Lorene Day, and Dr. Louise Caudill. Her three children traveled the train each day for their education at the expense of the Rowan County School Board. Neither Grace nor her children ever complained and they made the best of a bad situation.

Grace loved the church and was active in the Morehead First Church of God. She was a strong disciplinarian and her three children attended Sunday School and Church with her. Grace always volunteered to assist in lodge, church, and community activities. Usually she would remain after everyone left to help clean up. Although Grace had a speech impediment, it did not slow her down. Grace Storey was an honest, hard working, community minded citizen of Morehead, who contributed to Morehead's growth. When Grace Storey's daughter Louise got married, Judge and Mrs. Caudill hosted a grand reception for the bride and groom at their home. Many Moreheadians attended wishing the young couple much happiness for the future.

OTHER BLACK FAMILIES MOVE HERE

George and Lena (Johnson) Wright moved to Morehead from Bath County in the early 1940s. Lena worked for Mrs. Anna Clay and had an apartment in her home. (Later she had a son and named him William after Mrs. Clay's youngest son, William Earl.) George, a veteran of WW II, ran his own window cleaning and shoe shine business. He worked out of Frosty's Barber Shop at the corner of Main and Hargis, and lived in one ofthe rooms upstairs over the shop. Later, they moved to a house behind Lane Funeral Home. (Now Morehead National Bank.) Among other families Lena worked for were the Oscar Patrick and O.B. Elam families.

George brightened the day of many Moreheadians, greeting everyone with a smile and a friendly hello. He was friendly and enjoyed being with people and knew about everyone in Morehead and their family. (When this writer played basketball in high school, he was a strong Viking fan and attended most home games.) George was a solid citizen of the Morehead Community for almost 40 years. He was a man of deep faith in God and discussed his faith with this writer on many occasions. He recently had open heart surgery and is living in a Veterans Nursing Home in Ohio. His wife, Lena, lives in Lexington, Kentucky.

Jason Hemphill and Hattie Thomason were two other black residents of Morehead. Jason worked at the Haldeman Brick Yard, and Hattie worked for the Dr. E.D. Blair family. Jason attended the East End Church of God. Later he attended the Clearfield Church of God Tabernacle and was always ready to testify to his faith in God. Commenting on the brevity of life, Jason would say, "You've heard people say here today, gone tomorrow, but I say to you here today, gone today." Jason is now gone, along with many of the old black families in Morehead. But they remain a Morehead Memory and inspiration to those who had the privilege of knowing them.

Early Packhorse Librarians crossed rough terrain to deliver books to inaccessable places in Eastern Kentucky. (1934)

CHAPTER ELEVEN

Arts and Entertainment;
Movies, Music, Radio, Etc.

THE COUNTY FAIR

The Rowan County Fair was an institution steeped in this county's earliest history. The fair had its beginning in 1913 when plans were made to hold a "chautauqua" in Rowan County. (It was a type of fair.) "Chautauqua" was an Indian word meaning a ceremonial gathering. It was originated at Lake Chautauqua, New York, in 1874 by the Methodist Episcopal Church as assemblies for religious studies. The program was soon extended to include educational, musical, and dramatic entertainment. A "chautauqua" soon became a generic name for programs given by traveling entertainers usually performing at rural county fairs. It became an institution in the early history of our nation. Also it became a popular gathering for the purpose of education and entertainment, in the form of lectures, concerts, and plays. Those gatherings were usually held either outdoors or in a large tent.

ROWAN FARMERS HOLD CHAUTAUQUA

In the fall of 1913 Rowan made plans to become the first mountain county to hold a chautauqua, and it was planned for September of that year. But Madison County jumped ahead of this county and booked all of the talent Rowan had counted on securing. However, local leaders were not to be deterred. They held their

Cattle being shown at the Rowan County Fair, 1937. (Photo: MSU Archives)

chautauqua the following summer, closing with a grand homecoming week, and a greater Rowan County Convention. This event, spearheaded by School Superintendent Cora Wilson Stewart, was actually the forerunner for future fairs in our county. Beginning in the 1920's, county fairs sprang up throughout Kentucky. Each county tried to make their own fair the "fairest of them all." Rowan County was certainly no exception, and on the first Friday and Saturday in October of 1925, Rowan's first fair was held. It was called a Community Fair, and had a very modest beginning on the campus of Morehead State Teachers College and Normal School. It was the brainchild of Agriculture Professor Henry C. Haggan, County Extension Agent C.L. Goff, School Superintendent Harlan Powers, and Morehead State College President Frank Button. The first fair was called a Community Fair, and its purpose was to promote city, county, and college cooperation. It was a noble purpose and the first Community Fair was housed in five rooms of the college administration building. It was declared a success by everyone.

FAIR INTEREST INCREASES

Interest in and support for the Community Fair grew rapidly, and by 1927, "represented a tremendous step forward in the development of Rowan County." Even a heavy downpour of rain on that Friday, October 8, 1927, failed to dampen the enthusiasm of the exhibitors. Although the crowd was down on Friday due to the rain, attendance was excellent on Saturday.

Rowan's Community Fair was growing and becoming more successful each year. Its idealistic purpose also expanded to bring all of Rowan Countians together and to develop a better relationship between the farmer, merchant, parent, and school. Prizes were awarded for the best examples of canning, baking, sewing, fruits, and vegetables. The prizes, ribbons, and catalogs were paid for by local merchants, who reaped tremendous benefits from the thousands of people that eventually attended these fairs.

FAIR COMMITTEE CHANGES SITE

With the construction in 1928 of the new modern Morehead High School Gym and auditorium, the site of the fair was moved from the college to the new Gymnasium on Second Street and Tippett Avenue. Not only the site of the fair changed but the name of the fair changed. Therefore, by 1930, under the leadership of new School Superintendent Lydia Messer Caudill, Rowan's Community Fair became known as the Rowan County School and Agricultural Fair. Greater emphasis was placed upon school participation emphasizing the educational importance of the fair. Added to the list of usual fair exhibits were art, athletics, music, and livestock. Not only ribbons were awarded for winners in their areas, but prize money was also provided by the local merchants.

Roy Cornette became Superintendent of Rowan County Schools in 1934. Working with local community leaders, he began to enlarge and expand the Fair, with the schools taking an even more active part. Planning began with the appointment of a Fair Committee which met July 8, 1935. Mrs. Lester Hogge was elected president of this committee. Other committee members included Henry C. Haggan, Head, Agriculture Department MSC; Rev. B.H. Kazee, Pastor Baptist Church, Secretary; Dr. H.L. Wilson, Treasurer; Roy Cornette, Head of School Dept.; C.L. Goff, Agriculture; Mrs. C.U. Waltz, Home Department; and Austin Riddle, Athletics. This same committee served for five years, improving and enlarging the fair each year.

Rowan's 1935 Fair was held on October 3, 4, and 5 in the Morehead High School Gymnasium. It was decided that because of the great number of floats, exhibitors, and participants, that an extra day (Thursday) was needed for registration, and building temporary pens to house the animal exhibits. Also, detailed plans were made for the first School Parade.

TEACHERS INVOLVED—PARADE ADDED

All Rowan County Teachers met Friday, September 13, 1935, to finalize plans for the fair. The teachers met in the Morehead High School Gym, and the program was as follows:

Morning Session 9:30 a.m.
Assignment of tests for scholarship events
   (Art, Music, Literature)
Devotional Exercises - Rev. T.F. Lyons
Roll Call - Secretary
Aims and Purposed of the Fair - Mrs. Lester Hogge
Registration of Exhibits - Rev. B.H. Kazee
Group Singing led by Murvel Blair

Agricultural Department - C.L. Goff

Afternoon Session 1 p.m.

How to Prepare School Exhibits - Goldie Dillion
Art in School Exhibits - Lillian Messer
Preparation for the Parade - Frank Laughlin
Athletic Events (Track & Field) - Austin Riddle
Open Discussion - Questions by Teachers - Roy Cornette
(Scholarship Tests for grades 5-8 held at this time)
Business Meeting - Ira Caudill, president.

The first teachers meeting every school year throughout the remainder of the 1930s involved primarily planning and preparation for the Fair. Very detailed planning for the fair did not include how to get the children into town. That problem was left up to the ingenuity of the individual teachers. There were no school busses for these early fairs, and it was up to teachers and parents to bring the children into town. Some walked, and some came in cars, cattle trucks, wagons, and on horseback. (Many schools held pie suppers to pay for a truck to haul the children into town.) But they came to town to march in the parade and celebrate the fair. It was a great day in the life of the community.

TEACHERS MARCH IN PARADE

Each school and teacher was required to march with a banner or a float in the parade. (However, first and second grades were not required to march.) Banners and floats carried by the children proudly represented their school and community. For instance, the banner carried by the Sharkey rural school children had a picture of a shark and the picture of a key; thus making "Sharkey." Also, the Little Brushy School carried a banner with the word "Little" printed next to a pile of brush, followed by a "Y"; therefore, "Little Brushy". They worked hard building banners, floats, and preparing exhibits of livestock, cooking, canning, and sewing.

The 1935 Fair, considered one of the county's best, brought seven thousand people into Morehead. They came from Haldeman, Farmers, Elliottville, Clearfield–and all points east, west, north and south. They came from schools such as: Charity, Bull Fork, and Clark. They came from Haldeman, Hardeman, and Holly, and from Ditney, Dry Creek, McKenzie, and Minor. From Mt. Hope, Oak Grove, Waltz, Wess Cox, Razor, and Perkins, and from forty other schools. But they came and were happy to be here.

Fair Day More Exciting Than Christmas

Fair Day was the most exciting day of the year in the life of Rowan's school children. Christmas paled by comparison to Fair Day for those depression age children. They expected little for Christmas and received very little. They understood their parents could not afford to buy them much for Christmas. BUT FAIR DAY– That was something else. Each child in each home was up long before daylight. They completed their chores, put on their Sunday best over-alls, or gingham dresses, and began the exciting journey to Morehead. There they proudly participated in the parade, prizes, and other activities. If they won a blue ribbon for any activity, they were as proud as any Olympic athlete because they understood they represented their school. The athletic events were held at old Jayne Stadium, and few had such things as athletic shoes so most everyone took off their heavy shoes and participated barefooted.

Some examples of the 400 events listed in the 1935 School Fair were:

SCHOOL EVENTS

Athletics - Austin Riddle, Supervisor. High jump, broad jump, baseball throwing, and 75 yard and 100 yard dash.
Kindergarten - Norma Powers, Supervisor. Clay molding, hand writing, and best booklet.
Emergency Education - Katherine Caudill and Oscar Patrick, Supervisors. Best academic display, and domestic art display.
Elementary School - Ellen Hudgins and Mae Meadows, Supervisors. Best posters, hand drawings, poems, and maps.
Booklets - Ella May Boggess and Mable Alfrey, Supervisors. Best health, animal, arithmetic, and birds.

PUBLIC EVENTS

Cooking, Canning - Mrs. E. Hogge and Mrs. T.F. Lyons, Supervisors. Best canned fruits, vegetables, fried chicken, cake, and candy.
Sewing and Handwork - Mrs. Ernest Jane, Mrs. Sadie Fielding, Supervisors. Best quilt, dress, apron, handkerchief, and hooked rug.
Flowers - Mrs. C.E. Bishop and Mrs. Gertrude Synder, Supervisors. Best Vase of dahlias, zinnias, roses; and Best Potted Plants, ferns, and artificial flowers. Also best field crops of potatoes, hay pumpkins, watermelons, and tobacco. Also best garden crops including tomatoes, turnips, beans and onions. Also orchard products of apples, peaches, and pears.
Livestock - Henry Hagan, Supervisor.Best calves, pigs, chickens, and sheep.

MISCELLANEOUS EVENTS

Awards were given for best hog caller, chicken caller, fiddler, and hoe down dancer. (This event attracted more spectators than any other event.)

The Rowan County Fair continued every year until 1939. That was the year of the very destructive flash flood that hit Rowan County on July 4th. There were 25 people drowned on that dreadful night. Buildings, roads, bridges, and crops were devastated. Therefore, the Fair Committee elected not to hold the fair in 1939, but resumed in 1940 and 1941 until WW II stopped it again. Although the fair resumed in 1946, there never seemed to be the enthusiasm and interest that was there before the war. The nation, as well as Rowan County, seemed to have lost their innocence and became too sophisticated to participate.

FAIR FADES SLOWLY AWAY

Before WW II everyone looked forward to the fair and marching in the parade. They eagerly became involved in the events, but the post-war era brought grumbling from teachers, children, and parents. They complained that too much time was spent on the fair. Therefore, the Rowan County Schools and Agriculture Fair died a natural death in the 1950s.

In 1956 Rowan County celebrated its centennial year with a major Morehead parade and other activities, but the County Fair had disappeared. It has now been replaced by the excellent Hardwood and Harvest Festivals. But these events seem to be economically based, whereas the old fair was educationally based. Both are important, and as we approach the new millennium–we must not forget this. Maybe we need a Rowan County Schools and Technology Fair to replace the Rowan County Schools and Agricultural Fair.

LOCAL LOTTERY: DRAWING

In the summer of 1936, this nation had not yet recovered from the depression of 1929. Morehead seemed to be slow in feeling the results of the depression, but Morehead's merchants were quick to try to counteract its results. In June, 1936, the local Chamber of

Commerce organized a "local lottery." Playing on our basic instincts of getting something for nothing and to encourage more local shopping, a lottery was organized. This "lottery" was referred to as a "Drawing," actually awarded $50 in cash every Saturday afternoon at 3 p.m. First prize was $25, second was $10, third was $5, and five other prizes of $2 each. You had to be present to win, so every Saturday afternoon the swimming hole at blue hole in Triplett Creek emptied. Also the vacant lot where we played baseball (where the Adron Doran University Center now stands), vacated. Baseball and swimming seemed to lose their luster when there was the possibility of winning $25 cash.

In order to be eligible to win you had to spend at least .25 at one of the 26 local participating merchants. (Notice only two names as such, are still in business: *Dixie Grill* and *Battson Drug Store*.) So for every .25 spent, you would receive 1 ticket. You kept your stub and wrote your name on the ticket, and then you dropped it into the box provided at each store.

MOREHEAD—A SATURDAY TOWN

Beginning Saturday afternoon on June 13, 1936, huge crowds began to gather on the courthouse lawn where the first drawing was held. There were hundreds present from throughout Rowan and surrounding counties. After all the tickets had been collected and placed in a large wire mesh horizontal drum with a heavy handle at one end, the drum was placed on the back of a flat bed truck and delivered to the courthouse where the drawing took place. (It was moved to a different participating store every Saturday.) The truck with the tickets would usually arrive a few minutes early. Then you could drop your tickets into the drum until the 3 p.m. deadline. Those of us who dreamed of hitting this $25 jackpot waited until the last minute, because we were sure we had a better chance of winning that way. (Many are still scheming up ways today that will help them win the lottery).

At the appointed hour a child would be selected from the audience and after the round metal drum was cranked vigorously the child would begin pulling out the winning tickets. (Didn't this beat a computer selecting the winners).

The tension would build as the first number was called. As each name was called everyone hoped that the winner would not be there to collect, then another name would be called. As the last winner was announced our childish dreams were dashed, but we could look forward to next Saturday when we might win. But that next Saturday never came for me. Even though the "local lottery" continued for several years, I never won.

Dreams Are Dashed

Today I'm sure people who buy lottery tickets have wonderful dreams about how they would spend their million dollar winnings. But none of these dreams could comparewith the visions I had of what I would do with the $25 first prize. This nine-year old lad had dreams of a new, red bicycle with a siren on the side and a basket on the front. (His parents could never afford to buy him one at that time). In his mind's eye he would cruise up and down Main Street with greater joy than today's "cruisers" in their air-conditioned, "souped up" trucks. He dreamed of coasting down the "Saints Church" Hill (N. Hargis Avenue now) with the wind whistling through his blond hair. He dreamed of reaching the rite of passage of all the young boys in Morehead then, to be able to climb the Saints Church Hill on your bicycle without setting your foot on the ground.

I never won Morehead's Local Lottery, which was a good thing for me because I learned early in life that you rarely get something for nothing. Listed below are the lucky winners at that first "Local Lottery" (that first drawing in Morehead, June 13, 1936):

$25 L.C. Porter, Morehead

$10 F.D. Burrows, Haldeman

$ 5 Everett Hall, Morehead

$ 2 J.H. Reynolds, Farmers

$ 2 Sarah Parsons, Morehead

$ 2 Corrine Bradley, Morehead

$ 2 Maude Peters, Morehead

$ 2 Warren C. Lappin, Morehead

MOREHEAD'S MUSIC MAN
Birth of A Ballad

Musicians "play" an important part in the history of a nation, in the history of a community, and Morehead's music man was Jilson Setters. He was an internationally known singer of ballads and folk songs. He was an important part of Morehead's history from the 1930s to the 1940s. Blind "Jils" could be found on the courthouse lawn under an oak tree on court day singing and playing his unique style of music. He usually attracted a crowd that applauded his music.

Jean Thomas, the Traipson woman and collector of ballads, relates in her book, *The Sun Shines Bright,* that she came upon a blind folk singer named Jim Day in Morehead and took him as her protege. She changed his name to Jilson Setters, and he became a world famous folk singer. But he was known in Morehead as "Blind Jim" Day.

It was rumored that he was a grandson of Johnny Day, one of the participants in the election day 1887 shooting that started the Rowan County War. Everyone lovingly called him "Blind Jim" because his eyesight was so poor he could not distinguish between the denominations of paper money, so he dealt in change only. He was blind but he was a famous folk singer because Jean Thomas, a court reporter and famous collectorof folk songs, heard him sing, wrote down many of his songs, and took him to New York City to perform in Carnegie Hall. Later, she took him to Europe and he performed his beautiful Elizabethan music before the King and Queen of England.

Travelers Treated to Folk Songs

The Greyhound Restaurant and Bus Station in Morehead in those days was a busy lunch and dinner stop for cross country travelers (now Main Street Music and Video). It was also the place where high school kids "hung out", drank cokes, ate burgers, and played the juke box and danced the jitterbug. When buses stopped at the Greyhound Restaurant on Main Street, and as the passengers left the bus they might see "Blind Jim" sitting on a low stool at the entrance to the restaurant. He would have his fiddle under his chin and there would be a large tin cup setting on the ground in front of him. He would begin by tapping his 1-2-3 and start playing his fiddle vigorously. Then he would begin singing one of the old folk songs or ballads of Eastern Kentucky. Such songs as "Barbara Allen", "Sourwood Mountain", "Dear, Dear, What Can the Matter Be", "I Wonder as I Wonder", and the "Round County Trouble", (a local ballad with fourteen verses.). He often made up a song or changed the words to fit the occasion. His songs praised his friends for their good deeds, and criticized his enemies for their actions.

I heard John Jacob Niles, the great singer and collector of folk songs, say many years ago at a concert at Vanderbilt University, that he first heard the song "I Wonder as I Wonder" when it was sung by an old woman in Morgan County, Kentucky, as she sat rocking on her front porch. He wrote the words down and the song made him famous, and he made the song famous.

"ROUND" COUNTY WAR FAMOUS

"Blind Jim" would entertain the travelers as they got off the bus, and as they prepared to board. One song that he would sing was "The Round County Trouble". His metal cup would ring as the change clinked against the metal cup. It was said Blind Jim could tell the amount of the gift by the "clink" or "clank" sound as it hit the bottom of the tin cup. He would always nod his head in thanks to those who gave, and never missed a note. He made a good living and enjoyed his music at the same time.

"Jim" would sometimes become a traveling troubadour, buy a ticket, and board the bus heading for Lexington, Huntington, Ashland, or Cincinnati. There he would perform his music, receive a good offering, then return to Morehead, sleeping on the bus. It was on those trips that he was able to share his beautiful ballads throughout this region.

"Blind Jim" would often sing about the Rowan County War because he was a decendant of Johnny Day, who many thought fired the first shot that started the bloody Rowan County feud. According to the book *Folk Songs of the Southern United States*, there are two versions of this song. One was called *The Round County Trouble*, and the other was *The Tolliver Song*. Both songs warn of the terrible trouble that can becaused when whiskey, guns, and anger all come together. The authors were unknown. I cannot document it, but I believe Jim Day wrote one version of this song. I believe this because it was a song he made famous and it in turn made him famous. I have had people from other areas of the country ask me about the Rowan County War because Blind Jim sang about it. Jim's song was from an account that I'm sure was told to him by his grandfather. This is how ballads are born.

On one occassion during WW II, Jim was travelling by train from Lexington to Morehead. He had on his dark glasses, and with his rusty tin cup in front of him, was busy entertaining the passengers. He was picking his guitar, and rocking back and forth to the music, singing those familar folk songs. The train was crowded with servicemen and many were trying to sleep. Finally, Ward Rice, home on leave from the Navy, walked up to him and placed a five dollar bill in his cup, and said, "That's for you to <u>stop</u> playing." "Blind Jim" stopped immediately.

Jim Day met a tragic end while he was in Cincinnati playing and singing his folk music. As he started to cross the street outside the railroad terminal, he was struck by a bus. After a few days in the hospital, his long folk singing career ended in the death of the legendary folk singer.

SWIMMING POOL: MARDI GRAS

The building stands sadly neglected on the extreme northwest edge of the campus of Morehead State University, behind the President's home. A generation of students have passed by the forlorn looking brick building with broken windows and peeling paint, probably not even noticing the building. It gives the appearance that it has outlived its usefulness and is merely marking time until the wrecking ball pounds its sturdy walls into rubble. It is referred to as the "old swimming pool," and it once reverberated with joyful sounds of happy children laughing and screaming as they jumped or dived into the clear chlorinated water. Even today, this writer happily remembers those carefree summer days when the Breckinridge School children could go swimming every afternoon following a morning in summer-school. (Summer school was required by all Breck students and knowing that in the afternoon we could laugh, scream, dive, and swim in that beautiful pool, made it all seem worthwhile.)

When the pool was constructed in 1933, it was considered state-of-the-art and one of the most beautiful swimming pools in the south.

First Swimming Pool on the campus of Morehead State College, 1934.

The architectural design was of the Norman Period in keeping with a gymnasium-auditorium construction design. It was named the Senff Natatorium in honor of Judge Earl W. Senff, a member of the Morehead College Board of Regents. (Natatorium refers to an indoor swimming pool.) Etched in stone at the peak of the front of the building are these words "This swimming pool is dedicated to the ideal of a clean and vigorous youth." Those words were written by MSTC's eminent English Professor Emmitt Bradley, and formed the function for thefuture for that stately old building.

BOARD OF REGENTS APPROVED POOL

The College Board of Regents had discussed the possibility of constructing a swimming pool on campus for several years. However, there was never enough money available and it was always delayed. But in April 1932, President John Howard Payne, with the support of the Board of Regents, commissioned the Louisville architectural firm of Joseph and Joseph to design plans for an indoor swimming pool. Plans were first submitted to build the swimming pool in the basement of Button Auditorium where the auxiliary gym was located. Those plans were rejected. Later plans were submitted and accepted by the Board to build the pool on Battson Avenue, and connect it to Button Auditorium via a tunnel (that was the way we used to enter the swimming pool). Construction began in September 1932, under the direction of local contractor, Jesse L. Boggess, and College Superintendent of buildings and Grounds, William H. Rice. Mr. Boggess was a prominent local builder, (this writer's wife's uncle) who also built the President's home, power plant building, Morehead City Hall, and the old Peoples Bank building on First Street, plus many fine homes in Morehead. Mr. Rice was Superintendent of Buildings and Grounds at MSTC for 40 years.

MR. BOGGESS USED LOCAL LABOR

Mr. Boggess, taking advantage of the areas large un-employment rate, elected to go with local labor. He also refused to use power equipment which made the construction "very labor intensive," which was his purpose. Manpower and mule power were the primary power sources for the construction. Men who operated scoops pulled by mules dug the hole and shaped the earth. Wagons pulled by mules driven by local teamsters (literally, but not union) transported building supplies from the rail head to the building site. But it was a labor of love. The men appreciated the opportunity to work when jobs were scarce and, therefore, did quality work. Although crude construction methods were used, the swimming pool has never leaked a drop to this very day. However, the new Russell McClure Pool does seem to have a small leak.

The beautiful Senff Natatorium was built almost entirely by local labor and craftsmen. The exception was the tile work around and in the pool. The tile was installed by the Kena-Rosa Company of Louisville, under the supervision of Mr. J. Thurman. It was recognized as some of the most artistically, and practically designed tile work in the South. Also it was designed to be "a thing of beauty, and a joy forever."

Another unique feature of the pool was that the roof contained a large portion of glass skylights. These skylights could be opened and closed manually via pulleys and chains. This permitted the intense excess humidity, common to most indoor pools, to escape through the roof. Also the glass roof permitted natural sunlight to illuminate andhelp heat the pool, thereby saving on electricity. (This would have been impossible had the pool been built under Button Auditorium.)

When the pool was constructed attention was paid to conservation of trees and soil. There was a large oak tree on Battson Avenue that needed to be removed before construction began. However, Mr. Boggess and Mr. Haggan, (Professor of Agriculture) devised a way to save the tree. Mr. Boggess built a large semi-circular concrete wall, making a well half way around the roots, thereby saving the tree. (Although the tree is now gone, the wall still stands.) The tree stood for another fifty years and countless Breck Students climbed that tree while awaiting the pool to open on summer afternoons.

Construction was completed and the building turned over to the College on June 22, 1933. The pool was 90 feet long and 30 feet wide, with a depth of from 3 feet to 9 feet. The chlorinating system was designed to pump 100 percent of the water content of the pool through the system each day, thereby assuring a purer water quality.

STUDENTS "PLUNGED" INTO THEIR CLASSES

Soon aquatic performances, swimming classes, teams and swim meets were organized for intercollegiate competition. Coach Len Miller was appointed men's coach and Miss Louise Caudill was appointed women's coach. (Mr. Clell Porter was employed as caretaker of the new facility.) Soon the Daughters of Poseidon and the Aquamen were organized. These were college students with a special interest in water sports. They believed in themselves and became very competitive in intercollegiate aquatic sports. The late Miss Louise Caudill was a successful teacher and swimming coach long before she went on to become our beloved Dr. Louise, caretaker of local community health.

WINTER WATER CARNIVAL ORGANIZED

The Senff Natatorium was a heavily used facility year round. Many local students and local citizens utilized the pool. To be able to swim in the middle of winter made the winter go faster and helped reduce the winter doldrums that affected many Moreheadians. (Since no one went to Florida in those days.) Although no one in Morehead realized it, they were afflicted with Seasonal Affective Disorder (S.A.D. This is a malady marked by depression supposedly caused by lack of sunlight.) Therefore, a new use was made of the new swimming pool in an attempt to help students and residents overcome that disorder, when on March 1, 1934, the first Winter Carnival was organized on campus. It was a social recreational, therapeutic, and fundraising event to help raise money for the Morehead College Yearbook. The first year there were swimming and diving exhibitions. Also, there was a choreographed water ballet presented by the Daughters of Poseidon. It was under the direction of Miss Exer Robinson, Dean of Women. There was also an election of King and queen of the carnival. (This was Morehead's answer to the Mardi Gras). The queen of the first Winter Carnival was Ruth McKenzie from West Liberty, Kentucky. (A vote on your choice for Queen cost you 1 cent per vote, the election of a king did not come until later.)

KING AND QUEEN ELECTED

The winter carnival grew in interest and participation each year. In addition to the usual aquatic events, they began electing both a King and Queen. In 1937, the nominees for Queen were Beryl Motley and Linda Eaton. Nominees for King were Roger Caudill and Ruby Smith. The contest became heated and a rally and debate was held. Banners, parades, and caucuses made the campus a beehive of political maneuvering. Since a local man was nominated for King, the community also became involved.

MARDI GRAS ATMOSPHERE AND CORONATION

Finally, on Saturday, February 20, the doors opened into the beautifully decorated Gymnasium reflecting the carnival spirit. That year there were booths and barkers reflecting a carnival atmosphere. Such shouts as, "Hurry, hurry, come closer, see the spider woman!" "For one dime, see the colossal, stupendous, gigantic giant for one thin dime." Fortune tellers, food, bingo, and "chuck a luck" was available for a price. The carnival atmosphere changed to quiet anticipation when it came time to announce the king and queen.

At 9 p.m. came the drum roll in the background. An eerie hush came immediately over the crowd. The King and Queen of the Carnival were announced amid loud whistling and stamping of feet. The Queen was...Beryl Motley; the King was local resident, Roger Caudill. The royal couple was crowned in one of the most elaborate ceremonies this side of the Atlantic. After the King and Queen danced once together, the crowd danced until midnight, before the curfew rang. Everyone seemed to have fun, a lot of money was made for the College Yearbook, the Raconteur, and another Morehead Winter Carnival was history.

By 1940, Morehead College's winter Carnival became a water carnival again. Therefore, it was returned to its original site which was in the new swimming pool. Since it had moved away from the water to the Gymnasium, it had become very commercial. Therefore, believing that there were too many hurt feelings, too much commercialism, and too much energy spent in the wrong direction, the winter carnival became the new Water Carnival.

BATHING QUEEN SELECTED AT WATER CARNIVAL

In 1940, a bathing queen was selected at the Water Carnival. The bathing beauty contestants had to do more than just parade around the pool in a bathing suit. They actually had to get wet. They were required to participate in swimming, diving, or waterballet. Also, they were required to have good posture and figure. Every girl on campus was eligible to compete. They could represent their hometown, campus club, dormitory, or other organization. Morehead College had entered the age of the Bathing Beauty Contest.

On March 15, 1940, the first "bathing queen" was selected at Morehead College from among several lovely applicants. Admission to the affair was 25 cents, and each person received a ballot and was entitled to vote on their choice. The contestants were: Matty Center, Pauline Butcher, Isabel Pritchard, Jo Pack, Ruth Johnson, Margaret Horacek, Mary Crain, Martha Lewis, Thelma Strong and Gladys Allen.

Before the final vote there was a beautiful aquatic exhibition of swimming, diving, and choreographed water ballet. The water ballet was under the direction of Miss Louise Caudill in which the beautiful mermaids suddenly burst into full bloom from under the water. Arms and legs formed intricate designs of petals and flowers climaxed by a large M in the water. The Aquamen coached by Mr. Downing consisted of Chuck Morris, Stan Radjunas, E. Bell, Joe Jackson, and E. Vanderpool. These young men performed diving exhibitions and speed swimming much to the delight of the crowd, while the mermaids prepared for the final phase of the bathing beauty contest. The final phase included the traditional walk around the pool in their bathing suits accompanied by music, provided by J.N. Minish and E. Maynard. Ed Weicherz served as master of ceremonies. There was no interview or evening gown competition.

The time came to announce the results of the vote, accompanied by the traditional drum roll. The winner was local beauty Gladys Allen. Thelma Strong from Jackson was first runner up, and Gladys Lewis from Ashland, second runner up. While the crowd seemed pleased with the vote (I'm sure Gladys Allen had a lot of supporters there since she was a native of Morehead). Many of the Acquamen were unhappy. They were still in the water when the vote was announced and they immediately started a water fight that drenched Mr. Wicherz, the Master of Ceremonies. (What if this tradition had continued to the Miss America contests and Bert Parks would have been drenched upon announcing the winner?) That would have been better than the football tradition of drenching the winning footfall coach with Gatorade. However, the winter carnival was dropped during WW II, as a different tradition was established in the swimming pool.

SWIMMING WITHOUT SUITS

When the Navy trained electricians at Morehead College during W.W. II, they were required to attain certain swimming and endurance skills before completing their training. They swam without bathing suits. Many times the translucent windows in the rear of the pool were cranked open for ventilation. That provided passers by a clear view from outside. There was a well worn path behind the swimming pool where the girls strolled while the sailors swam.

Many of the local boys had a way of breaking into the swimming pool after hours. They also swam in the "buff." Usually a lower level window was left open enough to reach in and crank the window open enough for one boy to squeeze into the building. He would then open a back door and let the others in. Swimming and diving had to be done quietly in the dark so as not to attract Lee Cochran, the Campus Night Watchman. (Lee's claim to fame was that the President ran the college during the day–but he ran it at night.) Some of the most daring divers would climb out on the overhead steel beams and dive into the 9 foot depth below. (Always making sure the pool had not been drained.) Paul J. Reynolds told me that on one occasion one boy dived from the side of the pool in the darkness, and the water level had been lowered considerably. After that anyone breaking in after hours made sure there was always enough water in the pool before diving in.

Although the old swimming pool was kept open for special events, it formally closed after the new Russell McClure Pool opened in the Morehead State University Athletic Complex. The new pool is beautiful, and much more functional. However, to the thousands of Breckinridge children who learned to swim, dive, and water fight in the old pool, it remains a very special memory. Also, to those countless college students who perfected their swimming and diving techniques, it also is a special memory. All of those swimmers were also getting great aerobic exercise and didn't know it. Their lives were richer, happier and healthier as a result.

RADIO RECEPTION: POOR

In the early days of broadcasting, radio reception in Morehead was generally poor. The best that could be said was, it was intermittent and filled with static interference. It was also dependant upon the weather conditions, where you lived, (near power lines) and if you had other electric appliances in your home. Another factor was where your outside antenna was located. (An outside antenna was necessary for any quality of sound). However, even with one, there was always static interference that made for poor listening.

COMEDY, NEWS, AND ADVENTURE

This writer can remember in the late 1930s, living on West US 60, our radio antenna was connected to the clothesline at the rear of the house. Also, about the only radio station we could get was WLW (world's largest wave) from Cincinnati, Ohio. I grew up listening to Lowell Thomas' 15 minutes of nightly news at 6:45. His deep resonant voice proclaimed "Good Evening Ladies and Gentlemen, this is Lowell Thomas bringing you your nightly news of the world." We were quiet during those 15 minutes as he told us (amid the static and buzzing) about such people as the Deli Lhama, John Dillinger, Adolph Hitler, Mohatmas Ghandi, and he referred to such places as India, Tibet, Munich, Poland and Great Britain. Those places all seemed very irrelevant to me then. (Little did I realize in only a few short years, I would see some of those places.) Following the newscast, we might listen to Jack Benny, Fibber McGee, or Bob Hope. Then I might get to listen to the buzzing of the Green Hornet, or the fiendish laugh of The Shadow, as he said "The Shadow knows!" (My mother did not like for me to waste my time listening to those programs.) However, since there was no local radio, I listened to what ever we received. Therefore, even with poor reception, we still tuned in on the static filled air waves.

POOR RECEPTION STUDIED

In 1945, following WW II, the Morehead Board of Trade was determined to do something to improve radio reception in Morehead. They requested the Kentucky Utilities Company make a study to help determine the cause of the problem. Mr. Frank Maxey, local K.U. manager, and Mr. E.E. Curtis, district manager, agreed to try and identify the problem. They employed Mr. Holt of the Gilmore Radio Interests, (owners of WLAP Lexington, and WCMI Ashland) to try to identify the cause of the poor radio reception in this area.

Mr. Holt arrived in Morehead loaded with the latest equipment used to locate such trouble. Armed with a map of the city and his high tech equipment, he began plotting on the map those places with poor radio reception. After three days, he had the trouble spots all located and was ready to report.

His report said, "There was sudden disruption of services, creating a grinding effect in local radios. It was caused by appliances and electric motors." That problem could be corrected at a small cost. However, his report concluded that, "The basic problem of weak reception was because Morehead was located in a deep valley surrounded by high hills. Therefore, in order to bring in this weak signal, one had to increase the volume on the radio, thereby increasing the interference." His report said, "basically there was not much that could be done because of the high hills around Morehead." There is still a problem of clear radio reception in Morehead even in 2001.

In 1953, a group of local entrepreneurs decided Morehead needed a <u>local</u> radio station. Therefore, Bill Sample, President; Roy Cornette, Vice President; and Claude Clayton, Secretary, formed a company and made application to the Federal Communications Commission for an AM 1,000 watt daytime only radio station. Their application was approved in August 1954, and they were assigned the station call letters WMOR.

NEW RADIO STATION A LEARNING EXPERIENCE

Radio was raw and new in Morehead, and no one had experience in the operation of a radio station. (At that time there were no radio stations between Lexington and Ashland, except Maysville.) In August 1954, Bill Pierce was hired as assistant trafficmanager at the radio station. He was employed with the agreement that he would spend a few days each week at the Maysville Radio Station WFTM (Worlds finest Tobacco Market) learning the day to day operations of a radio station. Mr. Pierce recalled he observed such things as how they did the news, weather, call in shows, and local programming. The Maysville manager was hired as a consultant to help WMOR get up and running.

In the fall of 1954, Gerald Yentes and Don Holloway were employed as radio announcers. Bill Pierce said, "Before the station opened, we would all practice on the office inter-com". Also, at that time, Dr. and Mrs. Adron Doran would come down and critique their pronunciation, enunciation, and articulation. Mr. Pierce said, "They were extremely helpful with their suggestions". (It was with their help they developed their deep, resonant radio voices).

Although WMOR was only a 1,000 watt AM daytime only station, in January, 1955, the FCC (Federal Communication Commission) permitted them to go on the air from midnight until daylight for practice. That provided a five hour period of practice, and consisted mostly of spinning records, taking requests, and announcing news and weather. But it did allow them some "on air" experience which helped the announcers get over the "butterflies" in their stomach. The station reached a wide audience during those nighttime broadcasts. Bill Pierce said they would get letters from people in Australia, Hawaii, South America, and Alaska saying they had picked up their broadcasts.

CITY CELEBRATES OPENING DAY

On February 18, 1955, practice ended and radio station WMOR of Morehead went on the air amid much local fanfare and great celebration. Local resident, Don Young, who operated the central panel at that giant opening, recalled it was a new era for Morehead. "Radio had arrived in Rowan County!" The station began broadcasting with all new "state of the art" equipment for that time. The company realized the problem of weak radio reception in Rowan County and used modern equipment designed to insure a strong uninterrupted signal. Their offices were located upstairs in the Monarch Building on Main Street (near the present site of Arbys). The staff was headed by former Letcher County resident William Whittaker. Morehead native and electronics genius, Earl S. Young, was chief engineer, and Murvel Hall, assistant engineer. Other early staff members included Norma Ramey, secretary and traffic manager; Joanne Zingale, librarian; announcer and assistant traffic manager, Bill Pierce. Other announcers were Don Holloway, Don Young, Gerald Yentes, Al Knelty, Pee Wee Hall (later became the famous Tom T. Hall), Steve Young, and Bernie Fieler. Mr. Fenton Morris was the outside sales person.

Weather Forecast Very "Local"

During those beginning broadcasting days of WMOR, many of the local merchants were permitted to come to the studio and read their own commercials live. However, it took Frank Havens, owner of the Big Store, two and one half minutes to read his 60 second commercial. (He would ad lib the copy.) Also, Murvel Hall, the assistant engineer, frequently filled in as an announcer and would read the news and weather. Many times when Murvel gave the weather forecasts, he would say, "Just a minute folks until I look out the window". So without the benefit of radar, he examined the skies. If it looked cloudy up Evans Branch, (be-

Bill Pierce, Assistant Program Director of Morehead's First Radio Station WMOR, 1954.

hind Breckinridge), he would forecast rain, if not, he forecasted fair weather. On the weekends, Murvel would do whatever needed to be done to keep the station on the air. He hurriedly read the sports one Saturday and said, "The New York Yankees left for spring training yesterday with 28 roosters on the squad. (He meant to say 28 on the roster).

John R. Duncan, aka "Punkin Duncan", was an early D.J. on WMOR, 1954.

Bernie Fieler, an outstanding football player at Morehead State College, began his radio broadcasting career as a D.J. (Disk Jockey) at WMOR. Each Sunday afternoon, he played top ten popular jazzy music designed to attract the college crowd. Also, since he was an athlete, he soon began broadcasting sports. Little league was just getting started in Morehead and WMOR broadcasted their games live. That generated much interest in that program and helped make it a success.

JOHNNY'S JUKE BOX OR PUNKIN DUNCAN

Gary Pinkerman, who had previous radio experience in the Cincinnati market, was employed as program director. He began to expand programming to reach a broader audience. Local Breckinridge High School student, John Duncan, was hired in 1955 as an announcer and disk jockey. He continued there through high school and college. John R. Duncan began his career in radio by hosting a 3:30 p.m. Friday afternoon show called, "Johnny's Juke Box." He played the latest popular recordings and accepted call-in requests. It was a show that soon attracted the high school age group. As the young D.J. gained more experience, he was called upon to fill other roles at the station. He then began hosting an early morning program where he was known as "Punkin Duncan."

There he would read the news, weather and play country music. His main audience was the farm community. On this afternoon program, he became "JD the DJ." On that program he played rock and roll music aimed at the high school and college crowd. (Dr. Duncan said everyone at the station had to be versatile and fill many different roles in order to keep the station on the air.)

RADIO UNITES TWO LOVERS

The power of radio can be used in many different ways. While working at WMOR, John met a lovely young lady by the name of Gretta Brown. During their courtship, they decided to break up. But shortly afterwards, Johnny played a song on his show entitled "I'm Sorry." A song that lamented two lovers break-up and reconciliation. John dedicated that song to Gretta. His on-the-air apology was accepted, as they are still happily married.

Following his marriage, John also took on the job of outside salesman for the station. He succeeded in selling a one-time ad for the Highly Grist Mill in Salt Lick. After the commercial aired, he returned to try to sell him another one. Mr. Highly said he would take another one if they would turn up the volume so there would not be so much static interference. Johnny explained that broadcasting did not work like that. There was no volume control to increase the output of the station and reduce static.

TOM T. HALL, COUNTRY MUSIC LEGEND

Tom T. "PeeWee" Hall, one of WMOR's early announcers, had his own band called "The Kentucky Travelers." They frequently played live music on WMOR. Tom T. was an "off the wall free spirit." He would ad lib commercials and sing along with the recordings. Frequently, instead of playing records, he would pick and sing his own music (songs he had written). On one occasion, Mr. Hall brought a paper bag full of dried cow manure to the studio and set the bag on fire while "Punkin Duncan" was doing his early morning program. He kept everybody loose at the station.

During Tom T's time at WMOR, charity fund raising began the method of putting people "in jail" until they raised the "bail" needed to get out of jail. That "bail" was then donated to charity and you were released from jail. Today, when you agree to go to jail for a charity, you are given a phone and you begin calling friends for donations. But "PeeWee"Hall actually agreed to be placed in the Rowan County Jail in order to raise $500 "bail" for the March of Dimes. For three days and two nights, he ate jail food, slept in jail beds, paced the floor of the jail cell and did his broadcast time from jail. He succeeded in getting his fans and friends to raise the necessary $500 bail for the March of Dimes. Some of the songs he later wrote were based upon that experience in jail.

Long before Tom T. Hall arrived in Nashville, he was a celebrity in Morehead. His was one of WMOR's most popular programs. He had many fans throughout this area, most of them young girls who were constantly coming to the studio to get his autograph, or request a song. Most of his songs were about some of his own experiences growing up. "Old Men and Watermelon Wine", "Harper Valley PTA" and one about "eating fried bologna," were from his own experiences. Bill Pierce and John Duncan said they went on to school and received their Ph.D. degrees and taught in college. They were paid 30-40 thousand dollars per year. Tom T. Hall continued "pickin" and singing, became world famous and made millions per year.

FIRST FIRE SAFETY SLOGAN

In late 1950, WMOR ran a contest among Rowan County School children for thebest safety slogan for fire prevention week. Dozens of entries were mailed in, but no one ever got around to judging them. Danny Pierce was the host DJ one day when someone rushed in with a box full of entries. It seemed they were supposed to announce the winners that day on his program. However, no one had even looked at the entries. But undaunted, Danny said, "Folks it's time to select the winner of this year's Rowan County Fire Safety Slogan." He then reached his hand down into a box full of entries and pulled one out and said, "The winner of the Rowan County Fire Safety Slogan IS: "Never smoke in bed, burnt meat stinks."

Don Young, one of the disk jockeys at WMOR in those early days, recalled that PeeWee Hall's Kentucky Travelers Band used to play at Thackers Drive-in on Saturday nights. Don said he would be there and tape the show and play the music the next day. It was one of the few taped shows they played. Later Don was a DJ and played the top 40 songs each week. One week, the top song was the pop tune "Cherry Pink and Apple Blossom White," by Press Prada. The next week the top tune was "Rock Around the Clock" by Chuck Berry. Rock and roll had arrived and Elvis was on his way.

GOSPEL MUSIC, TEACHING AND PREACHING

Another popular musical group in the 1950s was Farris Dunbar and his Fox Valley Band. They were regulars at WMOR. They would carry all of their instruments up those dark, narrow, squeaky steps to the studio. There, they would pick and sing gospel, country and western music. However, they never made it big like Tom T. Hall.

Gospel music and evangelistic preaching were among the more popular radio programs of that time. Some of the evangelists were scheduled to preach each Sunday afternoon. Many times they would come into the studio and begin their program by saying "Folks, we don't have enough money to pay for this broadcast today. However, we have faith that some of you will come in to the studio right now before this program ends and help us pay for this broadcast. Many times their faith was rewarded, because people would come up to the studio before the program was over and pay for their broadcast time.

Mrs. Hazel Whittaker taught a Sunday School class every Saturday on WMOR for many, many years. It was one of the more highly received and supported programs at WMOR. Mrs. Whitaker was a faithful member of the Morehead Baptist Church and a Sunday School teacher. (She is fondly remembered today by her many friends.) Her positive sweet Christian spirit seemed to just permeate the airwaves throughout Rowan County."

One of the more popular programs on WMOR was "The Man on the Street." It was a live program in front of the station. The announcer just dropped a microphone out the front window down to the street level. (There were no air conditioned studios in those days.) On that program local people were asked their opinion about topics of local interest. Those topics included such areas as the price of tobacco, local politics, weather,sports, current events, and ethics. The announcers would take turns hosting that program and many times the results were hilarious.

October 18, 1956, the original owners of WMOR, Claude Clayton, Roy Cornette and Bill Sample, sold the station to another group of local businessmen. The new owners included: Frank Havens, Earl Young, J. Earl McBrayer, Tommy Combs, Joe Mauk, and William Whitaker. Local Real Estate Broker, Alpha Hutchinson handled the transaction that had to be approved by the Federal Communications Commission. (It was approved).

RUNNING PROGRAM ON WMOR

Mr. William Whitaker was experienced as a station manager, and J. Earl McBrayer, began a popular early morning call-in show called "Swap Shop." It was on the air six mornings a week at 7:30 a.m. for 30 minutes. If you had anything to buy, sell or trade, you called in live, gave the item, price, and phone number. It was the most popular program on the air. Retirees, housewives, business people, professional people, and students listened intently to items for sale and trade. Also, for the rest of the day, people would talk about the items listed that day.

The reason "Swap Shop" was talked about in the community was because of many of the bizarre items listed for sale or trade. One woman who had obviously called before, called again and said: "My husband (and she gave her husband's name) still has his rear end for sale." (Obviously she was referring to an automobile transmission.)

Bee Course For Deer Tracks

Another early "Swap Shop" caller said, "I will trade one bee course for deer tracks." Lest you think that was a crank call, let me explain, with the help of local bee experts Paul Ousley and Joe McKinney. A bee course can be determined by mixing a little sweet anise with honey and placed outside in an open pan. The bees will be attracted to it, and you wait near by, and as they are feeding on the bait, you sprinkle flour lightly on them. When they are through feeding, they will first rise up circling directly over the bait, then they will establish a direct course (bee line) to their bee tree. You watch the direction of their flight and keep time on how long it takes before those covered with flour return. You then know the direction and approximate distance to their bee tree. (That's how the old timers found bee trees.) Therefore, with very few deer in Rowan County in that time, the caller offered a bona fide trade of "one bee course for deer tracks."

Radio Station WMOR's "Swap Shop" ended in 1993 after almost forty years of continuous service to Rowan County. It was the longest running program in the station's history. There have been many numerous hosts of the program over those years, as well as many other bizarre requests. In 1999, Jim Forest, the present station owner, tells me WMOR-AM is still a 1,000 watt AM daytime station. However, with his staff of 5people, they also operate WMOR-FM, an 8,000 watt station that soon will increase to 25,000 watts.

Over the years, Radio Station WMOR has been a powerful influence in this community. Also, over the years, many, many people have worked at the radio station. (Some have gone on to become successful in larger markets.) However, they all have many memories of those early days at WMOR. We the listeners, have many memories of those golden days of Radio when that was about the only radio station received in Morehead.

MOVIES ON THE SILVER SCREEN

"A typical American has a fast car, a mortgage, pays alimony, and thinks moving pictures have grand opera beaten a mile"(Unknown)

In 1900 Morehead was a raw, rural railroad town with one normal school, one post office, one public school, four churches, six hotels, eight taverns, and a recent reputation for feuding. Except for an occasional school play or traveling vaudeville show, there was little in the way of entertainment. But that began to change when Mr. Ed Maggard, et. al., formed the Morehead Light Company in 1903. It was soon after the first electric lines were built in Morehead that the first movie house appeared.

In 1904 Mr. Millard Stevens built the first movie house in Morehead. It was called "The Nichelodium" and was located on the first floor of a two-story building on Trumbo Avenue. A very crude carbon arc projector projected dim flickering moving images on a white sheet hung on the wall. The film was made of celluloid and was highly flammable. The admission price was a nickel and the films were silent western action films. In 1908 Mr. Stevens sold his movie house to John Wall who moved the "theater" to Bishop Avenue.

Music Added For Drama

In 1909 Mr. Ed. Maggard bought an interest in the movie house. A piano was added to provide dramatic music to accompany the movies. Mrs. Elizabeth Young was the pianist who quickly mastered the art of playing faster as the horses ran faster and added a loud bang when the puff of smoke appeared as a gun was fired. Also, a dramatic crescendo accompanied the train as it bore down on the helpless heroine tied to the railroad tracks. All of that dramatic entertainment for only a nickel was the beginning of Morehead's movie houses.

In 1909 Mr. Maggard became so disgusted with the poor quality of the flickering image projected on the screen that he patented a shutter to improve the image. Also, in 1911, he and Mr. Bradley formed the Maggard-Bradley manufacturing company on Trumbo Avenue. They manufactured cosmograph motion picture projectors until the company was sold in 1918. Those projectors were called "Perfect Projectors."

Mr. Bert Willett migrated to Morehead from Buffalo, New York, in the early 1900s. Soon after arriving here, he and his son-in-law, John Knapp, purchased the mining operation of the Bluestone Company located five miles west of Morehead. In 1910 Mr. Willett purchased the old historic Gault House and began planning a new building on that site.

"Cozy" Comes to Morehead

In 1915 Mr. Willett borrowed $5,000 from a Farmers resident, Mrs. Laura Clayton (James M. Clayton's aunt). The money was used to tear down the old Gault House and build a new sawed stone building. Although the new building replaced one of Morehead's most historic buildings, the new building, became a part of Morehead history. It is historic because it is one of two buildings in the U.S. made of stone sawed to the same size as brick. The other building, located in Rosenberg, Texas, was owned by the Willett family until the 1960s.

In 1916 Bert Willett and John Knapp opened the new Cozy Theater in one section of their building on the corner of Main and College Blvd. The cheapest black and white silent films were about all that were shown to the packed house that seated less than 100. However, the admission was still only a nickel. Although all the films were silent, they were accompanied by a pianist, and soon the film content broadened to include murder mysteries (Fu Mauchu), love stories (Rudolph Valentino), drama (Shakespeare), as well as westerns (Harry Carey). However, the image of Morehead's movie houses was about to change.

In 1918 a young Canadian chemist/druggist arrived in Morehead riding his motorcycle. His name was Hartley Battson, and he was here to visit his parents who were teachers in the Morehead Normal School. After being here a few weeks, he decided to settle here, and he opened his drugstore in part of the Willett Building. In 1920 he bought John Knapp's interest, and in 1927 he also purchased Mr. Willett's interest in the Cozy Theater. Soon after purchasing the theater, Mr. Battson began to explore new movie merchandising methods.

ENLARGED AND IMPROVED

He purchased one of the locally manufactured cosmograph silent projectors and a new screen. Next, he added more comfortable seating and began renting better quality black and white films. In 1927 the Cozy Theater was enlarged and redecorated. Next he began to advertise in the *Rowan County News*. Also, Mr. Battson began another merchandising method. He hired local young boys to go down Main Street and up into the residential areas yelling what movies were playing at the Cozy that night. But the cityfathers did not approve of disturbing the peace and tranquility of

Morehead. (At first movies were shown only on Monday, Tuesday, Friday, and Saturday so as not to interfere with church services.) After receiving complaints about the noise, the city council enacted what might be called the "Cozy Ordinance." It was recommended by Mayor H.G. Wilson, and it specifically forbid "young boys from going about the streets of Morehead yelling commercial advertisements." (Maybe young girls could have been hired.)

Mr. Battson soon adopted another merchandising method that got around the town crier method of advertising. He once again hired young boys. However that method involved walking around town carrying signs of movies playing at the Cozy that night. They were known as "Battson Boys." No, not Don and Bill, Mr. Battson's very young sons, but other boys. They were paid one movie ticket for every hour walking around town carrying the sign. Among those early "Battson Boys" were: Paul J. Reynolds, Creed Patrick, Duval Payne, Harold Holbrook, Tommy Powers, Drexel Wells, Randy Wells, Irving Cash, Jr., Warren Hicks, and many others.

FIRE HAZARDS

The silent cosmograph projector manufactured in Morehead used a carbon arc light source. That involved using a white hot carbon electric wire. Also, the celluloid film used then was highly flammable. That volatile combination was an extreme fire hazard. Dr. Steve Young, son of Mr. Earl Young, who was the son of one of the early Cozy projectionists, recalled his dad saying, "They kept a big zinc bucket in the projection booth. The projectionist was instructed that if the film caught fire, they were to jerk the reel off the projector, and throw it in the bucket and out the window. Because of the fire hazard, the projectionist had to keep a careful watch on the projector at all time and could never leave the projection booth while the projector was running.

In 1929, with U.S. 60 completed, the Trimble Theater in Mt. Sterling began aggressive advertising in Rowan County. They advertised the Trimble Theater as "The most beautiful theater in the bluegrass." Also, they showed revolutionary "talking pictures." (Sound movies had arrived in Kentucky.) When the Trimble Theater in Mt. Sterling converted to sound movies, they began to attract Morehead movie goers.

Although Mr. Battson had just redecorated and purchased a new silent projector three years earlier, he recognized that if he was going to compete, he had to install a new sound projection system. Also, he redecorated and enlarged the seating capacity to 140. The total cost of new equipment and remodeling was $2,500. Next, Mr. Battson began renting the best quality of films available. The week of September 17, 1929, movies playing at the Cozy were: "Love Nest", "College Hero", and a Zane Gray film starring Jack Holt. Also, the following week a film called "College Love", billed as the "hottest film" on the screen appeared in Morehead.

TALKIES ARRIVE

On July 10, 1930, the first talking movie was shown in Morehead at the Cozy Theater. Soon the Cozy advertised "<u>only</u> talking movies shown all the time." Although the admission price was fifteen cents for adults and ten cents for children, the seats were usually filled. To meet the demand, the Cozy began to show films continuously. Morehead soon became recognized as the amusement center of Eastern Kentucky and people came from throughout Eastern Kentucky, to see and hear the "talkies." (Birth of a Nation" was shown in 1931.)

This writer can remember my uncle used to take me to the Cozy every Monday night. Of course as a small child, I was fascinated by movies. They seemed so real to me that I would frequently crouch behind the seats for fear of getting hit with a stray bullet.

Don Battson told this writer that in those early days people would throw candy or other objects at the screen's villains. Also, Walter Carr, said as a boy, "He would sometimes get into a fight over which western heroes horse could run the fastest--Hoot Gibson's, Ken Maynard's, or Wild Bill Elliott's." Yes, early talking pictures were more than just entertainment to the young people of Morehead. They seemed to be actually involved in the action.

MOVIE STARS ARRIVE

During the 1930s, stars of the silent screen would appear in person in Morehead to promote their pictures. One such star was comedy star William Haines who appeared on stage at the Cozy to promote his film, "Lovey-Mary." It was promoted as "one of his best films with an all star supporting cast" who added much to the mirth of the picture. There were 101 "mirth producing" situations. Mr. Haines was in Morehead for two days, Friday and Saturday nights, July 24-25, 1931, to publicize the film.

During the late 1930s, other screen comedy and cowboy stars came to Morehead to publicize their movies. On February 6, 1939, Will Bill Elliott appeared in person at the Cozy. He was dressed in cowboy attire with twin pearl handled 45 pistols worn reversed on his hips. He "wowed" the audience with his fancy "gun play," and rope tricks.

During that trip, Don Battson recalled, "Wild Bill stayed at their home over night." Don said "My mother cooked a gourmet dinner, and we dined in our fancy dining room." However, Wild Bill became fascinated with their eight antique cherry, rose-backed dining room chairs. He asked Mrs. Battson if she would sell them. Mrs. Battson priced the chairs for what she thought was an exorbitant price, and Wild Bill bought them. He had them crated up and shipped back to Hollywood. (Could anyone knowing that story ever look at tough, straight shooting, hard fighting Wild Bill Elliott the same again?)

REFRESHMENTS AND VAUDEVILLE

Mr. Battson soon recognized that the people at the theater were a captive audience, and they would buy refreshments if available. His drugstore and fountain were next door to the theater, and he began to pop popcorn in the drugstore and take popcorn and fountain cokes to the theater. His two young sons, Don and Bill, were the enterprising young lads who carried the cokes and popcorn up and down the aisles of the Cozy selling them to the audience. Later on Mr. Battson put in a small concession stand in the lobby and employed other people to sell the refreshments.

During the 1920s, vaudeville was still alive and well in Morehead. Although the movie theater was the dominant entertainment business in Morehead, traveling vaudeville shows continued to perform in town. Among those performing were Will Rogers and Bud Hawkins. Will Rogers went on to become America's great humorist and did not return to Morehead, but the Bud Hawkins show was an annual event in Morehead.

Beginning in 1928, just as regular as spring arrived, the Bud Hawkins players arrived. They were just about as welcome as spring itself, and the annual "Buds Coming" was a time for celebration. The Bud Hawkins Players were one traveling institution that was always welcomed in Morehead by young and old. The big tent was usually setup in the show lot on east Main Street where Larry Fannin's car lot is located in 1999. The older boys in town would work helping set up the tent for tickets. Bud arrived in Morehead for a three-night show May 28, 29, and 30, 1931. Although they had been sponsored by the American Legion in the past, that year the Legion allowed the Morehead High School Athletic Booster Club to sponsor the event. Not only were the people being entertained by one of the finest repertory companies in the land, but they were helping to support the Morehead High School Athletic Program. The Bud Hawkins Show was always a clean show for all the family. The play was always a comedy with "Bud" in the starring role. He was a "poor man's" Charlie Chaplain and usually played a clownish character with baggy pants. His shows were always a hit in Morehead, and many were disappointed when the show stopped playing in Morehead.

COZY CHANGED TO MILLS

In 1940 Mr. J.M. Mills purchased the Cozy Theater from Mr. Battson. Mr. Mills owned a chain of theaters in Maysville, Russell, and Washington, Kentucky Mr. Mills sold the theater to Warren Schafer in 1940. Mr. Schafer continued to operate the theater under the same name. Mr. Phil Chakers bought the Mills from Mr. Schafer in 1948 and continued to operate until the 1960s when the doors were closed.

Over the years many people were employed at the Cozy and Mills Theaters. Among those employed were: Earl Young, Grover Trumbo, Ernest Jayne, Bill Ferguson, Ben Johnson, John D. Epperhart, Kenneth Hamm, Mary Alice Calvert, and many others.

COLLEGE THEATER

In 1930 Morehead State College recognized the importance of a moving image and a sound track in education as well as entertainment. Therefore, the college installed a projection booth in the balcony of Button Auditorium and a 12 ft. X 18 ft. movable screen on the stage. After purchasing projection and sound equipment, the college had their own movie theater. The cost of admission was 10 cents, and the movies, even though they were shown only on weekends (Friday, Saturday and Sunday), were well attended. They were well attended because very few students went home on weekends and none had cars. Also, even if they did have cars, there were few roads. President John Howard Payne and the administration seemed to justify establishing the college theater because they took seriously their role of "In Loco Parentis," (in place of parents) to the students while they were under their care. Also, some believed that the local movies were "racy " with too much sex and violence. It was the intent of the College Theater to show more "educational" films and wholesome entertainment films. Also, the students were much less likely to get into trouble if they remained on campus.

EDUCATIONAL FILMS SHOWN

President John Howard Payne and the administration received a great deal of criticism for establishing the College Theater. Many parents believed the college should be educating their children not entertaining them. Many church leaders believed films inherently evil and should not be shown on campus at all. Also, many businessmen wanted to see the students downtown, and Mr. Battson, owner of the Cozy Theater, believed he suffered from un-fair competition. But the College Theater remained a viable part of the Morehead State College community for over 30 years.

At first the films shown at the College Theater were true to their purpose for establishing the theater. Such films as "Young Mr. Lincoln" starring a young Henry Fonda with Alice Brady and directed by John Ford. Another early film featured at the College Theater was "Music Goes Round" with Harry Rehman and Rachelle Hudson. Also, an educational film called "The Human Adventure" was shown on January 14, 1937. It was billed as an "eight reeler (2 hrs and 40 minutes) talking picture, which sketched the rise of man from savagery to civilization." It must have been required viewing by all students in Western Civilization courses. The film was produced by the University of Chicago, which was Dr. Warren Lappin's alma mater. Dr. Lappin was vice president at the College for many years.

The film was shown only to a limited number of colleges throughout the country, and the "Human Adventure" was not just another talking picture. It was in reality, "An air cruise, and an expedition into the lands where man rose up out of the jungle and made a conquest of civilization." Therefore, the College Theater was practicing their purpose of showing "educational films."

LESS EDUCATIONAL MORE ENTERTAINMENT

Later in 1937, James Fennimore Cooper's "Last of the Mohicans" was scheduled at the College Theater. This writer wanted to attend that movie but my mother was not too agreeable. However, when I assured her it was "educational" (I'm sure she knew that) and was shown at the College Theater, she reluctantly allowed me to attend. Later, as the attendance dropped at the school theater, it seemed that the college students wanted more entertainment and less "educational" type films. Therefore, more Hollywood extravagances were scheduled. Such movies as the risque "Follies Bergere" starring Maurice Chevalier and Merle Oberon was booked. The cast included the internationally famous Parisian chorus girls with Maurice Chevalier singing and dancing. Of course, the movie was well attended, and future films were more entertaining and less educational. The College Theater closed in the 1960s because more students wanted to go off campus.

TRAIL THEATER

In May 1937, early movie entrepreneur Ed Maggard was back in the movie business after a 30-year hiatus. He was chairman of the Morehead Consolidated Hardware Company when he announced his intention to build a new beautiful, modern theater in Morehead. It cost a hefty $25,000 and was financed by the Hardware Company. Mr. Maggard was the manager, and the name of the new theater was The Trail.

Ed Maggard served as architect, contractor, and builder, of the beautiful new modern Trail Theater which opened Saturday, December 25, 1937. The new theater was located on Wilson Avenue between Main Street and Sun Street directly across from the then new post office. The new movie house was 40 feet wide and 106 feet long. It was constructed on the site of the old Consolidated Lumber Company. It had a seating capacity of 430 plush, upholstered seats, all located on one floor. There was one aisle on each side that was carpeted. The floor sloped downward toward the screen, which made much better vision for the viewers. There was indirect lighting on the outside of the aisle seats that allowed the audience to move up and down the aisle without disturbing other viewers.

AIR CONDITIONED, WELL LIT THEATER

The lobby of the new theater was carpeted with plush wine colored carpet. The lobby walls were artistically designed with modernistic black art glass with aluminum trim, and listed the forthcoming films. There was a concession stand in the lobby and two spacious restrooms. The building was constructed entirely of brick, tile, and concrete and was completely fireproof. It had what was a first for Morehead (air conditioning). The air conditioning equipment was specially engineered and designed by Mr. Maggard. It was only fitting that the man who first brought electricity to Morehead be the one whofirst brought air conditioning to the city. Other equipment included the latest Simplex Projection and sound systems.

The marque outside had a large vertical sign: "Trail." Also, there were 500 bright, blinking lights that lit up the entire neighborhood around the sign and the marque. Black movable ten-inch steel letters that could easily be seen from Main Street, announced the feature film for the day. The admission price was 10 cents for age

12 and under, and 16 cents for adults. The Trail pledged to provide the latest films, including first run films in technicolor. Now that all films were "talkies," many were produced in spectacular living color. That new technology attracted many more film goers.

Trail Opened Christmas Day

The Trail opened its doors on Christmas Day (Saturday) 1937. The title of the movie was "Slim," with a cast that included Henry Fonda and Pat O'Brien. In retrospect, one might assume that it would have been a Christmas film. However, at that time, Hollywood producers had never made a Christmas film because they believed it would never be a financial success. That was because of the limited time period it would be shown and their mistaken belief that there was no market for re-runs since people would never pay to see a movie they had seen before. Also, Hollywood was reluctant to produce a secular film about such a sacred Christian holiday, and they were certainly not going to produce a film about the birthday of Christ.

First Christmas Films Produced

One of the first attempts at producing a Christmas film was the color animated version of the "Littlest Angel" produced in 1940 by Coronet Films, the world's largest producer of educational films. This writer worked for that company for three years as an educational consultant and can say with authority, it was that company's best selling "educational" film. It still remains popular to this very day. The first Hollywood Christmas film was Dickens' "Christmas Carol" that was released in 1938.

During the 1940s (WW II) there were a few films dealing with a secular Christmas theme, eg., "Holiday Inn" with Bing Crosby (1942), and in 1944, "White Christmas" with Bing Crosby, Danny Kaye, and Maysville native Rosemary Clooney. However, it was not until the 1946 Frank Capra produced classic "It's a Wonderful Life" starring Jimmy Stewart and Donna Reed, that Christmas films became popular. Although that film was not popular at first, it has grown in popularity over the years. That film was the inspiring story of George Bailey's Christmas eve visit by his guardian angel. It

Warren Shafer, owner of Morehead's Trail theater hangs kerosene lanterns under the marquee to give more light during the celebration of the end of the war in Europe, 1945.

was nominated for five academy awards and after almost a half a century it remains an American classic viewed by millions every year.

As he grew older, Mr. Ed Maggard grew weary of the day to day management of the Trail Theater. Although it was a successful venture, he decided to sell the theater. He met with Mr. Warren R. Shafer who seemed interested in purchasing the Trail.

TRAIL THEATER CHANGES OWNERSHIP

Warren R. Shafer owned a successful theater in Irvine, Kentucky (the county seat of Estill County). That theater burned in 1939, and he began to look around for another theater. It was then that Entrepreneur Shafer met Entrepreneur Maggard, and Mr. Shafer purchased the Trail Theater in 1939. However, he did not move his wife, Edna, and daughters, Barbara and Shirley to Morehead until 1940. Daughter Barbara recalled she was reluctant to move to Morehead because it seemed to her to be the edge of the universe, however, it turned out to be a wonderful place to live. After moving his family to Morehead in 1940, Mr. Shafer soon acquired a chain of Kentucky theaters by purchasing the Mills Theater in Morehead as well as theaters in Flemingsburg, Ashland, and Olive Hill. That made it possible for these theaters to get newer first run movies.

LOCALS COULD SQUEEZE A PENNY

Barbara Shafer, as a young teenager, worked at the Trail selling tickets on Saturdays and Sundays. She recalled that people from some of the surrounding counties would come to the theater early on Saturday afternoon bringing a paper bag full of sliced cheese and loose crackers. They would stay in the air conditioned theater eating cheese and crackers and watching the same movie over and over again until the theater closed at 10 p.m. But there were some local people who were pretty tight fisted with their money. Some would even bring their own paper bag to the movie and buy popcorn and not pay the 1 cent for the box. That was not surprising because there were two prominent banking families in Morehead known to squeeze a penny tightly. One wife of a prominent banker would go to Battsons Drug Store and order one half of a nickel coke and charge it. Another prominent Morehead banker would go into the Amos and Andy Restaurant and buy a cigar. They were two for a nickel and he would say everyday that was the 2 cent one. But the restaurant owner, Liz Martindale, soon put a stop to that by keeping a close record on the cigars purchased. On one occasion, Barbara Shafer recalled that one Saturday morning, her Dad received an irate phone call from a neighbor that lived up the street from the theater. The neighbor was very upset with the movie listed on the marque. So Mr. Shafer went to the theater to see why she was so upset. There on the marque was the title of the movie: "He Died with His Boots On," also, Shorts. (That referred to additional short subjects.)

SATURDAY AFTERNOON SERIALS

The bright lights of the Trail Theater were magnets that drew the young people of Morehead to the theater like gypsy moths to an open flame. The Trail was the place to be. All the boys and girls that could get 10 cents, flocked there on Saturday afternoon to see their favorite cowboy movie. It might be one of the outstanding stars such as Roy Rogers, Gene Autry, Tex Ritter, Hoot Gibson, Ken Maynard or others. Also, sometimes the Saturday fare included the latest episode of a Tarzan serial and you had to see how Johnny Weismuller, the jungle lord, survived the swim across the alligator infested stream. However, the serial might be "Shenna of the Jungle," or "Clyde Beatty in Darkest Africa," or the "Perils of Pauline," or another of the many exciting serials that brought the young people to the movies on Saturday afternoon. But whatever, the serial, it kept bringing the young people to the Trail on Saturdays.

Those Saturday afternoon matinees were sometimes pretty rowdy. The kids would smuggle fire crackers, soft drinks in glass bottles, and various and sundry other items that would give the manager headaches. Someone with a glass coke bottle at the rear of the theater would start the bottle rolling down the sloped floor under the seats. If the bottle rolled under your seat, you were supposed to keep it rolling. It was noisy and disturbing and brought Mr. Shafer up and down the aisles to try and locate the guilty party. Barb (Shafer) Hisle recently recalled that sometimes on her Saturday break from selling tickets, she would come into the theater and start a bottle rolling toward the front, and her Dad never did catch her for which she was very grateful.

WEDNESDAY: BANK NIGHT

Mr. Shafer tried several merchandising methods to increase attendance. One method was called "bank night." Therefore, Wednesday nights at the Trail were known as "Bank Night." Each time during the week that you attended a movie you could register for a cash drawing. Then on Wednesday nights, $10 was awarded to the lucky winner. If the winner was not present, the $10 was carried over until the next Wednesday. (That usually brought a full house.) There were occasional beauty contests, and amateur nights, where local people would sing, tap dance, or play an instrument. Those never really caught on and were soon dropped.

During the late 1930s, many young boys would sometimes sneak in at the Trail. There was an outside door at the rear of the building at the left of the screen. It was sometimes left unlocked, and you could enter that door and go down into the theater. This writer tried several times when he didn't have the price of admission to slip in but was only partially successful. Once when I found the door unlocked, I sneaked quietly into the darkened theater and sat behind a solid rail bannister on the stairs leading up to the stage, almost right against the bottom of the screen. I remained there throughout the whole movie afraid to go back into a seat in the audience lest I get caught. After the movie was over, I went back out the back door. That ended my sneaking into the movie. However, the brightly lit Trail Theater was a bright spot in the lives of the young people during the depression, war years, and post war years.

SHAFER SELLS THEATERS

While in Morehead, Mr. Shafer purchased a track of land just east of College Boulevard and north of U.S. 60. It is now where the new Courthouse, Jayne Stadium, and the Academic Athletic Center are located. It was to be a residential area and one street was built. However, the Shafer Addition never materialized because in 1948, he sold his chain of Kentucky theaters to Mr. Phil Chakers and moved to Daytona Beach, Florida. There he soon acquired two drive-in theaters and two regular theaters. He also owned a drive-in theater in St. Augustine, Florida. His daughter, Barbara, reported that in 1949, Mr. Shafer's Daytona Beach, Florida Drive-in Theater was rented to the Christian Church on Sunday for their outdoor church services. It was believed that was the first church in the nation to conduct outdoor worship services in a drive in theater.

Among those who worked at the Trail were: William Ferguson, Irvin Kash Jr., Frances Hunt, Stella Glover, Barbara Shafer, Mr. Brown, Kenneth Hamm, and many more.

MOREHEAD DRIVE-IN

Americans have long had a love affair with movies on the silver screen. But movies were always shown indoors and usually in plush theaters. Each city would compete to build the most luxurious theaters. However, that changed around the middle of the 20th century, when the seeds of the American drive-in theater were sown during WW II. A moving image and a sound track was a vital part of the training of the American servicemen during that era. They were shown films during every aspect of their basic training. Then they would probably go see a movie in the evening after they had viewed training films during the day.

MOVIES SHOWN TO SOLDIERS

Following their basic and advanced training, many men were shipped out to overseas bases and to combat assignments. But wherever they went, the Hollywood produced movies followed them. Even in the steamy jungles of the south Pacific, as soon as an island had been cleared of the Japanese, there would be movies shown to the men. There was usually a 8'x10' tripod beaded screen setup on a flat bed truck. Then a jeep parked about 40 ft. away served as a projection booth. The 16mm projector was hooked up to a gasoline generator for power, and the sound was connected to two speakers on each side of the screen. Therefore, you had an outdoor theater and the men would either sit or lie down on the ground as they watched the movie. Many times the movies would be shown in the rain as the men covered themselves with their "shelter-halves." Also, the Hollywood entertainers who come overseas, such as Bob Hope, had much the same venue for entertaining the troops, only on a much larger scale. Thus, the seeds of the outdoor movie theater were sown in the minds of many Americans.

DRIVE-IN MOVIES BEGAN IN CALIFORNIA

As the American men (and women) returned from WW II they began marrying by the millions. Soon there was a gigantic baby boom, as they began having children. Of course, the responsibility of a family and working or going to school interfered with their going to the movies. It was then that a theater chain in California built the first outdoor movie theater. It was called a Drive-in and it brought together America's love for the silver screen and their love of the automobile. It was a very convenient, informal way to see a movie, and it brought families to the outdoor theater, as they did not have to leave their car or get a baby sitter. Of course, it also brought lovers together on the back row of the Drive-in theater who never even knew the title of the movie.

By 1949 there were 1,025 Drive-in theaters in America, and by 1950 that number had more than doubled with over 2,200 Drive-ins. This method of film viewing seemed to have a bright future in 1949. In fact it was believed by many that Drive-ins would drive out traditional movie theaters.

MOREHEAD DRIVE-IN OPENED

In 1952 Mr. J.C. Conley from Paintsville, Kentucky, came to Morehead to establish a Drive-in theater. Mr. Conley owned the Paintsville Bus Line and other movie theaters in Paintsville and West Liberty. (At one time there were two Drive-in theaters in West Liberty.) In 1954 Mr. Conley formed a partnership with Morehead auto dealer, L.D. Fannin. Together, they continued to operate the Drive-in theater at the intersection of U.S. 60 East, and Route 32. (The 1999 location of the Rodburn Elementary School.)

VIEWERS TAKE SPEAKERS

The Morehead Drive-in theater had 500 parking spots, each on a slight ridge for better viewing and individual speakers and speaker stands for each spot. You removed the speaker from the stand and hung it in the car window when the movie started and replaced it when the movie ended. Unfortunately, some people forgot and drove off with the speaker still in their car. (This writer once did that.) Larry Fannin, son of Mr. L.D. Fannin, began working at the Drive-in at a very early age recalled: "Some time people would leave the speaker at the exit as they left, and sometime they would return it the next time they came." Larry also said, "On one occasion, they found a coffee sack full of speakers on top of Clack Mountain." (Perhaps someone thought they could hang the speakers in their car there and get the sound from the movie.) But the speakers could be re-wired and used again, and Kenneth Hamm and Jim Thomas were kept busy doing this. (Today's modern Drive-in theater broadcasts the sound through your car radio.)

In 1955 Mr. Fannin bought Mr. Conley's share in the business and began sole operation of the theater. Larry Fannin said one of his early jobs was selling tickets. Thetickets were first 29 cents for each adult and children under 12 were free. However, gradually the cost went up to 39 cents and then 49 cents and eventually reached $1.25 each. Larry recalled that many people would crouch down in the front seat, others would lie down on the floor in the back seat area, and occasionally some hid in the trunk. Larry said, "I could usually tell when someone was hiding in the trunk because the rear of the car was lower on the ground. He said: "If I became suspicious of a car, I would call Jim Thomas and he would check that particular car. They would then usually catch them unloading the stow aways from inside the car trunk. Also another way local movie goers would try and save the cost of a ticket was the fact that although the movie screen could not be seen from U.S. 60, it could be seen from Route 32. Therefore, almost every night, cars would be parked bumper to bumper up Route 32 where they could see the theater screen.

BUCK NIGHT, BLUEGRASS, AND COUNTRY

One memory in the minds of many Moreheadians was the Wednesday night "Buck Night" at the Drive-in. That was when the admission price for each car was $1 regardless of the number of people in the car. Therefore, as many as you could cram into a car was only $1." "Buck night" was always successful because after you got inside, you could spread out on top of the car or on a blanket on the ground to watch the move.

The Morehead Drive-in theater was always proud of the reputation of their concession stand. It was run by Mrs. Clara Collins, who specialized in real home cooked hamburgers and cheeseburgers from prime ground beef. Also, her barbeque and hot dogs were always in great demand. Mr. Fannin insisted on quality food because he and his wife both would eat there often.

From the 1950s to the 1970s, the Morehead Drive-in scheduled many stage performers. Among those booked could be called a list of who's who in the Bluegrass and Country music world. (Some were just teenagers then.) Those included: Ralph Stanley (Clinch

Mountain Boys), Bill Monroe (called father of bluegrass music), Keith Whitley, (now deceased), Tom T. Hall (Kentucky Travellers), Marty Stuart, Ricky Skaggs, June Carter, and the famous Flatt and Scruggs. Larry Fannin recalled that the stage performers were paid based on the number of cars in attendance on the night of their performance. He said: "Lester Flatt actually sat out by the gate and counted the cars as they entered the grounds. He was going to make sure the count was correct. Another popular stage show was the world famous Siamese twins. Jim Thomas, a long time employee of the Drive-in and at Fannins car dealership, said, "They always brought a full house because no one had ever seen people joined together like that."

DAYLIGHT SAVINGS TIME

Although some drive-ins furnished heaters to put inside the cars and were open allyear, the Morehead Drive-in was a seasonal business. It was open only from April to October and had to make it during those months. However, during the late 1950s and early 1960s attendance began to wane. That was at a time that daylight savings time was enacted into law. Larry Fannin said that in his opinion, "Daylight savings time was what destroyed the drive-in theater." That could be true because at one time Rowan County was on central standard time and then the time zones were changed and Rowan was in the eastern time zone. Then came daylight savings time, which was a two hour difference in time, therefore, it did not get dark until 9:30 in the summertime. With a starting time that late, working people and families just could not stay out that late. More than anything else, that destroyed the Drive-in.

Although Rowan County was a dry county and did not sell legal whiskey, many people would go to a "bootlegger" and buy beer, and come to the Drive-in and drink it. That caused some rowdiness and resulted in some arrests.

Mr. L.D. Fannin, in order to attract customers started showing X rated films. That boosted attendance for a while, but the family did not believe that was a wholesome business atmosphere. Therefore, they soon stopped showing those films. But they could not make a success of the business showing G films.

FANNINS' SELL DRIVE-IN

Mr. Fannin then sold the business in 1972 to Mr. O.J. Rodin who was a high school principal from Corbin, Kentucky, who also owned several other theaters. But the Morehead Drive-in theater closed in the late 1970s, a victim of "time" and television.

Larry Fannin began working at the Drive-in popping corn at the concession stand. He said its a wonder the beautiful Barbara Brown ever married him because he was always so busy working, he didn't have much courting time. However, they are now happily married with three children and four grandchildren. They still own the family car dealership in Morehead.

Mr. Jim Thomas, a long time employee of the Fannins began working at the Drive-in in 1952. He did all types of general maintenance work, and although he is now retired, he still works part-time for Larry Fannin. Kenneth Hamm was the projectionist at the theater and spent his entire life time working for the Fannins. Larry said Kenneth was a near genius and would do any type of skilled work. (He is now deceased.) Among those who worked at the Morehead Drive-in theater were: Mary Ellen Helwig, Shirley Mobley, Carol Patton, Jimmy Cox, Clyda Carter, Judy Thompson, Janice Caudill, Joyce Caudill, Joyce Tackett, Phoebe Butcher, Geri White, Buddy Black, Jim and Gary Thomas, and many more.

MOVIES ON THE SILVER SCREEN

Movie attendance began to decline during the late 1950s. That decline could be traced directly to the technology of television.

However, the so called "movie moguls" refused to believe their own surveys. They seemed to stick their head in the sand and refused to accept that television was keeping movie patrons at home. Therefore, when it finally dawned upon them that something was needed if they were to attract movie goers to the silver screen, they were at loss to know what to do.

The movie industry tried various technological innovations to combat television such as 3D. When a 3D movie was shown, the audience was given polariod glasses to wear. That was supposed to add depth to the height and breadth of the movie. It never quite caught on with movie-goers. Next came cinemoscope, metroscope, megascope, vista vision, and many other technical innovations, all with very little success in luring movie-goers back to the silver screen.

CHAKERES PURCHASED MOREHAD THEATERS

In 1948 Mr. Phil Chakeres, Chairman of the Chakeres Theater chain in Ohio and Kentucky, purchased the Trail and Mills Theaters in Morehead from Warren Shafer. Since Morehead was a college town with a large percentage of young people, the theater business was good. Also, because Morehead was not located close to a television station, good T.V. reception was slow to arrive in Morehead. Therefore, the movie business in Morehead seemed promising to the new theater owners.

In 1958 when Morehead College's high flying Eagles basketball team, coached by Bobby Laughlin, was scheduling nationally known universities teams, they played at the University of Miami (Florida). Phil Chakeres, owner of two Morehead theaters, was living in Miami and picked up the paper and saw Morehead was playing in Miami. He said, "Those are our boys, because we have theaters in Morehead." While the team and their followers were in Miami, he hosted a lavish party for them at a Miami Beach

The Morehead University Cinema held its grand opening January 11, 1968.

Hotel. He then attended his first basketball game and saw Morehead win over the University of Miami. They played at Morehead the next year and Morehead beat Miami badly. Coach Laughlin said Miami would never schedule Morehead again after that year.

Phil Chakeres' experience at Miami seemed to give him new insight into the future of Morehead State University. From that time, he began planning a new theater in Morehead, but it would be another ten years before those plans came to fruition.

Phil Chakeres and his two brothers, Harry and Louis, emigrated to this country from Tripolis, Greece, in 1900. They soon became American citizens, and in 1908, opened a Greek Restaurant in Springfield, Ohio. But after three years, they sold the restaurant and purchased the deteriorating Princess Theater in Springfield for $500. They soon realized they had much to learn about operating a theater. The first day they forgot to order films and were unable to open. But they determined to learn the business, and soon the Princess Theater was a successful operation.

In 1913 the Chakeres brothers opened the Majestic Theater in Springfield, Ohio, followed by the Hippodrome, and several other theaters throughout Ohio. In 1927 they built the State Theater, followed by the Capitol Theater in Columbus, Ohio. Following the untimely death of Louis Chakeres, his brother Phil was appointed the head of the company. Under his dynamic leadership, they formed a partnership with Warner Theaters whereby they acquired four more theaters. Then in 1948 the company purchased the Trail and Mills Theaters in Morehead from Mr. Warren Shafer. The Chakeres Company always believed in the future of Morehead as a market for movies on the silver screen. Therefore, almost 10 years after the Morehead-Miami basketball game, Mr. Chakers announced he was building a new theater in Morehead.

On January 11, 1968, at 7 p.m., the University Cinema held its grand opening. The title of the premier opening night film was "The Ambushers," with Dean Martin as Matt Helm. The University Cinema was billed as the "finest indoor theater in Kentucky or perhaps the nation." The theater seated over 500 people in luxurious chairs with an unobstructed view of the screen. The giant screen was 55 feet wide and 26 feet high, with unique picture window concept that enhanced motion picture viewing at its best. Also, the theater walls, ceiling, carpet, and sound system combined for almost perfect accoustics for sound listening. The building, of course, had all weather climate controlled comfort.

The lobby featured rotating art exhibits from Morehead State University's most accomplished art students. The luxurious lobby was spacious, attractive, and functional. It had a full service concession stand and restrooms. It was considered the landmark of Morehead's entertainment community, and represented an investment of over $500,000. It was the 40th theater in the Chakeres chain, and it was also considered the crown jewel of their theaters.

Thursday, January 11, 1968, was officially proclaimed University Cinema Entertainment Day by Morehead Mayor William H. Layne. Amid all of the whereases, herewiths, and therefores, Mayor Layne complemented the Chakers chain for their faith and investment in Morehead. He pledged the community cooperation and support of the cinema. Mr. Phil Chakers answered with this statement: "Welcome to our new theater. The wonderful world of movies unfolding in this new theater is only a part of the role we hope to play in this exiting community. May this theater bring you many hours of entertainment and escape from the cares and worries of a troubled world. Proudly and pridefully we dedicate this theater to you."

Contrary to what was going on in the rest of the nation, Morehead was still considered a profitable film market in the 1970s. Although television continued to cause the decline in film attendance, the University Cinema continues to show the latest Hollywood attractions on the silver screen. But the little box in the home and the video rental businesses, continue to erode theater attendance. Also, in the 21st century, the "web," "net," and the "laptop" continues to further reduce time and inclination for film viewing.

In an attempt to lure movie goers back to the silver screen, many large cities have built multiple screen theaters. Many of these theaters have 10 or 15 separate screens where the movie goers can select from a wide variety of films in an attempt to bring viewers back to the movies. The multiple screen format has been only marginally successful, and it would appear that America's love affair with movies on the silver screen is dying. It is a victim of small screens, dot coms, poor films, and multiple media stimuli. Will the University Cinema survive in the 21st century, or will it go the way of Morehead's passenger depot, bus station, and blacksmith shop? Will it become a victim of too little time and too much technology?

Throughout the past 96 years, Moreheadians have had an opportunity to see a movie on the silver screen. Although in the early years, the images flickered and faded a lot. Throughout most of those years movies have been very popular among Morehead residents. Sadly, the future of movies in the 21st century appears to be limited to home viewing. The new technology of cable and wireless transmission of a moving image and sound track into the home will make movie theaters a rarity limited to large metropolitan areas. Sadly!

CHRONOLOGY
Morehead Movie Theaters

Name	Opened	Closed
Nickelodium	1904	1918
Cozy (name changed to Mills in 1938)	1918	1938
College	1929	1972
Trail	1937	1990
Mills	1938	1968
Drive-In	1952	1975
University Cinema	1968	----

"ROUND COUNTY TROUBLES"
Ballad of the Rowan County War
Sung by local folk singer "Blind Jim" Day

Come all you fathers and mothers
    Sisters and brothers,
I will relate the history
    Of the Round County Crew,
Concerning bloody Round
    And many heinous deeds,
I pray you pay attention,
    Remember now it reads.

It was in the month of August,
    On election day;
John Martin was shot and wounded,
    They say by John Day.
Martin could not believe it,
    He could not think it so.
He thought it was Floyd Toliver
    Who shot the fatal blow.

They shot and killed Sol Bradley,
    Pure, sober, innocent man,
He left his wife and loving children,
    to do the best they can.
They wounded Ed Sizemore,
    Although his life was saved,
He seemed to shun the grogshop,
    Since he stood so near the grave.

Martin did recover -
    Some months had come and passed,
It was in the town of Morehead,
    The men both met at last;
Martin and a friend or two
    About the streets did walk;
He seemed to be uneasy
    And no one wished to talk.

He stepped into Judge Carey's grocery
    And stepped up to the bar,
But little did he think, dear friend,
    He'd met his fatal hour.
The sting of death was near him,
    Martin rushed in at the door,
A few words passed between them
    Concerning the row before

The people all were frightened,
    All rushed out of the room;
A ball from Martin's pistol
    Laid Toliver in the tomb.
His friends soon gathered round him,
His wife to weep and wail;
    Martin was arrested,
And soon confined in jail.

He was placed in jail at Round
    there to remain a while
In the hands of law and justice,
    To bravely stand his trial.
Some people talked of lynching him,
    At present though they failed,
Martin's friends removed him
    To the Winchester Jail.

Some person forged an order,
    Their names I do not know;
This plan was soon agreed upon,
    For Martin they did go.
Martin seemed to be uneasy,
    He seemed to be in dread;
They have set a plan to kill me,
    To the jailer Martin said.

They put the handcuffs on him,
    His heart was in distress;
They hurried to the station,
    Stepped aboard the night express.
Along the line she lumbered,
    At her usual speed;
They were only two in number,
    To commit the awful deed.

When they arrived at Farmer's
    They had no time to lose,
A man approached the engineer
    And told him not to move.
They stepped up to the prisoner,
    With a pistol in their hands,
In death he soon was sinking,
    He died in iron bands.

He was in the smoking car,
    Accompanied by his wife;
They did not want her present
    When they took her husband's life.
She heard the horrid sound,
    She was in another car;
She cried: "Oh, Lord, they've killed him,"
    When she heard the pistol fire.

The death of those two men
    Has caused great trouble in our land,
Caused men to leave their families
    And take the parting hand.
Relations still at war;
    O. will it never cease?
O, God, I would like to see
    This land once more in peace.

They shot the deputy sheriff,
    Bumgardner was his name;
They shot him form the bushes
    After taking deliberate aim.
The death of him was dreadful
    May it never be forgot;
His body was pierced and torn
    By thirty-three buckshot.

I composed this as a warning,
    Beware young man, my friend;
Your pistol will cause you trouble,
    On this you may depend.
In the bottom of a whiskey glass
    The lurking devil dwells,
It burns the breath of those who drink it,
    And sends their souls to hell.

APPENDIX

Rowan County Major Elected County Government Officials
1894-2000

1894 - D.G. Ham *(Circuit Court Clerk)*,Elijah Hogge *(County Court Clerk)*, A. Crostwaite *(County Judge)*, M.F. Fouch *(Sheriff)*, Hiram Bradley *(School Superintendent)*. J.W. Riley *(County Attorney)*.

1896 - D.G. Ham *(Circuit Court Clerk)*, O.J. Davis *(County Court Clerk)*, A. Crostwaite *(County Judge)*, M.F. Fouch *(Sheriff)*, Hiram Bradley *(School Superintendent)*. J.W. Riley *(County Attorney)*.

1898 - T.R. Tippett *(Circuit Court Clerk)*, William Caudill *(County Court Clerk)*,G.A. Nickell *(County Judge)*, JH. Fraley *(Sheriff)*, Hiram Bradley *(School Superintendent)*, J.W. Riley *(County Attorney)*.

1900 - T.R. Trippett *(Circuit Court Clerk)*, William Caudill *(County Court Clerk)*,J.E. Cooper *(County Judge)*, J.H. Fraley *(Sheriff)*, Hiram Bradley *(School Superintendent)*, J.W. Riley *(County Attorney)*.

1902   T.B. Tippett *(Circuit Court Clerk)*, C.P. Terrell *(County Court Clerk)*, R. Tussey *(County Judge)*, J.D. Caudill *(Sheriff)*, Miss Cora Wilson (1901-1905 *School Superintendent)* E.T. Young *(County Attorney)*.

1904- T.B. Tippett *(Circuit Court Clerk)* C.P. Terrell *(County Court Clerk)*, R. Tussey *(County Judge)*, J.D. Caudill *(Sheriff)*, Miss CoraWilson *(School Superintendent)* E.T. Young *(County Attorney)*, Elijah Hogge (D) William Caudill (R) *(County Boardof Election Commissioners)*.

1908 - T.B. Tippett *(Circuit Court Clerk)*, W.L. Day *(County Court Clerk)*, Jas. E. Stewart *(County Judge)*, G.W. Allen *(Sheriff)*, Miss Lyda Messer *(School Superintendent)*,T.W. Rose *(County Attorney)*, B.S. Wilson(D) H.C. Ellington(R) *(Board of Election Commissioners)*.

1910 - T.B. Tippett *(Circuit Court Clerk)*, W.L. Day *(County Court Clerk)*, J.W. Riley *(County Judge)*, J.D. Caudill *(Sheriff)*, Mrs. Cora Wilson Stewart (1910-1914 *School Superintendent)*,E. Hogge *(County Attorney)*,L.W. Dillon (D) H.C. Ellington(R) *(Board of Election Commissioners)*, J.W. Amburgey *(Surveyer)*.

1912 - T.B. Tippett *(Circuit Court Clerk)*, W.L. Day *(County Court Clerk)*, J.W. Riley *(County Judge)*, J.D. Caudill *(Sheriff)*, Mrs. Cora Wilson Stewart *(School Superintendent)*,E. Hogge *(County Attorney)*, C.L.Clayton(D) Sam Sorrel (R) *(Board of Election Commissioners)*, J.W. Amburgy *(Surveyer)*.

1914 - T.B. Tippett *(Circuit Court Clerk)*, W.T. Caudill *(County Court Clerk)*, J.W. Riley *(County Judge)*, Arthur Hogge *(Sheriff)*, J.H. Powers (1914-1930 *School Superintendent)*, J.W. Black *(County Attorney)*, S.S. Cassidy *(Road Supervisor)*, W.T. Hall *(Justice of the Peace)*, J.D. Johnson, W.S. Moore, W.J. Fletcher *(Magistrates)*.

1918 - L.B. Hogge *(Circuit Court Clerk)*, W.T.Caudill *(County Court Clerk)*, Arthur Hogge *(County Judge)*, N.L. Wells *(Sheriff)*,J.H Powers *(School Superintendent)*, D.B. Caudill *(County Attorney)*, H.N. Alfrey *(Tax Assessor)*, A.J. Alderman *(Justice of the Peace)*, J.D. Johnson, J.L. Sorell, W.S. Moore *(Magistrates)*.

1920 - L.B. Hogge *(Circuit Court Clerk)*, W.T. Caudill *(County Court Clerk)*, Arthur Hogge *(County Judge)*, N.L. Wells *(Sheriff)*,J.H. Powers *(School Superintendent)*, D.B. Caudill *(County Attorney)*, H.N. Alfrey *(Tax Assessor)*, A.J. Alderman *(Justice of the Peace)*, J.D. Johnson, J.L. Sorell , W.S. Moore *(Magistrates)*.

1922 - C.Crosthwaite *(Circuit Court Clerk)*, W.T. Caudill *(County Court Clerk)*, J.W. Riley *(County Judge)*, H.L. Roberts *(Sheriff)*, J.H. Powers *(School Superintendent)*, T.W. Rose *(County Attorney)*, A.M. Day *(Tax Commissioner)*, D.B. Cornett *(Justice of the Peace)*, Taylor McKenzie, W.D. Williams, Preston Cooper *(Magistrates)*.

1926 - C. Crosthwaite *(Circuit Court Clerk)*, W.T. Caudill *(County Court Clerk)*, T.A.E. Evans *(County Judge)*, John W. Fench *(Sheriff)*, J.H. Powers *(School Superintendent)*, T.W. Rose *(County Attorney)*, H.G. Cooper *(Tax Commissioner)*, W.T. Hall *(Justice of the Peace)*, Turner Crostwaite, W.V. Fletcher, Peyton Estep *(Magistrates)*.

1928 - Charles E. Jennings *(Circuit Court Clerk)*, W.T. Caudill *(County Court Clerk)*, T.A.E. Evans *(County Judge)*, Johns W. Fench *(Sheriff)*, J.H. Powers *(School Superintendent)*, T.W. Rose *(County Attorney)*, H.G. Cooper *(Tax Commissioner)*, W.T. Hall *(Justice of the Peace)*, Turner Crostwaite, W.V. Fletcher, Peyton Estep *(Magistrates)*.

1930 - Charles E. Jennings *(Circuit Court Clerk)*, John Butcher *(County Court Clerk)*, J.D. Johnson *(County Judge)*, Dan Parker *(Sheriff)*, J.H. Powers *(School Superintendent)*, J.W. Riley *(County Attorney)*, Marion Wilson *(Tax Commissioner)*, James Franklin, Dorsey Armstrong, Geo. Molton, W.F. Kegley *(Magistrates)*.

1932 - Charles E. Jennings *(Circuit Court Clerk)*, John Butcher *(County Court Clerk)*, J.D. Johnson *(County Judge)*, Dan Parker *(Sheriff)*, Lyda M Caudill* (1930-1934 *School Superintendent)*, J.W. Riley *(County Attorney)*, Marion Wilson *(Tax Commissioner)*, Sam Stamper *(Jailer)*, James Franklin, Dorsey Armstrong, D.G. White, W.F. Kegley *(Magistrates)*.

1934 - Joe McKinney *(Circuit Court Clerk)*, Vernon Alfrey *(County Court Clerk)*, Charles E. Jennings *(County Judge)*, Mort May *(Sheriff)*, Roy Cornette**(1934-1946 *School Superintendent)*, W.E. Proctor *(County Attorney)*, J.A. Lewis *(Tax Commissioner)*, J.B. Rose *(Justice of the Peace)*, Fred Burrows, Sherman Mabry, Ben Hamm *(Magistrates)*.

1938 - Joe McKinney *(Circuit Court Clerk)*, Vernon Alfrey *(County Court Clerk)*, I.E. Pelphrey *(County Judge)*, B.F. McBrayer *(Sheriff)*, Roy Cornette *(School Superintendent)*, Richard M.Clay *(County Attorney)*, J.A. Lewis *(Tax Commissioner)*, Albie Hardy *(Jailer)*.

1944 - J. McKinney *(Circuit Court Clerk)*, C.V. Alfrey *(County Court Clerk)*, Luther Bradley*(County Judge)*, Bill Carter *(Sheriff)*, Roy Cornette *(School Superintendent)*, Lester Hogge *(County Attorney)*, Peyton Estep *(Tax Commissioner)*.

1946 - Ernest Brown *(Circuit Court Clerk)*, Bernard Day *(County Court Clerk)*, Luther Bradley*(County Judge)*, Sam Green *(Sheriff)*, Ted L. Crosthwaite (1946-1951 *School Superintendent)*, E.M. Hogge *(County Attorney)*, Riley Cline *(Tax Commissioner)*.

1948 - Ernest Brown and Ottis Elam *(Circuit Court Clerk)*, Bernard Day *(County Court Clerk)*, Luther Bradley *(County Judge)*, Sam Green *(Sheriff)*, Ted L. Crosthwaite*(School Superintendent)*, E.M. Hogge *(County Attorney)*, Riley Cline *(Tax Commissioner)*.

1950 - Ottis Elam *(Circuit Court Clerk)*, B.P. Day *(County Court Clerk)*, Sam Greene *(County Judge)*, Chester Lewis *(Sheriff)*, Eunice Cecil (1951-1956 *School Superintendent)*, E.M. Hogge *(County Attorney)*, Riley Cline *(Tax Commissioner)*.

1952 - Herbert Bradley *(Circuit Court Clerk)*, B.P. Day *(County Court Clerk)*, Sam Greene *(County Judge)*, Chester Lewis *(Sheriff)*, Eunice Cecil*(School Superintendent)*, E.M. Hogge *(County Attorney)*, Riley Cline *(Tax Commissioner)*.

1954 - Herbert Bradley *(Circuit Court Clerk)*, Ottis Elam *(County Court Clerk)*, W.T. McClain *(County Judge)*, Carl Jones *(Sheriff)*, Eunice Cecil*(School Superintendent)*, Austin Alfrey *(County Attorney)*, Mrs. Marvin Wilson *(Tax Commissioner)*, Rube Thomas *(Jailer)*, Clark Lane *(Coroner)*.

1956 - Herbert Bradley *(Circuit Court Clerk)*, Ottis Elam *(County Court Clerk)*, Carl Jones *(County Judge)*, Sam Green *(Sheriff)*, Clifford Cassidy*(School Superintendent)*, Austin Alfrey *(County Attorney)*, Juanita Wilson *(Tax Commissioner)*, Buck Jones *(Coroner)*, Elmo Plank *(Jailer)*.

1960 - Herbert Bradley *(Circuit Court Clerk)*, Ottis Elam *(County Court Clerk)*, Carl Jones *(County Judge)*, Sam Greene *(Sheriff)*, Clifford

Cassity *(School Superintendent)*, Austin Alfrey *(County Attorney)*, Ollie Tabor *(Treasurer)*, Juanita Wilson *(Tax Commissioner)*, Tom Burns *(City Judge)*, Elijah Hogge *(City Attorney)*.

1962 - Herbert Bradley *(Circuit Court Clerk)*, Ottis Elam *(County Court Clerk)*, Carl Jones *(County Judge)*, C.E. Lewis *(Sheriff)*, Clifford Cassidy *(School Superintendent)*, Austin Alfrey *(County Attorney)*, Ollie Tabor *(Treasurer)*, Juanita Wilson *(Tax Commissioner)*, Tom Burns *(City Judge)*, Elijah Hogge *(City Attorney)*.

1964 - Herbert Bradley *(Circuit Court Clerk)*, Ottis Elam *(County Court Clerk)*, W.C. Flannery *(County Judge)*, C.E. Lewis *(Sheriff)*, Clifford Cassity *(School Superintendent)*, Austin Alfrey *(County Attorney)*, Ollie Tabor *(Treasurer)*, Juanita Wilson *(Tax Commissioner)*, Tom Burns *(City Judge)*, Elijah Hogge *(City Attorney)*.

1968- Wathan Armstrong *(Circuit Court Clerk)*, Ottis Elam *(County Court Clerk)*, W.C. Flannery *(County Judge)*, John Green *(Sheriff)*, Clifford Cassity *(School Superintendent)*, James E. Clay *(County Attorney)*, A.N. Alfrey *(City Judge)*.

1970 - Ralph Early *(Circuit Court Clerk)*, Ottis Elam *(County Court Clerk)*, Ottis Caldwell *(County Judge)*, Carl Jones *(Sheriff)*, Clifford Cassity *(School Superintendent)*, James E. Clay *(County Attorney)*, Ollie Sexton *(Treasurer)*, Juanita Wilson *(Tax Commissioner)*, A.N. Alfrey *(City Judge)*.

1972 - Ralph Early *(Circuit Court Clerk)*, Ottis Elam *(County Court Clerk)*, Ottis Caldwell *(County Judge)*, Carl Jones *(Sheriff)*, Clifford Cassity *(School Superintendent)*, James E. Clay *(County Attorney)*, Ollie Sexton *(Treasurer)*, Juanita Wilson *(Tax Commissioner)*, A.N. Alfrey *(City Judge)*.

1974 - Wathan Armstrong *(Circuit Court Clerk)*, Ottis Elam *(County Court Clerk)*, Ottis Caldwell *(County Judge)*, Jack Carter *(Sheriff)*, Clifford Cassity *(School Superintendent)*, H. Pennington *(County Attorney)*.

1976 - Wathan Armstrong *(Circuit Court Clerk)*, Ottis Elam *(County Court Clerk)*, Ottis Caldwell *(County Judge)*, Jack Carter *(Sheriff)*, Clifford Cassity*(School Superintendent)*, H. Pennington *(County Attorney)*.

1978 - Wathan Armstrong *(Circuit Court Clerk)*, Jean Bailey *(County Court Clerk)*, W.C. Flannery *(County Judge)*, Jim Nickell *(Sheriff)*, John Brock (1976-1987 *School Superintendent)*, John Cox *(County Attorney)*, Jim Barker*(Coroner)*, Roger Thomas*(Jailer)*, William Porter *(P.V.A.)*.

1986 - Wathan Armstrong *(Circuit Court Clerk)*, Jean Bailey *(County Court Clerk)*,Ott Caldwell *(County Judge)*, Jack Carter *(Sheriff)*, John Brock (1987 *School Superintendent)*, Harvey Pennington *(County Attorney)*, Wm. Porter *(P.V.A.)*, Dale Davis*(Jailer)*, Jim Barker *(Coroner)*.

1988 - Glenn Williams *(Circuit Court Clerk)*, Jean Bailey *(County Court Clerk)*,Ott Caldwell *(County Judge)*, Jack Carter *(Sheriff)*, Kenny Bland (1987-1993 *School Superintendent)*, Harvey Pennington *(County Attorney)*, Wm. Porter *(P.V.A.)*, Dale Davis*(Jailer)*, Jim Barker *(Coroner)*.

1990 - Glenn Williams *(Circuit Court Clerk)*, Jean Bailey *(County Court Clerk)*,Clyde Thomas *(County Judge)*, Jack Carter *(Sheriff)*, Kenny Bland*(School Superintendent)*, Harvey Pennington *(County Attorney)*, C.J. Baker *(P.V.A.)*, Roger Thomas*(Jailer)*, Jim Barker *(Coroner)*.

1992 - Glenn Williams *(Circuit Court Clerk)*, Jean Bailey *(County Court Clerk)*,Clyde Thomas *(County Judge)*, Jack Carter *(Sheriff)*, Kenny Bland*(School Superintendent)*, Harvey Pennington *(County Attorney)*, C.J. Baker *(P.V.A.)*, Roger Thomas*(Jailer)*, Jim Barker *(Coroner)*.

1996 - Jim Barker *(Circuit Court Clerk)*, Jean Bailey *(County Court Clerk)*, Clyde Thomas *(County Judge)*, Jack Carter *(Sheriff)*, Harvey Pennington *(County Attorney)*, C.J. Baker *(P.V.A.)*, Don Hall *(Jailer)*,   John Northcutt *(Coroner)*.

1998 - Jim Barker *(Circuit Court Clerk)*, Jean Bailey *(County Court Clerk)*, Clyde Thomas *(County Judge)*, Jack Carter *(Sheriff)*, Harvey Pennington *(County Attorney)*, C.J. Baker *(P.V.A.)*, Don Hall *(Jailer)*, John Northcutt *(Coroner)*.

[1]NOTE: When Rowan County was formed in 1856, the first County Judge was William Black; the first Sheriff was Isaac Johnson; and the first Jailer was James Black. The first State Representative from Rowan County was Harrison G. Burns.

[2] *Last Rowan County Superintendent of Schools elected by popular vote. Lyda Messer Caudill.

[3] **First Rowan County superintendent of Schools appointed by an elected school board. Roy Cornette.

BIBLIOGRAPHY OF SOURCES

Adjutant Generals Report to the Kentucky Legislature (1887)
Alderson, Warren M., Monograph

Baptist Church-100th Anniversary (Hazel Whittaker, et.al.)
Bath County Court Clerk
Bath County Public Library

George M. Calvert (unpublished letter)
Camden-Carroll Library, Morehead State University
    (Special Collections)

Denny Caudill (unpublished letter)

Etta Proctor Caudill (unpublished statement)
Olive Day Caudill (unpublished statement)
CCC Camp 578 Discharges and Achievements (F-4)
Christian Church (Brief History by Mary Alice Jayne, et. al)
Citizens Bank Historical Records
Chronicles of the 20th Century - Clifton Daniel

Disciples of Christ General Missionary Work

Elected Officials of Kentucky (1894-2000)

First Church of God (Brief History - Betty Lewis, et. al)
Fleming County Court Records

Journal of the Kentucky House of Representatives (1885)
Roy Holbrook (unpublished letter)

Illiteracy in the U.S. (Government Documents)

Kentucky Department for Libraries and Archives

Frank Laughlin (unpublished letter)

Medical Practitioners of Rowan County (1864-1950)
Methodist Church (A Condensed History by Reuel Buchanan)
Methodist Church Archives of Kentucky
Methodist Church Board Minutes

Methodist Episcopal Church Board Records
Morehead City Council Minutes
Morehead Fire Department Records
Morehead Women Club (First History)

Peoples Bank Historical Records
J.H. Powers (unpublished statement)
Post Office Archives - Government Documents (1828-1974)

Register of Patients of Dr. McCleese (1898-1922)
Rowan county Clerk Records
Rowan County Public Library
Rowan County Schools (Taylor Ellington - 8mm film)
Rowan County School Board Minutes
Survey of Rowan County Schools (1936) by W.H. Vaughn, et. al

SECONDARY SOURCES

Ashland Daily Independent
American Newspapers (1821-1936)

Bath County Outlook
Bible Sword - 1895
Breckinridge Eaglet

Country Life Reader - Cora Wilson Stewart

The Hite Place - Mabel Alfrey

Moonlight Schools, Cora Wilson Stewart
Morehead Advance (1898)
Morehead Independent (1934-1946)
More-Head Light (1927)
Morehead News (1962)

The Mountaineer
The Mountain Cruiser
The Mountain Scorcher
New York Times

The Quill (CCC Paper)

The Raconteur (MS)
Rowan County News
Rowan County School News

Trail Blazer

Viking Voice
Viking Yearbook
Yank, 1945

BIBLIOGRAPHY OF INTERVIEWS (1997-2000)

Adkins, Dale
Alderson, Raymond
Alfrey, Harvard
Allen, Hubert and Robert
Allen, Nora Ellis
Allen, Perry
Allen, Sonny and Merl
Alley, Bob

Baldridge, Jack
Baldridge, "Tub"
Barker, Cliff and Christine
Barker, Ollie
Battson, Don
Bishop, Robert
Blair, Don and Paul
Boggess, Jimmy
Bradley, Bill and Phyllis
Brown, Mrs. Galen
Buchanan, Reuel and Sue
Burns, Frank
Burns, Thomas R.

Calvert, Bill and Frankie
Calvert, George M.
Carpenter, Vivian Flood
Carter, Jack
Caskey, Mrs. O'Rear
Cassity, Fred
Caudill, C. Louise
Caudill, Katherine
Caudill, Mary
Caudill, Proctor
Caudill, Ron
Clark, Clyda
Clark, Thomas D.
Clayton, Billie (Caskey)
Clayton, Jimmy

Davis, Bill
Davis, Ralph
Dean, Lloyd
Duncan, John R.

Earley, Norton
Eldridge, Avenelle

Ellington, Barbie Casper
Ellington, Harold and Pauline
Ellington, James L.
Ellis, Janis C.
Ellis, Nellie E.
Ensor, Terry

Fannin, Larry and Barbara
Flannery, Jean
Flannery, Rufus
Fraley, Ruth Ann
Freeland, Kay

Gevedon, Loretta Barndollar

Halbleib, Suzie
Hardin, Phil and Margena
Hardin, Violet
Harr, Vernon
Hicks, Scotty
Hill, George, and Jean
Hinton, Frank O.
Hisle, Barbara Shafer
Hodges, Joe
Holbrook, Harold and Jane
    (Young)
Holbrook, John W., Jr.
Holley, Lois Ann
Horton, Roe
Hutchinson, Alpha

Jayne, Mary Alice
Jones, Kenneth and Chilma

Keith, W.L.
Kiser, Earl

Landreth, Jack and Joe
Lewis, Billy
Lewis, Vivian Evans

Mahaney, Nell Fair
Martin, Alvin E.
Mauk, Joe
Maynard, Hattie Caudill
McBrayer, Earl and Helen
McKinney, Hazel
McKinney, Joe and Evelyn
Moore, Annabelle
Moore, Lillian
Morris, Margaret Cornette

Needham, Joan Cecil

Oldfield, Donna
Ousley, Paul

Pierce, Bill
Poston, Glenn
Powell, Mary Northcutt
Powell, Mary Woods
Powers, Tommy
Proudfoot, Richard

Razor, Roberta Bishop
Reynolds, Paul J. and Mabel
Reynolds, Virginia R.
Richardson, Bill and Louvena
Riddle, Mabel
Russell, Roger and Jackie

Skaggs, Pat Crutcher
Sparkman, Garrad
Stamper, Bobby
Stokes, Rosemary
Spurlock, Bill

Taylor, H.K. and Audrey
Thomas, Jim

Wellinger, Sue
Wells, Nan Lytle
Wells, Randy
White, Hannah
Williams, May
Wilson, Marvin Jr.

Young, Steve
Young, Donald

For those that may have been missed,
my sincere appreciation and apologies.

JDE

POPULATION
Rowan County
1860-1990
(Rowan became a county in 1856)

Date	Population
1860	2,290
1870	2,991
1880	4,420
1890	6,120
1900	8,277
1910	9,438
1920	9,467
1930	10,893
1940	12,734
1950	12,708
1960	12,808
1970	17,010
1980	19,049
1990	20,353
2000	

*Source: Decennial Census of the U.S.